In Praise of Empires

OTHER BOOKS BY THE AUTHOR

WELLS AND WELFARE

METHODS OF PROJECT ANALYSIS— A Review

MEN OR MACHINES

UNEMPLOYMENT AND WAGE INFLATION IN INDUSTRIAL ECONOMIES

APPRAISING FOREIGN INVESTMENT IN DEVELOPING COUNTRIES
(With Martin Cave, Paul Hare and Jeffrey Thompson)

PRICES FOR PLANNING

THE POVERTY OF 'DEVELOPMENT ECONOMICS'

LABOUR AND POVERTY IN KENYA—1900–1980 (with Paul Collier)

THE HINDU EQUILIBRIUM—India c 1500 B.C.–A.D. 1980 2 vols.

THE REPRESSED ECONOMY—Causes, Consequences, Reform.

AGAINST DIRIGISME—The case for unshackling economic markets

THE POLITICAL ECONOMY OF POVERTY EQUITY AND
GROWTH—A comparative study (With Hla Myint)

UNINTENDED CONSEQUENCES—The impact of factor endowments, culture and
politics on long-run economic development

UNFINISHED BUSINESS—India in the World Economy

Edited volumes:

STAGFLATION, SAVINGS AND THE STATE (with Martin Wolf)

PUBLIC POLICY AND ECONOMIC DEVELOPMENT: essays in honour of
Ian Little (with M. Fg. Scott)

DEVELOPMENT ECONOMICS, 4 vols.

TRADE, DEVELOPMENT AND ECONOMIC POLICY: essays in honour of
Anne Krueger (with R. Snape)

In Praise of Empires

Globalization and Order

Order

Deepak Lal

palgrave
macmillan

First published in 2004 by
PALGRAVE MACMILLAN™
175 Fifth Avenue, New York, N.Y. 10010 and
Houndmills, Basingstoke, Hampshire, England RG21 6XS
Companies and representatives throughout the world

PALGRAVE MACMILLAN is the global academic imprint of
the Palgrave Macmillan division of St. Martin's Press, LLC and of
Palgrave Macmillan Ltd. Macmillan® is a registered trademark
in the United States, United Kingdom and other countries.
Palgrave is a registered trademark in the European Union
and other countries.

ISBN 1–4039–3639–0 hardback

Library of Congress Cataloging-in-Publication Data

Lal, Deepak.
  In praise of empires : globalization and order / Deepak Lal.
    p. cm.
  Includes bibliographical references and index.
  ISBN 1–4039–3639–0
    1. Imperialism. 2. Imperialism—History. 3. International relations.
  4. Globalization. 5. International economic relations. 6. United
  States—Foreign relations—2001—Forecasting. I. Title.

JC359.L295 2004
325′.32–dc22   2004049002

A catalogue record for this book is available from the British Library.

Design by Newgen Imaging Systems (P) Ltd., Chennai, India.

First edition: November 2004
10 9 8 7 6 5 4 3 2 1

Printed in the United States of America.

For my Yanks

Barbara, Deepika, Akshay

For these I set no bounds in space or time;
I have given them empire without end.
—Virgil: Aeneid, I, 278–9

Contents

List of Tables

List of Figures

Preface

This book is a greatly expanded version of the Wendt lecture ("In Defense of Empires") that I gave at the American Enterprise Institute in Washington, D.C., in October 2002. I am very grateful to Chris DeMuth and Nick Eberstadt for inviting me to give this prestigious lecture.

The theme of the lecture and this book has, however, been with me for some time. It concerns the role of empires in promoting globalization. I joined the Indian Foreign Service soon after my undergraduate studies at Oxford in 1983. After a brief sojourn in Tokyo to learn Japanese, I left the diplomatic life to take up life as an economics don at Oxford in 1986, but I have kept an interest in international relations. In the late 1970s when the Third World was demanding a New International Economic Order (NIEO), I began a project on the NIEO with my colleague at University College London, David Henderson, funded by the Nuffield Foundation. One of the academic advisors to our project was the late Hedley Bull, then professor of international relations at Oxford. Readers will see the influence of his writings on this book. The Nuffield project was aimed at looking at both the international politics and the economics behind the NIEO. Unfortunately, as the paths of the two collaborators diverged, with my departure for the World Bank to be their research administrator and David Henderson's to become the head of the Economics Directorate at the Organization for Economic Co-operation and Development in the early 1980s, this project remained incomplete. I did produce a pamphlet ("Poverty, Power and Prejudice") published by the Fabian Society on the politics and a small book on the economics of the NIEO (*The Poverty of "Development Economics"*), which has acquired some modicum of fame if not notoriety. This present book and its companion volume on international economic order in some ways will complete that interrupted project.

While the NIEO may be dead, the dirigiste dogma I castigated in *The Poverty of "Development Economics"* is not. In this present book, apart from its major defense of empires, I initially wanted to provide a detailed critique of the challenge to classical liberal views on economic policy mounted by the new dirigisme. But three of the readers of the first draft containing the critique—David Henderson, Angus Maddison, and my editor at Palgrave Macmillan,

Amanda Watkins—rightly felt that it did not mesh with the rest of the book and should be made into a separate one. This will become a companion volume on *international economic order*.

This more general book, *In Praise of Empires*, is a historical and cross-civilizational examination of the role empires have played to provide the order required for peace and prosperity, and how this imperial role has come to be thrust on the United States. Whether the United States is able and willing to fulfill it and the consequences for global peace and prosperity if it is not are the major themes of this book. It is bound to be controversial because of the strong passions the word empire arouses, not least in the United States. But I trust readers will find that my arguments are cogent and that the issues they raise are of great contemporary relevance—not least for the developing countries that have been the object of my study during my professional life.

This book is also my third essay that trespasses on the disciplinary territory of others since I was elected to the newly founded James S. Coleman Chair in International Development Studies at the University of California, Los Angeles. This interdisciplinary chair provides the necessary license for trespassing, as the study of economic development involves more than technocratic economics. The first of these essays, my book with Hla Myint, *The Political Economy of Poverty, Equity, and Growth*, looked at the political aspects of development; the second, *Unintended Consequences*, at the cultural impacts; and this, the third, looks at the international relations aspects. However, unlike the other two books, for which I found much of use for my purposes in the writings of the academics into whose specializations I was trespassing, I have not found the writings of their counterparts in international relations as useful. This is partly because much of academic "international relations" is premised on the existence of a world that has gone—the international system formed by the anarchic European society of nation-states after the fall of Rome. But, as I argue, that international system was the exception in human history, wherein imperial systems have predominated. If, besides encouraging a sober debate on the U.S. imperium among the general public—which judging from the torrent of recent books has begun—this book also helps academic international relations to take up the study of empires seriously, my purposes will have been more than fulfilled.

I have received detailed comments on the whole or parts of the earlier drafts from Surjit Bhalla, Harold Demsetz, Stanley Engerman, David Henderson, Jack Hirshleifer, Mats Lundhal, Angus Maddison, and Razeen Sally. I am most grateful. I have also benefited from the contributions of the participants and discussants at a colloquium I held at UCLA on "War and Peace" funded by the Coleman chair in November 1997. These included

Richard Baum, Leonard Binder, Robert Boyd, Paul Collier, Chandrashekhar Dasgupta, Brad DeLong, Jack Hirshleifer, Ronald Findlay, Michael Lofchie, Michael Mann, Marcus Noland, Sarath Rajapatirana, Richard Rosecrance, Paul Schroedr, Steven Spiegel, and Arthur Stein. As they have not seen what use I have made of their contributions and would by no means all agree with the thrust of my argument, they are obviously absolved of any responsibility for the contents of this book. Finally, for nearly a decade I have been associated with the Center for International Relations at UCLA and participated in their various research projects organized by its former director Richard Rosecrance and funded by the Carnegie Endowment. The interactions with the numerous participants in these projects and at the various conferences around the world have also been of great value in helping me to make up my mind on many of the issues discussed in this book. Similarly valuable were the comments by participants at the Wendt lecture at the AEI in Washington and at seminars at Timbro in Stockholm, at the University of Southern California, and at UCLA.

Finally, a personal word needs to be said about the author. In a television interview on a Swedish program called "Global Axess," relating to the Wendt lecture, the interviewer asked about my personal history and whether, as someone born and brought up in India, it wasn't strange that I should be arguing in favor of an American empire. So perhaps it is worth stating some personal facts. I was born and brought up in India and came to England to study at Oxford in 1960, where I lived till 1990 with brief sojourns in Washington at the World Bank, in New Delhi at the Indian Planning Commission, and while advising numerous international agencies and governments around the world. It was not till the late 1980s, when I had lived in Britain for nearly a quarter of a century, that I became a naturalized Briton. While my father's family had been collaborators of the British Raj, my mother's were fierce opponents and nationalists. My mother hurled bricks at the officials of the Raj during the Quit India movement; her brother went to jail and was subsequently a Congress party leader, mayor of Delhi, and a minister in Nehru's cabinet. I and my peers believed in the Nehruvian nationalist and socialist ideology of postindependence India. I married an American sociologist who was a student shop steward at Berkeley during the anti–Vietnam War movement. Our children are both U.S. and British citizens: one preferring for cultural reasons to live in England, the other in the states. My wife and I now divide our time between our three homes in Los Angeles, London, and New Delhi. This personal history can hardly account for my views.

It is evidence and experience, especially in working and traveling in most parts of the Third World during my professional career, which have led me to change my early views and come to those I currently hold. I hope the reader will come to this book with a similar independence of mind, shorn of preconceptions—particularly those characterized as politically correct—to judge the cogency of the arguments and evidence presented, for it concerns current issues of paramount importance to the United States and the world.

D.L.
Los Angeles and London
February 2004

Introduction

Four stories from my life provide some idea of the motivation, scope, and nature of this book.

First, in November 1999 I was in Seattle to address a conference organized around the meeting of the World Trade Organization. As I left my hotel early in the morning in the pouring rain, I saw a phalanx of bare-breasted women coming down the hill carrying a sign reading "Vegan Dykes against the WTO." Talking to the college students forming a large part of the army of demonstrators who later that day would turn the city into a battlefield, I wondered, as a development economist who has argued for globalization for nearly my whole working life, why this benign process had so inflamed the passions.

The second incident is now seared into everyone's memory. On September 11, 2001, I was in my study in London, when my teenage daughter, who is an inveterate surfer of television channels, came in to say I should come and watch, as a small plane seemed to have crashed into some tower in New York and wondered if it was close to Brooklyn where her granny lived. For the next several hours we both watched in horror as the subsequent events of that infamous day unfolded. Watching the constant replays of the two planes' balletic deathly dance into the twin towers, followed by the towers' spectacular implosion, I thought that this is what it must have felt like when the Arab tribesmen spilled out of their desert homeland in the seventh century, inflamed by a new religion, and swiftly conquered and destroyed the classical world of antiquity. For as Patricia Crone has written: "Of the Middle East in about 600 A.D. one thing can be said for certain: its chances of being conquered by Arab tribesmen in the name of a new religion were so remote that nobody had even speculated that it might happen. Islam came upon the world as a totally unexpected development."[1] Were we about to see a repetition of history, as the tribesmen's Islamist descendants from the ancient Arab heartland smashed into the towering symbols of the new U.S.-led liberal international order?

This led to reflections on a third incident, from the summer of 1967, at the height of the Vietnam War. I was working as a consultant to the UN's Economic Commission for Asia and the Far East in Bangkok and staying with a friend in the Indian diplomatic service. One evening we decided to take up an invitation from the U.S. embassy to attend a poetry reading. Expecting to hear poems by Walt Whitman and Robert Frost, I was astonished when the American servicemen hosting the event instead recited the poems of Rudyard Kipling, including the famous lines addressed to the United States:

> "Take up the White Man's burden—
> Send forth the best ye breed—
> Go, bind your sons to exile
> To serve your captives' need"[2]

This was particularly poignant as the verse was recited by a black captain. This imperial dream seemingly ended with the fierce domestic opposition the war caused in the following years and the U.S. troops' ignominious departure in helicopters from the rooftop of the American embassy in Saigon. Could this wounded and reluctant imperial power be expected to maintain the global order as other empires in the past, or would its Vietnam trauma lead to domestic opposition preventing the conversion of its undisputed global hegemony—having seen off the "evil empire"—into its own imperium?

This naturally led to reflections on empires and the bad name they have gotten in the modern world for being exploitative and for opposing nationalist ideals and claims. Would an American empire be able to obtain popular approval not only domestically but among those in the far-flung reaches of the new imperium? This brought to mind the fourth incident. In 1995 I was staying in Beijing with a very old friend, who was then the Indian ambassador to China. Beijing was hosting a UN Conference on Women, and the large number of female delegates were housed in a large tent city. One night the ambassador was woken by an agitated Chinese official asking him to rush to the tent city as the Indian delegates were rioting. On getting there he found that the trouble began when some American delegates went into the tents of their Third World sisters and tried to initiate them into the joys of gay sex. With the Indians in the lead, the Third World women chased the American women out of their tents, beating them with their slippers. This attempt to convert their Eastern sisters to their Western sexual mores obviously failed. But what would be the consequences if the new American imperium was to become a new international moral order, aiming to legislate its particular "habits of the heart" around the world?

These incidents relate to the major themes of this book. I will argue that globalization has been associated with empires. These empires have arisen whenever the international anarchical society of states has been replaced by a power with the material and military means to establish its hegemony. The order provided by empires has been essential for the working of the benign processes of globalization, which promote prosperity. Globalization is not a new phenomenon and has always been associated in the past with empires. This book argues that not since the fall of the Roman empire has there been a potential imperial power like the U.S. today. The themes covered in this book raise questions about the current international global order and the place of the United States within it. Is a U.S. imperium needed for the globalization which breeds prosperity? What form should it take—direct, colonial, or indirect empire? Will America be able and willing to run an empire? The United States has already faced hostile coalitions. What is the history and nature of resistance to U.S. hegemony? Before proceeding to deal with these questions in detail, it is important to define globalization and order—the subtitle of the book—and how they relate to empires.

GLOBALIZATION

Globalization is the process of creating a common economic space which leads to a growing integration of the world economy through increasingly free movement of goods, capital, and labor. Elementary economics tells us that this process is a potentially mutually beneficial process. It is, in the language of economic game theorists, a positive sum game. As an economic process in itself, it is value neutral. It cannot, as many have claimed, be an ideology.[3] However, criticisms have been raised against the impact of globalization and these concerns tend to have an ideological basis. The major concerns relate to globalization's distributional consequences, its political and cultural nature, and its possible fragility caused by the "creative destruction" of global capitalism. These criticisms have led to demands, from a wide political spectrum, for the process of globalization to be regulated and tamed through the creation or expansion of various international institutions to deal with the problem of global public goods.

Globalization is not new. It has been a cyclical phenomenon of history for millennia, being associated with the rise and fall of empires. By integrating previously separated areas into a common economic space under their Pax, empires promoted those gains from trade and specialization later emphasized by Adam Smith, leading to Smithian intensive growth.[4] Thus, the Greco-Roman empires linked the areas around the Mediterranean, the Abbasid empire of the Arabs linked the worlds of the Mediterranean and the Indian Ocean, the Mongol empire linked China and Central Asia with the Near East, the various Indian empires created a common economic space in the subcontinent, and the expanding Chinese empire linked the economic spaces of the Yellow River with those of the Yangtze. But, until the creation of the British empire in the eighteenth and nineteenth centuries, the imperial sway was usually confined to particular regions, and the resulting economic integration was not truly global. The first truly global empire was that of the British, and the nineteenth century saw the emergence of the first truly global economy, the first liberal international economic order (LIEO).

Before the nineteenth-century LIEO fostered by the British, the primitive methods of transportation limited the economic integration that could be achieved. The British LIEO, coinciding with the Industrial Revolution and the invention of the steam engine, led through the development of the railways, the steamship, and the telegraph to a substantial fall in global transport costs. This had important implications for the economic integration achieved as compared with other past empires. The goods traded along the channels created by past agrarian empires had to be of high value because of the high costs of transport and communications. These noncompeting goods—luxury goods (like Chinese porcelain or Dacca muslins) or more generally consumed primary products (like spices, tea, tobacco, coffee)—were not produced in the areas to which they were transshipped. Much domestic production in the areas linked by an empire would, therefore, not have been affected by the new imports. The main growth effects would come through the spread of knowledge and technology and the monetary effects of settling the trade balances between the newly linked regions.

The nineteenth-century LIEO for the first time saw domestic production being affected by the convergence in domestic and foreign prices for the mass of goods consumed. It led to specialization along lines of comparative advantage and Smithian growth. The distinctive nineteenth-century pattern of trade arose: the "North"—mainly Western Europe—specialized in the new industrial products, and the "South"—which included the current Third World and the areas of "new" settlement in the Americas and Australasia—specialized in primary products. This colonial international division of labor has been the target of economic nationalists in the South ever since, even though, as I will document, it generated spectacular Smithian intensive growth in their countries.

In the current phase of globalization, this process has gone even further, with the fragmentation of production processes, so that countries and regions specialize not in cars or shoes but in the components that make up these products. Thus, as I write this, I am wearing a custom-made sports jacket and flannel trousers that were ordered from Mr. Fitwell of Los Angeles. He took my measurements, and I chose the cloth from samples from around the world. The order was then sent by email to their headquarters in Hong Kong, where the cloth had been transshipped from its own location. It was cut by a Saville Row–trained cutter and sent to the neighboring city of Shenzen to be stitched by seamstresses from mainland China. The finished product was then sent to me in Los Angeles by Federal Express for final fitting. The whole process took less than 3 weeks, and the price was one-fourth of what an equivalent Saville Row suit would have cost.

The convergence of domestic and foreign prices of competing traded goods leads to countries specializing in producing and exporting the goods that use more of their abundant factors of production and importing the goods that use more of those which are scarce. This leads to income distribution effects with, *ceteris paribus*, the returns to the country's abundant factor rising relatively to that of the scarce. In a country with a lot of labor and little capital, opening up trade in competing goods will raise wages relative to profits. In the nineteenth century and in current periods of globalization, this has led to resistance to globalization from countries when their scarce factors are hurt by the opening up of trade. They have sought to use the political process to protect their incomes. With the revolution in information technology, various services that were locally provided, as they could not be traded, are now being traded internationally and being produced where the costs are the lowest. Many workers in service industries whose wages were protected by distance—set by local demand and supply conditions—find that the IT revolution's banishment of distance has made them compete with workers in a global labor market. Thus, recently, when I made a telephone booking for a flight and pointed out to the girl who answered that she had a nice Indian accent, she replied, "But I am in India." I shall examine the consequences of this fragmentation and globalization of production and of services which were previously nontraded in part II. The international outsourcing of services has added to the atavastic fear of foreign trade and globalization.

ORDER

The late Hedley Bull subtitled *The Anarchical Society*, his classic book on international relations, "A study of order in world politics." Following the Scottish philosopher David Hume, he maintained that there are three elementary and universal goals that any society must pursue if any social life is to exist. These are first, to secure life against violence which leads to death or bodily harm; second, that promises once made are kept; third, the stabilization of possessions through rules of property. By "order" in social life Bull meant "a pattern of human activity that sustains elementary, primary, or universal goals of social life such as these" (p. 4).

This definition of order is congenial to an economist, for it deals with the provision of the pure public goods of defense and the law, the primary function and duty of every state. This domestic order is an essential part of world order, the other part being the wider world political system, the international order. In this book I will be mainly concerned with the international order but, as Bull emphasizes, domestic order has primacy as it relates to the social life of individuals who are our fundamental concern, and not those lives of the artificial and sometimes changing societies and states they may constitute. This domestic order, as emphasized by economists, is essential to foster prosperity. The goal of an international order is to preserve the peace. This is an international public good, and its provision is the subject of the first part of this book.

Empires, which for our purposes can be defined as "multi-ethnic conglomerates held together by transnational organizational and cultural ties,"[5] have historically both maintained peace and promoted prosperity for a simple reason. The centers of the ancient civilizations in Eurasia—where sedentary agriculture could be practiced and yielded a surplus to feed the towns (*civitas*, the emblem of civilization)—were bordered north and south by areas of nomadic pastoralism: the steppes of the north and the semidesert of the Arabian peninsula to the south. In these regions the inhabitants had kept up many of the warlike traditions of our hunter-gatherer ancestors and were prone to prey upon the sedentary inhabitants of the plains. At times they attempted to convert them into chattel like their cattle.[6] Thus, the provision of a classical public good—protecting citizens from invaders—required the extension of territory to some natural barriers which could keep the barbarians at bay. The Roman, Chinese, and various Indian empires were partly created to provide this Pax, to protect their labor intensive and sedentary forms of making a living. The Pax of various empires has thus been essential in providing one of the basic public goods required for prosperity.

A simple thought experiment will help to show that in the past, despite nationalist rhetoric, an imperial Pax has usually succeeded in providing the essential public good of order. Consider an ordinary citizen of any ethnic and religious origin of either of the two supposedly benighted nineteenth-century empires extinguished by President Woodrow Wilson at Versailles: the Austro-Hungarian and the Ottoman. He in turn is considering the likelihood of his grandchildren living, surviving, and passing on their property to their children. Now consider a similar citizen of the postimperial successor states during the last century contemplating the same prospect. There can be no doubt of the great deterioration in life chances that has befallen the average citizen of the successor states. The situation in many ways is of course even worse in Africa with its millions of refugees and ethnic slaughter, even by comparison with the inhuman and brutal regime of Leopold's Belgian empire in the Congo. In many parts of the postimperial world, the main beneficiaries of the Age of Nations have been the nationalist predatory elites who have failed to provide even the most elemental of public goods—law and order—required for human thriving.[7]

The decline of empires was followed by both domestic disorder and a disintegration of the enlarged economic spaces they had created.[8] Thus, the Roman empire had through its Pax brought unprecedented prosperity to the inhabitants of the Mediterranean littoral for nearly a millennium. With its demise, the ensuing disorder and the destruction of the imperial economic space led to a marked fall in the standards of living of the common people inhabiting the fallen empire. As Samuel Finer notes: "If a peasant family in Gaul, or Spain, or northern Italy had been able to foresee the misery and exploitation that was to befall his grandchildren and their grandchildren, on and on and on for the next 500 years, he would have been singularly spiritless—and witless too—if he had not rushed to the aid of the empire. And even then the kingdoms that did finally emerge after the year 1000 were poverty-stricken dung heaps compared with Rome. Not till the full Renaissance in the sixteenth century did Europeans begin to think of themselves as in any ways comparable to Rome, and not till the 'Augustan Age' of the eighteenth century did they regard their civilization as its equal."[9]

Similarly, the periodic collapse of Chinese empires led to periods of warlordism and widespread disorder, until the Mandate of Heaven was passed on to another imperial dynasty which restored order. The Chinese have therefore always placed a very high value on the order provided by their successive empires. In our own times, the death of the nineteenth-century liberal economic order built by Pax Britannia on the fields of Flanders led to a near century of economic disintegration and disorder, because the British were unable and the Americans were unwilling to maintain an imperial global Pax.

In this context it is worth considering another thought experiment. As we shall see, by the 1870s, the British economic ascendancy which had underwritten their imperial Pax was coming to an end with the rise of two major new industrial powers, the United States and Germany. If the Americans had then joined the British in creating an Anglo-American imperium to maintain the Pax, the terrible events of the last century could perhaps have been avoided. The joint industrial and military might of an Anglo-American imperium run, let us say, by the equivalent of a Lord Palmerston could have prevented the Kaiser's gamble to achieve mastery in Europe, and one of the most pointless wars—the First World War—could perhaps have been averted. This in turn could have prevented the events that led to the rise of Hitler. Similarly, a joint Anglo-American imperium could perhaps have prevented the rise of the Bolsheviks. In a sense therefore, the rise of the two illiberal creeds—fascism and communism—which have blighted the lives of millions could perhaps have been prevented if, by the end of the nineteenth-century, the United States had taken over (in partnership) Britain's imperial role. Instead, Woodrow Wilson at Versailles destroyed the Age of Empire and, with the United States retreating into isolationism, left global disorder and economic disintegration to rule for nearly a century during the Age of Nations.

With the realization of the consequences of its failure to maintain an imperial Pax to promote peace and prosperity, the United States since the Second World War has at first surreptitiously, and since 9/11 more openly, taken on the imperial role. It is only in the last decade, with the defeat of the second of the illiberal creeds which ran riot in the last century and the undisputed emergence of the United States as the world hegemon, that the twentieth-century's global disorder and economic disintegration is coming to be reversed. But is the United States willing and able to maintain its Pax, which could underwrite the resurrection of another LIEO like that of the British in the nineteenth century? And if it is not, what are the likely consequences? What form of U.S. empire is likely to be sustainable and to promote the order required for the benign processes of globalization to work? Are the antiglobalization arguments of various activists of a self-proclaimed international civil society valid? Should the U.S. imperium promote democracy around the world? These are the central questions I want to raise in this book, but I hope I have said enough already to emphasize that globalization cannot be understood without understanding empires.

PLAN OF THE BOOK

This book is in three parts. In the first part, "Peace," I examine the alternative views on maintaining the peace required for globalization. I show how some simple economic models can explain why it can be expected that interstate anarchy is likely to be replaced by imperial hegemony, and what explains the extension and fall of these empires. A historical survey shows how empires have been natural throughout human history, how international anarchy has been usually replaced by the economically and militarily most advanced country establishing its hegemony. The period since the fall of the Roman empire in Europe has been the exception, with its anarchical European states system which has formed the implicit background for academic international relations. The European empires that arose were part of the ongoing struggle for the mastery of Europe among the various successive European powers which achieved a temporary dominance. Of these, the British, while being the last, also established the first truly global empire. The globalization this promoted in the nineteenth-century liberal international economic order was wholly benign and allowed many of the current developing countries to begin modernization. But, by the late nineteenth century, the United States had overtaken Britain in its economic size.

However, unlike the British, whose liberal international economic order was based on free trade and laissez faire, the United States has created a new LIEO which has rested on a number of dangerous economic fallacies which are discussed in the second part of the book, "Prosperity." Unlike Britain which acted upon the correct principle that it should unilaterally adopt free trade, the United States has relied on reciprocity. This will continue to create friction and disorder. The United States has also since the 1930s' New Deal and the populist antitrust legislation at the end of the nineteenth century wrongly eschewed laissez faire. This too will be shown to be inimical to maintaining global order. Many of the complaints of the antiglobalization brigades about the increase in world poverty and inequality flowing from globalization will be shown to be invalid, as will the growing demands that, because of the various financial crises of the 1990s, global capital flows should be controlled.

The most serious problem facing a new U.S. imperium is the self-image of the United States as the only moral nation pursuing universal values. But I will contest the purported universality of these universal values and argue that they are the specific values of a particular culture, Western Christendom. There are many, including the self-appointed spokesmen[10] of a mythical international civil society, who want its empire to transmit its moral values. A distinction between the cosmological and material beliefs of different civilizations (cultures) (see Lal [1998]) may be useful in explaining why one set of Western beliefs—the material—may command universal acceptance while another—the cosmological—may not. Material beliefs concern ways of making a living. As the environment in which one has to earn an income changes, these material beliefs will alter, as they have. They are malleable. The process of modernization—the move from the material beliefs of an agrarian to those of an industrial economy—will thus change material beliefs. By contrast, cosmological beliefs concern people's view of their place in the world and their relationship to others. They relate to morality and the beliefs associated with different religions. They concern questions of, in Plato's words, "How one should live." These cosmological beliefs of different cultures are difficult to change. The adoption of Western cosmological beliefs can be described as Westernization. The third part of the book, "Morality," will show that the so-called universal values are really the culture-specific values of Western Christendom, and that if they are forced on other civilizations, there will be resistance. While the Rest may voluntarily embrace the material beliefs of the West through globalization, they do not want to embrace its cosmological beliefs. They want to modernize but not Westernize. The same critique will be shown to apply to the broad "church" of antiglobalization activists who have their own diverse agenda fueled by what they see as the moral claims of an imagined international civil society. A U.S. imperium's attempt to link the transfer of its material to its cosmological beliefs could mean that the wholly benign change of accepting Western material beliefs, which accompanies the modernization promoted by globalization, will illegitimately be seen as also accepting the change in cosmological beliefs involved in Westernization. This could be exploited by cultural nationalists around the world to provoke a backlash against globalization.

The final chapter sums up my assessment of what form the U.S. imperium should take if it is to fulfill the hope expressed by Virgil for Rome in the epigraph and if, given U.S. domestic politics, this is likely to happen.

PART ONE

Peace

CHAPTER 1

Empires

In 1960 when I went up to Oxford, the recording of a theater cabaret called "At the Drop of a Hat" was all the rage. It was performed by a duo of former Oxford undergraduates—Michael Flanders and Donald Swann. One of their songs was "The Reluctant Cannibal." In it a cannibal father brings a roast leg of an insurance salesman for his children's supper to the log. This leads to resounding "yums" from the children. Except for junior, who pushes away his shell, gets up from the log, and says he will have no part of it as he doesn't eat people, "Eating people is wrong!" All the arguments of his father and siblings fail to persuade him, as he keeps repeating "Eating people is wrong!" Till his exasperated father says: "I give up, you used to be a regular anthropophagi. If this crazy idealistic idea of yours was to catch on, I just don't know where we would all be. It would just about ruin our entire internal economy. Fortunately, I suppose its catching on isn't very likely—why, you might just as well go around saying 'Don't fight people,' for example." Whereupon the son exclaims: "Don't fight people? Ha, ha!" and father and son roll about in helpless laughter, shouting "Ridiculous!"[1]

Alas, as evolutionary psychology is confirming and as the great political theorist Thomas Hobbes asserted, fighting and violence are endemic to human nature.[2] As Hobbes said, it leads to a "war of all against all" which makes life "nasty, brutish and short."[3] He noted "that in the nature of man, we find three principal causes of quarrel. First, Competition; secondly, Diffidence; thirdly, Glory. The first maketh men invade for gain; the second, for safety; and the third, for reputation. The first use violence, to make themselves masters of other men's persons, wives, children and cattle; the second, to defend them; the third for trifles, as a word, a smile, a different opinion, and any other sign of undervalue, either direct in their persons or by reflection in their kindred, their friends, their nation, their profession or their name."[4] To end this anarchical state of nature, a common power—Hobbes's Leviathan—is needed to provide that elementary security without which any social life is impossible. If this is true for maintaining domestic order, is a similar international Leviathan needed to provide order in an anarchical international system of states?

Empires have been the international analogue of a domestic Leviathan. But, empires need to be distinguished from hegemony. It is a distinction which goes back to Thucydides who noted that, in its alliance during the Peloponnesian War, Sparta controlled the foreign policy of its allies but allowed them considerable autonomy in their domestic affairs. By contrast, Athens in its empire controlled both the foreign and domestic policies of its allies. Thus, empires control both foreign and domestic policy, hegemons control only foreign policy.[5]

Also, as Machiavelli noted, this control of the domestic domain by an empire can take a number of forms. He wrote: "When those states which have been acquired are accustomed to live at liberty under their own laws, there are three ways of holding them. The first is to despoil them; the second is to go and live there in person; the third is to allow them to live under their own laws, taking tribute of them, and creating within the country a government composed of a few who will keep it friendly to you."[6]

The first option was taken by the nomadic empires. But they realized that if their imperium was to be maintained, they would have to move to the other two alternatives: formal and informal empire. In India, the British only ruled part of the country directly. The rest, consisting of princely states, were ruled indirectly through British political agents assigned to the native rulers. Wherever possible the British sought indirect rather than direct control to project their imperial power. This included areas like Latin America which were not part of their formal empire.[7] The Athenian empire was also an example of indirect rule, while the Roman empire was, like the British, a mixture.

What determines whether international anarchy is replaced by hegemony or empire? What determines whether the empire is ruled directly or indirectly? A theory I developed to explain the rise and fall of empires in India in my book *The Hindu Equilibrium*, combined with one developed by my University of California, Los Angeles colleague Jack Hirshleifer to explain how international anarchy is replaced by hegemony, helps to answer these questions.[8]

THE RISE AND FALL OF EMPIRES

The maintenance of international order raises the same issues that arise in maintaining domestic order. So we must begin by explaining how a state arises with a monopoly of coercive power within its borders. The state has to be given a monopoly of violence to maintain the peace, as Hobbes wrote, "covenants without the sword, are but words, and of no strength to secure a man at all."[9] From the historical record, the state as an institution arose with the development of sedentary civilizations. Before that, the stateless tribal societies studied by anthropologists in Africa are likely to have been the norm. Though warfare to take others' resources was endemic to these societies, it is with settled agriculture that organized means of protecting one's own or taking others' resources arose. The resulting monopoly of violence of the state could have arisen as the result of a Mafia-type protection racket whereby some roving bandits decided that, instead of making periodic raids, they could make higher returns from settling down and exploiting the villagers. Alternatively, it could have arisen because of the communal needs for the organization of peasant villages, as social contract theorists have claimed. Economic historians have not been able to resolve which of these routes—the predatory or contractual—gave rise to the state in the agrarian civilizations of Eurasia.

Nevertheless, there is some evidence from the earliest states established in the river valleys of the Tigris and Euphrates in Mesopotamia, the Nile valley in Egypt, and the Indus valley in India, that in these earliest Eurasian civilizations the state arose as a communal form of organization—a contractual origin. But, because of the encroachments of the nomads who besieged these civilizations from the northern steppes and the southern deserts, they were transformed by predatory intruders, roving bandits who turned into stationary bandits. Before examining the evolution of these ancient empires, I shall provide a framework to explain their rise and fall.

Domestic Order and the Predatory State[10]

Once sedentary agriculture came to be practiced in the ancient river valleys of Eurasia, we can expect that groups with a comparative advantage in taking (roving bandits) decided that their take could be increased if they settled down (became stationary bandits) and provided the basic public goods of law and order. These public goods financed by part of the tax takings would have led to the enforcement of property rights, which would raise the productivity of the economy and thence the tax revenue. But, the state would be inherently prone to predation because of its monopoly of violence within its territory. The aim of this predatory state (like that of the Mafia gang controlling a neighborhood) would be to maximize its net revenues, its net takings.[11]

Once established, the major threat to the predatory state lies in its being overthrown by rival predators (gangsters) who wish to seize its takings. The incumbent predator (Mafia leader), however, has a number of important advantages against any rival from within his own or some rival group seeking to overthrow him and take over his territory. The first advantage is that he will already have invested in the infrastructure of coercion—in the form of fortifications, armaments, roads, courtrooms, bureaus, etc., some of which the rival will have to invest in to challenge the incumbent. The incumbent will thus already have some sunk costs in his established system of coercion which the challenger will have to incur anew. Both will, of course, have to incur similar costs in running the state, in terms of expenditures on the police, the bureaucracy, the army, judges, etc. So it is the sunk fixed costs which provide a major barrier to entry for a rival challenging the current predator controlling the state.

For internal rivals trying to organize a coup, the military technology and the physical size of the naturally defensible territory will be vital. Other things being equal, a physically smaller territory would be easier to take over than a larger one, while the changing technology of warfare which makes large scale an advantage in the violence industry would tend to favor the incumbent. Thus, the cannon revolution in the fifteenth century allowed the development of larger centralizing states by eliminating local competitors hiding in their newly vulnerable castles.

For external rivals, amalgamation costs and geography will be important in making a successful challenge; in both these respects the incumbent may also have an important advantage. The incumbent may have been able to instill loyalty among the populace under his control for ethnic, nationalist, or ideological reasons. Given the resulting ethnic, linguistic, and religious differences between the external rival and the people in the incumbent's territory, the indigenous predator can count on a form of loyalty which the external rival cannot. This would require any challenger to spend extra resources to pacify and amalgamate a hostile population. Quite often external rivals have minimized these amalgamation costs by adopting the culture of the people they are taking over. The barbarians who destroyed the Roman empire and the successive nomads from the steppes who attacked China have followed this path of cultural assimilation with their newly acquired subjects.

Finally, given the existing military technology, the geography of the territory controlled by the incumbent may provide natural barriers to the entry of an external rival. The system of ancient Greek city-states was preserved because of its geography. But, with Athens's development as a sea power, the geographical barrier could be overcome. Later, in medieval Europe, as communications and military technology improved, larger nation-states could be created within natural geographical boundaries: the sea protected England, the Pyrennes and the Alps and the northern marshes provided the natural defenses of Spain, France, the Netherlands, and Italy. These raised the entry costs for external predators.

It is these barriers to the entry of challengers which allow the incumbent predator to extract revenue from his subjects. The higher the barriers, the greater the rent he can extract from his monopoly in coercion. But, if he raises his takings beyond the natural level allowed by these sunk costs and barriers to entry, a challenger would be able to displace him by providing his subjects the same protection for lower takings.

However, human beings are mortal. It would be rational for an individual predatory ruler to raise his takings from his prey in the later part of his life, even if this threatens his state with internal coups or foreign invasions. This is where the selfish gene enters. If the individual predator cares about his genes embodied in his progeny, he will wish to create a dynasty where his natural monopoly in coercion with its takings is passed on to his kin. This dynastic motive will then prevent him from acting myopically and allowing his profitable natural monopoly to become contestable by raising his takings above the long-run sustainable level. But, as the level of this sustainable rent and the accompanying tax burden is necessarily uncertain, it is as likely that, other things being equal, cycles of fiscal predation and thence the rise and fall of dynasties could emerge, as happened in India.

International Anarchy and Imperial Hegemony

If there are no natural geographical barriers preventing an easy conquest, competing predatory states will arise, each trying to extend its territory. For the revenue or rents available will rise as more territory with its inhabitants is conquered and incorporated into a particular state. But the extension of territory will also increase the costs of maintaining and running the state. So, given the relative costs and the benefits (revenues or rents) which can be extracted by an extension of its territory, there will be a natural limit to the geographical size of the state, where the marginal costs of acquiring new territory is equal to the marginal increase in revenue it provides.

With these natural limits to the size of the state governed not only by geography but by the state of communications, transport, and military technology, as well as the productive capacity of the economy, a number of competing states in a particular region could arise. This occurred in ancient times in the vast alluvial Indo-Gangetic plain in northern India, when the costs of any single state conquering all the others were too high, and in the ancient system of city-states in Greece, when protected from each other by their geography. They then comprised an anarchical international society of states.[12]

Anarchical equilibrium, however, breaks down if one of the competing states obtains an improvement in its military technology or in the productivity of its economy, which it can turn into a decisive military advantage, allowing it to overcome its rivals and establish its hegemony or empire. But, as with the domestic predatory state, the imperial state would also face rising fiscal costs of expansion.

These rising costs would to some extent be mitigated by another important source of revenue which historically has arisen with empire: long distance trade. Till the nineteenth-century transport revolution based on the steam engine, long distance trade was expensive and consisted mainly of high-value and nonbulky goods, which most often were not produced in the receiving areas. This long distance trade was even more precarious than sedentary agriculture, as it was more susceptible to the depredations of roving bandits. Providing protection to such high-value trade would offer even higher rents (above those available from protecting agriculture) once the stationary bandit had established his protection regime. Thus, a symbiosis developed between long distance trade and empires: empires facilitated trade and taxing trade provided the means to extend the empire.

Slaves were another important form of takings from warfare and a motive for the extension of empires. All the Eurasian civilizations faced the common problem of providing an adequate supply of labor to work the land which was abundant. Slaves provided an important addition to the domestic supply of labor. A continuous and numerous supply of slaves depended on warfare. Slavery has been ubiquitous throughout human history.[13] One of the motives behind Rome's continual wars to extend its territory was to augment the supply of the slaves on whom its agriculture depended. The Islamic empires with their dependence on mamelukes to protect and run their empires were also dependent on a steady supply of slave labor.

Thus, an asymmetric improvement in one state's military technology or a rise in its economic productivity that can be translated into military superiority leads to the breakdown of the international anarchy of states into hegemony. What leads to the conversion of this hegemony into an empire? Other things being equal, empires, which seek to control both the domestic and foreign policies of other states, will be more costly than hegemony. Control of foreign policy is equivalent to reducing the threat from a potential external predator. If the threat from external predation can be contained because of an asymmetric military advantage and the costs of amalgamating a foreign population into an empire are high, a hegemony is likely to be preferred to an empire. But if an empire is established and the amalgamation costs are high, the imperial power may choose to minimize these costs by ruling indirectly, as in the Athenian empire. The main gains from an indirect empire are likely to be the gains from expanding and protecting long distance trade. Depending on the relevant costs and benefits, there may be an optimal mix of direct and indirect empire, where the marginal benefit (from increased revenue) equals the marginal costs (in terms of amalgamation costs) of converting the indirect into direct empire.

THE EVOLUTION OF THE ANCIENT EMPIRES

We can now turn to an examination of the rise and fall of the ancient empires. The oldest go back to the origins of civilization.

Mesopotamia

In Mesopotamia about 4000 B.C. settled agricultural communities with cities began to appear. This civilization was based on vast irrigation works to make use of the annual flooding of the Tigris and Euphrates. The labor effort involved was coordinated by priests supervising the allocation of land, maintaining boundaries, storing a part of the harvest in temple granaries, and directing work gangs to clear the canals and strengthen the dikes each year.[14] These independent Sumerian states apparently arose from an implicit contract for organizing the communal effort needed to sustain them, where the priests also promised the divine management and intervention that all prescientific societies invoked for their survival. From the archaeological evidence it appears that there was no war during this early rise of the Sumerian cities to statehood. None of the 13 cities which are known to have existed had walls. Sumeria was a civilization without domestic strife because of the awesome authority of its priest-kings. There was no intercity war because there was no clash of interests. External aggression was deterred by the difficult terrain surrounding the fruitful valley. As neither the camel nor the horse had yet been domesticated, there was no means of mobility for the nomads from the western desert or the eastern steppes.[15]

But, with the growth of population and the spread of cultivation in the valley, these previously disconnected states increasingly began to collide. The priests who controlled these city-states were unable to manage this intercity warfare. Equally serious were the raids which began with the domestication of the horse and the camel by the more warlike people on the fringes of the river valley. With the extraordinary powers delegated in time of war to the wielders of the sword, the institution of kingship arose through military relationships being superimposed upon an older religio-political system.[16] Kingship then became the normal practice in peacetime.

So, by the third millennium B.C., an interstate system (similar to that in ancient Greece) seems to have emerged.

These Sumerian cities were united for the first time under the lordship of Lugalzaggisi ca. 2375 B.C., but it was not till the barbarian conquest by Sargon of Akkad ca. 2340 B.C. that the first Sumerian empire was created. The Akkadians combined barbarian prowess with organization to form a powerful military force which by ca. 2000 B.C. had created the world's first empire stretching into Syria, Lebanon, the Zargos mountain range separating Mesopotamia from northern Persia and Southern Turkey.[17] At its boundaries were the jealous predators, envious of the wealth of the plains and on the alert for any military weakness. Persisting local loyalties undermined the empire from within, but most serious were the problems of administering a geographically far-flung empire with the available means. Sargon's grandson Naram Sin tried indirect imperialism by replacing local rulers with his own relatives, but they did not always prove loyal to their kin.

So the Akkadian empire collapsed and it was only when Hammurabi ca. 1700 B.C. conquered the newly emergent city-states that a new Mesopotamian empire was created. This proved more enduring, as in the intervening period four conditions for the development of a secular and centralized authority had developed. These were, according to William McNeill: "(1) the development of an imperial political theory and of a wider political loyalties against the unmitigated localism which had characterized the first Sumerian age; (2) the development of a bureaucracy and a professional army; (3) the improvement of administrative technique, especially through the use of written communications; (4) the increase in intercity and interregional trade and the appearance of an independent merchant class."[18] But this empire, along with the other ancient Eurasian empires, was to be conquered ca. 1525 B.C. by the nomads from the steppes who had developed a fierce, new, and decisive instrument of war—the chariot.

These charioteers proved invincible against the unarmored foot soldiers of the agrarian empires. But the technology was soon disseminated, and ca. 1365 B.C. the native Mesopotamians overthrew the Hurrian invaders, who had destroyed Hammurabi's empire, and created their own empire, the Assyrian. By going on the offensive and extending their boundaries, they solved the perennial problem faced by Mesopotamia—the encirclement of its rich but naturally defenseless land by predators. Their multiethnic empire included parts of Arabia, Iran, Turkey, and modern Syria and Israel.[19] They created a professional charioteer army, recruited without ethnic discrimination, which was, Keegan observes, "able to campaign as far as 300 miles from base and to move at speeds of advance that would not be exceeded until the coming of the internal combustion engine."[20]

Egypt

It is not known whether the settlements in Egypt that had grown up along the valley of the Nile and were ruled by local chiefs were united peacefully or by war under a single king, Menes, about 3100 B.C. This established the kingdom which was to survive for 3000 years under the pharaohs. Unlike Mesopotamia, until the domestication of the camel, Egypt was protected by its geography from invaders from the deserts on both sides of the valley. The threat from the south was eliminated by the Egyptian conquest of Nubia (1990–1785 B.C.) and the establishment of an extensive series of forts. The threat from the sea to the north became manifest during the second millennium B.C. It was met by moving the capital from Memphis to Thebes, by raising a standing army, and by using the delta as a natural barrier.[21] With this extension and defense of the empire to its natural territorial limits, Keegan says, the ancient Egyptians for "fourteen centuries of what must have seemed a fixed normality to the generations which lived and died within their span, may very well have been spared the reality of war . . . altogether."[22]

This peace was shattered by the invasion of the barbarian charioteers, the Hyksos. They began infiltrating from the Sinai desert ca. 1730 B.C. and established their rule in the north. Even though the Hyksos tried to assimilate to Egyptian culture, they were hated as foreigners. By ca. 1570 B.C., a local princeling in Thebes, having adopted the chariot, led a rebellion which drove the Hyksos out of the Nile valley. Like the Assyrians, the Egyptians had learned the technique and ethos of imperial war making from the charioteers. Thereafter, no longer feeling safe behind their desert barriers, they extended their frontiers far from the Nile to the uplands of northern Syria. Their long isolation from the rest of the world came to an end, and they became a great imperial state which became part of the complex power struggles of the Middle East for the next thousand years.[23]

China

China had established an independent civilization in the valley of the Yellow River from about 3000 B.C. This was also attacked by charioteers from the steppes who established the Shang dynasty (1523–1028 B.C.) which in turn was overthrown ca. 1050–25 B.C. by the Zhou (a native southern dynasty), who had learned chariot warfare. Like most barbarian invaders, the Shang had been Sinified. Subsequent dynasties unified China, and the Qin dynasty ca. 217 B.C. created a bureaucratic authoritarian state, where various ethnically diverse people were unified as Hans through the bureaucratic device of writing their names in Chinese characters in a Chinese form. This bureaucratic authoritarianism developed very early. William Jenner notes that the reference manuals of a petty bureaucrat of the Qin regime show that "it kept detailed, quantified central records of the state of the crops almost field by field in every county of the empire. Maintaining that sort of control would be a daunting task for a government equipped with computers and telecommunications. Doing it before the invention of paper, when all the data had to be gathered, stored on strips of wood or bamboo, would have been impossible without an enormous bureaucracy."[24] This bureaucratic authoritarian empire has lasted to our day.

But it has by and large been a status quo empire, concerned more with maintaining internal order and fighting off any barbarian intrusions. Its foreign policy has followed the advice of the third-century Chinese Machiavellian philosopher Han Fei Tzu, who said that neither power nor order can be found abroad, but rather are matters of domestic government.

India

The fourth of the ancient agrarian civilizations was created in the Indus valley about 2500 B.C. Little is known about this civilization as its script has still not been deciphered. From the archaeological remains, it appears that the Indus valley civilization was based on utilizing the annual flooding of the great river. As in early Mesopotamia, it seems that there were no kings and warriors and that it too was a theocracy, where the priests organized the communal effort on which this form of agriculture depended. But, the massive fortifications which have been uncovered suggest that there must have been some warfare, perhaps to protect the rich harvest stored in the granaries from raiders from the adjacent mountainous areas. Dietmar Rothermund suggests that, "perhaps there was no warrior elite but bands of peasant soldiers trained for this purpose."[25]

By about 1500 B.C. charioteers from the steppes, the Aryans, completely destroyed this civilization. So unlike the other three agrarian civilizations which absorbed the barbarians, nothing of this ancient civilization survives. In time a new Aryan civilization was built, which initially consisted of a large number of feuding kingdoms in the fertile Indo-Gangetic plain. The taming of elephants in the great forests of southern Bengal and Orissa allowed the war elephant to stamp out the chariot as an instrument of warfare. Sitting on a platform tied to the back of an elephant, archers could direct a shower of arrows at the single warrior in a chariot. This new instrument of warfare changed the decisiveness of battles for the states which could afford them, for war elephants were difficult to maintain. In medieval India the price of a good war elephant was equivalent to 500 ordinary horses.[26] As several hundred elephants were required to form an efficient army corps capable of traversing long distances and trouncing the enemy, the considerable investment required could be provided only by a large empire. The war elephant thus had a centralizing tendency. The anarchy of the feuding states in the plains was replaced by the Mauryan empire (ca. 300–200 B.C.). This empire also created the bureaucratic framework for ruling the subcontinent which has survived to our day.[27] Though the imperial unity of the whole subcontinent has been ephemeral in Indian history because of the centrifugal tendencies dictated by geography and cycles in fiscal predation, the imperial ideal has animated every ruler of India.

Greece

In ancient Greece[28] the relatively indecisive patterns of warfare based on the phalanx, but lacking cavalry and effective missiles, led to the coexistence of a large number of city-states. But the increasing wealth of Athens and its deployment in the buildup of a large navy provided a militarily decisive instrument, as it now commanded the sea. This allowed it to turn many of the city-states into its dependencies in its new empire (466 B.C.). But it was defeated by a counter coalition led by Sparta in the Peloponnesian War (431–404 B.C.), which commanded a higher fighting intensity given the combined resources of the coalition; by adopting the new military technology of sea warfare, they countered the asymmetric[29] advantage of Athens. However, Sparta failed to establish its own hegemony, as the decisiveness parameter was too high for independent city-states to survive without allies but not high enough for a single hegemon to emerge.

The integration of infantry, siege weapons, cavalry, and missiles in a disciplined force gave Philip II of Macedon (356–336 B.C.) a decisive edge. Alexander the Great (334–323 B.C.) was the first to use these military innovations in land combat, uniting the Greeks and then using the decisive force of cavalry in the famous victory over the Persians and in the creation of another empire. But this empire did not last. Given the geographically large area to be controlled, the military decisiveness was not high enough to maintain hegemony, and the empire collapsed into an anarchic system of 3 or 4 states, each based on combined land and sea power, which lasted for 150 years. It was not till the Romans achieved asymmetric military decisiveness through superior organization, rather than through any special innovation in weapons or tactics, that Rome achieved imperial hegemony in the Mediterranean (ca. 133 B.C.).

Rome

Rome's main organizational innovation was the creation of the first professional army with the centurionate as its core. The Roman centurions were long-service unit leaders drawn from the best of the enlisted ranks. They formed the first body of fighting officers in history. They imbued the legions with backbone and transmitted the code of discipline and the accumulated store of tactical expertise by which Rome, over five centuries, waged successful, nearly continuous wars against numerous enemies.[30] With the growth of the empire, the army enlarged its recruitment from its Italian base to other nationalities, making the military a multinational institution united by a common duty owed to Rome.[31]

The conversion of the republic into an empire in all but name by Augustus (29 B.C.–A.D. 14) led to the creation of a centralized imperial bureaucracy to administer and finance this complex and highly centralized military state. The borders of the empire were stabilized by fortifying its scientific frontiers on the Danube, Rhine, the Scottish highlands, and the edge of the Sahara. Like the Chinese, the Romans treated the peoples beyond the pale as barbarians. Though they found it expedient to deal with them through diplomacy, they were not considered to be Rome's equal.

This imperial system was eventually undermined by growing problems in raising revenue and by the dilution of the nature of the professional army which formed its base. The first dilution occurred with Constantine (A.D. 312–337), who introduced sizable formations of cavalry and reduced the strength of the infantry on which the Roman army had relied since its inception. The second and fatal dilution came, says Keegan, when Theodosius (A.D. 375–395) accepted large units "of barbarian 'federates' who served not as the auxiliaries of old had done in units raised and officered by imperial officials, but as allies under their own leaders. This step, once taken, could not be withdrawn."[32] The barbarians were within the gates. The Western Roman empire collapsed.

The Steppes

For 2000 years since the Scythian raids into Mesopotamia in the seventh century B.C., the nomads of the steppes threatened the outer edges of civilization in Europe, the Middle East, India, and China. They came in waves, which William McNeill has ascribed to the altered carrying capacity of the grasslands of their steppe homeland caused by climatic change.[33] In these climatic cycles, moist seasons that allowed good grazing and hence animal and human infants to thrive were followed by harsher times making it difficult for the enlarged populations to survive. Migration within the steppes did not help, as the area as a whole suffered from these climatic variations. The nomads then sought their emergency rations by preying upon the sedentary agrarian civilizations on the edge of the steppes. They could have avoided this cycle of plenty and want if they had permanently left the steppes to conquer and settle in sedentary areas. The Mongols and Turks did establish tribute-yielding empires over settled peoples. This liberated them from the cycles of famine on the steppes, but they always longed for the nomadic way of life. Keegan writes, "What the nomads wanted was the best of both worlds: the comfort and luxury that settled ways yielded but also the freedom of the horseman's life, of the tented camp, of the hunt and of the seasonal shift of quarters."[34]

The Mongols. Nevertheless, these nomads did create or take over two great empires, one of which—that of the Ottoman Turks—lasted into modern times. It was Genghis Khan who, after uniting the Mongolian tribes in 1129, began the conquests which by 1258 under his grandson had stormed Baghdad, overrun the whole of northern China, Korea, Tibet, Central Asia, Persia, the Caucasus, Turkish Anatolia, and the Russian principalities. They raided India, campaigned in Eastern Europe, and even reached Vienna and Venice. Kublai Khan, Genghis' grandson, extended the eastern frontiers by including the whole of China and founded the Yuan dynasty which ruled till the end of the fourteenth century. The Mongols controlled Burma and Vietnam, failed to capture Japan and Java, and continued their raids into India, where in 1526 a descendant of Genghis, Babar, founded the Moghul (Mongol) dynasty. They thus created the largest land-based empire in Eurasian history.

This empire linked the ancient civilizations of China, India, and the Middle East, and the long distance trade promoted by their Pax was an important means of bringing new ideas and technology from the East to the West.[35] But like other horse people, they were unable to translate their conquests into permanent power. Genghis was a great military administrator, who offered a career open to the talents of all. His division of his army "into tens, hundreds and thousands—there were eventually to be ninety-five 'thousands'" anticipated the modern Western system of military organization where regiments contain squadrons which comprise sections.[36] But, this administrative ability "was extractive, not stabilizing, designed to support the nomadic way of life, not to change it. His system included no means for legitimizing the rule of a single successor, even in the eyes of the Mongols themselves, let alone of their subjects."[37]

Yet, their victories were astonishing. They did not have any advantage in military technology. Keegan argues that ultimately it was their pitiless and ruthless conduct of war that brought success, and that after they were Islamized, their war making was also infused with the force of an idea. But Genghis did not accept any "of Islam's palliating morality," such as showing mercy to strangers, and instead created terror in the people he opposed. "The tools of war making already at his disposal—the horse warrior's mobility, the long-range lethality of the composite bow, the do-or-die ethos of the *ghazi*,[38] the social elan of exclusive tribalism—were formidable enough. When to these ingredients was added a pitiless paganism . . . it is not surprising that Genghis and the Mongols acquired a reputation for invincibility. Their minds as well as their weapons were agents of terror, and the terror they spread remains a memory to this day."[39]

But, equally important was superb battlefield information.[40] Their scouts and messengers took along three or four extra horses, tethered, so they could switch mounts when one got tired. These "arrow riders" allowed the generals in the high command, far from the field of battle, to be well informed about occurrences within 3 or 4 days, while a sophisticated semaphore system for communication between field forces allowed a rapid battlefield response to changing circumstances. Moreover, the Mongols also had decentralized command in the field. They could therefore have both an overview and local initiative on the battlefield. The secret of their success was that the Khan could "advance his armies on a wide front, controlling them with a highly developed system of communications."[41]

Genghis Khan, like Alexander the Great, was motivated by glory. When told by his generals that life's sweetest pleasure lay in falconry, he purportedly replied: "You are mistaken. Man's greatest good fortune is to chase and defeat his enemy, seize his total possessions, leave his married women weeping and wailing, ride his gelding and use the bodies of his women as a nightshirt and support."[42] This pursuit of booty along with glory also succeeded in a massive spread of Genghis's genes, as has been recently confirmed in a study examining the chromosomes of 2,123 men from across Asia.[43] It found that an estimated 16 million males in a vast swath from Manchuria to Uzbekistan and Afghanistan are the direct descendants of Genghis as they carry his unique bits of DNA in their chromosomes.[44] Genghis's fighting thus allowed him to propagate his selfish genes to an unparalleled extent, apart from the glory.

The turning point for the Mongols in the heartland of civilization in the Middle East came in 1260, when their advance was finally stopped. They were defeated by the mameluke army of Egypt, which had learned from the Mongols and developed even faster means of strategic communications than the Mongols arrow riders, using carrier pigeons. It allowed them to mass a timely and effective defense.[45] As John Keegan notes, this battle "marked the power of one horse people, organized as a professional force and supported by the revenues of a sedentary state, to overcome that of another still living by pillage and animated by the primitive values of tribalism and vengeance."[46]

Yet the very success of Mongol arms carried its own nemesis. Besides the usual pattern of conquerors from the steppes being absorbed or else being repulsed by the agrarian civilizations they conquered, two other unintended consequences flowed from the success of their arms in the thirteenth century. The first was the introduction of the plague bacillus which Mongol horsemen had brought back from their campaigns in Yunan and Burma, where it was endemic in the local rodent population.[47] Once established in the steppes, the bacillus decimated the population. For two centuries after 1326 (when the Black Death hit Europe), there was rapid depopulation and even the abandonment of some of the best pasture land in Eurasia. However, by the time some form of immunity had been established and the steppes population began to recover, the Mongols were faced with the second consequence of their previous expansion, the diffusion of military technology, particularly gunpowder from China to the West. The steppes nomads found that the firearms developed in Europe by about 1550, and rapidly diffused to the other sedentary civilizations, could now counter nomad archers on the battlefield. The nomads' military superiority was finally eroded. By the eighteenth century the diffusion of gunpowder weaponry led to the final eclipse of steppes peoples' military power,[48] and the progressive encroachment of the Chinese and Russian empires into their grasslands.

The Ottomans. Another steppes people, the Turks, were more successful in creating a long lasting empire. They had infiltrated the Abbasid empire of Islam and gradually took over political control in Baghdad. But till 1258 they cloaked their usurpation of effective authority by keeping members of the Abbasid family on the throne. Thereafter, till the end of the First World War, the Ottoman empire they established was to be the core of Islamic civilization with vital outposts in India, Africa, and Southeast Asia.

Over the years they created an effective standing army, based on the pattern of the mamelukes—slaves who were part of the sultan's personal household—the Janissaries. They also had an obedient feudal army of Turkish warriors. Moreover, the slaves from the sultan's household also went out to the provinces as the sultan's agents. Thus the military and administrative cadres were dominated by these slaves. When the number of available slaves dried up, the Ottomans took to conscripting slaves from the Christian villages of the Balkans. The administrative structure they created provided a Pax which was tolerant of ethnic and religious diversity. However, they could not keep up with a resurgent West, and with Kemal Ataturk's Young Turk revolution, the successor state to the Ottomans ceased to be the center of Islam and became a secular republic.

The Russians. The other empire which expanded into the steppes was a successor of the Mongols who in 1240 had destroyed the first Russian

Kievan state. This had been established by Vladimir in 980 and had adopted Greek Orthodox Christianity as the state religion. After the fall of Constantinople in 1453, Ivan III, the ruler of Moscow, declared independence from the Mongol horde and laid claim to the inheritance of the Kievan state with the assumption of the title Sovereign of Russia. That began the Russian expansion to the south and the east. By the fifteenth century Muscovy's rate of expansion exceeded that of any Western state. In the great age of European expansion, while Western Europeans were creating their short-lived maritime empires, the Russians created one of the largest, and most long-lived, land-based empires in Siberia.[49]

It was an autocratic state, which has been called a "tribute collecting hierarchy,"[50] in which the noble landowners had total authority over their peasant serfs, and the czar had unchallenged and complete authority over the nobles. With its divorce from Latin Christendom, Russia was soon left behind in the technological changes which led to the rise of the West. It has since then periodically tried to catch up with the West, first under Peter the Great in the first quarter of the eighteenth century, then in the second half of the nineteenth century after the abolition of serfdom by Czar Alexander II, and for a third time under Stalin in the 1930s. In the first two efforts, the Russians sought to emulate the individualism which had led to the rise of the West, but in the third, they adopted another body of Western thought, the collectivist body of Marxist thought that had arisen in the late nineteenth century. With the failure of this experiment in 1989, not only did its empire collapse, but Russia is again turning to the more individualistic and liberal traditions of the West in order to modernize.

THE INTERNATIONAL SYSTEM SINCE THE FALL OF ROME

The Anarchical European States System

After the collapse of the Roman empire, Europe fell into the bleak Hobbesian state of a continual war. The fragmented political systems arising with the end of the Roman Pax saw constant strife and the dominance of warrior aristocracies. These warriors provided local protection and created societies whose existence was based on the view that there would be permanent war. The Roman church provided some form of legitimacy to this anarchic system after it had found a way to reconcile its notion that, in the divine order, peace was the normal condition, even though in the real world its own survival depended on the protection and favor of various warlords. St. Augustine had squared this circle in *The City of God*. War was part of mankind's fallen state. Mankind was both citizen of the City of God and of a worldly kingdom, and every man had a duty to render unto God what was God's and to Caesar what was Caesar's. Fighting against the enemies of Christendom was entirely just, while war among Christians had to be accepted as part of man's fallen condition.[51] But rules had to be laid down for this sinful activity and from this arose the notion of a just war.[52]

Despite Charlemagne's coronation in A.D. 800 as the Holy Roman Emperor, Europe remained an area of warlordism. The emperor could not afford the expense of maintaining the mounted knights who provided the mobile forces needed to defend the far-flung frontiers of this notional empire. For the alienation of land to the barons had deprived the emperor of a source of revenue; there was not much he could do to enforce his imperial authority. Thus, after the collapse of the Roman empire, no successor state was able to create an equivalent of the Roman army, as none was able to provide the necessary fiscal base. A myriad of small principalities came to form the medieval Christian international society. This began the European speculations on the conditions for maintaining order in an international anarchical society.

By the early fifteenth century, the cannon, by making it possible to batter down castle walls, ended the long inconclusive phase of indecisive siege warfare on which the medieval anarchical system had survived. Though there were improvements in the art of fortifications, their economic cost put them beyond the resources of the smaller units, leading to their amalgamation into the larger nation-states of Europe. But no hegemon was to emerge, as there was no asymmetric military innovation that would have increased the decisiveness in conflict in favor of the innovator. Nor was there any productive innovation that would have increased the resource base of the competing European powers.

With the Reformation, even the notional unity of Christendom was shattered. The new nation-states came to sanction the particular schismatic religions of their kings, which they then sought to impose by force of arms on the relevant schismatics of other nations. The resulting wars of religion ended in a stalemate and the Peace of Westphalia of 1648. This established the first modern anarchical international order. It recognized the sovereignty of states in their internal relations with their subjects to maintain domestic order, while in their external relations they were part of an international society of states—albeit anarchical—in which international order among them was to be maintained by the preservation of a balance between powers, if necessary by wars aimed at maintaining this balance.

But this process of creating nation-states was occurring when the long and slow divergence between the West and the Rest had already begun. The development of cannons and guns meant that aspiring monarchs now had the means to bring their overmighty barons, ensconced in their hitherto impregnable castles, to heel. But to pay for these new military artifacts, they had to raise taxes. They found that they could only do so by coming to some sort of terms with representative bodies of their working subjects, hitherto the lowliest of the three estates. For in all these regions (as in the other Eurasian civilizations), a common social stratification had arisen between those who wielded the sword, those who were the keepers of the book, and those who pushed the plow.[53]

In England, the original warrior aristocracy destroyed itself by internecine warfare in the Middle Ages and, from the time of the Tudors, was replaced by an oligarchy of landowners and merchants which subordinated both Crown and Church to the interests of a bourgeois culture more concerned with maximizing wealth than military power.[54] But the Enlightenment provided a challenge to the way of thinking about war and peace which had dominated the *ancien régime* of the estates. The rising bourgeoisie challenged not just the Church but also the Crown. Rousseau argued that Man's inherent nature was not as dark as painted by Hobbes, but rather was a tabula rasa, which had been poisoned by the institutions of the *ancien régime*. War was not a natural state but only the result of this social system, which therefore had to be destroyed. Thus began the idealist tradition of international relations which continues to have contemporary resonance.[55]

The anarchical society of European nation-states created by the Peace of Westphalia persisted, as none of the constituent states were able to achieve the military and economic superiority required to establish their hegemony. Thus, the anarchical order was stable. Some quantitative evidence for the underlying reasons for this stability can be gleaned from table 1 and figures 1 and 2. These figures are derived from the data for the world and its principal regions that Angus Maddison has heroically assembled for the population and per capita incomes from A.D. 1000 to the present. There are two major correlates of power: larger populations can mobilize more warriors and, if they are richer, can translate their relative economic strength into an asymmetric fighting force to protect their own resource base and/or increase it by seizure from others.[56] Despite obvious limitations, the Maddison data allow us to provide a summary of the relative strengths of the various powers that formed the European system from 1500 till 1998. (As Germany did not become a state till the nineteenth century it is only included in figure 2.) The table and figure 1 also include the major non-European civilizations of India and China. Figure 1 normalizes the *relative* GDP of the various powers around Russia (with a value of 100) for the period 1500 to 1998. Figure 2 shows the absolute GDP levels, excluding India and China, and considers just the European balance of power (but includes the U.S.) from 1500 to 1950.

Table 1. GDP, GDP per capita, and population for major countries, 1500–1998 (million 1990 international $)

Year	China	France	India	Netherlands	Russia(1)	Spain	United Kingdom	USA	Germany
					Country				
GDP (million 1990 international $)									
1500	61,800	10,912	60,500	716	8,475	4,744	2,815	800	0
1600	96,000	15,559	74,250	2,052	11,447	7,416	6,007	600	0
1700	82,800	21,180	90,750	4,009	16,222	7,893	10,709	527	0
1820	228,600	38,434	111,417	4,288	37,710	12,975	36,232	12,548	
1870	189,740	72,100	134,882	9,952	83,646	22,295	100,179	98,374	71,429
1913	241,344	144,489	204,241	24,955	232,351	45,686	224,618	517,383	237,332
1998	3,873,352	1,150,080	1,702,712	317,517	1,132,432	560,138	1,108,568	7,394,598	1,460,069
GDP per capita (1990 international $)									
1500	600	727	550	754	500	698	714	400	0
1600	600	841	550	1,368	553	900	974	400	0
1700	600	986	550	2,110	611	900	1,250	527	0
1820	600	1,230	533	1,821	689	1,063	1,707	1,257	
1870	530	1,876	533	2,753	943	1,376	3,191	2,445	1,821
1913	552	3,485	673	4,049	1,488	2,255	4,921	5,301	3,648
1998	3,117	19,558	1,746	20,224	3,893	14,227	18,714	27,331	17,799
World Population for Major Countries (in 000s)									
1500	103,000	15,000	110,000	950	16,950	6,800	3,942	2,000	0
1600	160,000	18,500	135,000	1,500	20,700	8,240	6,170	1,500	0
1700	138,000	21,471	165,000	1,900	26,550	8,770	8,565	1,000	0
1820	381,000	31,246	209,000	2,355	54,765	12,203	21,226	9,981	0
1870	358,000	38,400	253,000	3,615	88,672	16,201	31,393	40,241	39,231
1913	437,140	41,463	303,700	6,164	156,192	20,263	45,649	97,606	65,058
1998	1,242,700	58,805	975,000	15,700	290,866	39,371	59,237	270,561	82,029

Source: Angus Maddison, *The World Economy: A Millenial Perspective* (Paris, OECD, 2001). Tables B-21, p. 264; B-18, p. 261; B-10, p. 241
(1) refers to the former USSR area

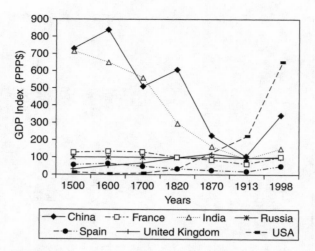

Fig. 1. Index of GDP for major countries, 1500–1998 (Russia equals 100)

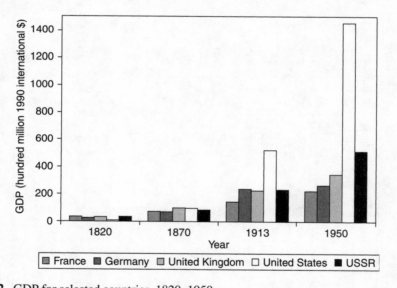

Fig. 2. GDP for selected countries, 1820–1950

Source: Maddison, Angus. *The World Economy: A Millennial Perspective*, OECD 2001, Table B-18.

Higher GDP, other things being equal, can, if desired, be translated into military power. Thus, from figure 1, it is clear that the great powers in 1500 were the non-European empires of China and India. But they went their separate ways and were only tangentially connected with the European states system until they felt the Western impact with the rise of the gunpowder empires. Among the Europeans, there seems to be almost a stalemate, with some rising then falling, with no clear dominant economic and military power (figs. 1 and 2).[57] Any military innovations that were made, such as the adoption and adaptation of artillery for sea warfare or the importance of drill in creating cohesive standing armies, were quickly diffused among the competing European powers. This is the anarchical society par excellence.

Islam

The Ottomans also formed part of this European system, if not least as the object of fear and loathing on the part of Christendom till their weakness became manifest after they were repelled in 1683 from the gates of Vienna. Thereafter, the Ottoman empire became the "sick man of Europe," over whose decomposing body the European great powers were to squabble for over a century. The Ottomans were the inheritors of an alternative civilization and imperial system: Islam. The reasons for the rapid success of the nomads from the Arabian desert in destroying and conquering antiquity has continued to baffle historians. Beginning with their defeat of the Persian army at Qadisiyah (near today's Baghdad) in 637, they conquered Syria (in 636), Egypt (642), the whole of North Africa (by 705), and crossing into Spain, reached the Pyrenees (711). Though their siege of Constantinople failed in 677, they were back in 717.

Keegan notes that these victories were astonishing as the Arab armies were of poor quality and, unlike the imperial armies they faced, had no experience of intensive warfare. Nor did they enjoy any advantage in equipment or military technique like the horse people of the steppes, who had periodically created an asymmetric military advantage in their raids into the sedentary civilizations of Eurasia. The Arabs had few horses and used camels to cross terrain that civilized armies could not penetrate. Then, before a battle, they would transfer to their led horses to launch their unexpected attacks. But unlike the regular armies, they were ready to take flight into the desert to fight another day if the opposition proved too strong. They were thus irregular "primitive" guerrilla fighters, whose major form of feuding in their desert homeland had been the raid. Nevertheless, as Keegan notes: "it is a general rule that primitives lose to regulars over the long run; harassment is an effective means of waging a defensive war, but wars are ultimately won by offensives and the Arabs were certainly on the offensive during the era of conquests. The conclusion must be that it was Islam itself, which lays so heavy an emphasis on the fight for the faith, that made them so formidable in the field."[58]

Islam and also the lure of booty: these two factors were responsible for the prophet Mohammed's success in conquering Arabia. The new faith he created claimed that the Arabs were the descendants of Ishmael, the son of Hagar, the Egyptian concubine of Abraham. So, both the Jews who descended from Isaac, the son of Abraham's wife, Sarah, and the Arabs who descended from Ishmael have a common monotheist history as descendants of Abraham with independent genealogies, and Mohammed claimed to be an Abrahamic prophet like Moses and Christ.[59] He thus integrated religious insights borrowed from Judaism and Christianity with a religious articulation of the ethnic identity of his Arab followers. This appealed to the newly urbanized Arabs who were attracted to Judaism and Christianity as the religions of civilization, but who were too proud to accept a foreign faith. This created the religious nationalism that provided the ideological motor behind the Arab conquests. It also led them to create a new civilization, unlike their barbarian cousins from the steppes who conquered the ancient Eurasian civilizations only to be absorbed by them.

The second factor in the rapid Muslim conquest was the material return in the form of the "take" by fighting—booty. From its inception, with Mohammed's use of the sword to convert and conquer, Islam had offered these more material rewards to the faithful. With their dramatic conquests, it appeared God smiled on Muslims.

After a series of civil wars, the original Arab empire collapsed into a number of different states. But ultimately, another set of barbarians from the steppes converted to the new religion and established another Islamic empire—that of the Ottomans. The Ottoman empire became intimately involved with the European states system. The Islamic threat it posed persisted till the raising of the siege of Vienna in 1683. The Ottomans established their own regular disciplined infantry but this was based (like the Islamic military system from its early days) on slaves. But from table 2, which shows the annual revenues of various European powers—which can be taken as a proxy for relative economic and military strength—for various dates from the fifteenth to the seventeenth centuries, it appears that the Ottomans did not have any asymmetric economic or military advantage which would have allowed them to establish a European hegemony.

Beyond Europe

The theories of international relations which influence thought and action in international politics to our day arose to explain war and peace in the anarchical European states system established after the collapse of the Roman empire. But, this was not the most common form of international system in history. At the time these theories were developed, in Eurasia—outside Latin Christendom—there were the Arab-Islamic system stretching from Spain to

Table 2. Estimated annual revenues of states from the fifteenth to seventeenth centuries (in million gold ducats)

Italian states (1492)	Other European states (c. 1600)	Non European states (various dates)
Naples 1.6	Spain (Castile) 9.0	Iran (1492) 3.0
Venice 1.0	France 5.0	Byzantium
Milan 0.6	Venice 3.9	(early middle
Florence 0.3		ages) 7.08–8.0
Papacy 0.2		(early 14th century) 1.0
Genoa 0.1		Ottoman empire (1527–28) 9.7

Source: H. Inalcik: in Inalcik and Quataert (eds.) (1994) *An Economic and Social History of the Ottoman Empire*, vol.1, Tables 1.20 and 1.21, pp. 81–82.

Persia, the international system of the Indian subcontinent, the Chinese system, and the Mongol-Tartar system of the Eurasian steppes. Some of these systems, such as the Arab-Islamic and the Indian, consisted of a number of independent states, but they were all Imperial systems. As Hedley Bull and Adam Watson note: "at the center of each was a suzerain Supreme Ruler—the Khalifa or Commander of the Faithful, the Emperor in Delhi, the Mongol Great Khan, the Chinese Son of Heaven—who exercised direct authority over the Heartland; and around this empire extended a periphery of locally autonomous realms that acknowledged the suzerain's overlordship and paid him tribute."[60]

Outside Eurasia, in the Americas lay the empires of the Aztecs and Incas, with advanced civilizations albeit based on Stone Age technology. These were governed by a small ruling group who had established their dominion after a long period of warfare over a subject people who accepted their dominion without loyalty.[61] Geographically isolated, these Amerindian empires did not confront outside pressures until the appearance of the Iberian conquistadors in the sixteenth century. Similarly, despite their interactions though trade, the ancient Eurasian empires rarely collided because of the high costs of transport and waging war at a long distance from their homelands. The major threat they faced was of being taken over by the barbarians from the regions of nomadic pastoralism to the north in the steppes and the south in the Arabian desert. Even then, except for the Arabs who created a distinct Islamic civilization, the other nomadic conquerors soon adopted the culture and ancient political institutions of the empires they had conquered.

In Africa, the north became part of the Arab-Islamic system, as did the small trading states such as Zanzibar on the eastern coast. Ethiopia remained one of the oldest Christian states. The rest of sub-Sahara Africa before the European expansion in the eighteenth and nineteenth centuries, consisted in part of hereditary kingdoms such as those of the Zulus, the Ashanti, and the Buganda, but was mostly populated by preliterate stateless societies. They have been studied extensively by anthropologists. These were truly anarchical states in the Hobbesian sense and yet they maintained order without the institutions of government, thus giving the lie to the presumption that without Leviathan there could be no order. This order was provided "through the strong moral or social sanctions possible in small and culturally homogenous societies, through religious or supernatural sanctions and through the enforcement of law by decentralized measures of 'self help.' Students of the modern system of states have noted resemblances between the devices for maintaining order in these anarchical societies of primitive peoples and those that provide a modicum of order among modern states, in the absence of government."[62]

Thus, it would appear that the real precursor of the anarchical state system that developed in Europe was the system of social interaction that had developed among our Stone Age ancestors. International relations theorists claim that, despite the attempts by Charles V, Louis XIV, Napoleon, and Hitler to resurrect another Roman empire, the European states system was distinct from the other regional international systems in the world. Bull and Watson claim "that it came to repudiate any hegemonial principle and regard[ed] itself as a society of states that were sovereign or independent. This non-hegemonial society was not without its historical precedent: the city states of classical Greece, the Hellenistic kingdoms between the death of Alexander and the Roman conquest, perhaps 'the period of warring states' in ancient China may all be thought to provide examples."[63] But, as we have seen, perhaps this repudiation of hegemony by the post–Roman European states system was making a virtue of necessity. For along with these other examples of anarchical international systems, it was an exception. The dominant international system in world history has been hegemonic and imperial rather than anarchic.

The Gunpowder Empires

The disruption of the ancient spice trade between Europe and South and Southeast Asia by the Ottoman presence led, in part, to the European voyages of discovery in the sixteenth century to circumvent the Porte. The subsequent establishment of their empires in the non-European world followed. This seaborne expansion was based on the development of the armed sailing ship in the sixteenth century. First developed in England, it was rapidly diffused among the other European maritime powers. Its precursors were the sailing ships developed in Northern Europe which shed their galleys of oarsmen and were suitable for oceanic travel. They had transported Columbus to America in 1492, and then the conquistadors who destroyed the Aztec and Inca civilizations with the few horses they transshipped. These horses had terrified the Amerindians, who had never seen any, since their hunter-gatherer ancestors had destroyed them over ten millennia before. Combined with the guns and the new germs the conquerors brought with them, most Amerindians were rapidly subdued. The Americas were colonized first by the Spanish and Portuguese, and later in the north by the English and the French.[64]

There was no similar asymmetric technological military advantage to allow the European powers to establish their empires in the eastern Eurasian civilizations. In fact, till the eighteenth century, the armed sailing ship only allowed the Europeans to establish small trading posts along the Indian Ocean and the China seas, because the naval gun could not project power inland and the Europeans' supply lines to their home countries were greatly stretched. In this early phase of their interaction with the East, European relationships with the native powers were ones of caution and equality, based on mutually beneficial trading interests. However, the Moghul empire in India had not organized cannon-armed seagoing fleets and so could not guarantee its coastline's security.[65] By contrast, China and Japan had in effect shut off their countries to outside contact.

The Chinese under the Ming (1368–1644) had begun a seaborne over-seas expansion which had seen the fabled Chinese admiral Cheng Ho's "treasure ships" cruising the Indian Ocean (1405–53) from Borneo and Malaysia to Ceylon, East Africa, and the Red Sea, asserting Chinese suzerainty, and sealing the relationships with exchanges of tribute and trade. William McNeill argues that everything about these expeditions surpassed anything Europe could field: "more ships, more guns, more manpower, more cargo capacity, were combined with seamanship and seaworthiness equivalent to anything Europeans of Columbus' and Magellan's day had at their command."[66] He speculates that if the Chinese had continued with their seaborne explorations, they could have discovered the west coast of America "half a century before Columbus blundered into Hispaniola in his vain search for Cathay. Assuredly, Chinese ships were seaworthy enough to sail across the Pacific and back. Indeed, if the like of Cheng Ho's expeditions had been renewed, Chinese navigators might well have rounded Africa and discovered Europe before Prince Henry the Navigator (1460) died."[67] But it was not to be. For as part of what I have elsewhere termed the closing of the Chinese mind,[68] the Ming emperor in 1436 banned the construction of seagoing ships, and China became for all practical purposes a virtually closed polity and economy.

In Japan the Tokugawa shogunate (1600–1868) had pacified and unified the country by ending the chaos induced by medieval baronial warriors.
As in Europe they had done this by destroying the fortresses of rebellious
samurai with the cannons and guns that Portuguese traders had brought to
Japan in 1542. Tokugawa Ieyasu's siege of the fortress of Osaka in 1614
marked the consolidation of Tokugawa power.[69] But having established its
centralized authority, the Tokugawa disarmed the populace, made the manu-
facture of guns and cannons a government monopoly, and in 1636 proclaimed the policy of *sakoku*, whereby the country was closed to foreigners
and foreign contacts. After the Shimbara rebellion by native Christians in
1637, fought with gunpowder, the authorities began to see both guns and foreigners as a threat to national security and domestic order. Thus, both China
and Japan had closed themselves from any trade-induced intrusions by the
Europeans by virtually eliminating all foreign trade,[70] and escaped the establishment of those trading outposts which were to be the launching pad for
European expansion in India and Southeast Asia in the next phase of the
establishment of European hegemony and empire in the East.

This early European expansion was an intercontinental continuation of
the conflict within the anarchical society of European states for an unachiev-
able mastery over Europe. For as figure 2 shows, the major European powers
were relatively closely matched in terms of their GDP. With the prevailing
mercantilist ideology, the trading advantage from acquiring overseas trading
outposts was seen as a way of stealing an economic edge in the European
power game. But apart from the Americas, this did not lead to an establishment of empires. That came in the eighteenth century with the inland extension of their power from their trading posts. This overseas inland incursion
was the byproduct of the creation of domestic professional armies to fight
their European battles between 1660 and 1720. This involved the instilling
of discipline by drill, a logistical infrastructure involving regular pay to create loyalty, administration to move supplies over ever, longer, supply lines,
and command by bold and skilled officers.[71] A modern version of the Roman
legions had been reborn. This greater social efficiency of the European
armies gave them an asymmetric military advantage over the native armies,
which the French in 1746 under Joseph Dupleix were the first to recognize in
India.

Heavy field artillery was known in India since the days of the thirteenth
century sultanate and used along with the cavalry.[72] Guns and muskets were
known since Babar's lightning raids over Northern India (1526) established
the Moghul empire. But the Indian marksman was an individualist, and the
loading and cleaning of the guns then available took time. The drill revolution of the late seventeenth century in Europe[73] changed this. Gustavus

Adolphus of Sweden found that small companies of musketeers, trained to take turns in firing salvos while their fellows reloaded their guns could, with the precise timing enforced by the drill sergeants, have the effect of a human machine gun. The French governor Dupleix imported this method into India, recruiting native infantry and training them in European drill at his trading post. In the siege of Madras in 1746, 230 European soldiers and 700 native infantrymen (sepoys) routed an Indian army of 10,000 deploying cavalry and elephants. The lesson was learned by the British. At the battle of Plassey in 1757, because of this organizational superiority and the treachery of the local ruler's subordinates, Clive with a force of 3,000 (of whom 800 were European) repelled a native army 50,000 strong.

The third stage of European expansion in the mid-nineteenth century, which included the British penetration and control of most of the Indian sub-continent, the carving up of the Chinese melon, the opening up of Japan, and the scramble for Africa, followed the Industrial Revolution and its technological and scientific advances. The steamship and the railways, the introduction of quick-firing, long-range firearms made possible by the development of high explosives, and the growth of medical knowledge which allowed the Europeans to penetrate the disease barrier that had hith-erto protected the tropical areas—particularly in Africa—from their minis-trations[74] allowed the European expansion to become imperial. This was the period when Britain as the leading industrial and commercial power estab-lished the British empire, having with its allies defeated the French attempt at mastery of Europe at Waterloo in 1815. It is apparent in figure 2 that Britain had the highest GDP from about 1820 to 1870.

The Evolution of American Hegemony

With the spread of industrialization to Europe and to Britain's ex-colony in the Americas—the United States—this British lead was eroding as first Germany and then the United States challenged it. The European anarchical state system was embroiled in two wars as another European power attempted to gain mastery over Europe. Because of the European expansion of the previous centuries, these wars drew in the whole world. As the various European powers were roughly equivalent in economic and military strength, there was the danger of a stalemate. This was only resolved when the country with the fastest growing GDP, the United States, threw its weight behind Britain and its allies. From 1913 on, the United States had the world's largest economy and potentially the most powerful military (see figure 2). Nevertheless, the peace Woodrow Wilson tried to implement after the First World War was based on implicit Kantian notions of internationalizing the

European society of states and maintaining international order through collective security.

After the Second World War with the invention of nuclear weapons, there was a military and ideological standoff between the two superpowers, the United States and the USSR. There was no obvious asymmetric military advantage that either side could establish. This was recognized by the doctrine of mutually assured destruction. When that confrontation ended with the collapse of the Soviet Union in 1989, it left the United States as the sole superpower. As figure 1 shows, its economic strength is overwhelming. What of its military strength?

The military historian John Keegan has demonstrated that the decisive factors in the last century's two World Wars were American industrial strength and the key role played by naval strength in controlling the sea. For example, in the Second World War "of the 750,000 aircraft produced by the principal combatants during the war, 300,000 originated in the Untied States, of which 90,000 were built in 1944 alone."[75] This ensured that "in any future conflict between conventional forces conducted as a struggle for national survival, industrial capacity, rather than any other factor, would be decisive."[76] But that is not all.

In the 1990s, America's military capacity has changed qualitatively because of another technological revolution in warfare. It was exhibited in the Afghanistan and Iraq campaigns in 2002 and 2003 and is likely to further increase the decisiveness of warfare in America's favor. This revolution in military affairs uses newly developed information technology (IT). It is leading to information-based operations which are finally lifting the fog of war.[77] As Edward Luttwak notes, the two classic aspects of conventional warfare are fire-power and movement: "Without fire to suppress the enemy's reaction, movement can only succeed against the void or the most feeble opposition, except at the price of casualties, perhaps huge. Without movement to exploit the firepower, there is only the grinding down of the enemy by sheer attrition, with no possibility of winning more quickly and cheaply by disruptive or encircling manouvres."[78] The firepower of ground forces including infantry, artillery and, tanks are all constrained by the supply of ammunition. The amount of ammunition modern tanks can carry for their guns could all be fired within an hour, while, in any significant battle, no matter what the means of transport, ammunition would run out for the infantry much before fuel or food.

It was hoped that with the deployment of air power and the development of smart bombs, fire power could be provided remotely, allowing ground forces to concentrate on maneuvers. The problem of substituting air power for ground power was not so much the inaccuracy as the chronic lack of continuity of air power, and even more the lack of timely knowledge. Information about the location of one's own and enemy forces on a changing battlefield and being able to communicate with those conducting the battle has been crucial for victory, as Genghis Khan demonstrated with the use of his arrow riders. With the advances in data processing and transmission, instant information has now become a reality. This was spectacularly demonstrated in the Afghanistan and Iraq campaigns, which saw the full use of the newly developed information technology and of unmanned aircraft such as the Predator to provide a continuous aerial survey of huge areas and even to fire a missile at a small human target (as demonstrated by the elimination of a Yemeni terrorist responsible for bombing the USS *Cole* in 2002). The new IT warfare also allowed a few U.S. special forces to summon accurate air strikes against the Taliban, much to the amazement of their Afghan allies. With ground troops now being equipped with hand-held computers and smart goggles that allow night vision, there has been a qualitative change in the nature of the war the United States can fight.

This new revolution in military affairs ultimately attempts to liberate movement from the encumbrances of firepower, allowing the exploitation of the full potential for maneuver, while at the same time making a much better use of firepower by liberating it from the inevitable fragmentation of the forces capable of movement. Such a system was proposed by the Soviet Union's general staff in the late 1970s which called it the Reconnaissance Strike system.[79] "The system's starting point was the computer-assisted fusion of intelligence from all sources to identify and locate all targets of potential interest. On that basis, the computer-assisted command headquarters would determine priorities among the identified targets, and select the most appropriate means to attack them from the full range of possibilities: ballistic and cruise missiles, manned bombers and fighter bombers, unmanned air vehicles, tube and rocket artillery, even commando raids. Finally, the system would issue computer-generated orders for each one of the separate but simultaneous attacks of an overall offensive, check to ensure their execution, assess the damage inflicted through more computer-assisted intelligence fusion, and order second and third attacks against insufficiently damaged targets."[80]

The Soviets could not establish this system because of their economic weaknesses and technological backwardness, particularly in information technology (IT). The United States is well on the way to doing so. When President Ronald Reagan upped the ante of military competition with his Star Wars campaign, the Soviets realized that they could no longer compete militarily with the emerging asymmetric United States advantage in the decisiveness of war. They have given up being a superpower.[81]

Furthermore, these U.S. military advances also represent the substitution of capital for men in warfare (as is appropriate for a capital-abundant and labor-scarce economy), thereby diminishing the need to put lots of ground troops at risk in what till recently were essentially wars of attrition. In past wars, highly populated poor countries were at an advantage, with their swarming techniques in fighting wars, as the value of life in terms of foregone earnings was low. But the recent technological advances have greatly reduced this asymmetric advantage. As the comparatively minimal loss of American, Afghani, and Iraqi lives in the campaigns against the Taliban and Saddam Hussein shows, machines can now defeat ill-equipped men. Given both the costs of developing and deploying these new weapon systems, as well as the lead the United States has developed in IT, it now has an overwhelming asymmetric military advantage, not only over the Third World armed forces against whom it has so far used them, but even over potential competitors such as the Europeans, Chinese, and Russians.

The trauma of the Vietnam War led to the natural aversion of the American public (and government leaders) to any loss of American lives (whose economic value is large in terms of foregone earnings). This resulted in a reluctance to use American military power that hobbled the U.S. giant. The new military revolution that will limit the number of American bodies directly under threat means that the aversion to losing American lives need no longer put a brake on the exertion of American military power. Thus, the United States today has an economic and military predominance unseen since the fall of Rome.

In terms of the analytical framework discussed earlier, this should have led to the breakdown of the anarchical society—on which most international relations theorizing has been based—and the establishment of an American imperium. Whether this has happened and should happen are among the major questions this book hopes to answer. From a historical perspective looking across civilizations, it should be clear that most of the international relations theories which are still current only apply to a special case—the anarchical society of European states established after the fall of Rome.[82] These theories will not be of much use in charting the route to establishing and maintaining order in a hegemonic or imperial international order.

THE MOTIVES, MECHANICS, AND RESULTS OF EMPIRE

Motives

The primary motive behind the ancient Mesopotamian empires, according to Rondo Cameron, "lay in the booty, tribute, and taxation that the conquerors could wring from the conquered and from the peasant masses."[83] This is very much the net revenue maximizing objective of the predatory state discussed earlier. But for Alexander the Great, Romans such as Julius Caesar, and Mongols such as Genghis Khan, there was also the search for glory. For the Mesopotamian, Chinese, Indian, late Egyptian, and Roman empires, there was also the objective of expanding the territorial area of the state to some natural boundaries which would keep the nomadic predators at bay. For the Spanish conquistadors as for the Islamic conquerors, booty and the desire to convert heathens were complementary motives. For the British and the Dutch, the reluctant extension of empire followed the almost accidental establishment of territorial control over distant countries by their trading companies, whose foreign exploits had been encouraged by their parent countries as part of their long drawn-out interstate competition in Europe after the Renaissance. The flag in these cases followed trade, and the motive of the metropolitan governments was as much to maintain a Pax to allow trade and commerce to prosper as it was to maximize the direct returns in terms of booty and tribute from their far-flung dominions. Thus, the motives for creating past empires were mixed and cannot be reduced to some simple single motive as theorists of imperialism from J.A. Hobson to Vladimir Lenin to Joseph Schumpeter have sought to do.[84]

Mechanics

What have been the instruments (the mechanics) of maintaining an imperial order? The most ancient of the empires I have briefly surveyed provides the answer. As McNeill notes, ancient Mesopotamia particularly during Hammurabi's reign had provided the essential instruments for maintaining coherent and stable, territorially extensive empires: "bureaucracy, law and market prices."[85]

Bureaucracy necessitated that people in distant parts of the empire accept that a stranger who arrived with a document appointing him a governor in the king's name had to be treated as such. Perfect strangers had to be persuaded to cooperate with other officials and to accept their claim that they were acting in an official capacity. Hammurabi's legal code enabled strangers to deal with each other and enforce their property rights. Similarly, market prices and legally enforceable rules for trading made effective cooperation among strangers possible.[86] The wider the territory in which the empire's writ ran, the more human relations became predictable. This creation of an imperial Pax maintained by standing armies with a professional officer corps (devised by the Assyrians) along with "the series of legal and customary definitions of merchant's rights and privileges facilitated trade over comparatively long distances and between mutually alien and distrustful populations."[87] The Pax thus led to both peace and prosperity.

The Roman, Chinese, and British empires—particularly in India—epitomize these mechanics of empire. The Roman empire began as a system of indirect rule. According to Arnold Toynbee, "The imperial government was to confine itself to the twofold task of keeping the local communities in harmony with one another and protecting them against attacks from the outer barbarians; and, for these limited imperial activities, a slender military framework and a light political structure were all that was required."[88] But from the reign of Marcus Aurelius (A.D. 121–180) on, a centralized, hierarchically organized bureaucracy came to govern the empire, partly because of the limited pool from which recruits to local government could be drawn. With this centralization of imperial government, Toynbee continues, "the self-complacent local magistrates and local councillors had been degraded into becoming the unwilling instruments of the central exchequer for extracting ruinously heavy taxes from the local notables."[89] In the post-Diocletian period, the army and administration were thrown open to any Roman citizen with the necessary education. This imperial bureaucracy went to pieces within seven centuries after its inauguration by Augustus.

By contrast the Chinese mandarinate, established by the Han emperor Han Liu P'ang in 196 B.C., was recruited on merit by an examination. This provided the Chinese state with the essential administrative spine which survived without interruption till A.D. 1911. It is now being recreated in the Communist state, since Deng Xiaoping initiated his reforms in the early 1980s.

In India, the agents of the East India trading company were converted into another remarkable civil service. Toynbee observes, "In this case as in that of the Roman equestrian class, the start may have been so bad as to be beyond hope of retrieving; yet in both cases, a predatory band of harpies was converted in a surprisingly short time into a body of public servants whose incentive was not personal pecuniary gain, and who came to make it a point of honor to wield enormous political power without abusing it. This redemption of the character of the British administration in India was due in part at least to the East India Company's decision to educate their servants for the new political tasks they had undertaken; and that training system that they created was superior even to that in force for Britain's own civil servants at that time."[90] With the British crown taking over from the company after the mutiny of 1857, a system of recruitment based on examinations was instituted, similar to the Chinese system. The higher reaches in the Indian civil service were, however, initially not open to Indians. This failure, unlike the Chinese and Romans' decision to allow open recruitment to positions in the instruments of imperial control, led—as it did in the other European gun-powder empires—to nationalist "creole" revolts which eventually destroyed the empire.[91]

In the case of the barbarian empires, the new rulers often took over the civil services of their predecessors. But in the case of the Ottomans, the sultans created an administrative class from their personal slave household. From these slaves recruited from all the ethnic groups in the empire and trained in the art of administration, an efficient, multiethnic, administrative structure was created which, unlike those of the European imperial bureaucracies, was not ethnocentric. In empires in which the bureaucracies were open to the talents of all, a common imperial culture emerged, which provided a means of amalgamating the diverse groups in the empire into a cultural and political unity. This reduced the dangers of nationalist revolts.

Empires produced two other public goods that were essential for their survival. The first was an efficient system of communications. This is an essential instrument for maintaining not only military control over far-flung dominions but also political control through both public and secret police forces.[92] Public transportation and an imperial postal service were integral parts of this communications system and date back to the Sumero-Akkadian empires. The imperial couriers of the postal system also served as spies, keeping an eye on the distant satraps. Even outside Mesopotamia, from the Chinese to the Incas, empires created vast communications systems to control their empires.[93] But, as the Romans and many other imperial rulers discovered, these communications systems, particularly the means for public transportation—the roads and bridges—could be a double-edged sword. For in a world where all roads led to Rome, the same roads could, and did, convey the barbarian destroyers of their civilizations. This fact has considerable contemporary relevance to the events of 9/11, in which terrorists used our modern means of transport and of postal delivery—the airplane and the internet—for their barbaric mission.

The second public good is a lingua franca to conduct official business, both within the imperial bureaucracy and with its subjects. As most empires had amalgamated a mixed bag of ethnic and linguistic groups into their Pax, a delicate issue was which local language should become the lingua franca of the empire. As anthropologists tell us that the language group is the most potent identifier of different cultures[94] and as cultures embody their different cosmological beliefs, the imposition of the language of one or the other linguistic group as the empire's lingua franca could lead to domestic disorder. Most empire builders made their own mother tongue the official but not exclusive language.[95] This linguistic flexibility of empires has been contravened in only three instances. The first was in the Ummayad Islamic caliphate (685–703), but this was changed when the Ottomans came to run the Islamic empire. In its heyday in the sixteenth and seventeenth centuries, the lingua franca of the Padishah's Slave-Household was Serbo-Croat, and the command language in the Ottoman navy, Italian.[96] The second instance was the linguistic monopoly imposed by the Spanish conquistadors of Latin America. With their eagerness to gather souls for their Christian mission, however, they had to compromise by allowing the Gospels to be preached in Quichua, the lingua franca of the Incas in the Andean world.

The third exception, that of the Chinese empire, was the most momentous. The Qin emperor Shih Hwang-ti (221–210 B.C.) gave exclusive currency to the ideographic language current in his own ancestral state; he created a Han Chinese identity by forcing all the diverse ethnic and linguistic groups in the country to write their names in these uniform characters in this new form. This also became the language of the mandarins and imposed a unity on the empire which has lasted to our day.

Results

The two major effects of empires have been that they have preserved the peace and promoted prosperity in the territories they encompassed.

Peace. Peace came before prosperity. After their often bloody ascent to power, peace was the primary public good all imperial rulers had necessarily to provide to maintain themselves and their authority over the territorial space they had acquired. Moreover, despite the current popular impression that empires are ephemeral, empires have been long-lasting. As can be seen from table 3, derived from Sam Finer's magisterial *History of Government*, most of them lasted much longer than the ex-colony that is now the world hegemon (the United States) has existed. In fact, in the long perspective of history, most people have lived under empires, which through their Pax have provided the basic order required for any social life to exist.

Prosperity. The empires also promoted prosperity by linking areas of diverse resources into a common economic space. The Greek city-states, which had turned the Mediterranean into a common cultural and economic Greek lake, began the process of specialization and urbanization that reached its apogee under the Roman empire in the first and second centuries of the Christian era. The long period of the Pax Romana allowed commerce to develop under the most favorable conditions. It eliminated the piracy and brigandage which had continued to threaten commerce in the Hellenistic era, and the Mediterranean became the major artery for trade and commerce. Though the Romans did not place a high value on commerce in their material beliefs, nevertheless, their Pax and the associated development of

Table 3. Life span of empires

Egypt 2850 B.C.–30 B.C.	2,820 years
China 221 B.C.–1912	2,133 years
Rome 509 B.C.–A.D. 476	985 years
Assyria 1356 B.C.–612 B.C.	744 years
Byzantine A.D. 330–1204	874 years
Venice A.D. 687–1799	1,112 years
Caliphate A.D. 632–943	311 years
Ottoman A.D. 1350–1918	568 years
Achemenian Persian empire 550–330 B.C.	220 years
Sassanian Persian empire A.D. 224–651	427 years
British Empire in India A.D. 1757–1947	190 years

Source: Finer (1997), vol. 1, pp. 31–32.

Roman law, and its spread with the expansion of the empire, created a large economic space with a coherent legal framework for economic activity. This provided strict enforcement of contracts and property rights and prompt (usually equitable) settlement of disputes. There was considerable freedom of enterprise, and one economic historian has described its economic policies as close to laissez faire.[97]

Similarly, the Abbasid empire of the Arabs linked the worlds of the Mediterranean and Indian Ocean, the Mongol empire linked China with the Near East,[98] the various Indian empires created a common economic space in the subcontinent, and the expanding Chinese empire linked the economic spaces of the Yellow River with those of the Yangtze. Finally, it was the British who for the first time in the nineteenth century linked the whole world by maintaining a Pax enforced by their navy. In all the other cases, too, the Pax provided protection against brigands and other predators. The institution of an empire-wide legal system, which—however imperfectly and unintentionally—did help in promoting trade and commerce over a wide economic space, led to those gains from trade and specialization emphasized by Adam Smith and thereby to Smithian intensive growth.

But each of the empires had its economic climacteric. With stagnant technology and the binding land constraint, they could not generate Promethean growth. They were in a high-level equilibrium trap with only extensive growth occurring—with output keeping pace with population growth and with per capita income stagnant. We have no quantitative evidence for the ancient empires, but heroic attempts have been made to piece together the per capita incomes and population of the three major empires at the beginning of the Christian era (India, China, and Rome) and are summarized in table 4.

India, which had reached its climacteric after it was united under the imperial Mauryas in the third century B.C. was by the beginning of the

Table 4. GDP and population for ancient powers, 0 A.D.

	GDP (in millions of 1990 US$)	Population (in 000s)	GDP per capita
Roman Empire	20,961	55,000	381
China	26,820	59,600	450
India-1	33,750	75,000	450
India-2	55,146	100,000	551

Sources: Angus Maddison, *The World Economy: A Millennial Perspective*. Paris, OECD, 2001. Tables B-21, p. 264, B-18, p. 261, B-10, p. 241, for China and India-1.
Goldsmith, R.W., "An Estimate of the Size and Structure of the National Product of the Roman Empire," *Review of Income and Wealth* 30(3), 1984, for the Roman Empire (tons of gold converted into US$ at the average 1990 price).
Deepak Lal, *The Hindu Equilibrium*. Oxford, Clarendon Press, 1989, for India-2 (1965 $ converted into 1990 $ using GDP deflator).

Christian era probably the richest and most populous. Thereafter, its per capita income fluctuated around this high-level equilibrium for the next two millennia (till the late nineteenth century). Population and the standard of living fell in the long periods (sometimes centuries) during which the country was engulfed by wars against invaders or else between feuding Indian chieftains trying to establish another pan-Indian empire.

The Chinese saw their efflorescence under the Sung in the eleventh century. This was based on linking the river valleys of the Yellow and Yangtze Rivers, an agricultural revolution based on wet rice technology, and connecting the rural economy with a national hierarchy of markets. Above all, there were remarkable scientific and technological advances, so many that China had developed all the ingredients necessary for an Industrial Revolution. Chinese per capita income rose to roughly $600 (in 1990 international $) and the population to 100 million.[99] But following the depredations of the Mongol invasions, there was a decline in the population to 65 million by the fourteenth century. When the Ming dynasty (1368–1644) replaced the Mongols and restored peace and stability, the population began rising again from 65 million to 400 million by 1800. But the incipient industrial revolution never occurred because of the closing of the Chinese mind,[100] and per capita income remained stagnant. China then experienced extensive growth into the modern period, with output rising with population at 0.4 to 0.5 percent per annum over these four centuries. It too had reached a high-level equilibrium trap, but at a higher per capita income than India's.

The third of our ancient civilizations, Rome, reached its climacteric in the reign of Augustus (29 B.C.–A.D. 14) who replaced the republic by the principate. The figures shown in table 4 are Raymond Goldsmith's estimates for A.D. 14, the date of Augustus's death. They probably represent the per capita income level when the Roman empire reached its high-level equilibrium trap.

"In the first and second century of the empire neither population nor product per head nor aggregate product increased noticeably, i.e., by say more than 0.1 percent and 0.2 percent per year,"[101] Goldsmith observes. Nevertheless, until the expansion of the United States and Russia in the mid-nineteenth century, the Roman empire was the largest political, economic, and monetary unit in the Western world. Its population and national product too was not surpassed by any Western economy until the nineteenth century. It was, according to Goldsmith, thus "the largest Western economic unit for nearly two millennia."[102]

But, unlike the Chinese, the Roman empire declined, and despite various attempts, no one has succeeded in establishing imperial hegemony over Western Europe thereafter. The causes of the decline of the Roman empire were ultimately economic.[103] The extension of the empire to its natural boundary meant that the average costs of maintaining the empire were rising and thus the sustainable rents it could garner were declining. As the treasures looted in the previous wars of conquests and the steady supply of slaves dried up, with the empire having absorbed most of the civilized Western world, foreign plunder no longer offered an independent source of revenue. As the past rents acquired during the empire's growth had been in part committed to a vast expansion of what we would today call a welfare state—which could not be cut without causing domestic disorder—and without an expansion of the domestic tax base, the empire faced an endemic fiscal crisis. It tried to close the deficit by levying the inflation tax through debasement of the currency. But this was not enough and the state had to raise the burden of taxation above the sustainable rate. Toward the middle of the fourth century, as this tax pressure grew, tax evasion and avoidance by high officials and large landowners also increased.[104]

The endemic fiscal crisis also led to the problem of maintaining the old military organization, as this "scarcity of means," Robert Bernardi says, "did not allow a satisfactory treatment of the men in military service, the area of recruiting was enlarged just in time to prevent the legions being filled with the poor and desperate. In this way, for budgetary reasons the sword passed in the Early empire from the hands of the Italici into those of provincials and from them, in the late Empire, into the hands of the barbarians . . . who served in autonomous military formations under their own chieftains . . . this system . . . turned out to be less costly than to equip anew, and to maintain, regular troops."[105] But by letting the barbarians inside the gates because of fiscal exigencies, the Roman empire had sealed its doom.

This vicious circle, whereby the creation of politically determined entitlements to income leads to an endemic fiscal crisis, can be observed later in the post-Renaissance mercantilist states of Europe and in our own times in the neomercantilist states of the Third and Second Worlds.[106] Three alternative outcomes ensued from these historical fiscal crises of the state: reform and economic liberalization to recover the tax base (as in England in the eighteenth and nineteenth centuries, and much of the Third World since the 1980s), revolution (as in France in 1789, and in much of the Second World in 1989), or collapse of the state (as in Rome and in many postindependent African countries).

The Chinese and Indian imperial states survived these endemic fiscal problems which led to the periodic overthrow of a dynasty until some other competitor was again able to recreate the empire. By contrast, the decline of the gunpowder European empires created after the Renaissance merely reflected the changing balance of economic and military power in their metropole's struggle for the mastery of Europe, as the empires were an overseas extension of this struggle.

But, before the revolution in administration of the sixteenth century and the growing monetization of the economy, the power of any state to tax was very limited compared to modern states. Thus, Goldsmith notes of the Roman empire that, "reflecting its economically liberal policies, very close to those which would later be called 'laissez faire,' but also due to limitations of an as yet only partly monetized economy, the share of the expenditures of central and local governments in the early Roman empire was very low, probably not above 3 percent for the imperial government and on the order of 5 percent for all government units. This is not only far below the figures to which we have become accustomed since World War I in developed countries, but also below those in less developed countries, where the share of public expenditure in 1960 averaged 8 percent, a ratio similar to that in England in 1688 and in the United States and in France in 1820."[107]

Foreign empires also taxed less than indigenous ones as our analytical framework predicts. Thus, in India, Maddison estimates that the fiscal exactions of the Moghul empire at its height in the sixteenth century (by which time it had been Indianised) was between 15 and 18 percent of national income. By contrast, the British Raj imposed a total tax burden of only 6 percent of national income.[108] For the British, unlike most of India's invaders, after a brief initial period (which ended with the 1857 mutiny) in which they attempted to assimilate and become a traditional Indian power—taking a robust delight in the country's mores and its women[109]—set themselves apart and above their subjects. This meant that, unlike any of India's previous rulers, the British were faced with the possibility of a nationalist revolt of the populace as a whole against their rulers. This meant that the entry costs for internal rivals had been considerably reduced, and the British found that low taxation,[110] while providing law and order more cheaply than had historically been possible, was the secret to success. With the end of alien rule and the accompanying danger of an internal nationalist revolt, the natural rents to be extracted once again rose to historic levels, and the tax revenues garnered by the newly independent Indian state were soon running over 20 percent of national income.

THE DIFFERENT CHARACTERISTICS OF EMPIRES

There are two important distinguishing features of empires which are worth noting, as these will allow the formation of normative judgments about empires in the third part of this book. First, empires can be distinguished as being either multicultural or homogenizing. The former included the Roman, the Abbasids, the various Indian empires, the Ottoman, the Austro-Hungarian, and the British, in which little attempt was made to change cultural mores of the constituent groups—or if it was, as in the early British Raj, an ensuing backlash led to a reversal of this policy. Contemporary India is an imperial state whose political unity is a legacy of the British Raj, but whose multiethnic character is underwritten by an ancient hierarchical structure which accommodates these different groups as different castes.

The homogenizing empires, by contrast, sought to create a national identity out of the multifarious groups in their territory. The best example of these is China, where the ethnic mix was unified as Han through the bureaucratic device of writing their names in Chinese characters in a Chinese form, and suppressing any subsequent discontent through the subtle repression of a bureaucratic authoritarian state.[111] In our own time, the American melting pot, making Americans out of a multitude of ethnicities by adherence to a shared civic culture and a common language, has created a similar homogenized imperial state. Similarly, the supposedly ancient nations of Britain and France were created through a state-led homogenizing process.[112]

Second, empires can be distinguished in terms of a crucial distinction, made by the British political philosopher Michael Oakeshott,[113] between two major strands of Western thought on the state: the state viewed as a *civil* association, or alternatively as an *enterprise* association. Oakeshott notes that the view of the state as a civil association goes back to ancient Greece. The state is seen as the custodian of laws that do not seek to impose any preferred pattern of ends (including abstractions such as the general or social welfare, or human rights). It seeks to maintain civil order. This view has been challenged by the rival conception of the state as an enterprise association— a view that has its roots in the Judeo-Christian tradition—in which the state is seen as the manager of an enterprise seeking to use the law for its own substantive purposes and, in particular, for the legislation of morality.

The Roman, Chinese, and most of the Indian empires embodied the civil association view of the state, as did the British. By contrast, the Spanish empire,[114] Leopold's Belgian empire in the Congo (almost literally in the business sense of enterprise), and the mutation of the Russian empire under Lenin and his successors embodied the enterprise view, as did the failed attempts at empire by Hitler's Germany and Tojo's Japan. The nomadic empires of the Arabs and the Mongols began as enterprise associations, seeking booty as well as conversions in the case of the Arabs. But partly because the continual garnering of rents from the subject populace required settling down among them, and partly because conversions reduced the tax base on which the *jizya*—the tax paid by infidels—was levied, the Arabs soon converted their empire into a civil association, a tradition continued by their Ottoman successors. Except in China where they were Sinified, the Mongols never succeeded in converting their enterprise association into a civil association, and the empire did not long survive its phase of plunder, compared to the empire established by their nomadic Arab cousins to the south. Thus, it would appear that empires commonly thought to have been evil are those that have subscribed to the enterprise view of the state and sought to serve some ideal which went beyond the maintenance of order.

CONCLUSIONS

Most of the world since civilization began has lived under empires, since anarchical international state systems have usually broken down into empires (controlling both domestic and foreign policy) rather than mere hegemony (controlling only foreign policy). In this sense, the anarchical system of European nation-states which arose after the collapse of the Roman empire has been an exception.

These empires have been established for a mixture of motives (including glory), but by and large the major motives have been those captured by the analytical framework of the predatory state. More recently, the European overseas empires were acquired almost by accident, when imperial authority was reluctantly exercised in territories often acquired by their traders. However established, their longevity has depended upon not overcharging for the public good of peace and order they provide. This has meant that in the perennial struggle of the prey to obtain this public good at least cost, empires controlled by foreigners have better served the interests of the indigenous population than states created by their own.

Given their territorial extent, empires have had to create a civil service, establish a legal code, and promote a means of communication and control as well as a lingua franca. The empires can also be distinguished by being either homogenizing or multiethnic. In the latter cases, their longevity has been preserved by throwing open the instruments of the mechanics of governance—the military and the bureaucracy—to all talents. Failure to incorporate natives into the governance of the empire has led to nationalist creole revolts which have destroyed the empire. If possible, indirect control has been preferred to direct control of empires, as this is less costly to the metropole.

By creating order over a large economic space, empires have inevitably generated Smithian intensive growth. But given limited technological progress (except for the exceptional period under Sung China), Promethean intensive growth remains a European miracle of the anarchical system of nation-states established after the breakdown of the Roman empire. But as I have argued in detail elsewhere,[115] it is incorrect to infer that it was this anarchy which caused the miracle. The period of Smithian intensive growth in the early stages of the empire usually petered out, and after this climacteric, most empires experienced only extensive growth.

The most common cause of the decline of empires is an increase in fiscal exactions, which because of the tax resistance, avoidance, and evasion they provoke, lead to an endemic fiscal crisis, which leads to the breakdown of the empire's military and bureaucratic infrastructure and the order they promoted. The prosperity resulting from the order of an empire is then also undermined, until (with the exception of Western Europe) another empire is created.

Finally, if we seek to judge empires normatively, a useful test is provided by distinguishing those which are, in Oakeshott's terms, civil associations from those which are enterprise associations. Most of the empires which have been regarded as evil fall into the latter category.

Given that the empires that did not overtly promote some enterprise for long periods of time and in large territorial areas did maintain the domestic and international order required for social life to flourish, the contemporary aversion to empire is puzzling. I take up the story of this strange evolution in the next chapter.

CHAPTER 2

From a British to an American Imperium

For the New Year celebrations at the end of the last millennium, the New Labour Party organized a party in the newly constructed Dome in London. This was to be the greatest display on earth to show off Cool Britannia. I watched the proceedings on television, as samba dancers from Brazil wobbled their half-clad extremities in front of the Queen. I could not help wondering how ludicrous it was that some natives of an ex-Portuguese colony had to be imported to prance about before the queen, when a similar show could have been put on with greater resonance by getting native dancers from her Commonwealth, the toothless association of former states which replaced the far-flung British empire. For if one reflected on the most important events of the last millennium compared with the first, the ascent of the English-speaking peoples to predominance in the world surely ranked highest.[1]

At the end of the second millennium Britain was a small island off the shore of the western outposts of Eurasia, whose rise had begun with a few trading posts established by its merchant adventurers around the world. Finding a power vacuum in crumbling empires or in empty lands populated by Stateless people, the British established a vast empire. They led the way to modernity, and at the end of the nineteenth century, Britannia's dominions and influence stretched to all four corners of the globe. In the last century, its outpost in the New World was to further extend this heritage, both economically and militarily. So from the perspective of global history, in the last millennium Virgil's hopes for Rome, which form the epigraph of this book, seem to have been fulfilled in large measure for the descendants of this "sceptered isle."[2] Yet, in those millennial celebrations in the Dome, there was no pride in these amazing British achievements. For in New Labour's modernizing project, Britain's past, and particularly its empire, had become politically incorrect. The postimperial guilt arising from a feeling of having exploited the Third World has given the E word a bad name in Britain and the West, as well as among the former imperial subjects.

But this was not always so. Here is a letter that King Bell and King Acqua of the Cameroons River, West Africa, wrote on 6 November 1881 to William Gladstone, the Liberal prime minister of the United Kingdom:

> Dear W. Gladstone,
>
> We both your servants have met this afternoon to write you these few lines of writing trusting it may find you in a good state of life as it leaves us at present. As we heard here that you are the chief man in the House of Commons, so we write to tell you that we want to be under Her Majesty's control. We want our country to be governed by British Government. We are tired of governing this country ourselves, every dispute leads to war, and often to great loss of lives, so we think it is best thing to give up the country to you British men who no doubt will bring peace, civilization, and Christianity in the country. Do for mercy sake please lay our request before the Queen and to the rulers of the British Government. Do, Sir, for mercy sake, please to assist us in this important undertaking. We heard that you are a good Christian man, so we hope that you will do all you can in your power to see that our request is granted. We are quite willing to abolish all our heathen customs. . . . No doubt God will bless you for putting a light in our country. Please to send us an answer as quick as you can.[3]

Gladstone demurred, and Germany snapped up the offer instead. This example provides both the major justification that can be provided for empires, while the reasons for Gladstone's refusal provide the main and still resonant arguments against empire.[4]

But how did this dominion of the English-Speaking peoples arise, and will it continue?

THE BRITISH EMPIRE

In her important book, *Britons*, Linda Colley argues that the nation which created one of the largest empires was forged after the Glorious Revolution of 1688 by a succession of wars between Britain and France. They were at war on sea and land between 1689 and 1697, 1702 and 1713, 1743 and 1748,

1756 and 1763, 1778 and 1783, 1793 and 1802, and finally between 1803 and 1815, when the Battle of Waterloo seemed to settle the rivalry in favor of Great Britain. During this period, the union of England and Scotland was cemented by the common feeling of Protestants being threatened by a Catholic power. The threat of a Jacobite invasion sponsored by the French receded with Britain's success in defeating France in the Seven Years' War (1756–63). As these wars had spilled over into their overseas territories, they also left Britain with large imperial acquisitions. But the French fought back by allying with Britain's progeny in the New World, whose declaration of American independence in 1776 succeeded in stripping Britain of its most valuable imperial possession. Nevertheless, the successful conclusion of the Revolutionary and Napoleonic wars left Britain as the paramount global power.

This constant battle with Catholic France created that feeling of being threatened by the Other, which generated a common patriotism among the Protestants who had joined to form Great Britain. In addition, the acquisition of an exotic overseas empire to counterbalance the loss of America also strengthened this feeling of Us against Them. Furthermore, for the Scots who had joined England, the empire provided opportunities to exhibit their ancient warrior spirit and, through the jobs it provided and the commerce it promoted, to profit.

The Glorious Revolution of 1688 had another consequence. In order to finance the French wars, the Bank of England and the national debt were created. This led to the financial revolution of 1694–96, which encompassed a vastly expanded credit mechanism and the rise of the bankers and stock jobbers who had an interest in expanding their lending abroad.[5] Also, despite the Navigation Acts and the mercantilist policies that followed in the late seventeenth and early eighteenth centuries, there had been a vast expansion in trade and commerce. In eighteenth-century Britain nearly one in five families drew its livelihood from trade and distribution. In addition, there were the farmers and manufacturers whose profits depended upon domestic and external trade.[6] All these groups had an interest in a state which provided both naval protection and a global order that allowed international commercial and financial transactions to take place. These commercial interests were in harmony with those of the landed ruling class, which was equally concerned about securing British interests abroad. This provided an important source of social and political stability and led to a cult of commerce becoming an increasingly important part of the British identity.[7]

After the creation of the national debt, the emerging financial interests of the City (London's business center) were increasingly accepted into the inner circles of political and social influence; their expertise was needed to finance the continuing wars, and the national debt was profitable for those who could afford to invest in it, including the landowners. This resulted in a partnership between landlords and financiers. They were to be the promoters of the "gentlemanly capitalism" which Peter Cain and Anthony Hopkins in their important book *British Imperialism* identify as the mainspring of the British Empire. It was in the interests of these gentlemanly capitalists to build a strong navy and to export the revolution settlement "by promoting a propertied interest abroad and by capitalizing on Britain's comparative advantage in finance and commercial service to supply credit, carriage and insurance, and thus to capture an increasing share of world trade. . . . Successful expansion, reinforced by colonial acquisitions, generated profits and revenues, helped to service the national debt, and contributed to employment and political stability."[8]

The separate landed aristocracies of England and Scotland had consolidated themselves into a British landed ruling class by the end of the eighteenth century. The profitability of land had risen as a result of the acceleration of population growth in the last third of that century, which raised the demand for food crops and led to an explosion in the price of wheat. This increase in their wealth meant that the Scottish aristocrats could now partake of metropolitan life—the hallmark of the gentleman. There was also a massive transfer of land by purchase and inheritance. These factors along with the increased intermarriage between the English and Scottish landed aristocracies led to their consolidation into a unitary class. They also increasingly turned themselves into a patriotic service class. They began to send their progeny to the great public schools and universities which trained this ruling class in patriotic virtue, and through the study of the classics—with its celebration of Rome—reminded them of their duty to serve and fight.

The new financial interests of the City did not have broad acres but their wealth was growing. Unlike the burgeoning new class of industrialists in the provinces, they were based in London and the southeast and could acquire all the accouterments of a gentleman. For the gentleman ideally required, write Cain and Hopkins, "income and preferably sizeable wealth, but he was not to be sullied by the acquisitive process any more than he was to be corrupted by the power which leadership entailed." The gentleman's code of honor placed duty before self-advancement. "In an order dominated by gentlemanly norms, production was held in low repute. Working directly for money, as opposed to making it from a distance, was associated with dependence and cultural inferiority." The gentleman reconciled his need for income and his disdain for work by participating in activities which were far removed from the mundane world of producing commodities, but which "enabled wealth to be accumulated in ways that were consistent with a gentlemanly life style."[9] The *rentiers* of the landed aristocracy obviously fitted this bill.

But so did the great financiers and bankers of the City. Their accumulation of wealth, residence in the metropolis, and the nature of their business—based on channeling the capital of others rather than making their own through sordid industrial activities—created acceptable indirect and invisible income streams. As their business could be conducted part time, they could pursue the gentlemanly life style of metropolitan London. By the end of the eighteenth century, they had been co-opted into the gentlemanly ruling class hitherto dominated by the landed aristocracy. The public schools and great universities acculturated their children in gentlemanly values, and many also took on the trappings of the landed aristocracy by acquiring their own estates.

With the end of the Napoleonic wars in 1815, the various alarms which had threatened Britain from Europe since the Glorious Revolution came to an end. But there were three issues left over after the Napoleonic wars. They all concerned issues of national identity now that there was no Other in the form of Catholic France to define an identity based on an embattled Protestantism. The first arose as a result of the incorporation of Ireland into the United Kingdom by the Act of Union of 1800 to prevent Napoleon using it as a base to attack England. This raised the question of Catholic emancipation, for how could the Irish Catholics be granted civic rights which were denied to the Catholic minority in Britain? Catholic emancipation was achieved in 1829, but the fierce religious nationalism of the Irish, many of whom never accepted their incorporation into the United Kingdom, was to haunt Britain to our day.

The second issue was parliamentary reform. This arose from the growing feeling that mass participation in the French wars should be rewarded by the extension of the franchise. Linked to this was the fiscal imperative of reducing the burden of the national debt which consumed nearly 80 percent of government revenues. The governing elite also realized that the mercantilist system, with its promotion of monopolies, damaged economic growth and was endangering social stability.[10] This led to a series of initiatives by the gentlemanly order to preserve itself. There were deep cuts in public spending after 1815, a reduction of tariff rates in the 1820s, and a return to the gold standard in 1819. The lineaments for the nineteenth-century British liberal international economic order based on Gladstonian finance, sound money, free trade, and laissez faire were gradually put in place. Meanwhile, the extension of the franchise by the Reform Act of 1832 met the popular demand for extending the rights of citizenship unleashed during the Napoleonic wars. It "put the seal of political acceptance on new property in the south of England as well as on that created by the Industrial Revolution in the provinces,"[11] Cain and Hopkins write, although the franchise remained limited till the end of the nineteenth century.

Equally momentous was the repeal of the Corn Laws in 1846. In the 1820s, both agriculture and industry faced problems. There was a growing imbalance between domestic output of food and population growth which led to a weakening of the hold of the landed interest as more food came to be imported. The import tax on food in the form of the Corn Laws had become more onerous. There was a need to move to a more open economy to quell the rising discontent. The new industries, particularly cotton textiles, also needed foreign markets to deal with incipient problems of domestic unemployment. The City provided a way out for these difficulties. With a reduction of tariffs, imported corn would solve the problem of food supply. The foreign exporters of corn would increase their purchasing power to buy British manufactures. This expansion of trade would be financed, insured, and transported by City merchants, while the additional revenues generated would reduce the tax burden and the national debt. The repeal of the Corn Laws was thus seen by the dominant landed aristocracy as a means of "placating and partially incorporating the most successful representatives of the new wealth produced by economic development"[12] while preserving its own power. But with the acceptance of free trade, within a generation the profitability of agriculture was eroded and with it the economic base of the landed interest. It was the City and the newly emerging professional classes[13] which were to continue the tradition of gentlemanly capitalism.

Cain and Hopkins note that despite Britain being the first industrial nation, the new industrialism never had much influence on British economic and political policies. This was largely because these new sources of wealth were never considered to be gentlemanly; moreover, being mainly located in the provinces, their owners could not partake in the glittering metropolitan social and political life which defined the gentlemanly order. Toward the end of the century some of the richer of these industrialists were grudgingly let into the establishment, but they could not overcome the ungentlemanly attributes of their calling. Nor, after the initial burst, were they the main contributors to Britain's growing economic power. For with the diffusion of the Industrial Revolution, in particular to the former colony—the United States—industrial leadership soon shifted to the New World. Where Britain remained paramount was in providing international services: shipping, insurance, and above all financial services. Through the empire they interwove a huge worldwide web of trade and commerce centered in London. As long as this financial and commercial preeminence was unchallenged, the economic sources of British power remained undiminished. It was with the replacement of London by New York as the world's financial capital after the First World War that the British empire was doomed.

The third domestic consequence of the end of the Napoleonic wars was that, even after the loss of the American colonies, the boundaries of the British empire had expanded so far that they included one in five of the world's population and by 1820 may have included as much as 26 percent.[14] How were these people, who were not British, to be treated? The banning of the slave trade in 1807 meant they could not be slaves. As the end of the slave trade had not ended slavery, the Anti-Slavery League comprising various religious denominations—mainly evangelicals—and secular propagandists such as the utilitarians succeeded in passing the Emancipation Act of 1833, which the British navy thereafter sought to enforce around the world. In Britain's newly acquired exotic possessions, Colonial Secretary Goderich declared in 1833, the aim was "to transfer to distant regions the greatest possible amount both of the spirit of civil liberty and the forms of social order to which Great Britain is chiefly indebted for the rank she holds among the civilized nations." This was to be accomplished by exporting its gentle-manly code, in part by creating a landed gentlemanly elite in the colonies, and also by exporting the British gentlemen being turned out by the public schools and the ancient universities to govern an empire on which the sun never set. India was the main arena for implementing a paternalist version of this policy. The imperial Pax was ideally to be maintained by a form of indi-rect imperialism, where "a cluster of economic satellites [were] managed by foreign beneficiaries of English culture,"[15] and if that proved impossible, direct rule by the gentlemanly guardians.

In enforcing this web, which Palmerston stated was aimed to "export abroad the same self-regulating system which was transforming British soci-ety,"[16] India was to become the jewel in the imperial crown not merely because of the commercial motives which had led to its acquisition, but because it provided the empire with its sinews—in the form of a large stand-ing army paid for out of Indian taxes, which maintained the Pax from Suez to the South China Sea. But this acquisition of empire and the maintenance of a global order in which, as Palmerston stated, "it is the business of government to open and secure the road for the merchant"[17] did not go uncontested in domestic British politics.

The Liberal party largely represented the radical and industrial interests of the provinces. The great economic dynamism of the private economy in Britain had led to a widespread demand for a small state and cheap govern-ment. Both middle-class and working-class radicals espoused this cause, as they saw it as a way to restrain aristocratic power, the national debt, and the Old Corruption which spent taxpayers' money on the politically influential.

Thinkers as far apart as Thomas Paine and John Stuart Mill had argued for freedom of individual choice. Gladstone was the major embodiment of this liberal strand in British politics. Cain and Hopkins write that he "epitomised a liberal consensus centered on middle class property, both industrial and non-industrial, but who also respected aristocratic and gentlemanly values and appealed to the artisan classes with their deep hostility to the state as an engine of repression and as a 'tax-eater.'"[18] This convergence of interests, between the non-aristocratic propertied classes and a large part of the working population, for a limited state allowed Gladstone through his great budgets to usher in that Age of Reform which made limited government—or laissez faire, its derogatory name—a reality.

But the Liberals had an ambivalent attitude to empire. Gladstone's reasons for not acceding to the request of Kings Bell and Acqua of the Cameroons River reflected classic liberal views about empire which resonate to this day, not least in the hearts of many of my libertarian friends. For though Adam Smith did not have much to say about empire per se,[19] his followers Cobden and Bright who (along with Gladstone as the leader of the Liberals) were the leaders of the anti-imperial party, maintained correctly (following in the master's footsteps) that the arguments used by the imperial lobby to justify empire as in the economic interests of the general British populace were flawed. Even today economic historians are unable to agree on whether or not the economic benefits of retaining and expanding the formal British empire after 1850 exceeded its costs.[20] The nineteenth-century classical liberals rightly maintained that, as foreign trade and investment were mutually advantageous (a non-zero sum game), no empire was needed to obtain these gains from trade. All that was required was free trade and laissez faire.

In addition, as they, unlike their American cousins, believed in the correct free trade doctrine—that despite other countries' protectionism, unilateral free trade was in the national interest—they did not want an empire in order to force other countries to free their foreign trade and investments. They rightly urged Britain to unilaterally adopt free trade, which it did with the repeal of the Corn Laws in 1846. But these classical liberals went further in believing that the interdependence resulting from a world knit by mutually advantageous trade and investment would also lead to universal peace. They were projecting onto the international arena the spontaneous order of a market economy in which seemingly conflicting interests are unintentionally harmonized. This was of course the view of the Enlightenment as codified in Kant's *Perpetual Peace*. The apotheosis of this English liberalism was the book written by Sir Norman Angell in 1911 called *The Great Illusion*. In the Liberal tradition he argues that war is economically irrational as it imposes excessive fiscal burdens, defeated powers seldom pay indemnities, colonies do not provide a profit, and "trade cannot be destroyed or captured by a military power." But "what is the real guarantee of the good behavior of one state to another? It is the elaborate interdependence which, not only in the economic sense, but in every sense, makes an unwarrantable aggression of one state upon another react upon the interests of the aggressor."[21]

But the Liberals did not altogether eschew empire, for as Angell states: "Where the condition of a territory is such that the social and economic cooperation of other countries with it is impossible, we may expect the intervention of military force, not as the result of the 'annexationist illusion,' but as the outcome of real social forces pushing to the maintenance of order. That is the story of England in Egypt, or, for that matter, in India. And if America has any justification in the Philippines at all, it is not that she has 'captured' these populations by force of conquest, as in the old days a raiding tribe might capture a band of cattle, but that she is doing there a work of police and administration which the natives cannot do for themselves."[22] This is the white-man's-burden argument for empire which meant that even Liberals were in favour of an empire to maintain a Pax.

The British Pax, which underwrote free trade and commerce around the world, was maintained by its naval supremacy, while its policy of maintaining a balance of power also prevented the domination of the European continent by a single power or combination of powers. By the end of the nineteenth century, industrial and technological primacy had passed from Britain to the United States. Both the United States' and Germany's GDP were rising rapidly. By 1913 the GDP of both (but most markedly that of the United States) would be greater than Britain's (see fig. 2). These were the rising powers challenging British hegemony.

Though an interminable debate continues about the causes of the First World War,[23] an important element for Britain's involvement was the German naval buildup and the threat this posed to Britain's naval supremacy, and thereby to the maintenance of its global empire. But when the British joined the war, which began with the assassination of the Austrian Archduke Francis Ferdinand by a Serbian nationalist in Sarajevo in August 1914, it effectively signed the death warrant for its empire. For this war and the next, which arose from it, would destroy the financial supremacy of Britain, which had ultimately provided the economic base to maintain its empire. Over the next century, the burden of maintaining a Pax would shift to its offspring in the New World.

THE IMPERIAL REPUBLIC

The ascendancy of the United States from a British colony to independent republic to, what the great French political sociologist Raymond Aron[24] aptly termed, an Imperial Republic can be briefly told. The period since the American War of Independence ended in the Treaty of Paris in 1783 can be broken down in a number of ways.[25] I find the older classification by Aron still the most useful. Throughout the history of the United States as an independent nation, the globalization engendered by Britain was the conditioning factor which influenced both its domestic and foreign policy. In the first period from 1783 till 1898 and the war with Spain, the United States initially had an uneasy relation with the old mother country. The young republic was surrounded by the old empires, the English to the north and the Spanish and French to the south. Protected as it was by distance, its major aim was not to be drawn into the continuing disputes of the European nation states while it expanded over much of North America. Even before independence, Americans had seen themselves as having the right of occupancy of the whole vast territory over which they sought to establish an empire such as the world had never seen. The chief justice of South Carolina, William Henry Drayton, in 1776 summarized these sentiments as follows: "Empires have their zenith—and their declension and dissolution. . . . The British period is from the year 1758, when they victoriously pursued their Enemies into every Quarter of the Globe . . . The Almighty . . . has made the choice of the present generation to erect the American Empire . . . And thus has suddenly arisen in the World, a new Empire, styled the United States of America. An Empire that as soon as started into Existence, attracts the attention of the Rest of the Universe; and bids fair by the blessing of God, to be the most glorious of any upon Record."[26]

By 1823 and the promulgation of the Monroe Doctrine, the United States had reached an equilibrium in its external relations which would last till the end of the century. Declaring the Americas as part of the U.S. sphere of influence, they warned the French and Spanish not to attempt to recreate their old dynastic empires in the continent. Through its accommodation with Britain, which rightly decided it would be best not to snuff out its wayward progeny, the United States got the British navy to enforce their doctrine. America could fulfill its manifest destiny by creating a large land-based empire in North America. The liberal international economic order (LIEO) the British promoted with free trade, free mobility of capital, and the gold standard allowed the new country with its industriousness and unique egalitarian and democratic institutions to develop. By the end of the century, it had become an economic colossus which surpassed the mother country in its economic wealth. Meanwhile, through a series of small wars and astute purchases, it was able to extend its territory over the whole of the area which is now the United States. But, as Aron notes of this period when the Americans were creating their land-based empire, there were certain traits of American external action which persist to our day, "such as the flare-up of public opinion (in 1792 and 1812), legalistic scruples, the swing between the will to power (expansionism) and an uneasy conscience, and a curious mixture of pragmatic and moralistic morality."[27]

In the second period from the war with Spain, which allowed the United States to mop up the remnants of the Spanish empire, till the entry of the United States into the Second World War in 1941, the republic was torn between imperialism and isolation. In the early part of this period, the United States had seriously begun to think about its future once Pax Britannica declined. One response was direct imperialism. But then it pulled back from this course and under Woodrow Wilson tried to create a new world order based on national self-determination and collective security, which we need to look at more fully as it has continuing resonance to our day. But, as Aron notes of this second period from 1898 to 1941, "it is a unit only in its inconsistencies, its abrupt changes of front, its inability to choose a line of conduct, and stick to it—in short the rejection of the inter-state universe in the form it had taken throughout the ages yet whose rules the United States itself had unwittingly used for its own benefit and at the expense of first the French and then the English, the Indians, and the Spaniards. The Americans have never recognized the similarity between continental expansion and the imperialism of other states."[28]

After America's entry into the Second World War with the bombing of Pearl Harbor, the American foreign policy elite began to rethink the United States' role in the world. The third period begins with the Truman Doctrine in 1947 and lasts to our day. During this period, Walter Mead writes, the Americans concluded, as they had in 1823, that "the national interest required a strong maritime power to uphold the balance of power in Europe and to maintain an international economic and political order in the rest of the world. By 1947 that power could no longer be Great Britain; it would have to be the United States. Atlas shrugged, and the United States would shoulder the sky. Since World War II, that choice has been and remains the cornerstone of American foreign policy."[29] Pax Americana was to replace Pax Britannica.

A number of astute observers, including Aron and George Liska,[30] writing during or soon after the ill-fated Vietnam War realized the obsolescence of the view still being peddled by isolationists such as Pat Buchanan and expressed in the title of his recent book, *A Republic, Not an Empire*. The United States, as Aron rightly emphasized in the title of his book, had become *The Imperial Republic*. The Cold War and the Vietnam War were mere episodes in the consolidation of this indirect imperial rule. But, with some notable exceptions, even today most of the discussion of American power and how to use it is based on a denial of this fact. This, as I shall show, has hamstrung U.S. foreign policy and the requisite debate about how best this empire can be run and maintained. One of the major reasons for this denial of its imperial ascendancy is the continuing resonance of the views of Woodrow Wilson and the illusion that the world can be run on Wilsonian lines.

WILSONIAN UTOPIANISM

Woodrow Wilson was a Utopian whose world view was a strange mixture of classical liberalism, Burkean conservatism, Presbyterianism, and social-ism.[31] According to Thomas Knock, he referred to himself as an imperialist on two occasions, but this was to be a form of economic imperialism, in line with his former student Fredrick Jackson Turner's frontier thesis which "implied that the U.S. required greater foreign markets in order to sustain its prosperity."[32] But "for every sentence he uttered on commerce, he spoke two on the moral responsibility of the United States to sustain its historic ideal-ism and render the service of its democracy. . . . During his campaign for the Democratic presidential nomination in 1912 . . . [he said]: 'I believe that God planted in us visions of liberty . . . that we are chosen and prominently chosen to show the way to the nations of the world how they shall walk in the paths of liberty.'"[33] The instrument for achieving this Utopia was to be the League of Nations, which would ensure collective security by bringing transgressors of the new order into line through sanctions. The traditional notion of national interest which had governed the European balance of power system was eschewed, to be replaced by a community of nation-states in which the weak and the strong would have equal rights. In his new world order, said Wilson, the only questions would be "Is it right? Is it just? Is it in the interest of mankind?"

This Wilsonian moralistic universalism was countered by the isolation-ist Jeffersonians and Jacksonians, and for the whole of the period 1898–1941, U.S. foreign policy is marked by inconsistencies and zigzags. It was unable to decide whether it should replace the British with its own imperium to maintain global order, or whether it should stay within its prosperous fortress and let the world order look after itself. As Aron notes, during this period "the United States was guilty not of any will to power but of a failure to become aware of the role imposed upon it by destiny."[34]

This failure led to the two greatest threats to the classical liberal order created by Britain: Fascism and Communism. From the thought experiment outlined in the introduction, these threats can in part be seen to have arisen because the United States failed to establish its political hegemony in 1918.

On 10 October 1916, John Maynard Keynes saw that financial hegemony had passed irrevocably across the Atlantic. He wrote in a memorandum to the British Treasury, "the policy of this country towards the USA should be so directed as not only to avoid any form of reprisal or even active irritation but also to conciliate and please."[35] By then the British were completely financially dependent on the United States.

Nor, as Keynes bitterly complained in his brilliant *The Economic Consequences of the Peace,* did Wilson succeed in fulfilling the pledge in his Fourteen Points—whose acceptance by Germany ended the war—that no Carthaginian peace as demanded by the victors, particularly France, would be imposed on Germany. Keynes believed that Wilson had been hoodwinked by the "Welsh wizard," David Lloyd George, into acceding to Georges Clemenceau's desire to dismember German military and economic power, and that Wilson had convinced himself that the two prime ministers were in accord with his Fourteen Points. By the time Lloyd George realized his mistake, he could not "in five days persuade the President of error in what it had taken five months to prove to him to be just and right. After all it was harder to de-bamboozle this old Presbyterian than it had been to bamboozle him; for the former involved his belief in and respect for himself."[36]

Robert Skidelsky rightly notes that "Keynes's criticism of Wilson's character hinged on a mistaken assessment of the President's priorities. Wilson conceded on points that Keynes thought important, but which Wilson did not."[37] For Wilson's main purpose was to get his League of Nations: "From Wilson's vantage point, if this League were incorporated into the general settlement, then he could feel confident that he had kept his faith, that the most important objective of the Great War had been consummated, and that any injustices done by the treaty of peace itself could be redressed later with relative ease."[38] Of course, with the failure of Wilson to persuade the Senate to accept the treaty setting up the League, and the turn to isolationism of the United States, the flawed treaty did, as Keynes feared, lead to "the bankruptcy and decay of Europe . . . [which] will affect everyone in the long run, but perhaps not in a way that is striking or immediate."[39]

The most trenchant criticism of Wilsonian universal moralism and the whole idealist theory of foreign relations was provided by E. H. Carr in his *The Twenty Years' Crisis* in 1939, just before the beginning of the Second World War. The League of Nations, as the realists had always maintained, proved a broken reed. It failed to maintain the peace.

This Wilsonian universal moralism was resurrected after the Second World War with the United Nations. Once again, the anthropomorphic identification of states as persons, and the presumption of an essential harmony of interests between these equal world citizens was proclaimed, with those

breaking international norms being brought into line through collective economic sanctions. These sanctions, as the 1990 detailed study by Gary
Hufbauer and his associates shows, have been ineffective and inefficient in
serving foreign policy goals,[40] while the historical record yields two conclusions about blockades and sanctions. First, that any treaty signed before a
war to restrict actions has a high probability of being cast aside once the
shooting starts. Second, that sanctions by international bodies unless
enforced by force are almost meaningless.[41] Thus, the League of Nations fell
apart when Italy ignored its sanctions.

As part of maintaining their Pax, empires have also put a lid on ethnic
conflicts. President Wilson's invoking of the principle of national self-
determination—as he proclaimed the new moral Age of Nations to replace
the immoral old Age of Empires—let the ethnic genie out of the bottle. As
Dean Acheson noted in a speech at Amherst College, December 9, 1964, this
high-sounding principle "has a doubtful moral history. He [Woodrow
Wilson] used it against our enemies in the First World War to dismember the
Austro-Hungarian and Ottoman Empires, with results which hardly inspire
enthusiasm today. After the Second World War the doctrine was invoked
against our friends in the dissolution of their colonial connections. . . .
On the one occasion when the right of self-determination—then called
secession—was invoked against our own government by the Confederate
States of America, it was rejected with a good deal of bloodshed and moral
fervor. Probably you will agree it was rightly rejected."[42]

Moreover, as Niall Ferguson, a historian of the First World War, has
noted, the principle of self-determination was in part responsible for
the Second World War. At the end of the First World War about 13 percent of
the total German-speaking population was outside the Reich. "The adoption
of 'self-determination' as a guiding principle of the peace was fatal because
it could not be applied to Germany without aggrandizing her far beyond the
territory of the pre-1919 Reich. The choice was between an organized
hypocrisy, which denied Germans the right of self-determination granted
to others; or an irresistible revisionism, which would end by granting the
Germans a substantial part of the annexationist aims of 1914–18. From
the outset, there was inconsistency: no Anschluss of the rump Austria to the
Reich; but plebiscites to determine the fates of Schleswig, southern East
Prussia and Upper Silesia."[43] The principle of self-determination could not
be applied without renewed violence in Central and Eastern Europe.

Today, the most common form of deadly conflict is a civil war in the
name of cultural self-determination. Some interesting recent research
by Paul Collier and his associates[44] on the causes of civil war finds that the

relationship of ethno-linguistic fragmentation in a state and the risk of a civil war is an inverted U in shape. The most homogeneous as well as the most fragmented are least at risk of civil war. Thus, there is likely to be a bipolarity in the institutions best able to deal with ethnic diversity. One characteristic, considerable fragmentation, is to be found in most empires. The other, homogeneity, is surprisingly a course advocated by Keynes during the Second World War in his speculation about the ideal political postwar order in Europe. Robert Skidelsky reports on one of Keynes's fancies:

> A view of the post-war world which I find sympathetic and attractive and fruitful of good consequences is that we should encourage small political and cultural units, combined into larger, and more or less closely knit, economic units. It would be a fine thing to have thirty or forty capital cities in Europe, each the center of a self-governing country entirely free from national minorities (who would be dealt with by migrations where necessary) and the seat of government and parliament and university center, each with their own pride and glory and their own characteristics and excellent gifts. But it would be ruinous to have thirty or forty entirely independent economic and currency unions.[45]

But as Skidelsky notes "this pleasing picture of a re-medievalised Europe did not survive in later drafts." This homogenized solution, which as Keynes recognized could involve ethnic cleansing, has clearly been eschewed by the West—as witness its actions in Bosnia and Kosovo. This reflects the hopes stemming from the Enlightenment of much progressive thought over the last two centuries that transnational and modern forms of association, such as class, would transcend primordial forms of association, such as ethnicity and culture, of which nationalism is an offshoot. But, contemporary history continues to show the power of these primordial forces.[46]

The Keynes solution is feasible in a globalized economy where size does not matter for prosperity—demonstrated by the shining examples of the city-states of Hong Kong and Singapore—as long as there is someone to maintain a global Pax. The events in Bosnia and Kosovo show that the United States and its allies have (rightly in my view) chosen to impose a regional Pax by partially reconstructing parts of the Balkan Austro-Hungarian empire. The High Representative of the UN in Bosnia and the chief administrator of Kosovo are the equivalents of British viceroys in areas of direct imperialism and political agents in those of indirect imperialism. Similarly, the recent Afghan peace is underwritten by an allied police force and another form of indirect imperialism, much as the British sought to do through their residents in Afghanistan during their imperium.

DOMESTIC BASES OF U.S. FOREIGN POLICY

Wilsonianism has only been one strand in the domestic politics which has determined U.S. foreign policy. Walter Russell Mead in an important book *Special Providence*[47] has identified four separate foreign policy schools with domestic support in the United States.

Besides Wilsonianism, which apart from its English liberal roots was also fed by the nonconformist missionary tradition of the country, the other schools (using labels associated with other past U.S. presidents) are: Hamiltonians, Jeffersonians, and Jacksonians.

The Hamiltonians[48] were the party of merchants and industrialists. They were the clearest in seeing the importance of the international order maintained by Pax Britannica for the promotion of U.S. enterprise both domestically and internationally. They were the first to see that as the British empire declined, America would have to replace it. But though they believed in free trade, they did not subscribe to unilateral free trade as did the British. They believed in reciprocity. So while they were for opening foreign markets, and were major proponents of the Open Door policy in the nineteenth century that prevented China being colonized by one or another of the European imperial powers which would have shut out American commercial interests, these bankers and manufacturers did not see the case for allowing foreign goods to trade freely in the United States. Unlike the British who believed in the theoretically correct free trade doctrine, that free trade was to Britain's benefit even if other countries did not reciprocate, the Hamiltonians would only allow foreign goods access to U.S. markets if other countries reciprocally opened up their markets to U.S. goods. Also, following the arguments advanced by Alexander Hamilton, they were in favor of tariffs to protect infant industries. During "the zenith of Hamiltonian power," writes Mead, " . . . from Abraham Lincoln's election to the outbreak of the Great Depression . . . American tariffs were at the highest levels in [U.S.] history."[49] After the disastrous Smoot-Hawley tariff in the interwar period, the Hamiltonians gradually shifted from protectionism to free trade, and since the Second World War—often in association with the Wilsonians— have been the main proponents of rebuilding and maintaining another liberal international economic order with, Mead continues, "freedom of the seas, the open door, and an international legal and financial order that permitted the broadest possible global trade in capital and goods."

The Jeffersonians[50] were often opposed to the Hamiltonians and the Wilsonians. They have considered the most vital interest the preservation of American democracy in a dangerous world. They have, Mead observes, "consistently looked for the least costly and dangerous method of defending

American independence while counseling against attempts to impose American values on other countries."[51] They are suspicious of both big business and a big government, believing that both jeopardize the liberty of the republic. They are libertarians. They are against foreign entanglements and wars, as these extend the powers of the state. They have never been able to come to terms with the need for the United States to take over Britain's imperial responsibilities. For them, American liberty is precious and fragile. They do not want the American republic to be transformed into an intercontinental empire because, as John Quincy Adams said, "She might become the dictatress of the world: she would be no longer the ruler of her own spirit."[52] They have been the isolationist party.

Domestically, the Jacksonians have probably been the most influential party, as they comprise what has been called middle America. Walter Mead states: "the Jacksonian school represents a deeply embedded, widely spread populist and popular culture of honor, independence, courage, and military pride among the American people."[53] They are America's warriors. Though Americans like to believe that they are a pacific people protected from foreign adventures and threats by two vast oceans, they have, nonetheless, apart from the major wars—the two world wars and those in Korea and Vietnam—fought a large number of what Rudyard Kipling called "savage wars of peace."[54] Thus, U.S. Marines staged 180 landings abroad between 1800 and 1934. Though the annexation of the Philippines was the only case of direct imperialism, these other small wars, writes Max Boot, were "'imperial wars'—a term that, American sensitivities notwithstanding, seems apt to describe many U.S. adventures abroad."[55] In the period to about 1890, the United States military power was used to pacify the Indians at home as it expanded to the West, and to act as a junior constable to Britain's world policeman "often working hand in glove with the British to defend freedom of the seas and open markets in China, Japan, and elsewhere."[56] These forays—like the earlier war waged against the Barbary states of North Africa—were aimed at opening up the world to Western commerce. In the second period, beginning with the 1898 war against Spain till 1941, the United States turned the Caribbean and much of South America into its indirect empire. Even Woodrow Wilson partook in this extension of the American imperium with his goal of teaching "the South American republics to elect good men."[57] His intervention in Mexico in 1914 and the occupations of Haiti and the Dominican Republic in 1915 and 1916 were part of this pattern. In all these foreign adventures, the U.S. administration could count on the support of the Jacksonians.

Like the Jeffersonians, the Jacksonians are highly suspicious of elites. Both groups are civil libertarians and deeply committed to the Constitution and the preservation of the liberties of ordinary Americans. But there are also deep differences between them. These became apparent during the Cold War, with the Jeffersonians being the most dovish, the Jacksonians, the most hawkish. Mead notes, "suspicious of untrammeled federal power, skeptical about the prospects for domestic and foreign do-gooding (welfare at home, foreign aid abroad), opposed to federal taxes but obstinately fond of federal programs seen as primarily helping the middle class (Social Security, Medicare, mortgage interest subsidies), Jacksonians constitute a large political interest."[58] Though unfashionable among the two coastal elites, they express the social, cultural, and religious values of the large swath of Middle America. It is the political philosophy of the American heartland rather than the two coasts, and it represents the views of white Protestant males of the lower and middle classes.[59]

The Jacksonians are the descendants of the Scotch-Irish who settled in the Carolinas and Virginia, the Old West, and the south and south-central states. But Jacksonian populism has moved beyond these ethnic and geographical limits. Over time most urban immigrant groups have assimilated to this quintessentially American culture. "Jacksonian values play a major role in African American culture. If anything, the role of Jacksonian values in African American life has increased with the increasing presence of African Americans in all military ranks,"[60] Mead writes. This culture emphasizes rugged individualism, honor and respect for ordinary people, economic success based on hard work, absolute equality of dignity and right, and a constant search for self-improvement. This democratic and populist culture, which is pervasive outside the two coasts, provides the vision of a country in which the average person can live their lives free of any cultural, economic, or spiritual inhibitions. It is what attracts so many ordinary people to the United States from around the world, while it is also the reason why so many sensitive souls particularly from the elitist educated classes in Europe and their outposts on the east and west coasts of the United States find this culture crass and vulgar.[61]

In foreign policy, the Jacksonians are America's warriors. They are realists who have no truck with Wilsonian moralism. "For the Jacksonians the world community Wilsonians want to build is a moral impossibility, even a moral monstrosity."[62] They believe that international life will remain violent and anarchic. They have little regard for international law and practice. They accept the need at times to fight preemptive wars and to assassinate foreign leaders with bad intentions. They separate issues of war and morality. They believe that if a war is worth fighting, it must be fought completely; it should be fought to achieve strategic and tactical objectives with as few U.S. casualties as possible. There is nothing wrong in civilian targeting in war if it will bring about the enemy's capitulation. Finally, wars must end in victory, but foes who have surrendered unconditionally should be treated magnanimously. It is the mass patriotism and the martial spirit of the Jacksonians which has made the American imperium possible. Given the political weight in a mass democracy of this large constituency, the other schools competing to run U.S. foreign policy ignore it at their peril—as do what some in America have called "the surrender monkeys" of Europe!

CONCLUSIONS

The United States is indubitably an empire. It is more than a hegemon, as it seeks control over not only foreign but also aspects of domestic policy in other countries. But it is an informal and indirect empire. After its nineteenth century colonial adventure in the Philippines, it has not sought to acquire territory. Nor is it like the Spanish and many of the ancient predatory empires a tribute-seeking empire. It is an empire which has taken over from the British the burden of maintaining a Pax to allow free trade and commerce to flourish. This Pax brings mutual gains. Given the well-known human tendency to free ride, the United States like Britain in the nineteenth century has borne much of the costs of providing this global public good, not because of altruism but because the mutual gains from a global liberal economic order benefit America and foster its economic well-being. It has not in this promotion of globalization or global capitalism—as some would derogatively label it—yet been forced to take direct control over areas which have fallen into the black hole of domestic disorder, as was the case, for instance, with the British takeover from the crumbling Moghul empire in eighteenth-century India.

Given the varied contradictory currents in domestic politics regarding America's relations with the world, since the Second World War the imperial mission has been pursued surreptitiously by a foreign policy elite which has shown a remarkable consensus about the aims of U.S. foreign policy.[63] These aims are not only to maintain U.S. military superiority for purposes of national security, but also "to maintain international order, thereby enabling the process of globalization to continue and the American people to reap its rewards. As Secretary of Defense William Cohen [in the Clinton administration] explained 'economists and soldiers share the same interests in stability.' By tapping American military power, 'we are able to shape the environment in ways that are advantageous to us and that are stabilizing to the areas where we are forward deployed, thereby helping to promote investment and prosperity . . . business follows the flag.'"[64] These are sentiments which the gentlemanly capitalists promoting the nineteenth-century British imperial Pax would have heartily endorsed.

Moreover, the maintenance of a global liberal international economic order through a Pax Americana requires—as did Pax Britannia—supremacy over the seas and nowadays over the air, along with bases on the relevant sea and air lanes to both protect the homeland and keep the channels of trade and commerce open and free of "pirates." Though, because of the exigencies of the Cold War, the United States in order to maintain the Pax had to station ground troops in Europe and Asia; this need disappeared with the end of the Cold War in Europe and will, when the problems on the Korean peninsula are finally sorted out, also make ground troops redundant in the Far East. Particularly if the promise held out by the revolution in military affairs (discussed earlier) is borne out, the United States will not have to occupy recalcitrant states for long to impose its will.

Furthermore, the United States has created four regional military commands with their respective commander-in-chiefs (CINCs), who in effect divide up the world between them. The CINC of the Pacific command (PAC), based in Pearl Harbor, holds sway over the Pacific and East Asia; the CINC of the European command (EUR), based in Stuttgart, is responsible for Europe, Africa, and parts of the Middle East, including Israel. The CINC of the central command (CENT) based in Tampa, looks after the rest of the Middle East, including the Persian Gulf, Central Asia, and the Horn of Africa; while the domain of the CINC for the Southern command (SOUTH) is South America and the Caribbean. Their role after the end of the Cold War, as General Anthony Zini (CINCCENT) noted, is "like that of a proconsul of the Roman empire." They are now engaged not in planning war campaigns but in a mixture of "political, diplomatic and military concerns" relating to governance in the regions they oversee.[65] But unlike past empires, there is no matching imperial civil service to run the empire once the military task has been done. This has come to haunt the U.S. in the task it faces in Iraq.

Given these realities of empire and the U.S. pursuit of its imperial mission since the end of the Second World War, the illusion has nevertheless been maintained among the general public that America is not an empire. Many domestic and foreign observers of U.S. foreign policy like Liska and Aron realized early on that America had turned itself into the imperial republic. Even many liberal and non-Marxist scholars have recognized that America is an empire.[66] Arthur Schlesinger Jr. wrote: "who can doubt that there is an American empire?—an 'informal' empire, not colonial in polity, but still richly equipped with imperial paraphernalia: troops, ships, planes, bases, proconsuls, local collaborators, all spread around the luckless planet."[67] Yet, even today officials refuse to admit that the United States is an empire. President George W. Bush, we are told, "dislikes the whole idea of empire, and he routinely makes a point of warding off the 'imperialism' label."[68] This is a great pity, for as this book will argue, it is important that there be acceptance in U.S. domestic politics of its imperial power. The real debate about how best to use that power could then sensibly ensue, for empires come before imperialism.

With the publication of the new National Security Strategy of the United States in September 2002, setting out what is being called the Bush doctrine, some sort of debate seems to have begun. This document's tenets include the maintenance of overwhelming military supremacy, more active promotion of democracy and free markets abroad, and preemptive action against threats from failed and rogue states, especially those with or seeking weapons of mass destruction. It seems, despite Bush's disavowal to signify the continuation of an American imperium, the strategy has for the first time brought the question of the American empire and how its imperial power should be used in the post–Cold War world to the fore.

There seem to be three positions in the current U.S. debate which can be identified. The first is based on the hope that the empire will just go away. The second argues for handing over the empire to a multilateral committee at the United Nations. The third is identified with those neoconservatives labeled democratic imperialists. According to Ivo Daalder, of the Brookings Institution, democratic imperialists want to "'use American power, and the values behind it, to remake certain parts of the world in America's image— a more democratic and prosperous place.' Unlike traditional, predatory imperialism, democratic imperialism has its goal 'to make countries free, open to globalization—on the assumption that, if countries are like us, they're less likely to be a threat. It's very idealistic.'"[69] That is why on the issue of the aims of the new imperialism there is a convergence of views between neoconservatives and the Wilsonian Democrats in the U.S. and new Labour in the U.K. But the first of these positions is unrealistic—it amounts to saying "stop the world I want to get off." The second is infeasible, and the third is confused and dangerous and a sure way of creating disorder.

It might help to give a preview of my detailed argument in Part III of why this democratic imperialism with its whiff of Wilsonianism, which seems to infect the latest U.S. National Security Strategy document, is confused and dangerous. It is confused because it conflates different forms of liberty (even abstracting from the positive liberty advocated by socialists of various hue). One must at least differentiate between economic, civil, and political liberty. The first relates to free markets, the second to the rule of law, and the third to democracy. If the purpose of the present Pax, as it was for the British in the nineteenth century, is to promote and maintain a liberal international economic order (LIEO), the relevant liberties are civil and economic. Political liberty, as we shall see, may be desirable for all sorts of reasons, but to put it above domestic order can damage the LIEO by setting up that feared clash of civilizations. The purpose of the American imperium, in my view, should be as it was for the British in the nineteenth century, to promote that globalization which leads to modernity. The ensuing prosperity will do much more to fend off threats to peace than attempts to thrust Western cultural mores and values down recalcitrant throats. What the new imperialists need to remember, I will argue, is that the modernization they rightly seek in the world does not need and may in fact be hindered by attempts to promote Westernization.

CHAPTER 3

Challenges to the American Imperium

What are the tasks the new American imperium can be expected to perform? Will these inevitably lead as many observers have suggested to imperial over-stretch and the decline of the empire? Is the very existence of the empire likely to lead to the formation of a countervailing coalition to contain the empire? And finally, what are the dangers to international order and how should the imperium respond to them? These are the questions we need to answer if, as I have argued, the existence of an American imperium is now an inescapable fact but, unlike past empires, one that is clearly not going to be motivated by territorial expansion or the predatory motive of booty.

TASKS

In discerning the tasks required of a nonpredatory imperial power, it is useful to see how it differs from a mere great power. George Liska admirably summed up the difference: "an empire is a state exceeding other states in size, scope, salience, and sense of task." The size which is relevant is the size of its material resources summarized by its gross domestic product (GDP) relative to other states. The scope of its interests and involvements is coter-minus with the international system itself, which today is global. The salience of the imperial state lies in that no other state can ignore it. Its task is to create and maintain a world which harmonizes the particular interests of the imperial state with the interests of the commonweal. "An empire or imperial state is . . . a state that combines the characteristics of a great power, which, being a world power and a globally paramount state, becomes automatically a power primarily responsible for shaping and maintaining a necessary modicum of world order."[1]

In an imperial order the relationships with other states are defined in their relationship with the dominant power as allies or potential rivals. The system is managed by alliances but these, unlike an interstate system where they are instruments of conflict, are instruments of control. Much of the diplomacy conducted by the imperial state is management diplomacy as Liska labels it, rather than the maneuver diplomacy which characterizes interstate systems.[2] In the imperial system, order is maintained by "the widely shared presumption of the ultimately controlling power of the imperial state; this is true even if the manifestation of the controlling power is only intermittent, because the countervailing dynamic continues to operate most of the time."[3] This is a different form of maintaining order than the reciprocal countervailing pattern of the distribution of antagonistic power in an interstate system through a balance of power.

Liska also lists the immemorial instruments of empire and compares the contemporary versions with those of Rome. The first is the wide diffusion of a pro-American party in friendly and dependent lands, like Rome's aristocratic party vis-à-vis the Macedonian party in Greece. Second is a military force which has overwhelmingly superiority in both organization and weapons and is kept so in part by preventing the diffusion of crucial weapons to friends and foes alike. But there are certain aspects of consolidating its empire for which America will have to find functional equivalents to Roman strengths. America will need some substitute for Rome's unified or dual citizenship, which enabled its army and bureaucracy to be multiethnic and meritocractic, and Liska notes, it will need "a relatively small, highly professional military establishment, organized for mobile offensive-defensive warfare at more or less remote—and in America's case ever-shifting—imperial frontiers, [which would] become the equivalent of the Roman legion."[4] With the new military revolution and the establishment of the proconsular regional CINCs, the latter may now be coming into existence. Finally, there is the growing appeal of American ideals and culture, or what has been termed its "soft power." This is already happening, in particular with the spread of English as the global lingua franca.

MEANS

But does America have the means to fulfill these imperial tasks? Would it not lead, as Paul Kennedy argued in the late 1980s, to "imperial overstretch" and the nationalist backlash which has undermined past empires?[5]

Relative Economic and Military Strength

On the first question, the three major correlates of military power and hence the means to sustain an imperial role are population size, gross domestic product (GDP), and the ability and willingness to convert economic into military power.[6] As we are concerned with the dangers of declining power, the relevant variables are how the relative current levels of population and GDP will alter in the future. These will obviously depend on the current and likely future growth rates of these variables, with the growth rate of GDP being jointly determined by the rate of growth of population and of productivity.

Table 5 shows the latest UN estimates of population in various countries from the year 2000 to 2050. These projections take account of current trends in fertility and mortality, as well as in net migration, in each of the countries. It is clear from this that India will be the most populous country in 2050, with China coming close but with its population beginning to decline as the fertility rate falls below replacement levels. The United States continues to have a growing population through both natural increase and immigration, as does the UK to a lesser extent. By contrast, Japan, France, Germany, and Russia will see a mild to rapid decline in their populations. This is likely to adversely effect their future GDP growth rates, as is the projected long-term declining trend in the Chinese population growth rate. Only the U.S., UK, and India are likely to have positive effects on GDP growth from their demographics. Europe (including Russia and Eastern Europe) as a whole will have a decline in population.

These divergent trends in population growth rates which are one determinant of economic growth rates are likely to be reinforced by divergent trends in productivity. India and China can as latecomers expect to use already known technology to obtain productivity gains through catch up. What of the European countries and the United States? In the U.S., productivity in the nonfarm business sector rose at an annual rate of 1.6 percent per annum between 1970 and 1995. In the seven years from 1995 to 2002 it rose by 2.6 percent per annum. There seems to be no sign that this productivity surge is dying out. Thus, productivity growth averaged 3.1 percent between the beginning of the current recession in the third quarter of 2000 and the third quarter of 2002.[7] There has been no similar productivity surge in Europe and Japan. Their productivity rise since 1995 is less than that in earlier years. In large part this is because of the failure, in particular of Europe, to adopt the information technology (IT) revolution, which in turn is partly due to the economic framework in which their businesses operate. Thus, the big difference in the productivity increases between the U.S. and Europe has been in the sectors that are substantial *users* of IT equipment and software.[8] As the revolution in military affairs (RMA) taking place in the U.S. (discussed

Table 5. Population estimates (UN) 2000–50 (millions)

Year	China	India	Japan	US	Europe	France	Germany	Russia	UK
2000 1	1,275	1,017	127	285	728	59	82	146	59
2	1,322	1,097	128	300	725	61	83	142	60
3	1,364	1,174	128	315	720	62	83	138	60
4	1,402	1,246	127	330	713	63	83	133	61
5	1,429	1,312	126	344	705	64	82	129	62
6	1,445	1,369	123	358	696	64	82	124	63
7	1,451	1,417	121	370	685	65	82	120	64
8	1,448	1,455	119	382	674	65	81	115	65
9	1,439	1,486	116	391	661	65	80	110	65
10	1,421	1,512	113	400	647	65	80	106	66
2050 11	1,395	1,531	110	409	632	64	79	102	66

Table 6. Military expenditures as a percent of GDP, major powers, 1988–2000

	1988	1989	1990	1991	1992	1993	1994	1995	1996	1997	1998	1999	2000
China	2.7	2.7	2.7	2.5	2.7	2.1	1.9	1.8	1.8	1.9	2.0	2.1	2.1
France	3.7	3.6	3.5	3.5	3.4	3.3	3.3	3.1	3.0	2.9	2.8	2.7	2.6
Germany	2.9	2.8	2.8	2.2	2.1	1.9	1.7	1.7	1.6	1.6	1.5	1.5	1.5
India	3.1	2.9	2.7	2.5	2.3	2.4	2.3	2.2	2.1	2.2	2.2	2.4	2.4
Russia	15.8	14.2	12.3	0	5.5	5.3	5.9	4.1	3.8	4.2	3.2	3.6	4.0
UK	4.1	4.1	3.9	4.2	3.8	3.5	3.3	3	2.9	2.7	2.6	2.5	2.5
US	5.7	5.5	5.3	4.7	4.8	4.5	4.1	3.8	3.5	3.3	3.1	3.0	3.1
EU	1.7	1.7	1.7	1.7	1.7	1.7	1.7	1.7	1.7	1.7	1.7	1.7	1.7

Source: Stockholm International Peace Research Institute, Military Expenditures Database.

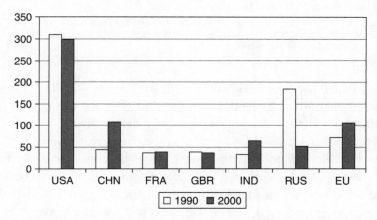

Fig. 3. Military expenditures: major powers, 1990 and 2000 (in billions of PPP$)

in chapter 1) is based on advances in IT, the Europeans are also likely to fall well behind the frontier of military technology. Unlike the U.S., where the rise in productivity has been accompanied by a substantial rise in employment (until the latest recession), in Europe employment has stagnated. Because of these differing trends in population growth and productivity, the European Commission's recent "Economic Review" predicts that the annual growth rate in Europe during the next fifty years will be only half that in the United States.[9]

These differences in growth rates of GDP and population will obviously translate into differences not only in economic but also in military strength. I have assembled some figures on the share of military spending in GDP of the United States and other potential great powers from the late 1980s, together with their total military spending in purchasing power parity (PPP) dollars for 1990 and 2000 (table 6 and fig. 3). The table shows that if there was any imperial overstretch it was in the former Soviet Union. The current share of military expenditure in GDP of the successor state, the

Table 7. Growth rate to catch up with U.S. military expenditures

	2020	2050	2100	Actual GDP Growth Rate 1973–98
China	8.5	5.2	4.1	6.84
France	14.3	7.4	5.2	2.10
UK	14.6	7.5	5.2	2.00
India	11.8	6.4	4.7	5.07
Russia	12.7	6.8	4.9	−1.15
EU	6.5	4.4	3.7	na

Assumptions
$ U.S. real PPP GDP will grow at a constant 3% per year (average from 1988 to 1998)
$ Military expenditures / GDP will stay the same as in 2000

Source: *World Development Indicators* for PPP GDP in 2000; *Stockholm International Peace Research Institute Database* for Military expenditures / GDP; A. Maddison: *The World Economy—A Millennial Perspective*, OECD, 2001, Appendix C Table C I -b.

Russian Federation, remains much higher than anyone else's. Figure 3 shows that the military expenditure of the United States in 2000 was greater than that of any of the other great powers by a massive margin.

I then examined how fast the GDP of the other great powers would have to grow to achieve parity with the United States in terms of military PPP$ at various dates. I assumed that the U.S. GDP (in terms of PPP) would continue to expand at the average rate of 3.3 percent per annum as it has done over the last 12 years, and as we have reasons to believe it will continue to do for the foreseeable future; and that the shares of military expenditure in GDP of each country will remain unchanged from those for 2000—so that none of these countries (apart perhaps from Russia) will have to choose between guns and butter.

It is apparent from table 7 (which also gives the PPP growth rates of GDP over the 1973–98 period in these countries) that based on past and current performance and future prospects, the only potential competitors to U.S. military power are the Chinese (by perhaps midcentury) and the Indians by the end of the century. Given the U.S. technological lead, these potential dates for military catch-up are likely to be even later. Thus, it appears that, as one military analyst notes, the IT-based RMA "will continue to favor heavily American military predominance. It is not likely that China will, in any meaningful way, close the RMA gap with the USA."[10] So, for at least this century, it is unlikely that U.S. military power will be challenged. The claims by various political scientists[11] that Europe will soon be able to challenge U.S. military and economic superiority are based more on hope than experience. Of course, any peering into the future based on current trends is fraught with well-known dangers. But the above divergences are now so great and the prognosis for the currently sclerotic economies of Europe and the collapsed ones of Russia and Japan remain so bleak that it is unlikely these trends will be reversed in the near future.

Administering an Empire

If the economic and military means for maintaining an American imperium are at hand, what of the imperial bureaucracy which the experience of other empires shows is required to run an imperium? The Americans already have in place the military proconsuls in the form of the regional CINCs to deal with the military threats around the globe. What will be the equivalent of the fabled Indian Civil Service (ICS) and the Indian Political Service which provided the agents to run the direct and indirect British Empire in India? Will the creation of such an imperial civil service be costly in terms of both material and human expense and threaten the self-esteem of local elites, provoking a nationalist backlash?

We can provide some rough idea from the experience of the British empire of the administrative cost of running an empire based on both direct and indirect imperialism. At the end of the Second World War, writes J. Cole, "the elite administrative division of the colonial service in Africa, including District officers and central secretariats but not railway, agriculture, or other specialist departments numbered slightly more than 1200 men. These were spread over more than a dozen colonies covering nearly 2 million square miles, with an estimated population of 43 million . . . the Sudan Political Service, which reported to the Foreign Office, had some 125 senior officials for a territory twice [the size of] the American state of Texas. For a population of 353 million, the Indian Civil Service had a maximum strength of 1250 covenanted members, whereas the relatively well-manned Malayan Civil Service possessed some 220 elite administrators for a mere 3.2 million people."[12] That is a total of less than 3,000 civil servants from the metropole to run the empire. This can be compared with the huge numbers of nonclerical officials in the transnational organizations—the UN, the World Bank, the IMF, and WTO—currently seeking to run the postwar Wilsonian international political and economic order (table 8, which does not include the 2,000 World Bank officials outside Washington and the 65,000 UN officials outside its headquarters).

These small numbers of metropolitan civil servants were supplemented by a large army of English-speaking "creoles." In India, in his famous minute on education, Lord Macaulay stated that the English wished to create an English-educated native middle class "who may be interpreters between us and the millions whom we govern; a class of persons, Indian in blood and colour, but English in taste, in opinions, in morals, and in intellect."[13] He did

Table 8. Employment in major international organizations

UN headquarters	8,700
World Bank	10,000
IMF	2,650
WTO secretariat	550
Total	**21,900**

Source: UN, World Bank, IMF, and WTO websites.

also foresee that this could in time lead to the creation of the class which would contest and replace British rule. Thus, in the Charter Debate in 1833 in the British Parliament he said: "It may be that the public mind of India may expand under our system till it has outgrown that system, that by good government we may educate our subjects into a capacity for better government; that, having become instructed in European knowledge, they may, in some future age demand European institutions. Whether such a day will ever come I know not. But never will I attempt to avert or retard it. Whenever it comes, it will be the proudest day in English history."[14]

It was these "Macaulay's children," as we may call them, who were to overthrow the empire. Their nationalist revolts were part of that "creole nationalism" which, as Benedict Anderson argued, overthrew Spanish colonial rule in the Americas. The major complaint of the "creoles" (people of Spanish descent born in America) against the peninsulares (persons born in Spain) was that, even though in every respect—language, descent, customs—they were indistinguishable, they had an inferior status because they were born in the New World. In India, Macaulay's children in India also had an inferior status, despite being English in every respect except in "blood and colour." It was this racism of the British empire which was ultimately to undo it by fueling "creole nationalism." But in its early phase, the British Raj had behaved like a traditional Indian power. The notions of racial exclusiveness which came to characterize its late imperial phase were alien to India's early British rulers who exhibited a more robust delight in both the country's mores and its women. It was the shock of the Mutiny of 1857, and the arrival of English women in India, which turned the British in India from "nabobs" to "sahibs."[15]

One of the strengths of the United States is that in its public and, increasingly, private philosophy, racism no longer plays a part—witness that two of the leading lights dealing with foreign policy today are African Americans. Moreover, the United States and many other countries are recognizing dual citizenship, with even the most nationalist such as India planning to follow suit. With the growth of a cosmopolitan class (culturally and often personally linked) of primarily U.S.-trained technicians and executives at work in many different countries, the core of a global, "Roman" political and economic elite—open to the talents of all—already exists. It could run this new U.S. imperium.

Moreover, if, as I argue in the next part, there is a case for closing down many of the multinational institutions that were created to manage a very different world at a time when the United States was unwilling to openly embrace the burden of empire, the multinational bureaucracies of some of the technical multilateral agencies could be absorbed into the new imperial bureaucracy. Many of these international civil servants on retirement choose to remain in the United States and acquire U.S. nationality. It is not difficult to imagine a system in which they could have dual nationality, creating a truly multiethnic international civil service to run the empire.

HOSTILE COALITIONS

There are a number of influential voices in the United States and in Europe which have argued against the United States assuming the imperial role. In the recent debates preceding and following the Iraq war, the issue is usually put into the code words of unilateralism versus multilateralism. The former is supported by those who favor U.S. assumption of an imperial role; the latter by those who want the United States to follow the failed Wilsonian policies of relying on collective security and international sanctions to deal with rogue states through the United Nations. The Bush administration has been caught in the middle. In its rhetoric it is Wilsonian, denying it is an empire. But in its actions it behaves as an imperial power. This has led to much confusion in the public mind. Hopefully, the debate in the forthcoming presidential election will remove this dissonance between rhetoric and reality.

To clear the air, it is useful to sort out what is really in dispute between the unilateralists and multilateralists. Their positions cannot be defined by traditional political categories such as Left and Right, as these disputes cut across the political spectrum. Moreover, like so many other disputes in which antagonists seem to be arguing about the style of particular policies, they are really questioning the substance. Thus, despite protestations to the contrary, the disputes between unilateralists and multilateralists is not, as is often claimed, about means but about ends, not about the feasibility but about the desirability of empire. This obfuscation is possible as in the public debate neither side is willing to acknowledge the fact that the United States is an empire or to begin the required debate about the sort of empire it should be.

The resulting confusion shows up in a number of ways. It is claimed (for instance, by many opponents of the Iraq war) that the United States should use diplomacy to get its way rather than military force. Though force may sometimes be necessary, it should be applied by an internationally sanctioned multilateral force, albeit led by the United States, as in the first Iraq war. Without this multilateral route, the United States will not be able to get its way, as its unilateralism will lead to the dissipation of its soft power and the formation of a hostile coalition of other powers combining to thwart its will.[16] Prima facie this seems an argument about the feasibility not the desirability of the United States asserting its imperial power. But is it?

Consider the first claim of the multilateralists that diplomacy should wherever possible trump military force in achieving U.S. imperial aims. There can be no dispute between unilateralists and multilateralists on this score. It is always cheaper to get one's way, if one can, by talking rather than fighting. As we have seen, the Romans at the height of their imperial power did not eschew diplomacy to get their way with the barbarian states on their borders. But they made sure their velvet glove enclosed an iron fist. The multilateralists' objection is to a U.S. fist not controlled by the UN. But why should they object if their end is the imperial one of maintaining the U.S. Pax, and the UN is unwilling or unable to sanction the deployment of a U.S. fist or provide one of its own?

Europe, Russia, China, India

The multilateralists' answer is that using the U.S. fist alone would be counterproductive as it would induce the formation of a hostile coalition of other powers to thwart the ends of the United States. But is this plausible? As Thomas Donnelly says, there is no sign or prospect in the foreseeable future of anyone being "willing to employ [the] traditional tools of international politics—in the form of military force or economic restrictions—to constrain the global leadership of the United States."[17] Given the great imbalance between the United States and all its competitors (documented in figs. 1 and 3 and table 5), it is unlikely that the future holds out the prospects of another Peloponnesian war with Sparta organizing a coalition against imperial Athens.

The French fondly hope to do so, and some claim that the European Union has already constrained American power.[18] It is difficult to see how anyone could believe this after President Jacques Chirac's failed Gaullist attempt to constrain the United States in unseating Saddam Hussein. As this failed Franco-German attempt also opened deep fissures within the EU, with Britain and Donald Rumsfeld's "new" Europe siding with the United States against the "old" Europe of France, Germany, and Belgium, the very future of the EU as well as NATO must now be open to question. In the true correlates of power—relative military and economic strength—there is no chance of a united Europe challenging the United States in the foreseeable future. Moreover, the viability of the ongoing project to create a political unity out of the different polities with their distinct historical identities in Europe is also in serious doubt. Nor, despite its progenitors' hopes, is the straitjacket provided by European monetary union likely to provide a route to such political unity. It is as likely to lead to its breakdown.[19]

Finally, now that the French and Germans have shown that if they have their way—and for them that is the only way for a united Europe to come about—the focus of the EU will be to constrain U.S. power, it must be in the interest of the United States to see that a politically united Europe does not emerge. Until now, the United States had looked upon a united Europe as a bulwark against the Soviet Union, but with the end of the Cold War, this is no longer required. It must be in U.S. interests to see Europe remain a congeries of independent states, happy, as in the past, to be free riders in the world order maintained by the U.S. imperium.

If Europe is likely to be a paper tiger, is there any danger of a coalition forming against the United States amongst the other potential great powers, Russia and China? Most observers see this as unlikely,[20] if not least because of the markedly divergent demographic trends in the two regions, and the Russians' continuing fear of large-scale Chinese encroachment in their contiguous and sparsely populated territory in Siberia. Moreover, with both countries more concerned with using the international economic system to engender prosperity, they are unlikely to take actions which undermine the political guarantor of this LIEO. Finally, regarding the serious external threat that they both face from Islamist terror, their interests rather than being divergent are congruent with those of the United States.

Nor is the other potential great power—India—likely to challenge the U.S. imperium. It too shares the same threat from terrorists, and with the recent strategic partnership proclaimed jointly by President George W. Bush and then–Prime Minister Atal Behari Vajpayee, India is likely to be a close ally instead of a rival of the United States. Thus, the likelihood of a serious coalition forming against the United States which can countervail its power is extremely unlikely for the foreseeable future.

If no hostile coalitions are likely to form as a counter to the exercise of imperial power by the United States, and there is no need to eschew diplomacy in its exercise, what is the real reason for the multilateralists' complaint against the unilateralists? It is that the country's recent actions do not correspond to the Wilsonian utopianism to which they—and in its rhetoric, the Bush administration too—seem to subscribe. Furthermore, with the professionalization of the U.S. academy and the influence of its certified members on public policy, academic international relations practitioners have great influence on public policy. Unfortunately, the contemporary academic international relations theory these Ph.D. practitioners have learned has by and large been devised for the anarchical European states system which developed with the fall of Rome. This has made them unable or unwilling to recognize the immense change taking place with the rise of a U.S. empire to parallel that of Rome. How to maintain an empire is not what they have been taught in their classrooms. Empires are looked upon as being outmoded. Hence, the unreal debates based on the assumption that the United States is not an empire.

In the debates on the management of the presumed anarchical international society of states, both sides in the U.S. debate are ironically idealist followers of Kant, who wish to establish the "democratic peace" predicted in his *Perpetual Peace*, either through force (many of the neoconservatives) or through persuasion, example, and sanctions through the multilateral institutions of the UN (many of the center-left). The former are at least in some ways in tune with the changed times and are supportive of many of the policies required to maintain the American imperium, though, as I argue in part III, their aims are misguided. The latter though are living in cloud-cuckoo-land. They are basically suspicious of the exercise of American power. Some, like the libertarians on the Right, who are Jeffersonian in their foreign policy views, fear the exercise of U.S. power, as they believe it threatens liberty at home. They would just like the empire to go away. Others, like many of the liberals in the Democratic party, want to use international institutions, particularly the United Nations Security Council, to constrain U.S. power because they see an international order based on Wilsonian ideals and institutions as the only moral international order.

The United Nations

But the UN, like its Wilsonian predecessor, the League of Nations, has proved to be a broken reed in maintaining the peace. It merely provides a forum for the weak to unite to tie the U.S. Gulliver down with a thousand strings, as the three powers of the old Europe—France, Russia, and Germany—had hoped to do before the start of the second Iraq war. The calling of their bluff in the lead up to the Iraq war shows how ineffectual is their soft power. The Security Council has been largely irrelevant since its inception, having been bypassed in nearly all the conflicts since the Second World War, except for the Korean and first Iraq wars. With the demeaning behavior demanded of the United States to get the Iraq resolution through in early 2003 by trying to outbid the French to get the vote of Cameroon on the UN Security Council, no self-respecting power and certainly not one as powerful as the United States should, or is likely to, put up with this remnant of the old international order.

The UN is now likely to die a long drawn-out death by perpetual neglect or opportunistic utilization in the interests of the imperium. It is of little use and in a rational world would be wound up. But given the interests of the failed bureaucrats and politicians from around the world who strut through its corridors and collect massive rents in the form of tax-free salaries and pensions, it is unlikely that there will be any agreement among its self-seeking member states for its demise. The United States might also not wish to pull the plug if it can utilize the UN to provide a moral fig leaf for the exertion of its power.

Popularity

But will attempts by the United States to maintain its Pax make it unpopular? Alas, this is inevitable, as it has always been the fate of imperial powers. I remember coming to England from India in 1960 on a P & O liner, which then used to ply these old colonial routes, and meeting the wife of a British diplomat returning from a posting in New Delhi. Her husband's previous postings had been in British colonies in Africa. At dinner she was constantly bemoaning the fact that there had been no riots outside the British embassy in Delhi in contrast with their African postings, and that this was an unmistakable sign that Great Britain had ceased being Great.

Envy, jealousy, even hatred are the inevitable and unenviable consequence of disparities in economic and military power. But should the dominant economic and military power then actively seek to become poorer and weaker so it may be loved, or to prevent the remote possibility of other potential powers ganging up against it in the future? Or should it instead recognize that its dominance will lead both to emulation by many—the soft power idealists so often talk about—and to fear and loathing among others. Preventing the latter from spilling over into global disorder has in fact been one of the essential tasks of imperial statesmanship. To undertake it sensibly, one has to recognize that one is an imperial power. The nub of my case is that the United States, even more than any other economically and militarily dominant powers in the recent past, has acquired an empire but is reluctant to face up to the resulting imperial responsibilities because in its domestic discourse it refuses to face up to the reality. Facing reality would involve developing a theory for the beneficent exercise of its imperial power. Wishing the empire would just go away or that it can be managed by global love and compassion is not only to bury one's head in the sand but to actually promote global disorder.

DISORDER

If we look at the current threats to global or regional political and economic order, there would seem to be a convergence rather than divergence in the interests of the United States and other potential great powers. There are clearly two major regions of the world where disorder rules: first, the vast region spanning the Islamic world in the Middle East and Central Asia, and second, the continent of Africa. The World Bank has recently identified potential failed states. Most of them are in Africa or part of the Islamic world. September 11, 2001, showed how failed states can provide a safe haven for terrorists who can directly threaten life and property in the American homeland. The maintenance of international order thus means ensuring that there is also domestic order in states which, if they fail, could become terrorist havens.

Africa

Historical Evolution. The tragedy of Africa lies in its rich natural resources, its relative scarcity of labor, and its history of colonial penetration. Before its encounter with the West, much of Africa consisted of stateless societies in which a community of five to ten thousand people was ruled by a chief. At the beginning of the colonial period, such communities accounted for about 100 million people, half the population of Africa. The other half lived in the larger kingdoms, accounting for another 100 million.[21] The initial European contact with these states was confined to the coast, where Western goods—mainly guns—were traded for ivory and slaves. The disease barrier and the seemingly impenetrable interior constituted formidable obstacles. Inland transportation was difficult and had to rely on human bearers who were relatively expensive. This was because labor was scarce in a continent whose fragile soils did not permit the evolution or adoption of plow-intensive agriculture.

It was the discovery by two French chemists in 1829 that quinine could be an effective prophylactic against malaria which, by 1848, allowed Europeans to penetrate the continent without succumbing to the deadly disease. Till then the death rate among Europeans had ranged between 46 and 72 percent of those infected. The development of the steamboat meant dispensing with expensive overland transportation dependent on scarce and expensive local labor. In 1854 the combination of quinine and the steamboat allowed the *Pleiad* to steam up and down the Niger with no deaths. Thereafter, regular journeys began along the Niger allowing British commercial and eventually political domination of the Nigerian hinterland. But it was when the gun revolution of Europe was introduced into Africa that the

Europeans achieved overwhelming coercive power. From the breech-loading rifle in the 1870s to the Maxim gun at the turn of the nineteenth century, the Europeans had an overwhelming advantage over native armies—even over those which had acquired some of these marvels of military technology through trade.[22]

In the late nineteenth century, local treaties with the chiefs created the colonial empires during the famous scramble for Africa. The most notorious example of this was the Congo Independent State created in 1885 by King Leopold of Belgium as his personal property. The artificial boundaries which arose continue to haunt contemporary Africa, for these boundaries in many cases cut across the traditional boundaries of tribe and ethnicity. But as Roland Oliver notes, traditional "African polities were mostly very small, and that nearly all of the new European colonies comprised within their frontiers many times more indigenous groups than they divided. It was quite normal for a single one of the newly defined colonies to comprise two or three hundred earlier political groupings."[23] Many of these precolonial states comprised common linguistic and cultural clusters, which for administrative reasons were amalgamated into a single unit, the tribe. This process was further augmented by the activities of the Christian missionaries who standardized related dialects into a smaller number of written languages.

This European partition of Africa was motivated less by greed than the exigencies of the continuing conflict between the powers seeking a mastery over Europe. Thus, even Leopold who hoped to profit from his imperial adventure found that, apart from the short boom in rubber prices at the turn of the century, he was faced by bankruptcy and had to be bailed out by the Belgian government.[24] Much of the African labor employed to maintain the new apparatus of administration and control had to be coerced in one way or another, partly because its supply price was always high (being set by the fairly comfortable alternative subsistence existence afforded by the balance between scarce labor and abundant land). By the late nineteenth century various forms of direct and indirect control had been set up by the colonial powers, with the waters being further muddied by the white settler communities which were established in eastern and southern Africa.[25] Whereas the internal autonomy of the precolonial political units was undermined by the creation of these colonial states, there were a few—most notably today's Botswana—which obtained special dispensations from the British to preserve their internal autonomy and hence their tribal elites.

By 1914 the Europeans had completed their occupation of African territories. In the interwar period, they undertook the task of development as a trust for their new subjects which they expected would take nearly a century. This was the period when the great mineral wealth of the continent began to be tapped and the introduction of new cash crops—often based on peasant farms rather than plantations—began to spread prosperity to the countryside. But with the granting of Indian independence in 1947, the century envisaged for colonial development and welfare was severely shortened, and beginning with the granting of independence to Ghana in 1957, by the mid-1960s most of Africa was being run by Africans. South Africa had to wait till 1990 for its own deliverance from minority white rule.

The African Crisis. But 40 years after independence, the great hopes of a bright autonomous future for Africa have been belied. So much so that there is no other part of the world where the Four Horsemen of the Apocalypse have galloped with such fury and left devastation in their wake. The per capita income of the subcontinent has stagnated and in some countries has fallen below its pre-independence levels. The one exception has been Botswana whose economic performance till recently was comparable to those of the Asian tigers. By 1998 one third of sub-Saharan Africa's 42 countries were involved in international or civil wars.[26] By 1989 there were 4 million officially recognized refugees and another 12 million displaced in their own countries as a result of these wars.[27] Famine, which had disappeared with the introduction of the motor truck in the 1920s, reappeared in country after country in the 1970s and 1980s, largely because it was used as a tool of coercion in numerous civil wars. Large parts of the subcontinent are being ravaged by AIDS, and in the 38 countries highly affected, the UN estimates that the population by 2015 will be 91 million less or 10 percent lower than it would have been without AIDS. Even in the African miracle economy of Botswana, one in three adults is HIV positive, life expectancy has fallen from 65 years in 1990–95 to 56.3 years in 1995–2000 and is projected to fall to 39.7 years in 2000–5.[28]

There are a number of reasons for this dismal picture.[29] Two are part of the colonial heritage. The developmental and welfare phase of colonialism was relatively short. At independence only about 3 percent of the population of working age had secondary or higher education. They formed the nationalist elites who, as in so many other ex-colonies, sought to create a nation in their newly inherited domain by pursuing economic nationalism. But the artificial boundaries created in Africa meant that the task of nation building was compromised by claimants "across the border." Peoples put into administrative straitjackets which bore little relationship to their own sense of ethnic identity have fought on behalf of that identity or else against attempts to be submerged in states dominated by other tribes.

The third reason for the African crisis was that, like past nation builders, these nationalist leaders chose to use dirigiste means to develop. These policies proved to be a disaster. In part this was due to the relative abundance of natural resources, which proved to be a precious bane. In my comparative study with Hla Myint, *The Political Economy of Poverty, Equity, and Growth*, we showed the importance of relative resource endowments in determining economic outcomes. The major difference is between the natural resource rich and labor poor countries of Africa and the labor abundant and natural resource poor countries of East Asia. Given their natural resources, the opportunity cost of labor, and hence the price at which it can be drawn into modern activities such as manufacturing, is much higher in Africa than in East Asia. If the African countries industrialize, their comparative advantage could lie in the relatively capital-intensive industries. But given the paucity of their human capital, the limited size of the domestic market, and the lumpiness (fixed size) of investment in such industries, it is almost inevitable that if they are set up, it will be by governments—with all the inefficiencies that entails, as witness the disastrous policy of developing heavy industries in Kwame Nkrumah's Ghana.[30] By contrast, the comparative advantage of labor abundant East Asian countries lies in labor-intensive industries which can be small scale and do not require as much skill or capital.

These difficulties in industrializing are compounded by the rents provided from the exploitation of natural resources. These rents provide a tempting source of revenue for the predatory state. This inevitably leads to the politicization of economic life with deadly struggles between different groups to control the state and these natural resource rents. Given the relatively uncertain future of any incumbent who succeeds in capturing the state, he must always be looking over his shoulder for coups d'état to unseat him and capture the state and its valuable natural resource rents. The incumbent will thus naturally have a very short time horizon—and hence what economists call a very high rate of discount of the future—which will lead him to loot as much of the rents he can in as short a time before he is killed or overthrown. The stationary bandit will in effect turn into a roving bandit. The history of the African region around the great lakes over the last 40 years bears this out.[31]

There is, however, one shining African exception to this dire tale: Botswana.[32] It has had one of the highest rates of economic growth in the world, comparable to those of the fast-growing East Asian newly industrializing countries. Moreover, its stellar economic performance is based on the natural resources that were found after its independence—diamonds. Whereas in other parts of Africa—namely Angola and Sierra Leone—the endowment of diamonds has been a major source of political and economic disintegration, this has not happened in Botswana for one major reason. Unlike the artificial states created by the Europeans in the rest of Africa within which the traditional tribal elites were marginalized or disestablished, and replaced after independence with new, small, half-educated indigenous elites, the British allowed Botswana to keep its old tribal chieftains and elites. They have behaved like old tribal chiefs and shared the new-found wealth by promoting economic development for their citizens instead of looting it for their own purposes. The biggest threat to Botswana today is from AIDS, with one in three of the working age population infected with the virus.

The other beacon of hope for the continent is South Africa, where Mandela's eschewal of populism and advocacy of racial harmony has provided hope for a large multiracial and relatively well-governed state. Unlike the rest of Africa, it has a much larger and better educated black middle class, and the attempts of the ANC to reconcile the white population to black majority rule seem to have been more successful than anyone could have expected. But these are still early days. With a large black underclass still waiting to see some tangible gains from independence, South Africa may be sitting on top of a volcano unless it can grow rapidly enough to satisfy these demands. The problem of Africa, therefore, as in the continually repeated current mantra of the multilateral foreign aid agencies, is governance. There can be little hope for Africa unless the tropical gangsters breeding domestic disorder are suppressed and the basic order needed for any social life to exist is restored.

But (sadly) with the ending of the Cold War, Africa does not represent a strategic challenge to the United States or any of the potential great powers. Its strategic importance in the nineteenth century lay in guarding the sea lanes to India, the jewel in the British imperial crown. That reason no longer applies. Apart from justified humanitarian concerns about the plight of its people, there is little that the rest of the world has to lose or gain from engaging or disengaging from Africa. Given the dismal failure of the Western development program in Africa, based on conditional aid channeled through governments run by predatory elites, little short of costly direct imperialism is likely to provide that good governance which everyone now maintains is the prerequisite for the economic advancement of the continent. But, as in Afghanistan, failed states can become havens for terrorism. With the northern part of sub-Saharan Africa forming part of the Islamic world, the United States might find as it did in Afghanistan that to scotch the terrorist snake, it has to restore domestic order in these otherwise strategically unimportant states, although the botched intervention in Somalia must give any U.S. administration cause to pause.

I would expect, therefore, that increasingly, as is already evident and lamented by these African elites, Africa will be marginal to the world economy and polity. Perhaps in their pursuit of ethical imperialism—as a British foreign policy advisor to Tony Blair has recommended[33]—the EU or its old imperial constituents, the UK and France, will be willing to spend men and materiel to establish and maintain their own imperium. This would allow Africa the period of peace and good government it needs for prosperity. But I fear that in the changed circumstances, any contemporary plea similar to that of Kings Bell and Acqua is likely to fall on deaf ears. In any case, there is no danger of any great power coalition forming against the United States in Africa. For the United States and the world, the best policy toward Africa, if direct imperialism is ruled out as being too costly, is to keep markets for African goods and capital flows to Africa open, and leave it to the Africans to sort out their own problems.

Islamic Countries

The Islamic world poses a more serious challenge. In rightly trying to distinguish the direct threats posed to national and global security after September 11 from Islamists as distinct from Islam (in no small measure to protect the substantial Muslim minorities in many Western countries), many commentators and world leaders have gone out of their way to say that in the war on terror, the enemy is not Islam. At one level this is true. As the doyen of Middle Eastern studies, Bernard Lewis, once remarked to me, the Islamist threat is greater for other Muslims than it is for the West.[34] But once one seeks to understand the reason for the rise of Islamic fundamentalism and its seeming attraction to large numbers in Muslim countries, it is difficult to escape the conclusion that it has something to do with the nature of Islam itself.

Historical Roots. The best way to see the problem is to go back in time before the rise of the West. At the end of the first millennium, the dominant world civilization was that of Islam, described by their poets as providing "tastes of paradise."[35] This paradise was shattered by the rise of the West, though it was not till the Ottomans were turned back after the siege of Vienna in 1683 that this Islamic world went into relative decline. By the end of the First World War and the dismemberment of the Ottoman empire, it was clear that Islam was a defeated civilization. This, of course, was also true at that time of the other great Eurasian civilizations—the Indian, the Chinese, the Japanese—in their encounters with the West.

There were two responses of these civilizations to the Western onslaught in the nineteenth century. The first was that of the oyster, which closes its shell. The other was to modernize, to try to master the foreign technology and way of life, and to fight the alien culture with its own weapons.

Japan is the prime example of a country which chose the latter route. India and China seesawed between the two responses and took nearly a century to truly come to terms with modernization. Some Islamic countries—in particular, Attaturk's Turkey and Mehmet Ali's Egypt—also took the second route, but only partially. The other remedy, that of the oyster—in which Muslims sought to purify Islam from all the corruptions that had crept over the centuries into Muslim lives and thereby to regain Allah's favor—has had much greater resonance. While the other civilizations have come to realize that modernization does not entail Westernization,[36] and hence ancient cosmological beliefs can be maintained even when material beliefs have to change to modernize, it was, as William McNeill notes, Islam's misfortune that, despite many voices (e.g., Sir Sayed Ahmad in nineteenth-century India) stating that modernity could be reconciled with Islam, "the two remedies seemed always diametrically opposed to one another. Reformers' efforts therefore tended to cancel out, leaving the mass of Muslim society more confused and frustrated than ever."[37]

Until the Muslim world wholeheartedly embraces modernization, recognizing this does not involve Westernization and the giving up of its soul, there is little hope of the Islamist threat to other Muslims and to the rest of the modern world being eliminated. But how is this to come about?

Here we need to go back to the fate of the Arabs after they had created their glittering civilization at the turn of the first millennium. The most important fact is that from the thirteenth century until the twentieth century no Arab government existed in the Middle East. An empire created by the sword was overthrown by the sword by outside invaders whose only commonality with their new subjects was their religion. The region had thus been ruled by a succession of foreign Muslim military invaders from the Seljuks, Mongols, Turks, and the slave mamelukes. Saladin was a Kurd, not an Arab. When after the First World War the West acquired political power in the region, it was pushing out a power equally as foreign as its own. So no *Arab* nation had existed since the Middle Ages.

Aftermath of World War One. Most of the problems of the current Middle East arise from the peace imposed by the contending powers seeking the rich pickings from the dismemberment of the sick Ottoman empire. As the young Field Marshall Earl Wavell (who served under General Edmund Allenby in the Palestine campaign) observed about these peace treaties, "After 'the war to end all war' they seem to have been pretty successful in Paris in making a 'peace to end all peace.'"[38] The British during the advent and course of World War One had no additional territorial ambitions of their own in the Middle East. Their major aim was to ensure that their regional rivals, the French and the Russians, did not change the balance of power in the region, apart from a few minor territorial adjustments. Britain's purpose, as Churchill emphasized, was its traditional one of propping up the failing Turkish empire.

It was Lord Kitchener of Khartoum (who became secretary of war in Asquith's government at the start of the war) who changed the course of British policy. Kitchener aimed to seize the Arabic-speaking part of the Ottoman empire for the British, thereby creating a Middle Eastern empire to link and rival the one in India. Recognizing the importance but misunderstanding the nature of Islam, he sought to use it as a bulwark for the new Arabic empire by capturing its religious leadership in the form of the caliphate from the Turks for an Arab, whom they expected to be able to manipulate in the interests of their secular power. The person he had chosen for this role was the Hashemite Sherif of Mecca, a direct descendant of the prophet Mohammed. But what he had misunderstood is that, unlike Christianity in which the spiritual and temporal authority could be split, no such distinction was possible in Islam, where the whole of life including politics and governance falls within the holy law. The caliph is not merely a pope but also a prince who governs and leads his followers in both prayer and battle.

When the caliphate was offered to the Sherif of Mecca, he naturally assumed that he was being offered the kingdom of the Arabic-speaking parts of the Ottoman empire. Kitchener had also misunderstood the extent of Arab and Islamic disunity and fragmentation. "Thus the Kitchener plan called for Ibn Saud, leader of the fierce puritanical Wahhabi sect, to recognize the spiritual authority of the Sunni ruler of Mecca; but that was not a realistic possibility, for like so many of the dozen of contending sects into which Islam is divided, theirs were at daggers drawn."[39] By 1918 the British had become disillusioned with the Hashemites who had involved them in a losing conflict with Ibn Saud, who in 1924 conquered the Hejaz region with its holy cities of Mecca and Medina and drove Hussein ibn Ali into exile. The British ended up putting Hussein's sons Feisal and Abdullah on the thrones of the newly created states of Iraq and Transjordan as a consolation prize, even though Feisal proved to be "treacherous" and Abdullah "lazy and ineffective."[40]

The other event flowing from the settlements of World War One was the commitment to the establishment of a Jewish home in Palestine as part of the mandate given to Britain by the peace treaties. David Lloyd George, the wartime prime minister, was the principal agent in making this happen, despite the endemic anti-Semitism of the British upper classes. The clue to his motivation and that of other British statesmen in the nineteenth century (including Lord Palmerston) lies in the nonconformist and evangelical tradition which goes back to the Puritans. They believed that following "the Scriptures . . . the advent of the Messiah would occur once the people of

Judaea were restored to their native land,"[41] an idea that still has great resonance among the Religious Right in the United States and that underpins
their unwavering support for Israel.

In the Balfour Declaration of 2 November, 1917, addressed to the
most famous Jew in Britain, Lord Rothschild, the seeds of a conflict lasting
to our day were sown. It stated: "His Majesty's government view with favour
the establishment in Palestine of a national home for the Jewish people, and
will use their best endeavors to facilitate the achievement of this objective, it
being clearly understood that nothing shall be done which may prejudice the
civil and religious rights of existing non-Jewish communities in Palestine, or
the rights and political status enjoyed by Jews in any other country."[42] The
two parts of the commitment were contradictory and have proved to be so
down to our own day.

The post–World War One settlement of the successor states in the Arab-
speaking part of the Ottoman empire consisted of a League of Nations French
mandate covering Syria and Lebanon, a British mandate over a truncated
Palestine incorporating the Balfour Declaration, and British-controlled states
created for the Hashemite princes of Iraq and Transjordan. But by 1922 this
imposed settlement which had destroyed the old order was one in which the
British themselves no longer believed.[43] Moreover, with the demobilization
following the First World War and the emerging economic crisis, Britain did
not have the means to directly rule these vast territories. There was continuing
local opposition on religious or other grounds to the settlement. The Allied
hope that they were installing permanent successors to the Ottoman sultans in
the new states they had created was not fulfilled.

The Crisis of Islam.[44] In his enthralling history of the fall of the
Ottoman empire and the creation of the modern Middle East, David Fromkin
concludes that this was due to "a characteristic feature of the region's politics: that in the Middle East there is no sense of *legitimacy*—no agreement
on the rules of the game—and no universally shared belief in the region that,
within whatever boundaries, the entities that call themselves countries or the
men who claim to be rulers are entitled to recognition as such."[45] This is
part of a deep crisis of social and political identity, similar to one faced by
Europe after the collapse of the Roman empire. The issue is the same: "how
diverse peoples are to regroup to create new political identities for themselves after the collapse of an ages-old imperial order to which they had
become accustomed."[46]

In this search for a political identity, Muslims are not helped by an age-
old cultural trait. The empire which the Arabs created was a conquest society, and subsequent Islamic polities have never lost their militaristic nature.
The great fourteenth-century Arab historian Ibn Khaldun saw the medieval

Islamic polity he observed as consisting of a settled, nonpolitical society and a tribal state, either imported or imposed by conquest.[47] Whereas the Chinese, for instance, in their cyclical view of history saw settled rule as the norm and a change of dynasties as the result of the loss of virtue of an old tired dynasty, the Islamic polity never accepted the notion of settled rule.[48] Ibn Khaldun considered it effeminate. This has been the black hole of the Islamic polity from its inception.

The social ethos of the political culture of Islam "is imbued with martial values and the spirit of the army"[49] unlike any other existing culture. "In the Arab world, military rule *is* political legitimacy; it is the only authentic form of government which has ever emerged in the Arab world."[50] It makes "glory, honor, pride, form—the virtues of chivalry—into the prime motors of the social ethos."[51] The democratic constitutions imposed by the West in Egypt, Syria, and Iraq were quickly overturned once the West's representatives departed, and the traditional military form of government clothed in various new civilian hues and ideologies was reestablished. In the Middle East "the question 'what is the army doing in politics?' is never raised. Of course the army is in politics: this has been its business since Mohammed, so to speak."[52] No better example of the continuance of this cultural trait in Islamic countries is provided than by the fate of the successor states of the British Raj in the Indian subcontinent—India, Pakistan, and Sri Lanka. Their respective armies had a common heritage and training as part of the imperial Indian army. All three countries had similar Westminster-style constitutions at their independence. But only the two non-Islamic polities—India and Sri Lanka—have succeeded in maintaining them and keeping the army out of politics.

The tragedy of the modern Middle East is that once the Ottoman empire was replaced by Western protectorates, the successor states were not directly administered by the Western powers and hence the traditional sociopolitical elites were not replaced by new modernizing ones. Instead, these older elites kept their hold on their society.[53] This has meant that the modernization which the Middle East so badly needs did not take place.

The Militants. Western education and other trappings of modernization, instead of creating modern rational societies, have in part led to the Islamist backlash. The hijackers who flew into the World Trade Center were not poor, illiterate peasants, but the children of well-off middle-class parents, who had been given a technical education. An enormous industry has grown up to explain their motivations.

Studies of the educational and socioeconomic status of Islamic militants by Sa'd al-din Ibrahim and Valerie Hoffman find that in the Arab world, and in Muslim states from Iran to Pakistan, there is a consistent pattern.

Fundamentalists are mainly students and university graduates in the physical sciences with rural or traditionally religious backgrounds. They are the recent beneficiaries of the expanded university systems, were raised in a traditional family, and have had to make recent adjustments to a modern urban intellectual and cultural environment.[54] In his study of Egyptian Islamic militants, Ibrahim concluded that "the typical social profile of members of militant Islamic groups could be summarized as being young (early twenties), of rural or small-town background, from middle and lower-middle class, with high achievement motivation, upwardly mobile, with science or engineering education, and from a normally cohesive family."[55] The role of graduates of the natural sciences in Islamic fundamentalism is also borne out by Hoffman's educational profiles of the Marxist and the Islamist guerrilla movements which overthrew the Shah of Iran. The Islamists were mainly students of the natural sciences, the Marxists of the humanities and the social sciences.[56]

So why are these natural science students from traditional lower-middle-class families turning into Islamists in the Muslim world? It might be because these Muslim countries are not growing fast enough for them to get jobs to which they believe they are entitled by their education.[57] But as Malise Ruthven rightly notes, this does not explain the rise of Islamists in Malaysia and Indonesia, whose economies have been performing spectacularly.[58] A more cogent reason is provided by a major conclusion of the American Academy of Arts and Sciences' (AAAS) Fundamentalism Project. Islamists, like other religious fundamentalists among the Hindus in India, the Buddhists in Sri Lanka, the Protestants in the United States, and new religious movements in Korea and Japan, "are concerned with defining, restoring, and reinforcing the basis of personal and communal identity that is shaken or destroyed by modern dislocations and crises."[59] All these fundamentalisms represent a crisis of identity forced by modernization.

In particular, Ruthven says, it is caused by the failure to integrate "the dual identity of the village Muslim and the applied scientist. . . . The religious mind inherited from the village or suburb is conditioned to believe that knowledge is 'Islamic,' that all truth is known to, and comes from, Allah. The scientist operates in a field of epistemological doubt."[60] For the devout Muslim the real scandal is that knowledge acquired through doubt has proved more powerful in creating material prosperity than the revealed knowledge of their religion.[61] During the earlier phase of Islam's expansion, its stupendous conquests which provided the booty for the Islamic community's prosperity were seen as proof of God's approval. The success of the post-Enlightenment West then becomes unbearable. "One way out of the dilemma in which the dual identity of the villager-turned-scientist is reinforced by the epistemological dualism of religion (certainty) and science (uncertainty)," Ruthven continues, "is to pretend that religion already contains the truths of science."[62] But for those trained in the natural sciences, such an escape from their dilemma is not possible. They could just accept their dual identity, but for many this is not possible. "The intransigence of the world, its refusal to conform to the 'straight path' laid down by 'God and his Messenger' is experienced for them in our time as acutely as it was experienced by Nietzsche and his contemporaries a century ago, when the demise of the metaphysical divinity was afflicting the sentient minds of Europe."[63] The September 11 hijackers, therefore, were not motivated, argues Ruthven, by "some naive faith in a paradisiacal future, but the final solution they found to a profoundly tragic personal predicament. The pre-Kantian metaphysical deity taught in the mainstream academies of Islam had failed them catastrophically. In a world dominated by the post-Enlightenment West, the Argument from Manifest Success was collapsing everywhere. These highly educated products of Western technical education. . . . [found] their faith in the benign and compassionate deity of Islam begin to wobble. Their final act was not a gesture of Islamic heroism, but of Nietzschean despair."[64]

But why has this Nietzschean despair leading to murderous acts of terrorism occurred in Islam and not the other civilizations also faced with the task of reconciling tradition with modernity? The AAAS's project concluded that this was because unlike other civilizations, it is not possible to separate the mosque and state in Islam.[65] Whereas in most other civilizations a distinction can be made between the public and private spheres, and hence duality in the beliefs relevant to each can be accommodated, this is not possible in Islam. Moreover, if this duality is enshrined in a political system which legitimizes a secular constitution, the fundamentalist imperative to legislate their personal beliefs has to play out in the political arena. As Bernard Lewis has noted, "For Muslims, the state was God's state, the army God's army, and of course, the enemy was God's enemy. Of more practical importance, the law was God's law, and in principle there could be no other. The question of separating Church and state did not arise, since there was no Church, as an autonomous institution, to be separated. Church and state were the one and the same."[66] It is only in the twentieth century that the question of privatizing religion became an issue, and then only in Turkey, the only Muslim nation to legally formalize the separation of church and state.[67] So ultimately it is Islam itself which is at the root of the problems for the Muslim world in coming to terms with modernity.

While this might provide a reason why Islamists should seek to overthrow the apostates ruling their own countries, why do they want to wage *jihad* (holy war) to destroy the foreign United States and other infidels?

There are two reasons: one is found to be in common with the inhabitants of many other Eurasian civilizations, the other is again peculiar to Islam.

The common reason is an aversion to Western habits in the domestic domain, particularly those concerning sex and the family. It is not commonly recognized that the Western family revolution predates the Industrial Revolution and can be traced back to the papal Revolution instigated by Pope Gregory I in the sixth century. The Catholic Church came to support the independence of the young in choosing marriage partners, in setting up their own nuclear family units, and entering into contractual rather than affective relationships with the old. (Friar Lawrence egging on the young lovers in *Romeo and Juliet* against their families' wishes is emblematic of this trend.) This was in contrast to the traditional Eurasian pattern where the explosive primordial and ephemeral emotion of love was socially controlled, and marriages were arranged by extended families which also had a duty for the care of their old.

But, as anthropologists and psychologists have shown, love is a universal but ephemeral emotion with a biological basis. In the primordial environment, it had been vital for males and females not only to be attracted to each other to have sex and reproduce but also for the males to be attached enough to the females to look after their young until they were old enough to move into a peer group and be looked after by the hunter-gatherer band. The traditional period between successive human births is four years, which is also the modal period for those marriages that end in divorce today.

All the Eurasian civilizations sought to curb the effects of this ephemeral emotion as it would have been destructive of their way of making a living. Settled agriculture requires settled households. If households were in permanent flux, there could not be settled households on particular parcels of land. To prevent this, they used cultural constraints to curb this dangerous hominid tendency by relying on arranged marriages, infant betrothal, and the like, restricting romantic passion to relationships outside marriage. The Catholic Church sought to curb the dangers to its own settled agriculture arising from the papal family revolution by separating love and sex and creating a guilt culture in which all forms of sex were fiercely denounced. But once the Christian God died after the Enlightenment, this lid was removed and the West went back to the sexual and family practices of its hunter-gatherer ancestors.[68]

No greater testimony to the rage felt by traditional Muslims to these new-fangled domestic habits of the West can be provided than by the life of one of the founders of the contemporary Islamist movement, Sayyid Qutub. He was born into a small well-educated family in a small village in upper Egypt in 1906 and brought up as a devout Muslim. When his family fell on hard times, he went to live with his uncle in Cairo and attended a reformist Islamic teacher training college. He was a nationalist who also acquired a wide reputation as a literary figure and was well acquainted with European culture and literature (in translation). But he was shocked by the unveiled women he saw in Cairo. Unwilling to choose a bride from such women and not having the connections to get a traditional bride, he remained celibate for all of his life.

In 1948 he was sent on a government grant to investigate American methods of instruction and curricula in secondary and primary schools. His experiences on the sea voyage to America and of college life in the United States were to turn him into an Islamist. The trouble began when he gave a lecture on Islam on the ship to counter one given by a Christian missionary. A Yugoslav woman refugee sat in rapt attention and Qutub believed this was due to the sublime power of the Koran, until she appeared "drunken and semi-naked" at the door of his cabin. "For a virgin (one presumes) of forty-two, this direct encounter with female sexuality 'in the raw' was profoundly unsettling,"[69] writes Malise Ruthven. In America he was shocked by what he saw as the vacuity and amorality of the society. He was even more shocked when a woman at the college he attended said that sexual intercourse was a purely biological matter which had nothing to do with morality. He was shaken by the social mixing of the genders and his sexually charged encounters with American women. He was appalled by the vulgarity of American popular culture and its lack of appreciation of European high culture. He came back an Islamist.

Valerie Hoffman argues that sexuality is at the heart of the identity crisis of the young men who become Islamists. They are caught between the allure of the loose Western mores and the restrictions of their own societies. Similarly, the British historian J. B. Kelly, writing of the Western carpetbaggers in the Arabian Gulf after the oil boom in these traditional societies, states: "many aspects of their behavior—whether it is their copious consumption of liquor, the cheerful vulgarity of some of their pleasures, their careless profanity, their casual sexual improprieties, or the heedless freedom they accord their own women and the lack of restraint these show in their dress and deportment—have, in one way or another, shocked or offended, and in some cases corrupted, the local Arab inhabitants. . . . And when they experience for themselves, as many now have done on visits to Western countries, the easy availability of Western women, their contempt for Western Christendom, for a civilization in which men hold their women in such low regard as to allow them to hire themselves out to men of alien race and hostile creed, becomes absolute."[70]

Jihad. The second reason why the Islamists have expressed their rage with the West in a *jihad* (holy war) goes back to some special features of Islam.

Islam considers itself a religion of peace. But this peace is conditional on the acknowledgment of the Islamic idea of God. As with most ancient scripture, the Koran can be read in contradictory ways. The justification for war for liberal interpreters is provided by the verses in which "the defense of religious freedom is the foremost cause for which arms may—and indeed must—be taken up," while for other interpreters the verses advocating aggressive warfare against infidels are considered authoritative. Thus, a famous "sword verse" states: "And when the sacred months are over, kill the polytheists wherever you find them, and take them captive, and besiege them, and lie in wait for them in every stratagem [of war]; but if they repent, establish regular prayers, and pay zakat, then open the way for them, for God is the dispenser of mercy."[71]

Once the Arabs moved out of their Arabian heartland, they embarked on a ceaseless war of conquest in which jihad was used both to spread the religion and to establish an imperial world state.[72] Jihad was not an individual duty but a duty of the state. There is also a *hadith* (narrative tradition) which states that there is both a lesser jihad concerned with war and a greater jihad on an individual level concerned with the struggle against evil. But, this hadith is not accepted by militant Islamists, as it is not included in any of the authoritative compilations.[73] The Islamists take a view of jihad closer to the classical authorities. Sayyid Abu Ala Maududi (1903–79) the founder of the Jamaat-i-Islami in Pakistan, which is similar to the Muslim Brotherhood in Egypt, believed that the law revealed to Mohammed was universal and timeless: "The Quran does not claim that Islam is the true compendium of rites and rituals, and metaphysical beliefs and concepts, or that it is the proper form of religious attitude of thought and action for the individual (as the word religion is nowadays understood in Western terminology). Nor does it say that Islam is the true way of life for the people of Arabia, or for the people of any particular country or for the people preceding any particular age (say the Industrial Revolution). *No! Very explicitly, for the entire human race, there is only one way of life which is Right in the eyes of God and that is al-Islam*" (emphasis added).[74] Jihad for him is an ultimate political struggle for the whole of mankind. "Islam wants the whole earth," he writes, "and does not content itself with only a part thereof. It wants and requires the entire inhabited world." This is, of course, the charter Osama bin Laden has nailed to his mast. There is clearly no political compromise possible with these claims; either we all become Muslims or we will be put to the sword by Islam's contemporary holy warriors.

From Nationalism to Islamism. But, even if we accept that these structural faults in Islam have been operative for nearly a century, why have the Islamists begun to pose a serious threat only in the 1980s and 1990s? Gilles Kepel drawing on the views of Ernest Gellner provides some answers.

Gellner, harking back to Ibn Khaldun, maintained that there is a high Islam and a low Islam. The former was the Islam of the scholars (the *ulemma*), the latter of the people. The low Islam was often syncretist and much influenced by the mystical form of Islam preached by the Sufis and their cult of saints. It believed in magic rather than learning. High Islam, Gellner writes, was concerned with "the three central, pervasive and actually invoked principles of religious and political legitimacy [within Islam]: the divine message and its legal elaboration, the consensus of the community, and finally sacred leadership by members of the House of the Prophet."[75]

The elites who came to power with the withdrawal of the West were mainly nationalists, as epitomized by Nasser in Egypt. They recognized that they had to come to terms with the low Islam or there would be social unrest.[76] In addition, the high Islam, from which the Islamists arose, was seen as a threat to the nationalist's modernizing ambitions and was ruthlessly suppressed, or the leaders of the more popular low Islam were sometimes used to counter high Islam. But the popular low Islam had little influence on the growing mass of educated youth in the cities.[77]

An attempt was then made to coopt high Islam. In Egypt, Nasser effectively nationalized Al-Azhar, the Islamic seminary which had instructed the ulemma for a thousand years, and sought to get its teachers and pupils to argue for the compatability of Islam with Nasserist socialism. But this attempt backfired, as the ulemma came to be looked upon as stooges of the state and could no longer fulfill their traditional function of mediating between the state and society. Kepel notes, "A vacuum had been created, to be filled by anyone ready to question the state and criticize governments in the name of Islam, whether that person had received clerical training or not."[78] The way was open for the Islamist followers of Qutub and Maududi in the Sunni world and of Ayatollah Ruhollah Khomeini in that of the Shias.

The Arab defeat in the six-day 1967 Arab-Israeli War saw the turning point in the fortunes of the nationalist regimes. They were divided between the progressives led by Nasser (including the Baathists in Iraq and Syria) and the conservatives led by the monarchies of Jordan and Arabia. But both groups were agreed on the confrontation with Israel. The shattering defeat in the war which had been started by the progressives destroyed any hope that socialist nationalism offered a solution to the Muslim predicament. This military defeat was compounded by the failure of Arab socialism to increase the economic pie sufficiently fast to allow the lower-middle classes and rural and urban proletariat to share in the material gains which had been promised at independence but garnered mainly by the traditional elites.

The Islamic intelligentsia financed by Saudi money then turned away from the nationalists and toward Islamism and the creation of an Islamic state as the answer to Muslim woes. In their pursuit of power, the Islamists mobilized to their cause two groups with different interests. The first was the burgeoning mass of the young from deprived backgrounds whose parents had come in from the country, and who formed the bulk of the urban poor. The other was the devout bourgeoisie; both the monarchical and military regimes had excluded them from political power and had damaged their economic prospects by their statist economic policies.[79] But though both groups were devoted to the creation of an Islamic state, they differed in their agendas for the state. The poor urban youth wanted it to follow a social-revolutionary agenda, while the bourgeoisie only wanted to wrest power for themselves from the traditional elites while maintaining the existing social hierarchies. These divisions were exploited by most of the existing regimes to prevent the Islamist takeover of their countries. The two exceptions were Iran and Afghanistan. In Iran, the political skills of Khomeini succeeded in not only deposing the shah but also in decimating his young radical support-ers and establishing a theocracy, supported largely by the *bazaaris* (mer-chants) and the rural poor. In Afghanistan, the Islamist takeover was the outcome of a civil war in which the Taliban was financed by Wahhabi Saudi Arabia, while military and logistical support was provided by the intelli-gence services of Pakistan in order to establish what they saw as their colony.

But the manifest failures of these two experiments in creating Shia and Sunni Islamist states has led to the decline of political Islam. Kepel sees the causes of this decline as the deflation of the utopian dreams once the Islamists came to exercise power, the conflicts between the different con-stituents of the movement, and the failure to institute democracy, with the major fault line behind the failure being the social antagonism between the devout middle class and the young urban poor. The disillusioned Islamists' references to democracy shows "the yearning of the middle-class and of a segment of the Islamist intelligentsia for an alliance with mainstream secular society whereby they can escape the trap of their own political logic."[80]

Kepel believes that the only path for the Islamic regimes is to absorb and integrate the social groups left out at independence. "They must assist at the birth of a Muslim form of democracy that would embrace culture, religion, and political and economic modernity as never before."[81] But given the structural features of Islam I have discussed, this hope might well prove to be in vain.

Wahhabism. Another source of continuing disorder in the Islamic world is the Wahhabism of Saudi Arabia. The kingdom of Saudi Arabia is not the descendant of any ancient Arab state but the result of a religious movement—the Wahhabi movement (a fundamentalist version of Islam) which created a state in central Arabia in the eighteenth century.[82] This state, along with Yemen, maintained its independence through the turbulent period when the British and the French held mandates over most of Palestine and the

Arabian peninsula. But Albert Hourani observes, "without known resources, with few links with the outside world, and surrounded on all sides by British power, [they] . . . could be independent only within limits."[83] It was the discovery of small amounts of oil in the 1930s that changed Saudi fortunes.

This oil was discovered, extracted, and exported by Western companies, and by 1960 the total Middle Eastern oil reserves were estimated to be about 60 percent of known world reserves. Given the erosion of international rules concerning property rights, and the growth of statism, the Saudi oil fields along with others in Iraq and Iran were nationalized. The Saudis, moreover, were protected by the United States. As Kepel points out, "In 1945, Franklin Delano Roosevelt flew from Yalta to Suez, where he met King Ibn Saud aboard the U.S. navy ship *Quincy*. They struck the deal that would eventually 'fuel' the cold war. Saudi Arabian oil flowed to the West, matching the Soviet's reserves. In return, the U.S. promised security to the dynasty. . . . But there was always a tension at the heart of the arrangement. On the *Quincy*, the King was adamant that he could not compromise on his opposition to a future state for the Jews in the Muslim land of Palestine. The U.S. dilemma ever since has been to reconcile its backing of Israel with its protection of Saudi Arabia."[84]

September 11 finally showed up the dangers in this Faustian pact, dangers that concern both money and ideology. The Saudis have maintained a tightrope act for half a century.[85] They have balanced their alliance with the infidels and the untold riches provided to the dynasty by maintaining what is probably the most virulent and medieval form of Islam in their own country, and used their new-found wealth to propagate it by financing mosques and Wahhabi preachers around the world. The *madrasas* (religious schools) in Pakistan which turned out the Taliban are all run by Wahhabis. The charitable donations all believers are required to make have often—perhaps innocently—ended up in charities which funded al-Qaeda. The Saudis have directly and indirectly funded the mosques and madrasas which preach hatred against the infidels—Jews, Christians, and above all Hindus—to young minds, who learn little if anything about the modern world.[86] But for the Saudis to eschew or put a stop to this funding would undoubtedly create a Wahhabi backlash in Saudi Arabia and end the dynasty.

For the rest of the world, the poison being spread by this Wahhabi evangelism is becoming intolerable. To see how pernicious it is, imagine what we would think if German schools only had lessons in anti-Semitism, or those in America were just teaching the young to hate blacks. But this ethnic and religious hatred is what is being taught in the large number of madrasas funded by the Saudis in Pakistan and many other countries around the world. If there is to be an end to the "war of terror," this poisoning of the Muslim mind clearly has to stop.

Arab-Israeli Conflict. Numerous commentators have argued that the reason this poison is still being successfully spread is the continuing Arab-Israeli confrontation and the anger this arouses in the Arab street. This provides the Islamists with an unlimited supply of jihadis. Without going into the historical rights and wrongs of the issue—on which the Arabs can claim to have a rightful grievance—this issue (despite Arab rhetoric) is merely another symptom of the Islamic world's failure to come to terms with modernity, as well as being the common tactic used by the Third World to externalize its domestic problems.

The Camp David accord brokered by President Clinton in 2000–1 gave the Palestinians virtually everything they had asked for except the so-called right of return, and yet Yasser Arafat turned it down and instead launched the intifada. He and every Arab government knows that no Israeli government can agree to the right of return, which in effect would involve the extinction of Israel. Apart from that, Israel's Prime Minister Ehud Barak had accepted almost every other Palestinian demand, and the rest were open to negotiation.

The amazing thing to me is that after 50 years the right of return is still an issue and is being kept alive by the large number of Palestinians still in refugee camps. Why are they still there after 50 years? On a personal note, my family and I, along with millions of others, lost their land and property as a result of the partition of India in 1947. We were refugees. Both the Indian and Pakistani governments provided some help, but most importantly the refugees themselves, after a little while, made new lives for themselves. There are no refugee camps on both sides of the India-Pakistan border with millions asserting their right of return.[87]

History is never just, and economists have been right to maintain that bygones are bygones. This is particularly important in that highly contested territory of Palestine. This came home to me in the late 1970s when a friend was carrying out a dig near the Wailing Wall. He took me down and showed me layer upon layer of corpses. The ones in each layer had killed those below them, and then they themselves had been killed by those above. To decide who has the original rights to the land in this fiercely contested territory, where might has been right for millennia, and to right historical wrongs on the basis of some principle of restitution would defeat even the wisdom of Solomon. For, as Julius Stone has maintained, why does "any moral priority attach to that 13th century old Arab conquest [of Palestine] against the still older Israelite conquest of the land from the Hittites and Philistines in the 13th century B.C., or as against the undoubted governance of the land by a succession of Jewish judges and kings for many centuries thereafter. . . . [I]f we are beguiled by titles based on ancient Arab conquest, we cannot consistently dismiss from history the even more ancient Jewish conquest. If, on the other hand, we are beguiled by more recent Arab conquest, then we must face the fact that, among other titles, the present state of Israel rests on its own ability in our own age to defeat open aggression from the Arab states of the region, more than once and against heavy odds."[88] Sensibly, losers in these continual shifts in fortune through history have come to terms with their losses and continued with their lives.

The Palestinians could have done the same. There was plenty of land in neighboring Arab countries to provide them housing, and given the untold oil wealth that accrued to the Arab states in the area, there should have been no financial impediment to their rehabilitation. Yet 50 years later we have two generations who have lived in the misery of these camps, waiting for the Israeli state to be destroyed. There can be no peace on those terms with Israel. In the circumstances what should any prime minister of Israel (of whatever political allegiance) do in the face of the current intifada? I have never received any answer to these questions from any Arab leader with whom I have discussed this issue.

The only solution to the Arab-Israeli problem, therefore, also lies in the Muslim world coming to terms with modernity—accepting along with Israel the so-called road map, and with the other Arab states providing both land (if needed) and resources from their oil wealth to resettle the refugees. But this in turn requires that the Saudi, Iranian, Syrian, and Iraqi direct and indirect support for the intifada must end. What this suggests is that the current status quo in the Middle East is untenable. The primary task of a Pax Americana must be to find ways to create a new order in the Middle East, where the cosmological beliefs are preserved but the prosperity engendered by modernity leads to the ending of the belief in jihad, thus easing the confusion in the Islamic mind which has plagued it for over a century.

Reconstructing the Middle East. How this is to be done is not an issue open to easy answers. But there are a few points that can be made. It is accusingly said by many that any such rearrangement of the status quo would be an act of imperialism[89] and would largely be motivated by the desire to control Middle Eastern oil. Far from being objectionable, imperialism is precisely what is needed to restore order in the Middle East. It was the breakdown of the Ottoman empire and the botched attempt by the British to replace it with one of their own which is in large part responsible for the region's woes. But given the importance of Islam and the growth of nationalism in the region, the new imperialism cannot be direct. The purpose of the American imperium would be to maintain the threat or actual use of force to prevent any international disorder arising from the region. Additionally, some way has to be found for maintaining domestic order in the states in the region. As (with the exception of Egypt) the other artificial states have not become nations but are riven by tribal and religious rivalries, the demands by separate groups for their own states need not be denied. The form of government they choose should also not be made an issue, with the important proviso that all the governments should be required to maintain the civil and economic liberties essential for them to develop in a global economy. For ultimately the Muslim rage which has threatened the world can only be assuaged when, like the other great Eurasian civilizations, Muslims in the Middle East join the globalization bandwagon by recognizing that the modernization it entails does not require Westernization and losing their soul.

However, oil remains central to both the current problems and the solution for two reasons. First, despite the claims by the Greens that alternative forms of energy can replace oil as the major energy source propelling global prosperity, realistically this prospect is still a long way off. For the next 20 to 50 years oil will be required not only by the present industrial countries but, even more, by the rapidly industrializing ones like India and China to fuel their growth. With a large part of the world's known reserves of oil and natural gas still concentrated in Saudi Arabia and Iraq, these countries remain crucial for providing this essential fuel of global prosperity.

So far, given Roosevelt's compact with the house of Saud, the Saudis have continued to remain reliable suppliers of oil. But they are now faced with an existential dilemma, as their 50-year balancing act can be no longer be maintained. If they side with the United States and stop funding Wahhabi evangelism and clamp down on the charities funding al-Qaeda, they are likely to be overthrown by a Wahhabi rebellion. Classical liberals would say with Norman Angell that this does not matter. The successor regime would still have to depend on sales of oil to maintain its prosperity. But if Osama bin Laden—or someone of his ilk—is the leader of this successor state, we know that prosperity in this world means nothing to them if the withholding of oil supplies is likely to mean the destruction of the infidels. The nightmare would be an Iraq run by the likes of Saddam Hussein and Saudi Arabia run by a clone of bin Laden, both equally committed (though for different reasons) to choking the West and its allies.

The other choice the Saudis could make is, of course, to continue to use their oil wealth to fund Wahhabi fundamentalist evangelism across the globe. But, the poisonous jihadi mentality this would continue to breed is equally intolerable.

Either way it seems that the Rooseveltian pact will have to be revised if not abrogated. This is not the occasion to discuss the mechanics of the exercise of imperial power to reorder the Middle East to allow its people and those of the world to prosper under an American Pax. But there is the question: Whether in this task of establishing a Pax in the Middle East the United States will have to act alone? If one looks at a map of the Middle East and sees the countries currently threatened by the spread of Islamist hatred, they include Russia, China, India, and, of course, embattled Israel. If the maintenance of global order in the near future therefore means countering this Islamist fascism, clearly the United States is not going to find opposition from these quarters. Deals will no doubt have to be cut on the side, but there is no real conflict of interests which would allow a hostile coalition to build up against the United States on this issue.

What is more, there is at least one of these powers (apart from Israel), whose very existence as a multiethnic empire is jeopardized by the Islamist threat—India. It would seem to be a natural partner in any reordering of the Middle East to extinguish the jihadi tendency. It is worth remembering that India was the "jewel in the crown" of the British Raj, not because of its fabled wealth but because it provided the Raj with the largest land army in the world, paid for by Indian taxes. It was this Indian army that enforced the British Pax from Suez to China. Could something similar happen again in the new imperium? There are some straws in the wind. When I was in India in early 2002, the press was full of reports of an informal agreement having been reached for the Indian navy to jointly police the sea lanes from Aden to the Molucca Sea with the Americans. There were also reports of joint training exercises by U.S. and Indian special forces in the northern Indian plains (and not the Himalayas). More recently (2004), the U.S. president and Indian prime minister announced a strategic partnership in which America is willing to share its technology in various high tech areas including space. One can draw one's own conclusions. But it does seem laudable that some in the U.S. administration may at long last be taking the imperial task seriously.

Oil also remains central to the reconstruction of the Middle East as it has, as in Africa, proved a precious bane. So an important goal of the American imperium must be to depoliticize these natural resource rents. The vast rents from oil have not only financed fundamentalism but also the militaristic ambitions of rulers like Saddam Hussein. Furthermore, as in Africa, these natural resource riches have not allowed the development of alternative industries and viable forms of employment, so that a large part of the populations of these oil-rich countries have become pensioners of the state.[90] This is a reversion to Islam's earliest days when the tribes involved in the conquests were put into the equivalent of modern-day cantonments and pensioned off from the booty obtained by conquest.

To avoid these effects, a deployment of these rents on purely technocratic grounds is required. The example of Indonesia may be instructive.

There, the so-called Berkeley mafia of technocrats, who ran economic policy under Suharto, banked the oil revenues abroad and allowed them in only at a graduated pace to finance genuine development projects. An international analogue needs to be devised to prevent natural resource rich states from failing, and when failed, to promote their revival.

AN INTERNATIONAL NATURAL RESOURCES FUND (INRF)

I have recently suggested[91] an institutional response to counter the strong temptation for anyone controlling the state to appropriate the rents from natural resources for their own purposes. The various civil wars in Africa, including the ongoing ones in Liberia and the Congo, are fueled by the desire to control these rents. And, it was the rents from their oil that enabled Middle Eastern autocrats such as Libya's Muammar Qaddafi, Iraq's Saddam Hussein, Iran's mullahs, and the Saudi monarchs to pursue aims as diverse as funding global terrorism, developing weapons of mass destruction, and exporting Wahhabism. What is to be done?

The answer must be to find a way to depoliticize these natural resource rents as, in failed or failing states, the political struggle surrounds their capture. Lacking any assurance about their tenure, incumbent predators know their time horizon is understandably very short: they may be killed or overthrown in the next battle for the control of the rents. Hence, it is rational to get as much, as soon as possible, out of the country. Once we have such a failing state, an obvious solution, adopted, for example, by Alaska, is to distribute its oil revenues to citizens by writing checks through the tax system. But such a policy is not available in countries that have no functioning state.

An international extension of the UN's oil-for-food program in Iraq could provide a prototype for a solution. However, given the United States' understandable lack of confidence in the UN after its recent shenanigans concerning the Iraq war, another agency would have to be found for this long-term development task. Nor could the United States do it through a purely domestic institution because of the nationalist passions that this would unleash.

But there are two multilateral institutions—the World Bank and the IMF—which might be suitable for this undertaking. Both institutions, having fulfilled their original purpose, should logically be shut down.[92] But, like old soldiers, international institutions never die. The two should now be amalgamated and given a new role. They can call on the expertise of an international technocratic bureaucracy and, unlike the UN, are not subject to populist international pressure (though there may be doubts on this score about the present World Bank). And given their weighted voting systems, they are likely to be acceptable candidates to the United States. A conjoining of their staff to form an International Natural Resources Fund (INRF) would thus be desirable.

The purpose of the INRF would be to obtain the rents from the natural resources of failed or failing states, once they form part of the direct or indirect U.S. imperium. These revenues would be put in escrow by the fund for use *only in the country in which they were generated*. The funds from these country escrow accounts would be released only on the authority of the INRF for purposes determined by the fund's managers in consultation with the local government—mainly for social and economic infrastructure projects. These projects would be subject to the international bidding, controls, and monitoring procedures of the World Bank. This would depoliticize the deployment of the natural resource rents and remove one of the major reasons for the failure of states.

How could predators be prevented from attacking and capturing the mines and wells generating the rents? Here, the military prowess of an imperial power or a coalition of such powers is crucial. Such a power could follow the example of China during the interwar period. Foreign companies could lease territory which they could protect with their own police forces in return for royalties to the INRF. But even this privatized solution would require the imperial power to maintain "gunboats and Gurkhas" at the ready, in case some local predator decided to mount a challenge to the private controllers of these resources.

In time, as properly deployed resource rents led to general prosperity and the development of efficient political institutions, the INRF could hand back the escrow account to the local government. But this is likely to be a long haul, and it is an open question whether the United States has the will to sustain such nation building. But without it, the natural resources which should have brought prosperity to the populations of failed states will continue to be stolen by predatory elites and used to oppress them. Worse, they may be used to fund the global terrorism that remains a serious source of international disorder.

CONCLUSIONS

Our conclusions can be brief. The United States does have the potential means to fulfill its imperial tasks. Though this will make it unpopular, the dangers of hostile coalitions of other major powers forming against it are minimal. The advocates of "soft power" and the UN are either trying to constrain the American Gulliver with a thousand strings, or at best asking for the imperial task to be carried out with good manners. The major challenges to a U.S. imperium are to be found in the failed or failing states of Africa and the Middle East. There is little hope that the United States or any European power is likely to take on the required burden of direct imperialism in Africa's failed states, which will have to find their own salvation from their domestic disorder. Open western markets for capital and foreign trade (but not foreign aid) provide the West's best available response to their plight.

Dealing with the disorder in the Middle East requires assuaging the Islamist rage which, despite the rhetoric, has little to do with the Arab-Israeli conflict but more with the failure of many Muslim countries to come to terms with modernity. This could involve the ending of the United States' Faustian pact with the House of Saud, as well as indirect imperialism to introduce the economic and civil liberties needed for prosperity. In this imperial task of modernizing the Middle East, no attempt should be made to impose Western "habits of the heart." For it is the fear that modernization will involve westernization, particularly in the domestic domain concerning family and sexual mores, which lies at the heart of the Islamist rage.

As most of the failed or failing states in Africa and the Middle East are rich in the natural resources whose rents have been misused by their predatory elites, a depoliticization of these rents is required to restore order. An INRF maybe the answer.

PART TWO

Prosperity

CHAPTER 4

Liberal International Economic Orders

Empires have provided peace. They have also led to prosperity by creating their Pax over a common economic space. But it was only in the nineteenth century that the first truly global economic space was created when the British through their empire and control of the sea linked most of the world. This allowed the spread of its global gentlemanly capitalism and the creation of the first truly liberal[1] international economic order (LIEO), based on Britain's domestic policies of laissez faire, free trade, the gold standard, and the protection of property rights. The First World War dealt a fatal blow to the British empire. The economic troubles of the interwar years destroyed this first LIEO. After the Second World War, the United States as part of its new-found imperial role reconstructed a second LIEO. But there were important differences from its predecessor in the policies it followed, differences concerning government intervention, foreign trade, and exchange rates. In many ways these differences have led to the current discontents with globalization. Contrary to critics such as the Nobel Prize–winning economist Joseph Stiglitz,[2] this second period of globalization has promoted prosperity (including of the poorest) through the stupendous mutual economic gains to the countries participating in this new U.S.-led LIEO.

In this part of the book I will briefly outline how the two global empires—the British and American—have promoted global prosperity, the bases of these two LIEOs and their effects, and will evaluate the various objections to the spread of global capitalism in the current LIEO.

THE NINETEENTH-CENTURY LIEO

Created under British leadership after England's repeal of the Corn Laws in 1846, the nineteenth-century LIEO was based on a number of pillars.

Free Trade. In the mid-nineteenth century, both ideas and interests conjoined to allow Britain to *unilaterally* adopt free trade. The United States in contrast has from its inception never accepted the economically correct principle of a unilateral move to free trade. It has believed in *reciprocity*: it would only cut its tariffs in exchange for cuts by its trading partners. The underlying assumption is the erroneous one that foreign trade, like disarmament, is a zero-sum game—one should only disarm if one's opponent does so too.

Laissez Faire. Closely allied to the policy of free trade was that of laissez faire which Britain adopted in the mid-nineteenth century. Laissez faire circumscribed the role of the state. It viewed the state as a civil association and not an enterprise association, in Michael Oakeshott's sense (see ch. 1). The state was to eschew interference with the course of economic life and to involve itself in only the elementary and unavoidable functions in foreign policy, defense, and above all the legislation and administration of justice required to maintain domestic order. It remained the official economic policy of Britain till the end of the nineteenth century, when the rise of demos (the common people) and the growing resonance of another enterprise view of the state—promoting egalitarianism—was coming to the fore.

Gold Standard. The gold standard—with exchange rates irrevocably fixed against each other through their link to gold—provided the adjustment mechanism for balancing imbalances in trade and mediated the large flows of international capital which provided the financial means to develop the underdeveloped regions of the world, including the Americas and Australasia. But as this fixed exchange rate international monetary system depended on flexibility in the workings of the price mechanism in the participating countries, it was fatally undermined when, with the rise of trade unions in the developed regions, labor markets became inflexible.

Labor Mobility. There was also free mobility of labor across national boundaries during the British LIEO. This allowed the bourgeoning labor forces in India and China to find gainful employment in the mines and plantations in the tropics, promoted by the nineteenth century international division of labor. With the rise of welfare states in most industrial countries, this international labor mobility came to an end as immigration controls became ubiquitous. These barriers to free labor mobility were inevitable once the establishment of a welfare state created property rights in citizenship, with a citizen having a right to pick the pocket of his fellow citizens.

International Property Rights. Perhaps most important was the final pillar of the nineteenth century LIEO—the transnational legal system created for the protection of property rights, in particular of "foreigners." This system arose from the commercial treaties signed by European states in the mid-nineteenth century. These treaties provided rules for protecting international property rights which became part of international law.[3] The international disorder flowing from the First World War also destroyed this system of international property rights.

These pillars of the nineteenth century LIEO allowed the worldwide expansion of the gentlemanly capitalism of the City of London. The international legal framework was an integral element of Pax Britannica. Together with the economic integration through free trade and an international payments system based in the City of London, it allowed the empire to fulfill, as Peter Cain and Anthony Hopkins observe, a

> wider mission which can be summarised as the *world's first comprehensive development programme*. After 1815, Britain aimed to put in place a set of like minded allies who would cooperate in keeping the world safe from what Canning called the "*youthful* and stirring nations," such as the United States which proclaimed the virtues of republican democracy, and from a "league of worn out governments" in Europe whose future lay too obviously in the past. Britain offered an alternative vision of a liberal international order bound together by mutual interest in commercial progress and underpinned by a respect for property, credit, and responsible government, preferably of the kind found at home.[4]

And compared with the previous millennia, the results were stupendous. It was at the height of this nineteenth-century LIEO, from 1850 till 1914, that many parts of the Third World for the first time experienced sustained intensive growth. Lloyd Reynolds in his survey of the economic histories of 41 developing countries dated the turning points when developing countries entered the era of *intensive* growth (with a sustained rise in per capita incomes), as compared with the ubiquitous *extensive* growth of the past (when output growth just kept up with that of population) as shown in table 9.

Angus Maddison sums up the achievements of this period as follows:

> From 1870 to 1913 world per capita GDP rose 1.3% p.a. compared with 0.5% in 1820–70 and 0.07% in 1700–1820. The acceleration was due to more rapid technological progress, and the diffusionist forces unleashed by the liberal economic order of which the United Kingdom was the main architect. It was not a process of global equalization, but there were significant income gains in all parts of the world. Australia and the United States reached higher levels than the United Kingdom by 1913. Growth was faster than in the United Kingdom in most of Western and Eastern Europe, in

Ireland, in all the Western Offshoots, in Latin America and Japan. In India, other Asia (except China) and Africa, the advances were much more modest, but per capita income rose more than a quarter between 1870 to 1913.[5]

THE END OF THE FIRST LIEO

The nineteenth-century LIEO did not last. It was undermined first by a creeping and then a galloping dirigisme in much of the twentieth century.

The period of economic liberalism during the nineteenth century's great Age of Reform was short-lived in part due to the rise of another substantive purpose that most European states came to adopt: the egalitarian ideal promulgated by the Enlightenment. Governments in many developing countries also came to espouse this egalitarian ideal. The apotheosis of this version of the state viewed as an enterprise association were the communist countries seeking to legislate the socialist ideal of equalizing people. The collapse of their economies under similar but even more severe strains than those that beset less collectivist neomercantilist Third World economies is now history, though I cannot help remarking on the irony that it took two hundred years for 1989 to undo what 1789 had wrought!

The First World War marked the beginning of the end of this nineteenth century LIEO. As we saw in chapter 1, by the late nineteenth century, the

Table 9. A turning point chronology

1840	Chile	1900	Cuba
1850	Brazil	1910	Korea
1850	Malaysia	1920	Morocco
1850	Thailand	1925	Venezuela
1860	Argentina	1925	Zambia
1870	Burma	1947	India
1876	Mexico	1947	Pakistan
1880	Algeria	1949	China
1880	Japan	1950	Iran
1880	Peru	1950	Iraq
1880	Sri Lanka	1950	Turkey
1885	Colombia	1952	Egypt
1895	Taiwan	1965	Indonesia
1895	Ghana	–	Afghanistan
1895	Ivory Coast	–	Bangladesh
1895	Nigeria	–	Ethiopia
1895	Kenya	–	Mozambique
1900	Uganda	–	Nepal
1900	Zimbabwe	–	Sudan
1900	Tanzania	–	Zaire
1900	Phillippines		

Source: Reynolds (1985), Table 1, p. 958.

United States was by far the dominant economy, but after the First World War it retreated into isolationism. During the Great Depression—which was in part caused by its faulty monetary policy and its retreat into protectionism—the United States failed to do what Britain in the depression of the 1870s had done as the economic hegemon: to maintain open markets for trade and finance.[6] The interwar Smoot-Hawley tariff act and the "blue sky laws" (which banned U.S. banks from lending to foreign governments) in effect ended the LIEO.

Much worse, the turmoil of the interwar period also unraveled that complex web of international law and practice woven by the British in the previous century to protect foreign capital. From the start of the First World War till 1929 (when international capital markets effectively closed down), the United States was the largest lender, with its foreign investments increasing sixfold in the period, so that by 1929 its stock of foreign investment equaled that of Britain. But the weakening of British hegemony meant that the enforcement of the international rules created in the nineteenth century became problematic. In the interwar period the United States refused to take over the political and military responsibilities the British empire had undertaken earlier.

Chastened by the global disorder its interwar isolationism had caused, the United States sought a partial restoration of these nineteenth-century international rules after the Second World War. But it did not extend them to the newly decolonized Third World which experienced an explosion of economic nationalism. Given the anti-imperialist moralism which became a part of U.S. foreign policy after Woodrow Wilson, attempts such as the ill-fated Suez adventure of the British and the French in 1956 to prevent Nasser's nationalization of the Suez Canal were scuttled by the United States. There was no way in which anyone could thereafter stand against the new nation-states to assert their rights of national sovereignty over any purported international property rights. There was no bulwark against this disintegration of the international legal order.

Thus, much of the international turmoil the world has seen in the twentieth century can be traced to the failure of the United States to take over or become a partner of the British empire in maintaining global order in the last century. If the United States had used its emerging economic and military power to prevent the rise of the Bolsheviks, had not made the botched Wilsonian peace of Versailles, and had directly sought to prevent the rise of fascism, much of the blood-stained history of the past century could have been avoided, along with the nearly century-long hiatus in the continuation of the nineteenth-century LIEO. This would have allowed the benign nineteenth-century processes of globalization to proceed to modernize the world.

U.S. political elites realized during the Second World War that they had to take over from the British as the new imperial power, and we have seen how gradually they have fulfilled that ambition. The most overt attempt at succeeding the British in that role was in the effort to recreate a new LIEO under a Pax Americana.

RECREATING A NEW LIEO

After the Second World War, at Bretton Woods the United States tried to resurrect three of the pillars on which the nineteenth-century LIEO had been built—free trade, the gold standard, and free capital mobility. Whereas the British Empire had fostered these by example, treaties, and direct and indirect imperialism, the United States instead created transnational institutions—the General Agreement on Tariffs and Trade (GATT), followed by the World Trade Organization (WTO), the International Monetary Fund (IMF), and the World Bank.[7]

Trade. Rather than follow the correct British policy of adopting unilateral free trade and then allowing its hegemony to spread the norm, the United States chose the extremely acrimonious route of multilateral and more recently bilateral negotiations to reduce trade barriers. This is due to the fact that, unlike the British who have correctly seen free trade not as a zero-sum game and, since the repeal of the Corn Laws, adhered to this vision and its close cousin laissez faire[8]—despite various attempts by politicians like Joseph Chamberlain to stir the pot by demanding protection in the name of fair trade—the Americans have never accepted the classical liberal case for free trade. They have always looked upon trade as a zero-sum game. They have been protectionist. Only for a brief period between 1846 and 1861 was there a relatively liberal trade policy and even then the average ad valorem tariff on the 51 most imported categories of goods was 27 percent.[9] The original intellectual justification for protectionism was provided by Hamilton's flawed argument for infant industry protection.[10] But once U.S. industry had caught up with and even overtaken European industry by 1890, this argument was no longer persuasive, and the United States argued for the principle of reciprocity as the central principle of its trade policy. In his 1901 message to Congress, Theodore Roosevelt said: "Reciprocity must be treated as the handmaiden of Protection. Our first duty is to see that the protection granted by the tariff in every case where it is needed is maintained, and reciprocity be sought so far as it can be safely done without injury to our home industries."[11]

This principle of reciprocity has been the central tenet of U.S. trade policy ever since, and the twentieth-century hegemon has sought to achieve free trade through reciprocal concessions in the GATT and the WTO. But, as the antiglobalization riots from Seattle onward demonstrate, by perpetuating the myth that trade is a zero-sum game and that removing tariffs can only be done on the basis of reciprocity, the United States has ensured that issues of domestic policy will inevitably spill over into trade policy.

While the ostensible champion of free markets balks at accepting the principle of a unilateral adoption of free trade, an otherwise Communist country, China, has embraced this economically impeccable principle. It is instructive to note that one of the largest unilateral movements to free trade has occurred in China since Deng Xiaoping adopted the Open Door policy.[12]

It is time for the United States, too, to embrace the correct economic principle that unilateral free trade is to its own benefit. There would then be no need for the WTO's multilateral framework for doing deals on the erroneous principle of reciprocity and it could be shut down. Similarly, the network of trade-distorting bilateral and regional free trade agreements the United States is promoting should be rescinded, and instead it should open its borders to free movement of goods and services and capital, as the British did in midcentury and the Chinese are doing today.

Exchange Rates. The IMF was created to resurrect a variant of the gold standard—the gold exchange standard. The U.S. dollar was directly linked to gold, and all other currencies were fixed to the dollar and thus indirectly linked to gold. But unlike the strict gold standard, countries were allowed to change their fixed parity with the dollar in consultation with the IMF when they faced an unsustainable imbalance in their balance of payments. The United States alone did not have the option of changing its fixed parity to gold and thus other currencies.

This quasi-fixed exchange rate system policed by the IMF foundered as it was premised on controls on short-term capital flows. Such flows allow a speculative attack which can destroy a quasi-fixed exchange rate regime—as witness George Soros's successful attack on the pound during its ill-fated sojourn in the European Exchange Rate mechanism. But with the freeing of capital markets, it is not possible to distinguish between short-term speculative and long-term developmental capital flows.

When President Richard Nixon chafed at the U.S.'s inability to devalue the dollar in the face of the inflationary pressures caused by the Vietnam War, he abrogated the gold exchange standard by closing the gold window. The United States no longer was willing to change dollars into gold at a fixed price and the dollar began to float. With the generalized move to floating exchange rates, the need for the policeman of the Bretton Woods system— the IMF—also disappeared. This is not the place to go through the various and continuing changes in its role that the IMF has subsequently sought, but it clearly has outlived its initial rationale. The current international monetary system, which has been dubbed a "non-system,"[13] also has the advantage for international relations that unlike a fixed exchange rate system, it is decentralized and does not require any international cooperation[14] with its potential for international discord.

Development. The World Bank was the instrument chosen to channel capital for development to the Third World. Western capital markets had been closed to developing countries since their defaults and the passage of the interwar U.S. "blue sky laws."[15] The World Bank, or International Bank for Reconstruction and Development (IBRD) as its initial and still major component is called, was set up as a financial intermediary to fill this lacuna. Its intergovernmental ownership and guarantees allowed it to borrow at preferential rates in developed country markets and then lend the money at near commercial interest rates to the Third World. For those countries deemed too poor to borrow at these rates, a soft loan window—the International Development Association (IDA)—was established with money subscribed by Western governments.

The financial intermediation role of the World Bank was soon overtaken by its role as a multilateral foreign aid agency, in part to play its part in the Cold War both by tying the nonaligned to the free world and by promoting economic development. Western governments had also established their own bilateral foreign aid programs, more to compete for political influence in the Third World during the Cold War than to serve their professed aim of alleviating world poverty. As nearly all of these capital flows were mediated through multilateral or bilateral governmental channels, the access of developing countries to world capital markets was necessarily politicized. This was in stark contrast to the nineteenth-century pattern when private capital flowed from Europe to the rest of the world on market principles. The World Bank was to create another international development program, analogous to what the British had promoted in the nineteenth century through the propagation and enforcement of rules concerning international property rights and through direct and indirect imperialism. As these routes were eschewed, the only instrument available was the use of conditionality tied to these aid flows, to promote the appropriate development policies by changing state behavior in the Third World. But as with sanctions to serve foreign policy goals, this ever more stringent conditionality has been unsuccessful.[16] So the current development mantra is that "good governance is all." Now the stark choice facing the successors of Wilsonian idealism in foreign policy also faces them in international economic policy: can the order required for prosperity be promoted except through direct or indirect imperialism?

FROM PLAN TO MARKET

The interwar breakdown of the nineteenth-century international trading and payment systems which had transmitted the growth impulse around the world led the Third World to follow the communist world in turning inward.[17] This was ironic as the partial restoration of the LIEO under U.S. aegis did lead to a reduction in trade barriers, and within the developed world (grouped together in the Organisation for Economic Co-operation and Development) to a removal of the restrictions on capital flows and the exchange controls which had become ubiquitous in the interwar period. As a result, world trade boomed and income growth was unprecedented. The Third World, still traumatized by its interwar experience and aided and abetted by the seemingly new development economics, did not emulate the developed countries in liberalizing their controls on foreign trade and payments. A few small countries around the Pacific Rim, the so-called Gang of Four (South Korea, Taiwan, Hong Kong, and Singapore) bucked this trend and found that even a partial opening up of their economies allowed them to participate in the global boom—which has been called the postwar Golden Age. Their spectacular success in raising their growth rates by following outward-looking policies[18] finally had some effect in persuading other developing countries, first haltingly and more recently in a flood, to switch from their inward to outward-looking policies. But the real turning point for the Third World came with the OPEC coup of 1973 and its unintended consequences.

In 1973 OPEC (the Organization of Petroleum Exporting Countries) raised oil prices threefold. This brought the postwar Golden Age to an end. It also saw the emergence of demands by the Third World for a New International Economic Order (NIEO), in which their presumed commodity power would be used to redistribute income from rich to poor countries. Not having participated in the Golden Age boom, most developing countries caught in the time warp of their import substitution strategies did not reap its full benefits, claiming and getting their right to special privileges and exceptions in the emerging global free trade regime. The NIEO was their final attempt to replace this liberal trading order by a politically managed one. But within a decade the wind had gone from their sails. The supposed commodity power wielded by OPEC proved to be illusory. After the failure of another brief attempt at rigging it in the late 1970s, the price of oil has continued to decline in real terms ever since.[19]

But there was a momentous unintended consequence of the OPEC coup for the Third World. It arose from the disposition of the Middle East's sparsely populated countries' new-found oil wealth. The OPEC coup set in train a chain of events which were to dramatically change the postwar politicization of the disposition of international capital to the Third World. The OPEC countries could not conceivably absorb domestically the large surpluses derived from the oil price rise. They had to place them abroad. As Third World capital markets were underdeveloped, this in effect meant investing the surpluses in the West. But having obtained their new-found wealth through a political coup, the OPEC countries were fearful of placing it within the reach of governments' whose citizens they had robbed. It could be confiscated: a not unreasonable fear as shown by the subsequent sequestration of Iranian assets by President Jimmy Carter. So they placed their money in the offshore branches of the money center banks (the so-called eurocurrency market). These offshore banks had developed outside the jurisdiction and reach of their parent monetary authorities and governments in the 1960s to allow intermediation of capital flows to communist Europe—which had been equally wary of dealing directly with institutions that would be subject to political pressure from its Cold War adversaries.

The consequent explosion in the liquidity of these Western offshore bank branches led to a frantic scramble to lend this money. This recycling of the OPEC surpluses was also pressed by Western governments, who were concerned by the worldwide deflationary consequences of an increase in the worldwide savings propensity that was caused by the transfer of income from countries with relatively low savings propensities to those with high savings propensities. There were many eager borrowers in the Third World, in particular among the inward-looking countries of Latin America. Thus, the seeds of the debt crisis were sown.

This bank lending to the Third World was based on variable interest rates linked to LIBOR, the London Interbank Offer Rate. When, in the late 1970s, the United States and subsequently much of Europe adopted sound money policies to deal with the stagflation that had plagued them since the OPEC coup, world interest rates and the cost of servicing debt rose dramatically. As most of the Third World borrowers—mainly in Latin America but not in East Asia—had borrowed to deal with their longstanding fiscal deficits, they now found themselves unable to service their debts. Starting with Mexico, many in effect defaulted on their obligations. They were forced to recognize—as had the mercantilist states in the past—that the only way to restore their diminished control over the economy was through economic liberalization.[20] Thus began the long drawn-out worldwide process of reform whereby dirigiste inward-looking regimes are gradually being replaced by more market friendly outward-looking ones.

Economic liberalization has also provided many developing countries a new-found access to direct foreign and portfolio investments. For them, this is a more desirable form of borrowing than bank borrowing at variable interest rates, because the associated currency and income risks are shared with the foreign investors. More sustainable forms of capital flows are now available to developing countries willing to change their nationalist attitudes to multinationals.[21] These market-based capital flows now dwarf the politicized flows from bilateral and multilateral agencies, whether they be IBRD loans or various forms of foreign aid. The future of this politicized part of the world capital market is increasingly in doubt.[22]

Finally, the stagflation resulting from the OPEC coup also led to the replacement of demand management by supply-side policies in most developed countries. Beginning with the Thatcherite revolution in the UK, the worldwide movement toward privatization and deregulation—haltingly including labor markets—is reversing nearly century-old trends and the habits and intellectual beliefs they had engendered. With the spectacular collapse of the Communist economic system,[23] dirigisme for the first time in a century is in worldwide retreat. The most spectacular reversals in policies were those of China in the early 1980s and of India in 1991. Both came after endemic economic crises which were in large part the consequence of their past dirigisme.[24] Thus, apart from the two regions of global instability identified in the previous chapter—Africa and the Middle East—most of the Third and Communist worlds has, it seems, now embarked on that modernization which globalization offers.

There is, nevertheless, growing discontent with globalization. A large part of that discontent, as we shall see, is based on questions of morality. But there are also many economic sources of discontent, concerns about foreign trade and international capital flows, and questions relating to inequality and poverty. We turn to examining these in the following chapter.

CHAPTER 5

The Challenges of Globalization: There Is No Third Way

The globalization that the two liberal international economic orders (LIEOs) have promoted has led to a backlash, both at the end of the nineteenth century and increasingly today. Much of the criticism of the processes which have brought unimaginable prosperity to billions is unfounded. But underlying this discontent is a deeper reason. Today's critics like their nineteenth-century predecessors are against globalization because it promotes global capitalism, of which they disapprove. Their disapproval is based not merely on the erroneous belief that global capitalism promotes poverty and inequality but on an underlying belief in the immorality of capitalism. These are old objections, but should not for that reason be dismissed. Capitalism, it is believed, is based on the power of the economically strong to coerce the weak. It is fueled by that ancient Christian sin of greed. It is necessarily corrupt, as the rich steal from the poor, as witness the recent Wall Street scandals surrounding Enron and World Com. It leads to a growing concentration of economic and thereby political power in the hands of unelected and hence undemocratic captains of business who run the multinational companies which are the hallmarks and whipping boys of global capitalism. These bosses are only interested in feathering their own nests and keeping the rest of humanity as wage-earning helots in a consumerist society, whose advertising and the media feed various forms of mind-numbing sedation, leading to that bad faith which keeps the oppressed from recognizing their miserable state. The prosperity globalization fosters is only at the expense of destroying the natural world of spaceship earth. These complaints are as old as the Romantic revolt against the Enlightenment and its "disenchantment of the world." They are strengthened by the fears of the cultural nationalists that globalization and the modernization it brings is "a desert in which everything has been leveled, and all beauty been stamped out to create a mundane serviceable world of use objects."[1] Globalization is seen as a Faustian pact in which prosperity is bought at the cost of losing one's soul.

Many of the activists who have coalesced in the World Social Forum—which meets in Porto Allegre in Brazil as an anticapitalist camp at the same time that the rival camp of capitalists are meeting in the World Economic Forum in Davos, Switzerland—are also moved by these ethical and cultural complaints about global capitalism. As are the sundry philosophers, sociologists, political scientists, and most surprising some eminent economists who have condemned globalization for seemingly different reasons but whose complaints share the same ethical and cultural passions. In their diverse writings, recognizing the demonstrable failure of the countries of really existing socialism, whose creation was held out as the alternative to global capitalism by the nineteenth-century antiglobalizers, today's opponents of globalization seek a Third Way between the global capitalism of which they disapprove and the failed collectivism of the communist alternative.

But the writings of the noneconomists on the Third Way, as has been noted about one of its chief proponents, the sociologist Anthony Giddens, are "pretentious waffle . . . an airy and vapid mixture of the obvious and the obviously false, all of it smeared in unintelligible jargon. There isn't anything in his writing which sustains serious scrutiny."[2] The same judgment applies to the ruminations on globalization of the French sociologist Pierre Bourdieu and of the British philosopher John Gray.[3] But even if their twaddle is not impressive, it still raises the question: whether the social question[4] which animates their discontents and seemingly led to the unraveling of the nineteenth-century LIEO will also undo the new one? This is the fear expressed by the supposedly capitalist club of the World Economic Forum in Davos which issued a statement in 1999 saying, "we need to devise a way to address the social impact of globalization, which is neither the mechanical expansion of welfare programs nor the fatalistic acceptance that the divide will grow wider between the beneficiaries of globalization and those unable to muster the skills and meet the requirements of integration in the global system." Instead of finding a Third Way, they offer merely more hot air, a prescription for "'compassionate government' that some political leaders are now advocating as an alternative to the old dichotomy between right and left."[5] This is merely a commendation of window dressing of the inescapable processes of globalization by that new breed called spin doctors, a plea for mutton dressed as lamb. Fueled in part by the recent financial scandals on Wall Street, the forum's support for corporate social responsibility, which they see as meeting the complaints of the social activists and their demand for a stakeholder rather than shareholder capitalism, is altogether more dangerous, as it provides a window for the global salvationists of Porto Allegro to further their agenda. This could spell the death of the modern corporation which has been at the heart of the vitality and spread of global capitalism. So we need to examine the agenda of these so-called spokespeople of an imaginary international civil society and the challenge they pose to globalization.

The agenda of these global salvationists has been given surprising support in a recent book by Joseph Stiglitz, Nobel Prize winner and former vice president of research at the World Bank. This emerging academic icon of the antiglobalization movement makes a factual statement: "A growing divide between the haves and have-nots has left increasing numbers in the Third World in dire poverty, living on less than a dollar a day. Despite repeated promises of poverty reduction made over the last decade of the twentieth century, the actual number of people living in poverty has actually *increased* by almost 100 million. This occurred at the same time that total world income actually increased by an average of 2.5 percent annually."[6] He cites World Bank statistics for his conclusion. This puzzled me, as on the basis of the 1996 Lal-Myint detailed comparative study of the post–Second World War economic histories of 25 developing countries, one of the firmest conclusions was that growth above a certain level invariably decreased poverty. So, how was it possible that at a time in which the two largest Third World economies—India and China—with the largest numbers of the world's poor in 1980 had grown spectacularly at average rates between 6 and 8 percent in the two subsequent decades, the numbers of the world's poor had grown? Similarly, if these two of the poorest countries were growing at nearly twice to thrice the rate of the rich countries, how could this statement made in the World Bank's World Development Report for 2000–2001 be correct: "The average income in the richest 20 countries is 37 times the average in the poorest 20—a gap that has doubled in the past 40 years."[7] If true, these facts would support the rhetoric of the antiglobalizers, one of whom declaimed at the Doha meeting of the WTO in November 2001: "Globalization leads to the North getting richer, and the South getting poorer. . . . This is a direct consequence of globalization, and we need to stop this from continuing."[8] Or as another has stated, "the dramatic advance of globalization and neoliberalism, has been accompanied by an explosive growth in inequality and a return to mass poverty and unemployment."[9] Is this true?

The recent financial crises which removed the stripes from so many of Asia's tigers have also led to a backlash against free capital movements among many economists. There is the danger that, as a result, the recent conversion to global capitalism of many Third World countries will not last, as they eschew the classical liberalism embodied in the so-called Washington Consensus and also search for an elusive Third Way.

In this chapter I therefore want to examine whether the purported facts about the effects of the spread of global capitalism on global poverty and inequality are true, whether the fears of global capitalism expressed in many developed and developing countries are rational, and whether the Washington Consensus needs to be replaced by a Third Way.

POVERTY AND INEQUALITY

One of the abiding complaints against global capitalism has been the assertion that, while it might promote general prosperity, it leads to greater inequality and the perpetuation of poverty. Fortunately, an old colleague of mine at the World Bank, Surjit Bhalla, who now sensibly runs an economic research and asset management firm in New Delhi, has given the lie to this assertion in an important book, *Imagine There's No Country*.[10] Bhalla's response to the complaint concerns the misuse of statistics, as well as their unreliability in many cases,[11] to support ideological conclusions about the state of the world.

Having obtained access to the poverty data till recently closely held by the World Bank and utilizing the Bank's own methodology, Bhalla has meticulously estimated the headcount ratio (HCR) of the world's poor. He finds that the proportion of people in the developing world living below $1 a day in terms of 1993 purchasing power declined from 30 percent in 1987 to 13.1 percent in 2000, which is a much steeper decline than the reduction from 28.7 percent to 22.7 percent estimated by the World Bank.[12] Xavier Sala-i-Martin, using the same data but slightly different methods, reaches much the same conclusion.[13] There has been a substantial reduction in poverty in the developing world in the 1980s and 1990s. This was the period when China's opening under Deng Xiaoping, India's economic liberalization in 1991, and the gradual move away from planned to market economies in Latin America brought much of the Third World into the global economy. Outside the former Soviet empire, Africa—which has not integrated into the world economy and faces serious problems of governance—is the only

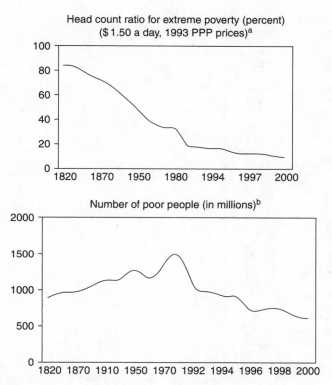

Fig. 4. World poverty, 1820–2000

Source: Bhalla (2002), p. 144.

[a] The poverty line of $1.50 a day, national account means, at 1993 prices, is roughly equal to the popular $1-a day, 1985-prices poverty line, when such a line is used with survey data.

[b] Computed by multiplying the estimated head count ratio by the world population.

region where poverty has risen. Contrary to Stiglitz, the World Bank, and the antiglobalization brigade, in the latest period of globalization which really began with the 1980s, there has been a historically unprecedented decline in Third World poverty.

Bhalla, using other data assembled by World Bank researchers, also computes how world poverty had changed from 1820 till 2000.[14] Figure 4 shows the changing head count ratio (HCR) of poverty and the number of poor in the world, using the same poverty line and methods of estimation he used for the post–Second World War poverty numbers. Table 10 shows the changes in income and the reductions in the world HCR of poverty for various periods. From these, three periods can be broadly identified: the nineteenth-century period of globalization; the interwar period from 1929 to 1950 when the process of globalization stalled and was reversed; and the period from 1950 forward when a new liberal international economic order was reconstructed. As the Third World did not join this till 1980, the true sec-ond period of globalization is from 1980. Bhalla then calculates what he

Table 10. Poverty reduction yield of growth

Time period[a]	Income		Head count ratio		Yield
	Change	Equivalent 20-year change	Change	Equivalent 20-year change	
1820–50	11.1	7.4	−2.4	−1.6	2.2
1850–70	19.0	19.0	−6.1	−6.1	3.2
1870–90	22.4	22.4	−3.6	−3.6	1.6
1890–1910	27.1	27.1	−6.1	−6.1	2.3
1910–29	21.9	23.0	−9.3	−9.8	4.3
1929–50	16.6	15.8	17.3	16.5	−10.4
1950–70	51.3	51.3	−12.4	−12.4	2.4
1960–80	42.9	42.9	−4.6	−4.6	1.1
1970–90	28.2	28.2	−14.6	−14.6	5.2
1980–90	11.2	22.4	−13.6	−27.2	12.2
1990–2000	12.6	25.2	−9.7	−19.4	7.7
1980–2000	23.8	23.8	−23.3	−23.3	9.8
Mean		**25.7**		**−9.4**	**3.5**
Standard deviation		11.6		11.5	5.6

[a] When a time period is either less or more than 20 years, the 20-year "equivalent" income or head count ratio change is presented, i.e., the actual change is multiplied by a fraction equal to 20 divided by the number of years; e.g., figures for 1910-29 will be multiplied by 20 divided by 19.

Note: The yield of growth is defined as the decline in poverty (head count ratio) brought about by each 10 percent growth in per capita incomes (data up through 1950) or per capita consumption (data for 1950 to 2000). Both income and consumption figures are national accounts based. The poverty line used is $1.50 a day, national accounts means, 1993 prices, for data for 1950–2000.

Sources: Bhalla (20002) p. 145. Derived from: Deininger and Squire (1996); World Income Inequality Database, available at http: www.wider.unu.edu/wiid; World Bank, *World Development* indicators, CD-ROM; for years prior to 1950, data taken from Bourguignon and Morrisson (2002).

calls the "poverty reduction yield of growth," the decline in the poverty head count ratio brought about by each 10 percent growth in per capita incomes—the bang for the buck in poverty reduction. From table 10 it is apparent that while the head count poverty ratio was falling during both the nineteenth century and current periods of globalization, it rose during the period of antiglobalization in the interwar period. Since then, during the second period of globalization, it has fallen, but the highest yield in terms of poverty reduction has been since 1980 when the Third World started to integrate with the world economy. The only region where poverty has not declined is Africa, which is also the region which is least integrated into the world economy. The largest decline in poverty has been in Asia, but Latin America and the Middle East have also seen declines in poverty. So poverty today is by and large an African problem, and it is the behavior of its predatory elites and their additional failure to join the globalization bandwagon which explains most of today's poverty. Thus, in 1980 when the number of the world's poor peaked, the majority of the world's poor were in Asia; today they are in Africa.

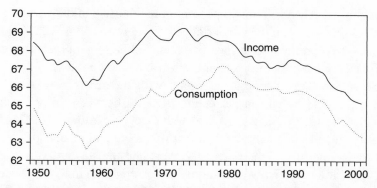

Fig. 5. World individual income and consumption inequality (Ginis), 1950–2000
Source: Bhalla (2002), p. 174.

What about income inequality? Much of the controversy has concerned the gap between rich and poor *countries* for which Bhalla finds that on a statistically sound reckoning, the gap declines from a factor of 23 in 1960 to 9.5 in 2000. Moreover, the largest decline in the gap between rich and poor countries has occurred in the two decades of globalization since the 1980s.

But, while some might find it of interest to see how the gap between rich and poor *countries* has changed with globalization, from the viewpoint of judging the changes in the welfare of *people*, we need to see how the incomes of the *world's citizens* have changed over the years. For this we need estimates of the distribution of income between all the people of the world, ignoring their place of residence (their countries). Bhalla has estimated these distributions for the post–Second World War period as has Sala-i-Martin based on the same data but using somewhat different methods. Their results are very similar.

A summary statistic to measure inequality is the Gini coefficient.[15] If there is complete equality, the Gini will be zero; if complete inequality, it will be 1. Figure 5 shows Bhalla's estimates of the Ginis for both the income and consumption of all the world's individuals from 1950 to 2000. These show a U-shaped pattern till 1980 as world individual inequality peaks, and then a steep decline from the 1980s, the period of globalization. So that by 2000 world individual inequality was at its lowest since the previous trough in 1958. No better picture can demonstrate the equalizing forces of globalization.

Finally, Bhalla also shows from his estimated income distributions for all the individuals in the world for 1960, 1980, and 2000 that there is the same equalizing effect of post-1980 globalization. But more important, he shows that there has been a massive growth of a world middle class in the era of globalization since 1980. Most of this growth in the middle class has occurred in Asia. In 1960 only 6 percent of the world's middle-class population was Asian, while in the industrialized world it was 63 percent. Today, 52 percent of the world's middle class is Asian.[16] This is the miracle that globalization in the most populous part of the world has wrought.

Since the Great Divergence began with the rise of the West in the eleventh century, the gap in per capita incomes between the West and the East (charted in fig. 1) began its inexorable course, leading to rising world inequality. It is only in the current era of globalization that this gap has begun to decline. It was the rise of the West and the stagnation of the great Asian civilizations which was responsible for this growing gap. It was only with their most recent attempt to modernize and catch up with the West by belatedly, and still half-heartedly, following classical liberal policies that these ancient civilizations have begun to close the gap. Growing global integration has been the motor for this transformation. Thus, contrary to the chants of the protesters marching through the streets of Seattle or Genoa, and despite the many financial crises which have plagued the developing world, globalization has been good for the world's poor and has reduced global inequalities.

CLASSICAL LIBERALISM, LAISSEZ FAIRE, AND THE WASHINGTON CONSENSUS

The complaints of the protesters against the so-called Washington Consensus are not justified either. The Washington Consensus arose as a result of the policy experiences of the Third World in the 1970s and 1980s, as the best way to promote poverty-alleviating growth. It is essentially an application of the nineteenth-century classical liberal principles of laissez faire, which have been unjustly caricatured as "the night watchman state," as assuming "a harmony of interests," and for assuming utility-maximizing rational actors. But all these characteristics are alien to the thought of the fathers of classical liberalism—David Hume and Adam Smith.[17] They do not look upon man as a rational utility maximizer with perfect knowledge.[18] Their central claim is that a free-market economy, by promoting the division of labor and by coordinating the division of knowledge (which necessarily exists in any society) through the price mechanism, can goad individuals to become more rational. The ensuing specialization allows a better allocation of a society's resources and leads to greater national wealth. But the free market is not considered to be one which has "perfect competition" as defined by modern-day economists, whose notion of market failure (to justify government intervention) is irrelevant, as it is based on judging an actual market economy by an unattainable Utopian standard.

Moreover, instead of there being a harmony of interests, a legal framework is needed, as David Hume noted, to mediate between clashing interests and reconcile individual self-interest with the public good. Classical liberals strongly believe in "liberty under the law" and therefore a *qualified*, not an absolutist *laissez faire*.[19] This liberty under the law is based on a procedural view of justice, where the latter, as Adam Smith put it, is "but a negative virtue, and merely hinders us from hurting our neighbors."[20] The law must be nondiscriminatory, applying to everyone without regard to particular circumstances. This rules out positive notions of justice—for instance, of the distributive sort—in part because then the law would be based on the discretion of fallible and most likely corrupt men to discriminate against some in favor of others.

Thus, the nature of the government is crucial in recommending policy. The great classical liberals from Hume to Smith to John Stuart Mill were aware of this. If, as I have argued elsewhere,[21] most states are predatory—even democratic ones, where the predators are the median voter and successful pressure groups—then *normative* analysis based on assuming the government consists of Platonic Guardians can go horribly wrong.

For the essential problem of political economy is to devise ways in which the state will provide the essential public goods at least cost in terms of taxation. This was clearly recognized by the classical liberals, whose recommendation of laissez faire was based on a realistic assessment of the nature of governments. The classical liberals were not hostile to the state, nor did they believe that governments had only a minor role in economic life. Their view of the state was positive and, as Lionel Robbins (1952) indicates, Adam Smith's famous statement of the three functions of the state, viz., (1) to protect society from foreign invaders, and (2) every member, as far as feasible, from oppression and injustice, by other members of society, and (3) provide and maintain various public works and public institutions which provided public goods,[22] is almost identical with Keynes's famous formulation in *The End of Laissez-Faire*: "the important thing for government is not to do things which individuals are doing already, but to do those things which at present are not done at all."[23] The ensuing principles of economic liberalism were clearly set out in Mill's *Principles*, and their clearest modern reformulation is in Friedrich Hayek's *The Constitution of Liberty*. In fact, the current Washington Consensus on economic policy for the world is essentially a classical liberal policy package: sound money, balanced budgets, free trade, and flexible exchange rates.[24]

From Smith to Hayek to Milton Friedman, classical liberals have maintained that equality comes into conflict with liberty, and a true "liberal is not an egalitarian."[25] Classical liberals have, however, always advocated public

transfers if private transfers are unavailable or insufficient to help the deserving poor,[26] and also, since the time of Mill, the public *financing* but not *provision* of merit goods, such as health and education for those unable to afford
them. Just as in the case of the economic package, the social package promoted by social democrats is increasingly coming to resemble these classical liberal prescriptions, except for merit goods. Thus, eschewing
egalitarianism in taxation—in practice if not in rhetoric—and by attempting
to reform welfare states to confine the benefits to the deserving poor, both
the New Democrats under Bill Clinton in the United States and New
Labour under Tony Blair in the United Kingdom are closer to the classical
liberal viewpoint than they imagine.

It was the rise of the enterprise voice of socialism and rampant nationalism, toward the end of the nineteenth century, which led to "the end of laissez faire," as Keynes called his influential pamphlet. The process began in
Europe with Bismarck's social insurance scheme in Germany and the welfare reforms instituted by the Liberal party under David Lloyd George in
Britain from 1906 through 1914. During the Great Depression and
Roosevelt's New Deal it spread to the United States. The resulting "embedded liberalism,"[27] as it has been called but which is more appropriately
termed "social democratic," became the dominant ideology, not least
because of the scribbling of economists. So that by the time of the Second
World War, the classical liberalism of the nineteenth century was replaced by
the Dirigiste Dogma. There has been a long battle against this dogma, particularly in the Third World, and despite the antiglobalization protesters' claims
that it is the classical liberal Washington Consensus which is responsible for
the Third World's continuing poverty, exactly the opposite is true. The parts
of the world—mainly Africa and areas in the Middle East—which have not
implemented this classical liberal package are the ones mired in poverty,
while in Latin America there are hardly any countries, apart from Chile, who
have in fact adopted the full package. Hence, to announce its failure
on account of half-baked liberalization attempts in many countries is rather
premature.[28]

Nor has the developed world by any means adopted the classical liberal
package. Most European countries including Britain turned their backs on
laissez faire at the turn of the last century. The United States by and large
held out till Roosevelt's New Deal led to "a shift in ideology—from a
skeptical view of government's ability to improve the functioning of the
economy to widespread faith in government's ability,"[29] and the consequent
expansion of government and the abandonment of laissez faire. Despite the
attempts by Ronald Reagan in the United States and Margaret Thatcher in
the United Kingdom to "roll back the state" in the 1980s, there has not been

Table 11. Growth of general government expenditure, 1870–1996 (percent of GDP)

Country	About							
	1870	1913	1920	1937	1960	1980	1990	1996
France	12.6	17.0	27.6	29.0	34.6	46.1	49.8	55.0
Germany	10.0	14.8	25.0	34.1	32.4	47.9	45.1	49.1
Italy	13.7	17.1	30.1	31.1	30.1	42.1	53.4	52.7
Japan	8.8	8.3	14.8	25.4	17.5	32.0	31.3	35.9
Sweden	5.7	10.4	10.9	16.5	31.0	60.1	59.1	64.2
Switzerland	16.5	14.0	17.0	24.1	17.2	32.8	33.5	39.4
United Kingdom	9.4	12.7	26.2	30.0	32.2	43.0	39.9	43.0
United States	7.3	7.5	12.1	19.7	27.0	31.4	32.8	32.4

Source: Tanzi and Schuknecht (2000), Table I, 1, pp. 6–7.

any marked reduction in the size of the state in these supposedly laissez-faire economies. To date, the hope of some classical liberals and the fear of social democrats that an increasingly integrated world economy would erode the tax basis of funding government expenditure (as mobile capital and skilled labor moved from high to low tax areas) has not been realized. As table 11 shows, there has been hardly any marked fall in the size of government in industrialized countries. What globalization has at best succeeded in doing is in slowing its growth since 1980.

Most of the growth of government since the Second World War has been due to the expansion of social expenditures which have taken the form of cash transfers to redistribute income, whereby social safety nets have been converted into systems of universal social benefits.[30] But the actual amount of redistribution achieved has been minimal and most of this social expenditure represents fiscal churning.[31] Moreover, where merit goods have been sought to be publicly provided rather than merely financed for the needy, the resulting inefficiency has added to that caused by fiscal churning. In light of the aging of the population in most developed countries, whether current publicly funded health and pension benefits are sustainable remains doubtful, since they are creating an intergenerational war by requiring taxation of the young to benefit the old.[32] Whether this will lead to another fiscal crisis of the state followed by liberalization as in the eighteenth and nineteenth centuries remains to be seen.[33] There are serious concerns about the U.S. fiscal deficit and future funding of Social Security and Medicare programs.[34] The current U.S. imperium seems to be on the road to a serious fiscal crisis, which as we saw in chapter 1 was the major cause of the fall of the Roman empire. The failure to adopt the classical liberal package in its economic and social policies may yet prove to be the Achilles heel of the U.S. empire.

FINANCIAL CRISES

The developing countries' main fear is that globalization, particularly of their financial markets, will lead to greater volatility in their national incomes and, as the recent Asian crisis has shown, to serious instability in which years of progress can be wiped out by some young traders on Wall Street pushing a few buttons on their computers. Many are asking for a new international financial infrastructure to manage global capital markets.

Volatility is an ancient worry of the Third World, earlier expressed as the purported adverse effects on growth of the export instability engendered by the integration of primary product exporting countries in the world economy. In a 25-country study covering the period since the Second World War, Hla Myint and I[35] could find no statistical evidence that volatility of growth rates affected long-run growth performance—a conclusion in consonance with the numerous studies of the effects of export instability on growth. Thus, Hong Kong has had one of the most volatile growth rates among developing countries while India, one of the most stable; but the long-run growth performance of Hong Kong puts the Indian performance to shame. Though there may undeniably be greater volatility in the national incomes of countries integrating with the world economy, this need not damage their long-run growth rates.

The Asian Financial Crisis

The financial crisis which hit some of the best run and most globalized developed countries in Asia has raised serious worries about the desirability of free capital movements in developing countries. Does the Asian financial crisis portend the beginning of the end of the decade-old trend of economic liberalization in the Third World aimed at integrating it into the world economy? To answer this question we need to briefly outline the threefold causes of this crisis: (1) the exchange rate regime; (2) the moral hazard in the domestic banking systems caused by the Asian model; (3) the international moral hazard created by the actions of the International Monetary Fund (IMF).

The Exchange Rate. The first cause was the quasi-fixed exchange rate regimes in many of the countries. It is increasingly becoming clear that in a world with a globalized capital market only two exchange regimes are viable: a fully floating exchange rate or a rigidly fixed rate as in the currency board of Hong Kong. These are the only ones which allow automatic adjustment to external and internal shocks without any need for any discretionary action by the authorities.[36] This lesson has now been learned by many countries in the Third World.

The Asian Model and Moral Hazard. The second cause of the Asian crisis was a systemic flaw in the Asian model of development. A central feature of this model—as seen most clearly in Korea but presaged by the development of Japan—is a close linkage between the domestic banking system, industrial enterprises (particularly the biggest), and the government.[37] The fatal danger of this model is that by making the banking system the creature of the government's will, it creates tremendous moral hazard in the domestic banking system. The banks having no incentive to assess the credit worthiness of their borrowers or the quality of the investments their loans are financing, as they know no matter how risky and overextended their lending, they will always be bailed out by the government. This can lead in time to a mountain of bad paper and the de facto insolvency of a major part of the banking system (as has happened in both Korea and Japan), not to mention the corruption that is inevitably involved in this type of development.

But as the example of the U.S. savings and loans crisis shows, this mess in the banking system can ultimately be cleared up if there is the political will. Korea does have the will and should bounce back fairly shortly. By contrast, Japan, which inherited a political system based on institutionalizing political paralysis from the Meiji oligarchs, shows no sign as yet of grasping this nettle, and its prospects must therefore remain a cause for continuing concern.[38]

The IMF and Moral Hazard. The problems of moral hazard for the domestic banking system created by this Asian model have been aggravated by the actions of the IMF and the entrance of foreign bankers as lenders in the newly liberalized capital markets. Of the three types of capital flows that can be distinguished—direct foreign investment, portfolio investment, and bank lending—the income and foreign currency risk of the first two types is shared by both the lender and the borrower because the investments are denominated in domestic currency. By contrast, foreign bank loans are usually denominated in dollars and the interest rate is linked to the London interbank offered rate (LIBOR). This means that if faced by a shock which requires a devaluation, the domestic currency burden of the foreign bank debt rises at equal pace with the changing exchange rate. If the debt is incurred by the private sector, this rising debt burden need pose no problem for the country, for if the relevant foreign banks run, the borrowers can always default on their debt.

But now enter the IMF. Ever since the 1980s debt crisis, the foreign banks faced by a default on their Third World debt have argued that this poses a systemic risk to the world's financial system; they asked, in effect, for an international bailout to prevent this catastrophe. The IMF has been more than willing to oblige. For since President Nixon's closing of the gold window in the early 1970s ended the era of the Bretton Woods adjustable peg exchange rate regime

(which the IMF had been set up to manage), the IMF has been like a character
in Pirandello's play *Six Characters in Search of an Author*. The debt crisis of the
1980s provided the IMF one such role, the rocky transition of the Communist
world from planned to market economy another, and the Mexican and Asian
crises a third. The IMF has increasingly become the international debt collector
for foreign money center banks. It should be shut down.

As regards the Asian model, it is dead. Countries are increasingly recognizing that what is derisively called the Anglo-Saxon model of capitalism
is the only viable one in the long run. It alone can deliver that prosperity
which a globalized economy offers in an unprecedented manner to all its
participants. Hence, most of the countries involved in the Asian crisis are
now moving toward adopting its institutional bases: transparent financial
systems and deeper financial markets which allow hedging of foreign currency risk, and either a floating or rigidly fixed exchange rate regime as in a
currency board or a monetary union.

Capital Controls

Yet, there are distinguished voices among hitherto mainstream economists[39]
who are arguing that developing countries should prevent or tax the free flow
of short-term capital to and from their economies through various forms of
capital controls. The examples of China and India—with their tight capital
controls—are cited as shining examples of countries which escaped the con-
tagion from the recent Asian financial crises. The temporary controls on outflows of capital instituted at the beginning of the crisis by Prime Minister
Mohammed Mahathir in Malaysia are commended. I believe these views are
profoundly mistaken.

We need to distinguish between transitory and permanent capital controls. While there may be a case for maintaining capital controls in the transition of repressed economies to full-fledged ones, thereby allowing time for
their domestic banking and financial systems to deepen, there can be none
for permanent capital controls. There may also be a case for temporary controls on capital outflows as instituted in Malaysia, but there is a danger, as
with emergency trade protection, that such controls will become permanent
(though this did not happen in Malaysia's case).

Maintaining permanent capital controls, besides being an important
denial of the economic freedom central to the efficient working of a market
economy, is also a denial of the associated efficiency gains.[40] Moreover, in
an economy with free trade with the rest of the world, capital controls will
always be leaky, as shown in the Bretton Woods era with the leads and lags
in payments associated with foreign trade being used to make the desired

capital movements. In addition, there are, as with trade controls, the costs of corruption and rent seeking.[41]

What of the tight controls on capital movements in India and China? In both countries the major motive today, as they have substantially liberalized various other aspects of their trade and payment regimes, is to maintain an undervalued nominal exchange rate—the dirty managed floating system in India and the fixed exchange rate (to the dollar) system in China. It is exchange rate protection, which leads to the inefficiencies associated with any form of protection, that eventually damages long run growth. It also leads to pressures for protection in the United States and Europe.[42] Furthermore, in order to maintain the undervalued exchange rate, they have to continually sterilize part of the capital inflows allowed, leading to rising foreign exchange reserves. As these reserves are usually kept in the form of U.S. government bonds, we have the absurd situation in China in which the undervalued exchange rate leads to larger trade surpluses than would otherwise occur, and these surpluses are then converted into U.S. government bonds. The Chinese and Indians are thus unrequitedly financing the burgeoning U.S. trade and fiscal deficits because of these misguided policies. It would make sense for both countries, once their financial systems have been strengthened, to abandon capital controls and float their currencies.

The conclusions of classical liberal economists on capital controls stand. Temporary controls on capital can be a stopgap measure. But, in the long run, concerns about the vulnerability arising from international capital flows are best met by pursuing sound macroeconomic policies, avoiding rigid exchange rates, and instituting supervision of domestic banks to reduce moral hazard and corruption.

The Global Financial Infrastructure

There has been much talk about restructuring the global financial infrastructure. Most of these schemes are implicitly based on an atavistic suspicion of speculation in capital markets. There are those who want to throw sand in its works by imposing the so-called Tobin tax on capital flows.[43] This would be an international tax levied on short-term capital flows to reduce them and hence stem their volatility. There can be no justification for this: consider the absurdity of imposing a similar tax on domestic stock market transactions so as to damp their volatility. Similarly, many of the current proposals to improve the so-called international financial architecture are misconceived. Clearly, with the IMF exacerbating rather than preventing debt crises, it can have no role in a liberal financial economic order, except perhaps as an international country-risk-rating agency like Moody's that can make use of its existing intellectual capital and access to national statistical data. The World Bank's intermediation role is also no longer required. Its only role left, if one believes this is needed, is as an aid agency. But foreign aid has been a failure;[44] it too should be shut down. This would demolish the now-archaic structure put in place at Bretton Woods to meet the very different requirements of a moribund international financial system inherited from the aftermath of the Great Depression.

Would any replacement be needed? No is the short answer. Without the IMF, there would be no international moral hazard exacerbating the domestic moral hazard already facing domestic banking systems worldwide because of deposit insurance. Although it would be logical to end this domestic moral hazard—which is endemic to any banking system with mismatched maturities—by ending deposit insurance, it is politically infeasible in this democratic age. Hence, the call for greater surveillance of bank portfolios by national or international authorities; but, as the governor of the Bank of England Mervyn King[45] has rightly noted, this amounts to a call for the nationalization of banks.

Nor is it credible for the IMF to be converted into an international lender of last resort. There are two functions that a lender of last resort has to perform, as set out in Bagehot's famous rules.[46] First, it should be able to create high-powered money quickly to lend to solvent banks in order to prevent a liquidity crisis. Second, it must be able to distinguish between good and bad paper and thus to judge the soundness of the banks to which it is extending liquidity, with insolvent banks being shut down. The IMF can do neither. It can lend only after lengthy negotiations with a country's government and the approval of its board. Also, it has no way of sorting out the good from the bad loans made (for instance, by foreign banks to residents in a country), and liquidating those that are bad. The lender-of-last-resort function for the money center banks involved in foreign lending must therefore continue to be provided by their parent central banks.

The proposal for the IMF to be converted into an international bankruptcy agency to prevent a minority of bondholders from obstructing an orderly restructuring of sovereign debt is its latest attempt to find a role. It has been prompted by the recent success of a vulture fund, Elliot Associates, in suing Peru for full repayment and interest on the $20 million of government-guaranteed commercial loans it had bought. Elliot Associates refused to accept the Brady bonds,[47] which other creditors were willing to accept in the restructuring. Instead, it obtained a judgment for $56 million and an attachment order against Peruvian assets used for commercial activity in the United States. It targeted the interest payments that Peru was due to pay to its Brady bondholders, who had agreed to the restructuring. Rather than be pushed into default on its Brady bonds, Peru settled.

But the proposal to convert the IMF into an international bankruptcy court to deal with the likes of Elliot Associates is flawed. Unlike a domestic bankruptcy court where the debtor has to disclose all his assets on which creditors can be given a fair share of their claims, no such provision is included in the IMF proposal and for a very good reason. Unlike domestic private debtors, to whom Chapter 11-type bankruptcy provisions apply, sovereign debtors will be *unwilling* to pay their creditors well before they are *unable* to do so, because when they default, it is only their assets in foreign jurisdictions which can be legally attached by their foreign creditors. There is no way in which their domestic assets can be attached. That Peru settled with Elliot Associates shows that the country was *able* to pay. Similarly, in the major 1990s debt crises in Mexico and Indonesia, both countries had large state-owned oil companies whose assets could well have covered their debt payments if they had been willing to use them. The IMF proposal would therefore reduce the limited incentives currently existing for sovereign borrowers not to overborrow and would lead future creditors to further curtail their lending to these emerging markets.

A simpler way to deal with the problem posed by a minority of creditors holding out in the restructuring of a country's debt is to adopt the practice of the London markets to insert collective action clauses into international bonds. These clauses allow a 75 percent majority in a meeting with a quorum to amend the bonds. This stops a minority of bondholders from preventing the restructuring of a country's debt. It is a decentralized and market-based solution, which the IMF too is now supporting. It is also favored by the U.S. Treasury[48] and the international banks. If widely adopted, there would be no need for the IMF as an international crisis manager.

Does this signify that there is no way to avoid the volatility of international capital flows and the periodic bubbles that occur in financial markets? The simplest way to an answer is to think of international capital markets as merely an extension of domestic stock markets. No one has credibly argued that domestic stock markets, despite their undoubted volatility and proneness to bubbles, should be shut down or have their operation circumscribed, as these purported cures would be worse than the presumed disease. And the same line of argument applies to competitive international capital markets.[49] Although international markets are volatile and subject to bubbles—and bubbles always burst—any public intervention will only make matters worse.[50] So I can only echo the sage advice of Lord Palmerston in 1848 when faced by calls for public action in the face of spectacular defaults on foreign bonds. In a circular eschewing any public action, he wrote: "The British government has considered that the losses of imprudent men who have placed mistaken confidence in the good faith of foreign governments would provide a salutary warning to others."[51]

FEARS OF DEVELOPED COUNTRIES

Pauper Labor Imports

For developed countries the major threat perceived from globalization is to the living standards of their poorest and least-skilled workers from trade with the Third World. The resulting protectionist response would be a serious threat to developing country growth prospects. There is a continuing and unsettled debate about the causes of the stagnation in the wages of low-skilled workers in the West (or historically high unemployment rates—which is the other side of the same coin—as in Europe). Whether low-skilled workers' wages are now set by those of Chinese and Indian workers (à la Stolper and Samuelson) or are stagnant because of technological changes in the West is unlikely, in my view, to be resolved. This is because of a massive structural change taking place in the global economy, which is as momentous as the first Industrial Revolution. The late Sir John Hicks had characterized the dominant feature of the latter as the substitution of fixed for circulating capital in the processes of production—as the factory replaced the "putting-out" system. The current structural revolution can be characterized as the replacement of human for fixed capital as epitomized by the communications revolution in the West.

Unlike heavy industry in which many of the larger Third World countries increasingly have a comparative advantage, much of industry supplying consumer goods seems to be going bespoke or custom-made. This means that instead of mass-produced consumer goods relying on long production lines—called Fordism by some in recognition of the revolution in standardized mass production of consumer durables achieved by Henry Ford—the current tendency is to produce differentiated versions of the same good more closely tailored to differing individual tastes. Variety rather than standardization is the name of the game in this designer world of commodities in the affluent West. Shifts in its variegated tastes are increasingly reflected in changes in differentiated products to meet this volatile demand. A new international division of labor, based on outsourcing and just-in-time production, reminiscent of the old national "putting-out" systems, is emerging, in which the design and sales capacities that are human capital intensive are located in rich countries. They then have virtual factories, with their production bases spread across the world, and use modern telecommunications to convert these designs into the differentiated consumer goods increasingly demanded in the West.

Both trade and technology will thus put a premium on skills in the West. A signal for the acquisition of these skills will be a widening of skill differentials—as is evident in the United States—and the stagnation of the wages of the unskilled (or if these wages are artificially kept high, as in Europe, to rising unemployment). But once, as a result of these incentives to skill acquisition, the necessary accumulation of human capital takes place, the levels of living of even those on the lowest rung of the current income distribution should rise. But this process will take time—witness the still-unsettled debate about nineteenth-century living standards in the United Kingdom when the previous major structural change was taking place. It appears that these living standards took a long time to rise as, for instance, the handloom weavers of the old "putting-out" system were converted into the factory workers of the modern age.

The Social Question

It was precisely this so-called social question that in part led to the unraveling of the nineteenth-century LIEO, as the redistributive and egalitarian politics emerging from the rise of the common people undermined that belief in classical liberalism which underlay the intellectual underpinnings of the LIEO. With globalization picking up where it left off before this so-called socialist impulse undermined the LIEO, the implicit philosophy underlying the so-called Washington Consensus on economic policy is underpinned by classical liberalism. In this sense, globalization has put an end to what might be called the Age of Keynes.

One of the consequences of the breakdown of the nineteenth-century LIEO was that convertibility of currencies and free mobility of capital was greatly attenuated and in many countries snuffed out by exchange controls, which were abolished in the UK only with the accession of the first Thatcher government. The bottling up of capital was essential for the Keynesian system to work. This was explicitly recognized in its international expression—the so-called gold exchange standard established at Bretton Woods, which required controls on what were deemed to be short-term capital flows to allow the adjustable peg exchange rate system to work, free from the speculative attacks which plague such systems.

The domestic consequence of this bottling up of mobile capital was that Keynesian remedies requiring the taxation of capital to subsidize labor would not work if capital was free to move and escape these arbitrary and exorbitant imposts. This is not the place to relate the story of how the world moved to free mobility of capital, but once it did, dirigiste states found it increasingly difficult to claim that they are able to promote national prosperity and welfare through fiscal policies to maintain full employment and increases in redistributive taxation. Globalized capital markets, by allowing the prey to exit, have diminished the power of the predatory state to maintain—let alone increase—its take. Even those imbued by the socialist impulse now recognize that their political prospects rely on two Clintonian slogans: "It's the economy, stupid" and "It's the bond market, stupid"!

There is also less danger today that the social question posed by the current phase of globalization will undermine the new LIEO as it did its nineteenth-century predecessor. This is because of the different nature of the losers in the North in the two eras and the mitigating actions they can take to preserve their prosperity.

The rise of the factory system in the nineteenth-century meant that the economic integration of the Atlantic economy by the LIEO led in each region to relative declines or stagnation in the real incomes of the factors of production which were relatively scarce and a rise in the incomes of the more abundant factors.[52] This meant that in the United States, which was labor scarce and natural resource-and-land abundant, the distribution of income moved against labor. This led to the growth of populist politics and creeping protectionism on grounds first propounded by Alexander Hamilton. In labor-abundant and land-scarce Europe, this nineteenth-century globalization led to landowners losing out relatively. This then led to political coalitions, such as the famous one between rye and steel in Germany, and growing protectionism justified by the infant industry arguments of Friedrich List.[53] The UK alone stood by its free trade creed, largely because having fought off the landed interests at the time of the repeal of the Corn Laws and being the first industrial nation, the prosperity of both its industrial capitalists and workers was enhanced by the cheap grain flowing across the Atlantic as a result of the LIEO.

While political action by threatened interest groups seemed inevitable to deal with the distributive consequences of globalization at the end of the nineteenth century, the situation is much more benign in the current phase of globalization. Whereas in the earlier phase the losers—the industrial workers in the United States or the landowners in Germany, for instance—could not acquire the means to prevent their relative decline, this is not so in the current situation in the North. The main losers are the unskilled, and unlike the industrial factory workers of the nineteenth century who could not acquire the physical or financial capital to stem their relative decline in incomes, today's unskilled *can* acquire the necessary *human* capital to share in the immense gains from globalization of their skilled compatriots in the North.

Second, and equally important, with most Northern economies becoming primarily service economies, many more workers will be employed in areas where the products produced are nontraded, i.e., sheltered from foreign competition. A hairdresser in south-central LA is not going to see his or her rates cut by competition from barbers in Bangkok. Many of these personal services require not just skills but also personal attributes like tidiness, punctuality, politeness, and trustworthiness. Mothers are hardly likely to employ a member of the so-called underclass as a babysitter or housekeeper even if the person is willing to accept the wages of a maid in India.

THE CORPORATION UNDER ATTACK

Most of the complaints against global capitalism have coalesced into an attack on the modern corporation, particularly in its Anglo-American and multinational form. It is argued that the corporation must accept various social responsibilities if it is to be acceptable. Various activist spokesmen for an imagined international civil society will otherwise take action, ranging from protests and consumer bans to public interest litigation and pressure on governments to regulate socially irresponsible corporations from disregarding the interests of society. Many of their claims about the inimical effects of multinationals on poor countries are false. But the recent scandals following the dot-com speculative bubble have furthered moral outrage at the behavior of corporations and have led to demands that governments should find ways of improving corporate governance. Many are advocating stakeholder capitalism over the shareholder capitalism enshrined in the Anglo-American classical liberal tradition, and many corporations have succumbed to the demands for corporate social responsibility.

For various historical reasons, the shareholder capitalism embodied in the Anglo-American corporation was not emulated by Japan or by the continental European countries.[54] They had a form of corporatism which has been called stakeholder capitalism in which there is collusion between industry, banks, governments, and trade unions—the so-called stakeholders. The outcome has been greater inefficiency as well as covert corruption than in the Anglo-American shareholder version, and (as we have seen) was one of the causes of the Asian financial crisis. But the Anglo-American version of corporate capitalism, with its separation of the ownership of the corporation from its management, leads to the danger that managers, instead of maximizing the value of the corporation to its shareholders, will use their positions to feather their own nests.

The major way to prevent managers from milking shareholders in the past was through the hostile takeover—hostile to the company's management but friendly to its shareholders. If a management was not maximizing shareholder value and was using the company's profits for its own ends, its share price would decline compared to other companies in the industry. A corporate raider could offer the shareholders a deal whereby he offered to buy their shares at a premium, take over the corporation, and serve shareholder rather than managerial interests. The existing management would, of course, be sacked. It is this market for corporate control which would control bad managers.[55]

In the late 1950s to mid-1960s there was a fairly unregulated market for corporate control in the United States. In the ensuing takeovers, shareholders received on average 40 percent over the prebid price for their shares. But following the howls of protest by threatened managers, Congress passed the Williams Act in 1968. This removed the highly profitable element of surprise in hostile takeovers and made it more expensive for outsiders to mount a successful bid. But it did not kill hostile takeovers; a wave of hostile takeovers followed in the 1980s which restructured U.S. business. Over half of U.S. corporations became targets, while many others restructured to avoid becoming targets. This led the managements of the largest U.S. corporations to petition state governments for protection from corporate raiders. The legislatures and courts obliged and the number of hostile bids declined precipitously. The takeovers that did take place were through friendly mergers in which the incumbent managers agreed to cede control in return for lucrative consulting arrangements, stock or stock options in the acquiring company, generous severance packages, and other bonuses. The managers in these mergers got the largest share of the premium being paid for control of the company, rather than the shareholders. Not surprisingly, as hostile takeovers declined from 14 percent of all mergers in the 1980s to 4 percent in the 1990s executive compensation soared. "Every statute, adjudication, or regulation that in any way inhibited the free functioning of the market for corporate control simply raised the real cost of ousting inappropriate managers. Dollar for dollar, every increase in those costs could be claimed by incumbent managers, either in greater rewards for themselves or in inefficient management policies. Until the real cost of wastefulness equals the cost of a successful takeover fight, they remain secure behind a legal barrier to their ouster, at least until the whole house of cards collapses."[56]

This is, of course, the predictable outcome of regulations which seek to tamper with the free functioning of the market—in this case, the market for corporate control. This attenuation of the market by making hostile takeovers more difficult was worsened by another feature of the post-war fiscal system, the double taxation of dividends. In both America and Britain, the profits of corporations which belong to shareholders were first taxed through a corporation tax. Then, when part of these post-tax profits were paid as dividends to shareholders, they were again taxed as part of their income. This greatly reduced the post-tax return to investors from shares in corporations. Most of their returns depended upon rises in the share price which in large part depended on the plowing back of the profits of the company into new and hopefully profitable investments. As one of the remedies to motivate managers to take account of shareholder value was to link their remuneration to stock options, both managers and shareholders had a common interest in seeing the price of the company's shares rise. This gave an incentive to managers to manipulate their share price through the fraudulent practices shown up by the Enron and other scandals during the 1990s stock market bubble. But though there is a lot of hand wringing at these clearly illegal accounting practices, as Harold Demsetz drily notes: "Indeed I wonder just how many shareholders might have objected to these misrepresentations if they had believed they would remain undiscovered."[57] The proposed removal of the tax on dividends in the United States will help corporate governance, for with the tax on corporate profits still in place, it will provide incentives for managers to retain less of post-tax profits and pay out more in dividends, which will shift resources from the control of management to shareholders.

The perceived ills of Anglo-American shareholder capitalism shown in the bursting of the 1990s stock market bubble are not therefore a sign of some decrease in corporate morality—though there have been some clearly illegal practices which are rightly being dealt with by the law. The ills stem from the perverse incentives created for managerial rent seeking by the regulations limiting hostile takeovers and the unintended effects of the double taxation of dividends. With the double taxation of dividends due to end, if all the regulations preventing hostile takeovers can also be repealed so that the unregulated market for corporate governance can once again do its work in providing checks on predatory managements, executive compensation will begin to fall, accountants will have less pressure to cook the books, and the Anglo-American corporation will pursue the innovation, efficiency, and profitability that has till now been its hallmark.

But there is one final cloud on the horizon. Various activists have been successful in persuading many people and corporations in the previous citadels of Anglo-American capitalism that corporations have a social responsibility to pursue sustainable development. We will discuss this issue in greater detail in chapter 6. Though this corporate social responsibility is not as yet being legislated in the bastions of Anglo-American capitalism, there are clearly pressures to do so. That would create a moral version of stakeholder capitalism and with dire results. Because, as David Henderson has shown in his devastating critique of this program of what he labels the global salvationists,[58] the objectives that are to be subserved are unclear, the means to subserve them and to judge their success are even more fuzzy.

However, as long as the pursuit of this moral agenda is not made compulsory in the Anglo-American shareholding countries, then as this form of capitalism is compatible with a thousand flowers blooming, companies which favor the corporate social responsibility agenda will have to compete with those interested in the traditional objective of maximizing shareholder value. If shareholders prefer these ethical companies, irrespective of their relatively poorer earnings because they serve alternative politically correct goals, they will bid up their share price relative to their earnings. If not, their share price will decline compared to their more politically incorrect peers with the consequent threat to their future survival. This has already happened to some of the firms and funds which have adopted this moral stance. In the recent bear market, the ethical mutual funds which eschewed holdings of tobacco stocks on ethical grounds have found that their performance has been worse than their more economically hard-headed peers, as tobacco shares proved more resilient to the downturn than other stocks. Similarly, Levi Strauss, which created the denim jean, embarked under its CEO Robert Haas on what has been described as "a failed utopian management experiment"[59] in which it "was intent on showing that a company driven by social values could outperform a company hostage to profits alone." The outcome was declining sales, profits, and share value. As Nina Munk entitled her article, this was "How Levi's Trashed a Great American Brand."

Conclusions

My conclusions can be brief. There is no Third Way. Departing from the so-called Anglo-Saxon model of capitalism leads to a dirigisme which undermines prosperity. Nor, unlike the nineteenth century, is there a danger of the social question undermining the newly emerging LIEO. It is threatened instead by the likely resistance in the Rest to the West's current moral crusade to legislate its values, which could undermine the Rest's acceptance of globalization. One of its more serious manifestations is the growing influence and power of various Western nongovernmental organizations (NGOs). They present a serious threat to the ongoing process of globalization and the prosperity it promotes. I turn to examine their agenda and the threat it poses in the next chapter.

CHAPTER 6

NGOs and Global Salvationism

In September 2000 I was in New York attending a jamboree organized by Mikhail Gorbachev around the UN Secretary General's Millennium Summit. This was supposedly to engage international civil society in ongoing debates on globalization. There were numerous sessions in which besides the usual suspects—the trade unions—there was a myriad of nongovernmental organizations (NGOs) whose representatives spoke by and large against globalization. But there was no focus to their complaints. Nor did they present any alternative to the spread of global capitalism, for they realized that the demise of already existing socialism had shown that the alternative socialist system around which critics of capitalism had cohered in the past was a dead end. As I thought about the plethora of disjointed complaints, it seemed that now anything which one did not like, including perennial problems like marital discord which are part of the human condition, was being blamed on globalization. The unifying theme, if there was one, was a cry for capitalism with a human face—an emotive demand which is deeply illiberal and a cover for another form of socialist enterprise. These NGOs are of importance as they are the storm troopers of the antiglobalizers.

The question therefore arises, who are these "global salvationists," as David Henderson[1] has aptly labeled them? How have their views come to have such resonance in the West? What are their true aims? Is there any international civil society and are these salvationists its spokesmen as they

claim? This global salvationist movement poses a major threat to the processes of globalization and the redress of poverty it offers to the Third World.

THE RISE OF THE NGOs

NGOs are pressure groups. They have been a feature of the political system in both the United Kingdom and the United States for 200 years. In the United Kingdom in the nineteenth century, many pressure groups arose to deal with the perceived evils of the emerging industrial capitalism. Many, such as the trade unions, were concerned with promoting sectional interests but many sought to promote causes based on a Christian morality which was increasingly threatened by various forms of secularism and the Darwinian revolution. They dealt with various causes, some involving international commerce, such as the abolition of the slave trade, but most concerned domestic issues, such as the rights of women, the extension of the franchise, as well as more directly moral issues, such as gaming and temperance.[2]

There is a view of pressure groups, which goes back to Alexis De Tocqueville[3] and was adopted by the influential American pluralist school of political sociology,[4] that sees their operations as a benign part of the political process. By contrast, the economist Mancur Olson sees them as essentially predatory, serving sectional interests at the expense of the common good. The political scientist Elmer Schattschneider saw many pressure groups as combinations of the well-heeled: "The flaw in the pluralist heaven is that the heavenly chorus sings with such an upper class accent. Probably about 90 percent of the people cannot get into the pressure group system."[5]

While Olson and other critics of domestic pressure groups criticized them for the promotion of sectional *interests*, the currently active internationally oriented pressure groups—which can be collectively included in the acronym NGO—are mainly dealing with specific *causes* whose resonance comes from some form of moral claim. But like the domestic pressure groups in the U.S. castigated by Schattschneider, they too reflect the ideals of the global rich even while claiming to speak for the global poor.

Of the several thousand NGOs which currently have a formal status in the UN system, only several hundred are from developing countries, and of the developed countries' NGOs an overwhelming majority are from the United States.[6] Most of these are environmental groups which have large bases around the world. Greenpeace, based in Amsterdam, has members and national organizations in 28 countries. They are also very well funded and bring large resources for lobbying and litigation. Of the U.S. environmental

NGOs, Conservation International has assets of nearly $10 million and income of $18 million; the Environmental Defense Fund, assets of $18 million, and income of $27 million; Greenpeace (US), assets of nearly $15 million and income of $9 million, while Greenpeace's global income is $101 million; the National Audubon Society, assets of $109 million and income of $106 million; the National Wildlife Federation, assets of $69 million and income of $102 million; the Natural Resources Defense Council, assets of $39 million and income of $26 million; the World Resources Institute assets of $47 million and income of $18 million; the Sierra Club, assets of $52 million and income of $73 million; the World Wildlife Fund, assets of $89 million and income of $320 million.[7] These resources dwarf those that many poor countries have to counter the lobbying and litigation in which these environmental NGOs engage.

Furthermore, given their large size, these NGOs are necessarily bureaucratic organizations. Their interest lies in creating scares to maximize their income and thereby the salaries, perks, and size of their bureaucracies.

Colonizing the UN

How have the NGOs come to have the influence they do? The crucial element has been their colonization of the UN and increasingly of its specialized agencies, including the World Bank under the current presidency of James D. Wolfensohn. Their entry into the international system was provided by Article 17 of the UN charter which provided for its Economic and Social Council (ECOSOC) to consult with nongovernmental organizations but in an arm's-length fashion, with an "insistence that the status is peripheral to the state."[8] Since the fall of the Berlin Wall, the UN shifted its focus from its traditional role of maintaining the peace to economic and social issues with a greatly expanded role for ECOSOC. It moved to center stage with the mandating of 9 conferences in the 1990s by the UN General Assembly, which were to produce a "global consensus on the priorities for a new development agenda for the 1990s and beyond."[9] Conferences were held on education, children, environment and development, human rights, population and development, social development, women, human settlement and food. Some of these touched on subjects in which the cosmological beliefs of many poor countries conflicted with those of the rich countries, most notably at the women's conference in Beijing in 1995—which I witnessed—and the population and development conference in Cairo in 1994, where the Islamic and Catholic countries opposed the pro-abortion agenda of the UN agencies dealing with population.

In each of these conferences the NGOs provided a parallel forum in which they networked with conference organizers. "As they became an integral part of the 1990s conference process, NGOs were transformed from arm's-length consultants to full participants in the development and implementation of UN policies and programs,"[10] according to Claud Barfield. UN Secretary General Kofi Annan enthusiastically endorsed this embrace of the NGO. In 1997 he stated, "I see a United Nations keenly aware that if the global agenda is to be properly addressed, a partnership with civil society is not an option, it is a necessity."[11] The UN Development Program—though not as yet the UN Secretariat—has endorsed the NGOs' demands for the UN constitution to be changed so that they have equal status with governments!

International Civil Society and Participatory Democracy

By analogy with domestic politics, NGOs and their apologists claim that they represent the world's citizens and hence an international civil society. But this claim is patently false. There are no world citizens as there is no world polity. There are only citizens of nation-states to whom—at least in democracies—their governments are accountable.[12] The chief characteristic of a state is its monopoly of coercive power. In democracies this power is granted to governments responsible to the electorate. As Martin Wolf of the *Financial Times* has cogently argued: "to grant *any* private interests a direct voice in how coercion is to be applied is fundamentally subversive of constitutional democracy. . . . Only elected government can be properly responsible for the making of law, domestically and internationally."[13]

The NGOs along with other pressure groups do compete to influence national politics. But if their claim that they represent civil society were true, those who embrace their ideas would be in power in national polities. They are clearly not, except in some countries of Northern Europe. So aside from their claim of representing a fictitious world citizenry, they are clearly not even representative of their own polities. Hence, they must attempt to hijack the bureaucratic international institutions to subserve their partisan and wholly unrepresentative ends.

Moreover, even the NGOs' moral claim that they represent the views and interests of this fictitious world citizenry is false. Shaffer has noted: "While northern environmental NGOs may be 'internationalist' in orientation . . . they do not represent a 'global civil society.' They have a specifically northern perspective, and often, even more specifically, an Anglo-Saxon one. Their representatives were raised and educated in the North. Almost all of their funding comes from contributors from the North. They obtain their financing by focusing on single issues that strike the northern public's imagination."[14]

The underlying theory behind the NGOs' claims, and the source of their popular appeal, is the wholly illiberal theory of participatory democracy. The Western notion of a liberal democracy is based on representative democracy. From the founding fathers of the American republic to liberal thinkers like Immanuel Kant, direct or participatory democracy on the model of the Greek city-states has been held to be deeply illiberal. Subject to populist pressures and the changing passions of the majority, it can oppress minorities. Greater popular participation does not necessarily subserve liberty. The great liberal thinkers have therefore been keen to have indirect representative democracy hedged by various checks and balances which would prevent the majority from oppressing the minority. Both James Madison and Immanuel Kant liked to call their preferred political system based on representative government a republic, rather than a democracy, which they saw as being of the direct sort and subject to illiberal rule by the mob. On the representative democracy model, people choose their representatives for a legislature which legislates, rather than the people directly writing and passing legislation. The ideal was best expressed by Edmund Burke in a speech to his constituents in Bristol: "Your representative owes you, not his industry only, but his judgment: and he betrays it instead of serving you if he sacrifices it to your opinion. . . .You choose a member indeed; but when you choose him, he is not a member of Bristol, but he is a Member of Parliament."[15]

But in both the bastions of representative democracy, the United States and the United Kingdom, there has been a gradual move toward direct participatory democracy. With the rise of the pollsters and the weakening of party loyalties, politicians, particularly those advocating a Third Way, have come to rely increasingly on focus groups to discover and pander to public opinion—a practice which Burke decried. Nowhere is this more evident than in the politics of California, where tasks like taxation and public spending are decided not by elected representatives but by plebiscites. The opening of the legislative process to greater scrutiny and accountability has paradoxically left these systems more open to influence by pressure groups. This has led to what has been called "Demosclerosis,"[16] with well-funded interest groups increasingly hijacking domestic politics. As Fareed Zakaria notes about these various attempts to democratize the system, to listen to the people, when the people do not have the time or inclination to monitor the legislators and various laws on a daily basis, "well-organized interest groups—no matter how small their constituencies—can ensure that governments bend to their will. Reforms designed to produce majority rule have produced minority rule."[17] The transference of such a system to the international arena would have even more dire consequences, and national governments, particularly those in developing countries, need to fiercely resist this NGO takeover in the name of a self-serving fictitous international civil society.

SUSTAINABLE DEVELOPMENT

What is the agenda of the NGOs? It is a left-wing agenda: to extend the U.S. New Deal's regulatory system to the international arena.[18] Marguerite Peeters has argued that the New Left has hijacked the economic and social programs of the UN. "The new model defies traditional values, national sovereignty, the market economy, and representative democracy. It demands radical changes in individual and social behavior and perceives culture as the last frontier of global change. The standard denounces as unethical the principles of modern industrial civilization, individualism, profit and competition."[19]

The genesis of a representative NGO agenda can be seen in the 1987 Brundtland report of the United Nations World Commission on Environment and Development, which recommended sustainable development as a global objective. It asserted that "sustainable development seeks to meet the needs and aspirations of the present without compromising the ability to meet those of the future." This is so vague and general a principle that, like motherhood and apple pie, no one could possibly object to it, and therein lies its emotive appeal. Being broad enough, it is open to different interpretations, and there is a voluminous literature which has developed. Perhaps the most widely adopted interpretation which has been widely accepted in the business world is that in the words of the World Business Council, sustainable development "requires the integration of social, environmental and economic considerations to make balanced judgments for the long term."[20]

Yet, this seemingly bland objective to which, it is claimed, no reasonable person could object, is not without fundamental disagreements. These concern what is to be sustained. "On the one hand, there are those who think of this in relation to human beings: their sole or main concern is with the sustainable welfare of people, now and for the future," David Henderson writes. "By contrast, others think in terms of ecosystems rather than humanity, so that sustainability is identified with ecosystem resilience. In the 2000 BBC Reith Lectures. . . . the leader of the Southern California Sierra Club . . . argued that sustainable development has become a buzz-word for human centered destruction of the wild planet. Such a view is common among environmentalists and their NGOs."[21] If it is human welfare that is to be sustained, there is nothing new in the notion of sustainable development.[22] But it is not generally human welfare they are concerned with, rather their concern is with preserving the ecosystem—Spaceship Earth.

THE GREENS AND ECOLOGICAL IMPERIALISM

Global Warming

I fortuitously got involved in debates on the environment when I was preparing the 1990 Wincott lecture. Its major theme was the illegitimacy of using arguments based on pecuniary externalities for international macroeconomic and exchange rate coordination. Pecuniary externalities being mediated through the market mechanism are Pareto-irrelevant as they do not effect the efficiency of the economy (see Buchanan and Stubbelbine). For balance, I hoped to argue that the global warming which was then making the headlines was a technological externality which was Pareto-relevant and would require international action.[23] Wanting to read up about global warming, I got in touch with the late Julian Simon who sent me a reading list as well as put me in touch with a scientist, Fred Singer, who though a respected atmospheric physicist was skeptical that there was any evidence of manmade global warming which needed to be countered. Having read the scientific literature I was appalled at how scientists, such as Stephen Schneider, openly admitted they were creating alarm about a phenomenon which they themselves recognized was highly speculative.[24] My lecture not surprisingly also ended up as an attack on this scientific attempt to bamboozle the public.[25]

My friend John Flemming, who was then chief economist at the Bank of England and also chairing a subcommittee of one of the UK's research councils, told me on reading the lecture that I would get nowhere by taking on the scientists who, at a meeting he attended to distribute funds for climate research, had explicitly said that they were not going to behave like economists by disagreeing with each other! Of course, the cornucopia of research funds that the climate change scare has generated provides a baser rent-seeking motive—well known to economists—for thus closing ranks. It would take me too far afield to describe the shenanigans of the International Panel on Climate Change, but just judging from its flip-flopping about even the likely extent of global warming, I think it is fair to say that the scientific basis of any great global catastrophe following from the undisputed increase in greenhouse gases which has and will accompany economic growth is highly insecure.[26] But the Greens had found a cause which resonates with the public, with any hurricane or flood or unseasonable warmth easily sold as a sign of global warming.

A number of points can be made from the ongoing controversies surrounding global warming. First, the greenhouse gases—CO_2, CH_4, N_2, and CFC's—are indubitably increasing and their emissions will increase with growing global economic activity. What still remains controversial is the purported link between this fact and catastrophic climate change.

Second, the global warming that has occurred to date is well within the climatic variations that have occurred over millennia, and even the highest estimate of the likely future rise in temperature is well within the historical pattern. Even the most rabid environmentalist does not expect a runaway greenhouse effect which will make the earth uninhabitable. As Schneider notes: "from the perspective of the overall existence of life on earth, even a 15 degree centigrade (27 degree Fahrenheit) temperature change is not threatening. For example, 100 million years ago dinosaurs roamed a planet some 15 degrees C. warmer than today, and tropical plant and animal forests have been found in high latitude locations such as Alaska."[27] The International Panel on Climate Change's expected rise in global temperature of 2.5 degrees C. by the end of this century is well within this range.

Third, the major economic effects of increasing CO_2—the major greenhouse gas—will be regional, with some regions gaining and others losing, particularly in agriculture. Moreover, industrialization and urbanization, the two great forces of economic progress over the last century, have made earning a living in developed countries virtually climate-proof. The same process of economic growth will have the same effects in developing countries.[28] The fact that millions have voluntarily moved from colder northern to warmer southern climates in the United States shows that even a sudden rise in temperature will not lead to a more drastic change in their local climates than they experience in their voluntary migration.

Fourth, the fear that global warming will lead to a rise in sea levels again represents distributional effects. Even if the projected rise in sea levels, which along with so many of the scientific predictions is now estimated to be much less than originally predicted, leads to the erosion of many coastal areas, this in itself is no worse than what is happening normally through sea erosion.[29] If some Pacific islands are threatened with extinction, the answer is to follow the example of the Naurians. The Pacific island of Nauru is made up of bird droppings—guano—which are valuable as a fertilizer. The Naurians have become rich by digging up their island and exporting it. They have used the revenues from their disappearing island's guano exports to create a trust fund to provide future income for themselves and their descendants. The Green NGOs and the various international institutions currently trying to convince developing countries to reduce their carbon emissions to prevent climate change should instead organize a trust fund to be paid out to the citizens of countries threatened by sea-level rises if the worst happens.

This last point raises the important question of whether, even if the most dire predictions of global warming turn out to be true, it is better to *adapt* to this global warming—as clearly humans have been doing for millennia in the long swings in climate—or to try and *prevent* it, as sought by the Kyoto protocol. A sophisticated cost-benefit study quantified the various alternative scenarios and the uncertainties surrounding both the extent of the likely climatic effects of the increase in greenhouse gases resulting from continued economic growth—not least its acceleration in countries such as China and India which contain the bulk of the world's poor—as well as the effects of this climate change on the economies of different regions of the world.[30] It shows that adaptation is less costly in welfare terms than prevention.

Still, the Greens will not be convinced by this because they invoke the precautionary principle: "it is better to be safe than sorry." This has some resonance with the public, as it has echoes of Pascal's famous wager about the existence of God: viz., if God did not exist, one would only have eschewed the *finite* pleasures from forsaking a sinful life; but if he did exist, a sinful life would lead to damnation and the *infinite* pain of Hell. In expected utility terms (as economists would call it), it was better to give up the finite pleasures from a sinful life for even an infinitesimally small probability of burning forever in Hell.

But as Julian Simon points out in his riposte to Paul Ehrlich's well-known restatement of this wager: "If I'm right, we'll save the world by curbing population growth. If I'm wrong, people will still be better fed, better housed and happier, thanks to our effort [all the evidence suggests he is wrong.JLS]. Will anything be lost if it turns out later that we can support a much larger population than seems possible today?" But, says Simon, note "Pascal's wager applies entirely to one person. No one else loses if she or he is wrong. But Ehrlich bets what he thinks will be the economic gains that we and our descendants might enjoy against the unborn's very lives. Would he make the same wager if his own life rather than others' lives were at stake?"[31] So it does come down to a question of values after all—not facts or logic.

Green Misanthropy

So what of the Greens' other scares? In the 1960s and 1970s there was general hysteria about a world food shortage and discussions of various models of triage—where, in a boat too small to hold all the shipwrecked, those who are the weakest from hunger and hence unlikely to be saved are simply pushed overboard. Bangladesh was the favorite candidate for this triage. The Green Revolution put an end to these speculations. Then there was the scare about the possibility of a nuclear winter, with the world entering a new ice age as a result of a war in which tactical nuclear weapons were used. When Mount St. Helens erupted and dumped dust clouds in the air and we did not get a new ice age, the nuclear winterwallahs retired into their warrens. Then there was the view propounded in the early 1980s that burning fossil fuels would lead to an ice age. So within a decade the same greenhouse effect was first expected to make us freeze and then frizzle!

Even though the Greens' changing scares have been countered by rational and scientific arguments, it has had no effect on them. For those who need the evidence which disproves the various Greens' scares till 1993, Julian Simon's *The Ultimate Resource*, provides a comprehensive compilation. More recently, Bjorn Lomberg, a Green environmentalist who sought to disprove Simon, found to his astonishment that Simon was right. His book *The Sceptical Environmentalist*, a detailed and scrupulous examination of all the available evidence on the various Greens' scares, is a tour de force which has predictably raised the hackles of the Greens. The ensuing debate has shown up the ideological motives of so many of the scientists in bed with the Greens. Lomberg found—as Simon before him did in a lifetime of arguments with the Greens—that trying to engage them in rational debate was futile. Their position is not based on reason but on faith. It is a new secular religion.[32]

But all their scares are without any foundations. The world is not running out of resources. The commercial reserves of nonrenewable resources have risen markedly since 1970 (with those for oil rising by 63 percent and natural gas by 163 percent), and declines in their price trends, as well as in their current consumption as a proportion of reserves, all point to a growing abundance rather than scarcity of many nonrenewable natural resources. The world is not going to starve because of the growth in its population. Even with low technology the world could support one-and-a-half times the 2000 world population, and over nine times that at the United Nations recommended calorie intake per head.[33] Lomberg, summarizing the evidence at the end of the millennium, writes of these scares: "We will not lose our forests; we will not run out of energy, raw materials or water. We have reduced atmospheric pollution in the cities of the developed world, and have good reason to believe that this will also be achieved in the developing world. Our oceans have not been defiled, our rivers have become cleaner and support more life. . . . Acid rain did not kill off our forests, other species are not dying as many have claimed, with half of them disappearing over the next 50 years—the figure is likely to be about 0.7 percent. The problem of the ozone layer has been or more less solved. The current outlook on global warming does not indicate a catastrophe—rather there is good reason to believe that our energy consumption will change towards renewable energy sources before the end of the century. . . . And, finally, our chemical worries and fears of pesticides are misplaced and counterproductive."[34]

So why do the Greens persist with their crusade? The reason is that, like any religion, their beliefs are not based on reason but on faith. For those who do not profess the same faith, the time has surely come to take on these new ecological imperialists. The first point of resistance is to recognize what they are seeking to do. Bluntly, they would like to perpetuate the ancient poverty of the great Eurasian civilizations—India and China—with, as they see it, their burgeoning unwashed masses increasingly emitting noxious pollutants as they seek to make their people prosperous and achieve parity with the West.

For as economic historians have emphasized, the Industrial Revolution which led to the rise of the West was based on converting the traditional organic rural economy that used energy derived from land (whose supply was ultimately limited) into a mineral-energy-based economy that uses fossil fuels (whose supply for all practical purposes is virtually unlimited).[35] It is by burning fossil fuels that the West has gotten rich and redressed that mass structural poverty which had been the fate of its masses for millennia. The same opportunity is now available to the developing countries. But the Greens, in subserving their dubious cause of global warming, want to deny the same means for the Third World's poor to climb out of poverty.

The Industrial Revolution in England and the globalization which followed was based on two forms of capitalism, one institutional, namely that defended by Adam Smith (because of its productivity-enhancing effects, even in an organic economy), and the other physical, namely the capital stock of stored energy represented by the fossil fuels. The Greens are, of course, against both forms of capitalism—the free trade advocated by Smith as well as the continued burning of fossil fuels—leaving little hope for the world's poor. Despite their protestations to the contrary, the Greens are the enemy of the world's poor.

The disengagement of the United States from the Kyoto protocol is therefore to be commended. India along with China rightly stood firm at Kyoto against any restriction of their CO_2 emissions. With the recent reluctance of the Russians to ratify the Kyoto protocol, perhaps it will finally be buried, and climate change cease to be an issue for the Greens to exploit.[36]

TOWARD WORLD DISORDER

The attempts by the ecology imperialists to curb the economic development of the Third World to save Spaceship Earth will be fiercely resisted. It is the major future source for global disorder. For major Third World countries and potential imperial powers such as India and China, it is imperative to confront the modern secular religious movement—the Greens—in their crusade to prevent economic development. First they must stand up to their own local converts—the modern descendants of what the Chinese called rice Christians and secondary barbarians. Second, they must refuse to accept the transnational treaties and conventions which the Greens are promoting to legislate their own ends. As many environmental ministries in developing countries have become outposts of local Greens converts, the economic ministries must play a central role in resisting ecoimperialism by having the last say on *any* transnational treaty or convention a country signs.

The UN and many of its specialized agencies have provided the antiglobalization environmental NGOs, as well as a host of others espousing Western politically correct causes, an institutional framework to push their agenda. It is time to shut them down. They do little to advance the cause of peace and prosperity which an imperial Pax is meant to promote. Even the more technocratic ones such as the World Bank and International Monetary Fund, as we have seen, have served their purposes, while others such as the World Health Organization seem to have stepped well beyond their purely technical arena to take up various politically correct but dubious crusades like those against smoking and obesity.[37] Others like the International Labour Organization (ILO), United Nations Industrial Development Organization (UNIDO), United Nations Conference on Trade and Development (UNCTAD), Food and Agriculture Organization (FAO), and United Nations Economic and Social Council (UNESCO) have also served whatever initial purpose they might have had and are all incubators of various antiglobalization agendas, staffed by rent-seeking international bureaucracies. They do not serve the interests of the U.S. imperium, and even less so those of the world's poor in whose name they claim to speak. They should all be closed, or else the United States should withdraw its financial support from them and let them fend for themselves.

But this is unlikely to happen because many of the causes espoused by the NGOs and these international agencies are part of the West's cultural values. It is the attempt to legislate these Western habits of the heart worldwide, as I argue in the next chapter, which poses the gravest danger to world order. It bears an uncanny resemblance to the ethical component of nineteenth-century imperialism which was in part responsible for the break down of the nineteenth-century LIEO. This imperialism was in part motivated by the civilizing mission embodied in the "white man's burden." Something similar is afoot today: the calls for ethical trading, ethical foreign policies, the insistence that everyone embrace the West's political system of majoritarian democracy are symptomatic of these trends. There are dangerous pressures in the West to use these multilateral institutions to legislate these Western values worldwide. The various proposals to introduce labor and environmental standards in the WTO and to tie issues of human rights to trade and investment under the rubric of ethical trading are of this ilk. They have neither logic nor ethics on their side.[38] Even if these protectionist attacks on the LIEO are beaten back, they can in the meantime lead to increasing international friction which could slowly unravel the new LIEO. Moreover, they tend to aggravate the suspicion of many developing countries that the newly emerging globalized economy will lead to a form of cultural imperialism that will undermine their ancient and cherished ways of life. It is to these broader issues of morality that I turn in Part III.

PART THREE

Morality

CHAPTER 7

Habits of the Heart

I have argued that empires have been natural throughout human history although they have taken different forms. The British in the nineteenth century created an empire of free trade, a liberal international economic order (LIEO). This depended, wherever possible, on exercising indirect rather than direct control through colonization. The U.S. empire is also an indirect empire; even less than the British does it seek colonization or territorial aggrandizement. It has sought to recreate another liberal economic order based on the free movement of goods and capital but not, as in the nineteenth century, of people. Unlike the British, the Americans have, however, adopted the illogical principle of reciprocity to achieve free trade. As the recent failure of the 2003 Cancun meeting of the World Trade Organizations shows, this attempt has run into the sands. The parallel U.S. approach in creating a series of bilateral trading agreements is also inimical to the promotion of genuinely multilateral free trade.[1] Like Britain, the United States has continued to promote free flows of capital. But there are many siren voices, not least among the clerisy, that since the financial crises in emerging markets in the 1990s are clamoring for controls on capital movement. I have argued that these controls are not only infeasible but undesirable. On, the other hand, the claim that the imperfect globalization which has occurred to date has worsened global poverty and inequality has been shown to be false. As in the nineteenth century, even the imperfect international economic order created by the American imperium has alleviated world poverty and reduced global inequalities. It is in the parts of the world—Africa and the Middle East— which have not participated in the global economy that the problems of poverty and inequality remain intractable. The fillip to poverty-redressing growth offered by globalization would be strengthened if the United States and European Union were to adopt the correct classical liberal principles of free trade and laissez faire.

As we have seen, this will not persuade many of those marching through Porto Allegre, as they are really against global capitalism. Much of their passion is fueled by a cultural and moral dislike of capitalism. However, the moral passions moving the global salvationists are in many ways shared by others in the West who do wish to create and maintain a new LIEO. They want to use the current American imperium promoting this LIEO to legislate their morality (what I call "habits of the heart") around the globe. Adherents of the Bush doctrine and many of the so-called neoconservatives who are said to have influenced its content want to use American power to promote human rights and democracy worldwide. There are others, mainly but not exclusively lawyers, who want to create an international moral order. Like the global salvationists, they seek to promote what they claim are universal human values. Far from being universal, these Western habits of the heart are the culture-specific ethic of, what remains at its core, Western Christendom. Their promotion will lead to that clash of civilizations prophesied by Samuel Huntington[2] and to world disorder.

For these reasons, I take issue with moral concerns about global capitalism and the desire to use the American imperium to promote a global moral order. I first take up the question of morality and capitalism, including ambiguous notions such as rights and freedom.

MORALITY AND CAPITALISM

In thinking about morality and capitalism, it is useful to distinguish between the *cosmological* and the *material* beliefs of different civilizations (cultures). Cosmological beliefs relate to our understanding of the world around us and mankind's place in it, which in turn determine how people view the purpose of their lives and interpersonal relationships.[3] These are the "habits of the heart," as I term them, the "morality" of different cultures. Material beliefs are about ways of earning a living, they relate to the material world and change as the material environment changes. The utility of capitalism is based on the material belief that it is the best institutional form to promote modern economic growth, as compared with alternatives such as socialism. Both cosmological and material beliefs are important in generating the legitimacy of different political systems.

There is considerable cross-cultural evidence that material beliefs are more malleable than cosmological ones. Material beliefs can respond rapidly to changes in the material environment. There is greater hysteresis or time lag in changing cosmological beliefs.[4]

One true story told to me by an old Indian friend can illustrate the point. She was the wife of a senior government official and an accomplished amateur singer of Indian classical music. She had arranged for her venerable teacher, who though modern in her ways had never been outside India, to give a concert at Royal Festival Hall in London. When the teacher arrived at her hotel in London she found it very comfortable with most of the facilities to which she had become accustomed at home. To her consternation, however, she found that unlike her and most Indian homes with modern toilets, there were no facilities provided for her to wash her bottom after performing her ablutions, as required by Hindu notions of pollution. She discovered a passable solution in an unfamiliar bidet in the toilet. But when she arrived to sing to a packed hall, no sound would emerge from her throat for a few minutes. As she sat gazing at the sea of washed faces, she was overcome with a feeling of overwhelming disgust at the knowledge that they were all monkeys with unwashed bottoms! She had readily adapted to the modern toilet (the material aspect of modern civilization) but could not overcome the cultural habits engendered by the cosmological beliefs of her civilization about pollution.

The cross-cultural evidence shows that it is the language group to which people belong which influences these cosmological beliefs—these worldviews, these habits of the heart. For most of the Eurasian civilizations, the geographical environment in which the civilizations arose also influenced these cosmological beliefs. As material beliefs can change but cosmological beliefs by and large do not, it is possible and has been the case that the same civilization can maintain its habits of the heart even with a change in its material beliefs and ways of making a living. In other words, different cultures are unlikely to change their cosmological beliefs even though they might change their material beliefs to conform to those of another civilization if that other civilization provides a way of making a better living. Thus, capitalism can and has been adopted by civilizations with very different habits of the heart or morality. They can modernize without Westernizing.

The contrary belief espoused by many in the West that modernization requires Westernization—that is, capitalism requires the adoption of Western habits of the heart—is based on a unique historical conjunction. In the West the change in material beliefs associated with the papal revolution of Pope Gregory VII in the eleventh century followed an unprecedented change in the cosmological beliefs of Christendom associated with the papal revolution of Gregory I in the sixth century (discussed in chapter 3). This first papal revolution changed the communalist cosmological beliefs that the West shared with the other great Eurasian civilizations by promoting individualism, primarily in the domestic domain. It was motivated by the Catholic Church's desire for bequests, particularly from rich widows, a motive which goes back to its inception.[5] Gregory I's family revolution overturned the common Eurasian pattern by promoting the independence of the young and by banning various domestic practices, common across Eurasia, to provide a male heir to inherit family property. The result was increased childlessness,[6] which in turn led the childless to leave their property to the Church.

This papal family revolution made the Church unbelievably rich. Demographers have estimated that the net effect of the prohibitions on traditional methods to deal with childlessness was to leave 40 percent of families with no immediate male heirs. The Church became the chief beneficiary of the resulting bequests. Its accumulation was phenomenal. In France, for instance, it is estimated that one third of productive land was in ecclesiastical hands by the end of the Seventh century![7]

But this accumulation also drew predators from within and without the Church seeking to deprive it of its acquired property. To deal with this denudation, Pope Gregory VII instigated his papal revolution in 1075 by putting the power of God—through the spiritual weapon of excommunication—above that of Caesar. With the Church newly entered into the realm of the material world, the new Church-state also created the whole administrative and legal paraphernalia that we associate with a modern commercial economy.[8] It replaced the material beliefs customary in all Eurasian agrarian economies with those based on contract.

This eleventh-century papal legal revolution (which changed material beliefs) arising from the consequences of the sixth-century papal family revolution (which changed cosmological beliefs) provided the essential institutional infrastructure for the emergence of Western capitalism and the dynamic that in time led to Promethean growth and the Great Divergence in living standards between the West and the Rest. But, the two revolutions though historically conjoined are not so by necessity. Japan, and increasingly India and China, are civilizations which have not altered their communalist cosmological beliefs to adopt Western ones based on individualism (and its subsequent mutations), but they have adopted the material beliefs of the West by taking over the legal and institutional infrastructure created by Pope Gregory VII's legal revolution to foster capitalism. These countries show it is possible to modernize without Westernizing, to accept capitalism without losing your soul.

Western cosmological beliefs even in their changed individualist form continue to be based on Christianity. I have argued that St. Augustine's

City of God with its narrative of a Garden of Eden, the fall leading to original sin, and a Day of Judgment has had a tenacious hold on the Western mind and still forms a major part of the West's cosmological beliefs. It has been echoed by the various secular mutations of Christianity including the philosophy of the Enlightenment, Marxism, Freudianism, and ecofundamentalism.[9]

This Christian cosmology has a number of distinctive features which it shares with its Semitic cousin Islam, and, in part, with its parent Judaism, but other features are not found in the other great Eurasian religions. First and most important is its universality. Neither the Jewish, nor the Hindu, nor the Sinic civilizations had religions claiming to be universal. You could not choose to be a Hindu, Chinese, or Jew; you were born as one. Second, this also meant that, unlike Christianity and Islam, these religions did not proselytize. Third, only the Semitic monotheistic religions have also been egalitarian; nearly all the other Eurasian religions believed in some form of hierarchical social order. By contrast, alone among the Eurasian civilizations, the Semitic ones (though least so the Jewish) emphasized the equality of men's souls. Louis Dumont (1970) has rightly characterized the resulting and profound divide between the societies of *Homo aequalis* which believe all men are born equal (as the *philosophes* and the American Declaration of independence proclaimed) and those of *Homo hierarchicus* which believe no such thing.

Neither individualism (promoted by the altered Western cosmological beliefs)[10] nor equality (arising from its Christian cosmological roots) are part of the habits of the heart of the great Hindu and Sinic Eurasian civilizations.[11] Islam, however, did not change the communalist component of its cosmological beliefs and does not accept individualism and its consequences in the family domain though, unlike the Chinese and Hindus, it shares the belief in equality with its Semitic cousin. There are thus no universal habits of the heart. Forcing one's own habits of the heart down the throats of other civilizations in the name of universality is to mount a *jihad*, whether the claimed universality of one's cosmological beliefs (values, morality) is Christian or Muslim.

JUSTICE AND FREEDOM

As briefly outlined in chapter 1, Michael Oakeshott has described two distinct Western views of the state. As a civil association, the state is neutral with respect to habits of the heart. Its purpose is to maintain that domestic order necessary for the existence of any social life. It does not pursue any purpose of its own such as promoting a particular morality, as does the state that is an enterprise association. Normative judgments about empires can be made on the basis of whether they are civil associations (the good empires) or enterprise associations (evil empires). The good empires have not tried to impose their own or a particular group's morality on the imperium. They have been content to maintain order. Those which did initially try to impose their own morality, such as the early British and Arab empires, rapidly changed course and ran their empires as civil associations.

There are three major enterprises that, Oakeshott claims, the enterprise association state has sought to enforce: nation building, the promotion of some form of egalitarianism, and a particular set of religious beliefs as in a theocracy. In my view, Oakeshott's taxonomy allows us to think clearly about the links between ethics, economics, and politics. The fog created by distinctions like negative and positive liberty and continuing attempts to reconcile the irreconcilable[12] can be readily dispelled by keeping in mind Oakeshott's distinction between these two interpretations of the state. The state seen as a civil association does not seek to legislate morality; the state seen as an enterprise association does.

But what is the morality that the antiglobalizers, the current followers of the enterprise view of the state, seek to foster? With the death of "really existing socialism" (the Soviet Union) in 1989, it was no longer feasible to argue against capitalism as the only remaining viable system to organize economic life. So, the antiglobalizers have changed their tack: they want to reform capitalism in the name of freedom and justice. Contemporary classical liberals (who view the state as a civil association) have found it difficult to counter these views because the notion of freedom remains central to their own traditions. In other words, even if we accept the civil association view of the state, what are the laws the state is supposed to enforce, and how do they promote the freedom that classical liberals value?

In a penetrating analysis, the philosopher-economist Anthony de Jasay has provided a cogent reworking of the principles underlying classical liberalism. It allows us to bypass the culturally specific justifications hitherto provided and to determine what in the notion of freedom could claim universal assent, even among civilizations with very different habits of the heart. Setting these out will also enable us to counter many of the moral claims (within the Western cosmology) on which current critiques of global capitalism are based.

Jasay begins with an audacious move. He argues that the concept of freedom is not essential for classical liberalism. "The notion whether freedom is valuable or a free society is good, ought not to enter at all into a properly thought-out political doctrine, liberal or other."[13] The reason for his rejection is that the two arguments on which individual freedom can be considered a final value open the way to relativism or circularity. For while individual freedom may be valuable to me, there is no reason it should be valuable to someone in a different culture. There are many cultures which have not valued it as the only or even *an* end. A second possible justification for individual freedom is that it allows us to choose what we prefer. But this ability to lead one's life as one chooses, or autonomy as others have called it, makes individual freedom merely of instrumental value. And the question then arises, what final value is this instrument serving? If we reply "freedom," we are in a circular argument, while if we posit some other final value, someone from another culture could once again deny this as being valuable.

The most basic reason for not relying on the concept of freedom to justify a classical liberal society and polity is that freedom, in ordinary terms, involves not having deliberate obstacles being placed in the way of individuals' actions. This immediately leads to the slide whereby being *free* to do something and being *able* to do it[14] are confounded. This results in our now calling, without the least semantic embarrassment, the freedom to choose and the set of things available to be chosen by the same name, freedom, distinguishing between them only by the misplaced adjectives negative and positive.[15] The discourse of freedom then degenerates into one about all good things, and their availability is also called freedom (an example is the recent book by the Nobel Prize–winning economic theorist Amartya Sen entitled "Development as Freedom"). Such discourse allows various policies forming part of the socialist enterprise view of the world to be smuggled in as being part of freedom.[16]

Instead, Jasay, relying on the English Common Law tradition, defines the basic rules which should govern a civil association, and which the state seen as a civil association should uphold: "The basic rule is that a person is free to do what is *feasible* for him to do. This presumption is subject to two compatability conditions. One relates a person's proposed actions to his own obligations, the other to harm to others."[17] The burden of proof lies on someone who wants to prohibit an individual's actions, either because he has an obligation—as in a contract or promises made—not to do it, or if it would harm others. This process is equivalent to the presumed innocence of the accused unless found guilty by due process.

In contrast to this English Common Law tradition of justice, there is an alternative which may be called the Continental system of justice, or of "public law" as Jasay calls it. Under this, unlike the Common Law tradition in which people are free to do what is feasible and not expressly forbidden by the two-sided (compatability) conditions, individuals in this alternative tradition are presumed to be forbidden from feasible actions unless those actions are expressly *permitted* by various rights granted under constitutional provisions. In fact, these bills of rights are only coherent if they provide a suspension of a tacit presumption that everything not covered by them is forbidden by "legislative discretion if not by legislative fiat." These rights ignore the central norm underlying classical liberalism that "whoever proposes to stop another from doing what is feasible must show a right to prohibit or obstruct the particular feasible action."[18]

But, just as with freedom as a final value, this norm of liberty too could be questioned by someone from a different culture. Jasay then uses an epistemological argument, not a moral intuition, to justify this liberty norm. The epistemological argument concerns what can be verified. Of the two alternative legal traditions, the Common Law based on a list of *prohibited* actions is more readily verifiable than the Public Law tradition based on a list of *permitted* actions. For *feasible* actions are limitless, and listing what we *must not* do is less onerous than listing what we are *permitted* to do. Even if the Public Law tradition accepted the liberal norm that individuals were at liberty to undertake feasible actions unless they harmed others or violated an obligation, it would have a problem. For it presumes that "*unless* it can be shown that the proposed action *is* harmless and breaches no obligation, it must *not* take its course."[19] If, as is usually the case, there is no clear boundary to the possible harms a particular action could cause, it will be impossible to prove (verify) that a feasible action is harmless. Similarly with obligations (which confer corresponding rights), it will be impossible to prove that some right has not been violated. In the Common Law tradition the *prosecutor* has to prove that the defendant has, in pursuing a particular action, violated obligations or caused harm to others. In the Continental law tradition it is for the *defendant* to prove that he has not violated *any* right or caused *any* possible harm.

The public law tradition based on bills of rights also leaves the judicial process open to all kinds of opportunistic behavior, in which innumerable third parties can make claims (spurious or not) of limitless harms and obligations being violated. These, in Jasay's view, "render ordinary processes of social cooperation excessively legalistic, litigious, costly and precariously dependent on judicial, administrative and regulatory review"[20]—a judgment corroborated by the experience of the leading rights-based polity, the United States.

RIGHTS

If we are to accept the liberty norm of the Common Law tradition based on *prohibitions* of feasible actions as being more sound because it is verifiable, unlike the Continental tradition based on *permissions*, what of property rights and human rights which so many votaries of freedom have sought to defend?[21]

Property Rights

So-called property rights are mistakenly called rights. If an individual is free to do something which is not wrong, that is it does not violate obligations and causes no harm to others, this liberty must include the freedom to do what he likes with his property—which includes his body as well as various material possessions such as his car or his clothes. *Liberties are different from rights.* I own a house which I am at liberty to do with what I will. Suppose I lease it out to a tenant through a contract. This contract obliges me to relinquish my liberty to use my property in certain ways by giving up the liberty to live in it, and gives the tenant a right to use it for the way and on terms stipulated in the lease. While the property owner has the *liberty* to use his property, the non-owner has to get the *right* to use it which is provided by the lease. Thus, whereas liberties are not conferred by anyone, rights require someone else to have agreed to fulfill some obligation.

But how do I come to own property which I am at liberty to use as I may? Much is acquired through the proceeds of work, other things through exchanges, such as assets, still others from gifts and inheritance. In each of these ways of acquiring property, besides those based on exercising my own liberties, I am also the beneficiary of others, who have exercised their liberty of using what they themselves own as they wish. These means of acquiring property meet the requirements of justice, as they are exercising a liberty without transgressing any obligation or causing harm to others.

But particularly for land a question arises: as we go back in history to a time when land was free and hence unowned, how could land which was a gift of nature be owned? It is only with the expansion of population that land would become scarce. It would then be appropriated and enclosed, largely for economic reasons as the marginal benefits to an individual from enclosing land were equal or greater than the marginal costs of excluding others.[22] As it was not owned by anyone else, no one else's liberties were thereby infringed and hence this appropriation cannot be called morally unjust. Moreover, in many cases the state claimed all land within its territory as its own, and it transferred ownership to others. This again cannot be considered unjust. But conquest and seizure have been equally important in acquiring land, and these actions would be morally unjust and calls for restitution would be justified. This is, of course, at the heart of the controversy about the right of return of the Palestinians in the Arab-Israeli dispute. As discussed in chapter 3, although the claim may be morally just, it is not expedient because most societies throughout history have recognized the chaos that would be caused by seeking to redress any fault in the historical descent of every current title to property, no matter how far back the chain of transfers stretches. They have, therefore, correctly applied some form of statute of limitations, if for no other reason than to recognize that the sins of their fathers should not be visited upon their grandchildren and great-grandchildren.

Human Rights

We have seen that rights arise from contracts—actual or implicit—which give rise to obligations that have been accepted by someone else. Thus, Jasay writes, "every right of one person has the *agreement* of another as its source, cause and evidence."[23] Agreement is crucial in generating rights and the corresponding obligations. Thus, what are often called social rights are not rights but *entitlements*. For instance, the right of the unemployed to unemployment insurance or the poor to welfare are not rights but entitlements created by the state, which can be changed or repudiated as they are not based on contract. By contrast a genuine right arising from a contract cannot be limited or withdrawn without the right's holder giving his consent. These rights are sometimes called *specific* rights.

In addition, it has been claimed that there are human rights—a *general* right arising from the assumption that being *human* in some sense provides a justification for some rights which go beyond specific rights. They are the modern descendants of natural rights.[24] Herbert Hart claims that they arise from the general right, namely "the equal right of all men to be free."[25] They include the right to free speech, to free worship, to walk about, to breathe. But this "right" is redundant in the Common Law tradition. One is simply free to undertake any feasible action which does not infringe one's obligations (the specific rights of others) and does not cause others harm.[26] It is only in the public law tradition that there would be the need to specify these rights because all feasible actions require *permission*, including these human rights to breathe, to be able to speak freely, etc. But as there are infinite number of such rights, it will be impossible to delineate them all, leading to endless legalistic disputes. Individual freedom of action is much better protected by the Common Law tradition where one is at *liberty* (free) to take any *feasible* action subject to the constraints of harm and specific obligations (rights).

CAPITALISM WITH A HUMAN FACE

I can now briefly outline the various ways in which many enemies of capitalism have used the notion of freedom and rights to insinuate various enterprise views of the state while seeming to subscribe to the classical liberal view of the state as a civil association. Most of these methods seek to provide justifications for redistribution. They are all ultimately based on denying that there can be a just distribution of property based on contract, transfers, and first possession constrained by the necessary expedient of a statute of limitations to rectify past unjust acquisitions, for they view property as arising from the mutual gains provided by social cooperation.

It is argued that much of the existing stock of wealth is the result of social cooperation going back to Adam and Eve. It is in that sense a social inheritance, and belongs to the whole of society. But largely for efficiency reasons, as the failure of "really existing socialism" has shown, it is inexpedient to rule out some private appropriation of this social wealth. Hence, some of this social wealth can be allowed to be converted into private property, on the terms and conditions specified by the co-owner, that is, society. One of these conditions is to prevent social exclusion from this social wealth of those disadvantaged due to lack of talent or luck who are unable to share in the benefits produced by social cooperation. Hence, the state as the co-owner of this social wealth should use its coercive powers to force the better off to give up part of their property or income to the disadvantaged.

This edifice is, however, based on the myth that it is impossible to trace the individual contributions to past and present social cooperation which has generated this social wealth. Hence, all wealth must be taken to be the wealth generated by society as a whole. While there is no doubt that cooperation between individuals has generated the wealth in the world, it is false to claim that no tracing of the individual contributions is possible. Everyone who has contributed through work was paid for their contributions in voluntary exchanges. Some of these payments were consumed and some saved and invested, with the resulting assets having the contributor's title to them. To coerce them to give away what is theirs, and which they are free to use as they see fit, would be unjust. Though undoubtedly everyone has contributed to the generation and accumulation of a society's wealth over the millennia, this does not mean that everything is owed to society. "*Nothing is owed*," Jasay rightly notes, "everything has been paid for, one way or another, in a manner and to an extent sufficient to call forth the contribution. There is no further common-pool claim overhanging the lot, for no payment must be made twice. He who sees an overhanging claim in favor of 'society' is seeing a mirage, or the wishful image of one."[27]

Equally tendentious is the claim that because of the social cooperation needed to get the mutual gains in a business or corporation, everyone is a stakeholder who must be consulted and, if necessary, assuaged. A corporation consists of a series of voluntary exchanges based on a contract in which the worker has an obligation to perform certain specified tasks in payment for the agreed remuneration. The obligation to consult may be given by the employer to the worker as part of the contract, thereby granting them a *specific* right matching the voluntarily agreed obligation.[28] But there can be no *general* right to consult stakeholders, unless one believes that the sharing of the fruits of cooperation cannot be assigned by the voluntary contract, and hence this social product has to be shared by continual negotiation or mediation by the co-owner of society's capital—the state. This would imply that the capital the employer deploys has only been implicitly leased to him, for reasons of efficiency, by the state on behalf of society which owns the capital. But this implicit claim is false. Once again, the employer has acquired his capital from his past savings, justly acquired, and he can do with it what he pleases. There is nothing which belongs to society which has been leased out to the employer.

Another illegitimate claim is that the economic power wielded by employers and corporations is coercive, as it forces the weak to give in because of necessity to the demands of the strong. But this is to mistake the *actual options* open to the weaker party for their *hopes* for a better deal. The first is part of the set of feasible actions they can take, based on the offer made by the strong, which does not infringe the rules of justice that permit the owner to dispose freely of his endowment as long as he does not violate the constraints of harm and obligation. The hope depends upon what turns out to be a false expectation. To use the coercive power of the state to enforce this hope of the weak would be to violate the strong party's liberty to use their endowments as they wish. It would be unjust.

Similarly, any other state coercion to take a person's justly acquired property and to give it to anyone else would also be ruled out in a state seen as a classical liberal civil association, unless all citizens approve of it by a vote. This would rule out redistributive taxes as being unjust. Would it also rule out public transfers to the destitute? Most societies have made provision for the destitute, those incapable of making any living. This social safety net has been provided usually through private transfers from other family members or public charity. With the disintegration of extended families in the West, because of the various processes discussed earlier about the course of individualism, these private social safety nets have become frayed. Public charity remains the only alternative; whether it should be voluntary or coercive will depend on particular circumstances. But unless the coercive power is voluntarily and unanimously given by free agents to the state, its exercise would be unjust. However, where private charity can be no longer be relied on to alleviate destitution, such near unanimity of agreement for some form of public transfers may be forthcoming.[29]

CONCLUSIONS

The major difference between the first liberal international economic order (LIEO) established under British leadership in the nineteenth century and the contemporary LIEO fostered under the U.S. imperium is that while the former embodied the classical liberal view of the state—viz, it did not seek to legislate morality—the latter is infected by the enterprise view in both its domestfic concerns for social welfare and its desire to export Western values such as human rights and democracy to the rest of the world. But the notion of human rights is, as Jeremy Bentham rightly observed, "nonsense on stilts."[30] A state seen as a civil association will seek to uphold its citizen's liberty to undertake feasible actions which are constrained only by avoiding harm to others and meeting one's obligations. Rights arise as the other side of a voluntary agreement between two parties, whereby one party willingly takes on obligations to the other party who thus acquires rights. This notion of justice and the associated notion of liberty (rather than the confused notion of freedom) underlies the English Common Law tradition. Rights-talk is based on the alternative Continental public law tradition in which justice requires agents to get permission to undertake feasible actions. As the set of possible feasible actions is infinite, this leads in these rights-based systems to endless legal disputes about what is or is not permitted. By contrast, in the Common Law tradition, as the list of prohibited actions is limited to those causing harm and to keeping one's obligations voluntarily arrived at, there is less room for dispute about the actions individuals are allowed. People are at liberty to do anything which is not prohibited by the two constraints on their liberties.

I have also argued that with the end of "really existing socialism," those still infected with the collectivist virus underlying the enterprise view of the state have shifted their focus from destroying capitalism to providing it with a "human face." The arguments for stakeholder capitalism and corporate social responsibility have been shown to be wanting. This desire by many current critics of globalization to use the state to legislate their preferred ethics is antithetical to the Western classical liberal tradition. These socialist impulses are atavistic. The state should—as it can if it chooses—restrict itself to providing the public goods which are an essential part of the infrastructure for efficient globalization and to upholding its citizens' liberty to undertake any feasible action which does not do anyone else any harm and which does not renege on obligations. All other aspects of morality are best left to the family and other institutions of a civil society.

CHAPTER 8

Nationalism and Democracy

Surveying the world at the onset of the new millennium, Michael Mandelbaum wrote, "The liberal Wilsonian triad—peace, democracy, and free markets—had attained the same status as literacy: widespread although not universal, dominant and unchallenged."[1] As the title of his book proclaims, these are *The Ideas That Conquered the World*. Have they? I have argued that far from the Wilsonian fantasy of collective security maintaining the peace, it was the Pax Americana created after the Second World War as a successor to the nineteenth-century Pax Britannica that first saw off the rival communist empire and is now the only feasible guarantor of global peace. Nor despite appearances has the free market triumphed. A form of the enterprise view of the state means that the laissez faire and free trade espoused and practiced by the British in the nineteenth century is nowhere in place. There has, of course, been a worldwide movement away from the planned to the market economy with the collapse of the countries of "really existing socialism," but this is a market heavily regulated and heavily taxed for various reasons, incorporating the egalitarian streak of the enterprise view of the state. But perhaps democracy has won the day, and we are at the dawn of the democratic peace that liberals since Kant have dreamed of? And even if it has not, do we need to promote democracy among the recalcitrant to ensure not only peace but also prosperity? Should the U.S.'s imperial power be used, as many in the current administration and its latest National Security Policy document desire, to bring democracy to the world? And what of national-ism? Can a Pax Americana be reconciled with the nationalist demon which President Woodrow Wilson legitimized when he ushered in the Age of Nations? These are the questions I will examine in this chapter.

NATIONALISM

There is a missing guest at Mandelbaum's feast of ideas that have conquered the world: nationalism. This is strange for two reasons. First, because it was the Wilsonian proclamation of the end of the Age of Empires and the dawn of the Age of Nations which so electrified the world at the end of the First World War. Second, whereas it is arguable whether collective security, free markets, and democracy have conquered the world, there is no doubt that, as the historian of ideas Isaiah Berlin has observed, "There was one movement which dominated much of the nineteenth century in Europe and was so perva-sive, so familiar, that it is only by a conscious effort of the imagination that one can conceive a world in which it played no part. . . . [B]ut, oddly enough no significant thinkers known to me predicted for it a future in which it would play an even more dominant role. Yet it would, perhaps, be no overstatement to say that it is one of the most powerful, in some regions the most powerful, single movement at work in the world today. . . . This movement is national-ism."[2] It is a European idea of the last 200 years. How did it arise?

Nationalism arose as a political doctrine in Europe at the beginning of the nineteenth century.[3] The doctrine holds that humanity is naturally divided into nations defined by distinctive cultures, and that the only type of government which is legitimate is national self-government.[4] Nationalism is different from both patriotism and xenophobia.[5] Nationalism divides human-ity into different primordial entities: nations. Language, race, culture, and religion constitute their different aspects. According to Eli Kedourie, nation-alism "claims that such nations must constitute sovereign states, and asserts that the members of a nation reach freedom and fulfilment by cultivating the peculiar identity of their own nation by sinking their own persons in the greater whole of the nation."[6] This is different from a loyalty to particular political institutions, as say in Britain and the United States.[7] Nor is national-ism a form of tribalism.[8]

However, it is important to note that Woodrow Wilson's notion of self-determination which launched the Age of Nations was based on a misconception of the difference between what Lord Acton in his essay "Nationality"[9] called the Continental and the Whig notions of nationality. The Whig notion, which goes back to Locke and which the Americans inher-ited, looks to representative government as the best guarantee of freedom.

John Stuart Mill, however, muddied the waters by his statement in his *Representative Government*: "It is, in general, a necessary condition of free institutions that the boundaries of government should coincide with those of nationalities."[10] But by nationality, Mill and the Whig tradition he represented did not mean the nation as defined by nationalists.[11] The Whig tradition was primarily concerned with individual liberty.[12] This is a very different notion of nationality from the Continental one based on that of a primordial nation defined by race or culture.

When Wilson, versed in this Anglo-American Whig tradition of nationality, went to Versailles, he thought that the various claimants to statehood believed in the same things as his revolutionary forefathers. But they did not, Kedourie says. "The Englishmen and Americans were saying, People who are self-governing are likely to be governed well, therefore we are in favor of self-determination; whereas their interlocutors were saying, People who live in their own national states are the only free people, therefore we claim self-determination. The distinction is a fine one, but its implications are far-reaching. . . . [I]n the confusion of the peace conference liberty was mistaken for the twin of nationality."[13] Thus was the virus of nationalism spread, which gave predatory nationalist elites the power to unleash the disorder caused by their self-aggrandizement in many parts of the Third World with the end of the Age of Empire.

The ex-colonial, new nation-states of Africa and Asia did not, however, follow the practice of "vernacular nationalists" in basing their nationhood on a particular territory within which a particular language was spoken. This was in large part because these Third World nationalists inherited states which had been created by imperial powers whose territorial borders were determined as much by realpolitik and the fortunes of war as by any coherence in terms of ethnic or linguistic homogeneity. These artificial boundaries were deemed to be sacrosanct by the succeeding nationalist elites, who then faced the problem the Austro-Hungarian empire faced during its period of official nationalism: what official language should it adopt? If the language of one group in a multilingual state is adopted as the official language, that immediately puts its speakers at an advantage and will be fiercely resisted by other groups. To allay these discords, like the Austro-Hungarians, the colonial nationalists have kept the old imperial lingua franca as the official language.

But they then face the problem of forging a sense of nationhood out of their multilingual polyglot inheritance—a problem similarly faced by the absolute rulers of Renaissance Europe. Like these European predecessors, Third World nationalist elites also adopted nationalism and dirigisme to modernize. This has proved to be a double-edged sword, for unlike the

German, Italian, and to some extent Slav nationalists whose task was to create a state for a preexisting cultural and political nation, most African and
some Asian nationalists inherited and cherished states created by colonial-
ists, within which they have since sought to create a modern nation.

The process of economic development, which all the Third World elites
seek to foster, involves profound changes over time in existing patterns of
income distribution and hence in the status hierarchy. This is to be thought of
not merely in the statistical sense but in terms of what happens to the
incomes (and status) of particular households over time. Even without any
marked change in the statistical measure of this distribution, economic
growth is likely to lead to a considerable and often rapid shuffling of the relative economic position and prospects of particular individuals and households. In a genuine nation-state, the ensuing resentment of the losers may be
mitigated by the solace they may find in the accompanying national gains.
The resentment is, therefore, unlikely to turn into the deadly conflicts to be
found in the pseudo-nation-states of the South, with their ancient and still
pervasive cleavages of race, religion, or tribe, where the shufflings can be so
easily identified as the humiliation of one subnationality by another. The
nationalist rhetoric of the political elite can then rebound (as it has done
quite often in the recent past) into demands to dismember the territorial state,
whose preservation was the prime end for which nationalism was conjured
up in the first place.[14]

Not surprisingly, therefore, it is in the relatively culturally homogeneous polities of East Asia that nationalism has performed the integrative
emotional and economic function it did in the West. In the more fragile and
pluralistic polities of Southeast Asia, South Asia, and Africa, by contrast,
nationalist rhetoric to gain independence from colonialism has created as
many problems of national integration as it was hoped it would solve.

After the post–Second World War wave of decolonization, these new
nation-states of the Third World found themselves caught in the vortex of the
Cold War, in which two land-based empires, those of the United States and
of the USSR and their respective allies, sought to woo or suborn these new-
born states. Many resisted by forming the grouping of nonaligned states,
which successfully played off the two behemoths for favors. With the collapse of the Soviet empire, its inhabitants suffered the same fate as those
at the demise of earlier empires. The lid which empires successfully place
on ethnic and cultural divisions was lifted, with ensuing disorder in the
name of various local nationalisms. The two remaining, major land-based
imperial states are China and India. Their imperialism is the direct type, with
China's being the homogenizing kind, India's, the multiethnic variety, as
discussed in chapter 1. Both face threats of subnational nationalisms

threatening the territorial integrity of their states, but their robust response has ensured that at least for the foreseeable future their empires will remain intact.

What of the new American imperium? Can indirect imperialism maintain a lid on the various divisions which still threaten disorder in so many failing or failed and rogue states, or will it have to resort to direct imperialism? From the recent outcomes in Bosnia, Kosovo, Afghanistan, and Iraq, it appears that, *faute de mieux*, a coalition of the willing of secondary powers led by the United States is maintaining direct control over these areas. But for how long will there be the will to continue doing this? The biggest danger comes not from serious threats of direct revolts against alien rule, but from the people of the occupying countries, especially in the United States. The continuing denial that it is an empire along with the moral resonance of the Wilsonian case against empires and in favor of nation-states are likely to erode the domestic bases of support over time. But is the moral case against empires and in favor of nation-states valid?

In the late 1960s I was a junior research fellow at Nuffield College, Oxford. A very distinguished political philosopher, John Plamenatz, was a fellow of the college. In 1960 he had published a small book *On Alien Rule and Self Government*.[15] This was the time when prime minister Harold Macmillan's famous winds of change were set to blow through Africa, and the British were to finally relinquish the empire they no longer had the will or means to maintain. In his book Plamenatz looked dispassionately, from a mainly utilitarian point of view, at the arguments for and against continued European rule over subject peoples. The balance sheet was mixed and depended largely upon the view one took of the capacity for self-government of the subject people. This capacity in large part depended on the experience they had gained during the colonial period in those arts of government which are required for modernization and which were pioneered in the West. He clearly saw the danger of handing the power over people—to whom the imperial powers had a moral responsibility of care—to predatory elites, particularly those who claimed the colonial inheritance on the basis of European ideals of national self-determination. Reading it today, after nearly a half century of the results of handing over power to predatory nationalist elites, one can only be impressed by Plamenatz's prescience. But he was reviled at the time and denounced as a racist or worse. Even though in his book and his remonstrances against his critics Plamenatz emphasized that he was only a naturalized Briton who had come to the UK from a backward country—Yugoslavia—albeit a prince. On purely utilitarian grounds, are the ordinary people in vast swaths of Africa, Asia, and the Middle East more free and prosperous today than under their colonial masters?

The major charge Plamenatz laid against the European imperialists was that of racism. It was the resulting damage to the self-respect of local elites which led to the revolts that undermined the European empires. He rightly contrasted this with the Romans who, instead of assimilating with the natives which would have cut them off from the imperial metropole, or keeping themselves aloof from the natives which would have underlined their alien status, created a truly cosmopolitan imperial elite. "They mixed with the powerful and wealthy among the natives to form a cosmopolitan class sharing a single Graeco-Roman culture. They did it without detaching the members of this class from the countries of their birth; it was not only possible, it was easy and natural, to have a double loyalty."[16] The United States, as I argued in chapter 3, has the same opportunity; if it behaves like the Romans, its imperium is less likely to be threatened by nationalist revolts.

DEMOCRACY

If nationalism is not a universal belief and on the basis of classical liberal ideals is to be eschewed, while empires are the best means for saving us from the disorder caused by nationalists, what of the related ideal of representative government which liberals have seen as the best means for preserving liberty? One of the proclaimed aims of U.S. foreign policy is to promote democracy around the world in the belief that its spread through the use of American power will lead to the democratic peace envisaged by many liberals. Democracy is also being touted as the best way to ensure prosperity, as it is argued that it promotes the good governance required for economic development. Promoting freedom is seen to be the desirable aim of the American imperium.

In examining whether this is feasible and not merely desirable, we need to make a crucial distinction between political, civil, and economic liberty (freedom). It is now a commonplace that economic liberty as embodied in the market is a necessary condition for development.[17] Similarly, civil liberty as embodied in the English Common Law with its impartial enforcement of contracts is also required for development. These two freedoms are better described as we saw in the last chapter as the general liberty to undertake any *feasible* action which does not harm others or break any obligations. But is political liberty as entailed by democracy also necessary to promote and sustain economic and civil liberties?[18]

Democracy and Liberty

The constitutional liberalism which arose in Britain and was adopted by America sought above all to protect civil and religious liberties.

Representative democracy arose along with the growth of constitutional liberalism. This meant that in these countries there were not only free and fair elections but also the rule of law and the protection of the liberties of free speech, assembly, religion, and property—the civil and economic liberties discussed in the last chapter. But while in the rise of the West this liberalism (which was the end) and representative democracy (a particular means) were conjoined, they need not be.

For even if there are free and fair elections—which is the *sine qua non* of democracy—the result may turn out to be *illiberal democracy*[19] in which the majority, instead of upholding these liberal civil and economic liberties, suppresses them. In many Muslim countries the autocrats are more liberal than the mass of the people, and if the majority had their way they would undoubtedly suppress even the liberties currently granted by the autocrats. The attraction of democracy is supposedly that it prevents the corruption of absolute power in autocracies such as those decried by Lord Acton. But, as attested to by the example of the innumerable autocrats who have been elected in many Third World nations and the successor states to the Soviet empire, this hope may not be fulfilled. Though the elections through which they gained power were not always as free and fair as in the West, by and large they still represented the popular will. Ever since the rise of Hitler and Mussolini through the ballot box, theorists of democracy have been haunted by the fear that popular participation may be exploited by demagogues playing to the irrational impulses of the masses.[20] Thus democracy and liberty are not coterminous.[21] While for classical liberals civil and economic liberties are the ultimate moral good, comprising the content of good governance, they are not necessarily served by one form of government, representative democracy. The fathers of the Scottish Enlightenment and the American Founders were well aware of this possible conflict between liberty and democracy.[22]

Democracy and Peace

What of the claim that democracy is needed to maintain the peace? Statistical evidence is purported to show that modern democracies never fight each other. This does not, however, show that democracies are more pacific. In fact, they have gone to war more often and with greater ferocity than other states. This is contrary to the belief of Immanuel Kant, the original proponent of the theory of the democratic peace. He argued that because in democracies the public who pays for war also makes the decision of going to war, they would be cautious and more pacific than nondemocratic states. They clearly are not. Furthermore, the purported statistical evidence is questionable. There have been only a small number of both democracies and wars over the last two hundred years, so one can have little confidence in the correlation. As one critic has pointed out, "no member of his family has ever won the lottery, yet few offer explanations for this impressive correlation."[23]

Moreover, there is no justification for the claim that unfettered democratic majoritarianism necessarily leads to peace. Michael Doyle observes, "Many participatory polities have been non-liberal. For two thousand years before the modern age, popular rule was widely associated with aggressiveness (by Thucydides) or imperial success (by Machiavelli). The decisive preference of [the] median voter might well include 'ethnic cleansing' against other democratic polities."[24]

The statistical evidence, for what it is worth, shows that while mature democracies do not fight each other, previous autocracies that are democratizing are more prone to go to war,[25] because, from both the historical and contemporary record, nationalism and democratization tend to go together, and the inflaming of nationalist passions usually leads to war and ethnic cleansing. Examples include France under Napoleon III, Wilhelmine Germany, Taisho Japan, and more recently Chechnya, Armenia, Azerbaijan, and the former Yugoslavia. I do not therefore find the oft-cited claim by international relations theorists, that democracy is needed to maintain the peace, persuasive.

Democracy and Prosperity[26]

Nor is there any necessary connection between democracy and prosperity. The historical evidence does not support any necessary connection between a particular form of government and the promotion of prosperity. In the postwar period one only has to consider the Far Eastern "Gang of Four" (Taiwan, Korea, Hong Kong, Singapore), or the more successful economies in Latin America—Chile, Mexico, and until the 1980s Brazil—to realize, as the former Prime Minister of Singapore Lee Kwan Yew has been proclaiming from the housetops, that there is no causal relationship between democracy and development.[27] Even in the rocky transition from the plan to the market, as the contrasting experiences of Russia and China show, *glasnost* may not help *perestroika*! This does not mean that authoritarianism or military autocracies are necessarily good for development either. The essential point is that various types of government, as long as they maintain the essentials of a market order, can promote development.

Statistical Evidence. However a number of cross-sectional statistical studies claim to have found a relationship between democracy and development.[28] But the statistical proxies used for the political variables in these studies do not inspire much confidence and are further plagued by the econometric problem of identification. In our 1996 book Hla Myint and I found no relationship between the form of government and economic performance during the 30-year economic histories of the 25 developing countries that we studied. Rather than the polity, the initial resource endowment, in particular the availability or lack of natural resources, was a major determinant of policies which impinged on the efficiency of investment and thereby the rate of growth. This was basically due to the inevitable politicization of the rents that natural resources yield, with concomitant damage to growth performance. By contrast, resource-poor countries, irrespective of the nature of their government, were forced to develop their only resource, their human subjects. Thus, the economic performance of resource-poor countries such as the Far Eastern Gang of Four tended to be much better on average than that of those with abundant natural resources such as Brazil and Mexico. Countries such as India and China whose factor endowments fall in between these extremes swerved between following the policies of their resource-abundant and resource-poor cousins, with a resultant indifferent intermediate economic performance. The difference in performance was further explained by the other major determinant of growth—the volume of investment. Thus while the efficiency of investment in India and China during both their dirigiste and more economically liberal periods was about the same, China's investment rate has been about twice India's, resulting in its growth rate also being twice as high. This might be taken as providing some support for the view that democracies will tend to have shorter-term horizons and hence discount the future more heavily (thereby saving less) than autocracies. But considering dictators such as Mobutu of Zaire or Marcos of the Philippines, it would be difficult to sustain this view.

Pressure Groups. By their very nature, democracies are plagued by pressure groups. An influential strand of American political sociology has argued that free competition among pressure groups leads, through a process similar to Adam Smith's "invisible hand," to subserving the general welfare, even though each group is only promoting its own particular interest. Perfect competition among interest groups, with the state acting as an umpire, is thus the political analogue of the perfect competition paradigm of the economist. As in the economic model with free entry and exit, the size of the associations would not necessarily pose a problem, because any untoward pressure by one group would call forth pressure by a countervailing group, if necessary one newly created for this purpose.

This benign view of pressure groups has been questioned by Mancur Olson.[29] Instead of assuming that all interests can be organized with equal facility, he asks the question, basic for an economist: what are the costs and benefits for individuals to join various interest groups?

Unlike the rather vague objectives assigned to participation in pressure group activity by political sociologists, Olson rightly looks upon these groups at least in the economic sphere as engaging in attempts to use the political process to obtain special economic benefits for their members. These benefits can in general be described as "subsidies"; pressure group politics is thus of necessity redistributive economics. Olson argued that small concentrated interest groups are more likely to form and succeed in their aim of influencing the democratic political process to their ends than larger, more diffused groups, for the payoff from any given "benefit" acquired through the political process for any individual member of a pressure group diminishes with the size of the group. Also, the larger the group, the more difficult it becomes for it to coalesce to subserve its aims because of the ubiquitousness of the free-rider problem in organizing collective action. A member who will gain from the collective benefit, even if he does not participate in its acquisition, will attempt to shirk bearing his share of the costs of the collective action if he can get away with it. An example of the relevance of Olson's theory is the stylized fact that in developing countries with a preponderance of farmers, agriculture is taxed for the benefit of urban consumers, while in developed countries it is subsidized at the cost of a much larger number of urban consumers.

Those larger pressure groups which do form and are effective, such as trade unions, attract members, according to Olson, by offering "selective benefits," not collective benefits. Thus, members may have to join trade unions if union membership is a condition for obtaining a particular job. But this is likely to leave the common interests of many large groups unorganized. As Olson concludes: "Only when groups are small, or when they are fortunate enough to have an independent source of selective incentives, will they organize or act to achieve their objectives. . . . But the large unorganized groups [with common interests] not only provide evidence for the basic argument of this study: they also suffer if it is true." Thus, far from being the benign social equilibrium of the political sociologists, for the economist, a pressure group equilibrium may not serve the commonweal.[30]

Mass Participation. Much worse, with the role that parties and party allegiance play in mobilizing a largely ignorant and apathetic mass electorate, in a competitive struggle for the peoples' vote which Joseph Schumpeter[31] identified as the most distinctive feature of democracy, democratic politics ends up as predatory politics, where the predator is the median voter. As Anthony Downs[32] has argued, politics is above all a redistributive game and no more so than in a democracy. In this game, it is not the welfare and moral arguments for redistribution discussed in the last chapter which are decisive but the interests of the median voter. Thus, if voters can be ranked along a single dimension (usually defined as the left–right spectrum), have single-peaked preferences, and there are only two political parties, then in a majoritarian democracy both parties will have an interest in converging on programs that appeal to the median voter. Assuming that all voters vote their economic interests, both parties will adopt programs which implicitly or explicitly redistribute income from both the rich and poor to the middle classes—the median voters. This middle-class capture of government transfers has been observed in majoritarian democracies in both rich and poor countries.[33] These transfer states necessarily involve deadweight efficiency costs associated with the transfers, which are not counterbalanced by any corresponding gains in reducing poverty (a possibly legitimate aim for state action, as argued in the last chapter) or increasing equality.

Despite these reasons for doubting whether democracy necessarily serves the ends of either liberty or prosperity, there is one virtue it does possess above other forms of government. It does allow the people to evict the incumbents. But even if desirable, is it feasible?

THE CULTURAL ROOTS OF GOVERNMENT FORMS

During the process of postwar decolonization, Sir Ivor Jennings went around parts of the former British Empire writing model democratic constitutions for the successor states. These were soon torn up or modified to kill their liberal spirit by many of the succeeding autocrats. For as Anthony de Jasay has quipped, a constitution is like a chastity belt whose key is left within reach, whereupon nature will take its course.[34] By contrast, India, one of the largest and poorest countries, has succeeded in maintaining a liberal democracy by and large for 50 years since its independence.

China and India

This success needs an explanation. It is to be found in the political habits of different cultures which have been formed as much by the geography of the territory where the relevant culture was formed as by any ideology.[35] For example, China, with its origins in the relatively compact Yellow River valley, constantly threatened by the nomadic barbarians from the steppes to its north, developed a tightly controlled bureaucratic authoritarianism as its distinctive polity which has continued for millennia to our day.

By contrast, Hindu civilization developed in the vast Indo-Gangetic plain, protected to a greater extent by the Himalayas from the predation of barbarians to the north. This geographical feature (together with the need to tie down the then-scarce labor to land) accounts for the traditional Indian polity which was notable for its endemic political instability among numerous feuding monarchies and its distinctive social system embodied in the institution of caste. The caste system, by making war the trade of professionals,

saved the mass of the population from being inducted into the deadly disputes of its changing rulers, while the tradition of paying a certain customary
share of the village output as revenue to the current overlord meant that any
victor had little incentive to disturb the daily business of its newly acquired
subjects. The democratic practices gradually introduced by the British have
fit these ancient habits like a glove. The ballot box has replaced the battlefield
for the hurly-burly of continuing aristocratic conflict, while the populace
accepts with a weary resignation that its rulers will, through various forms of
rent-seeking, take a certain share of output to feather their own nests.

The Americas

Both northern and Latin America shared similar resource endowments: an
abundance of land and scarcity of labor.[36] But very different polities and
societies developed in part because of the differing ecologies and religious
cosmologies of the two sets of Europeans who colonized the continent—the
English Puritans in the north, the Catholic Iberians in the south.

In the continental United States (except for its South), grains were the
most suitable crops for cultivation. As there were no economies of scale in
their production, the small family farm was suitable for their cultivation. It
was the gradual westward spread of the family farm which tamed the land-
abundant U.S. With no landlord class to support and protected by two vast
oceans from the need for a warrior class to fend off nomadic predators from
its borders, a unique egalitarian and democratic polity could develop.

By contrast, in the tropical areas of the Americas (including the southern states of the U.S.) the ecology favored the development of plantation
crops such as sugar and cotton which have increasing returns to scale. The
same is true to a lesser extent of tobacco and coffee.[37] Where climatic conditions in the Americas were suitable for cultivating tropical crops, the use of
coerced labor had enormous cost advantages over free labor, which led to
great social and economic differentiation in society with large inequalities of
income and wealth.

That these factor endowments (including the climate) rather than the cultural differences between the Protestant North and Catholic South were
responsible for the development of these different types of societies in the
Americas is illustrated by the case of the Puritan colony of Providence Island,
which developed the Caribbean and Latin American pattern of land ownership
and settlement rather than the North American one of its co-religionists.[38]

Cultural differences were vital, however, in the different polities that
were established in the areas of Iberian and Anglo-Saxon colonization.
Morse (1964) argues that Spain after the reconquest (from the Moors) was a

patrimonial state in which feudalism never developed fully. It was a centralizing state without the decentralization of rights of the manorial system. The patrimonial rather than feudal states that Latin America inherited were further distinguished by their Catholic lineage. In the Protestant colonies—as Luther succinctly expressed in his "Open Letter to the Christian Nobility"— the duty of Christians who found themselves in a land populated by pagans was not to convert the pagans but to elect their own religious leaders and to tame or exterminate the American Indians. There was no notion of saving one's neighbor in the Calvinist ethic, as for Calvinists only divine grace, not human action, can save man. So they felt no evangelizing mission.[39] By contrast, evangelism was the public justification given for the conquest and for the Spanish and Portuguese domination of Latin America. New Spain, even more than its parent state, adopted the neo-Thomism developed by Francisco Suarez and his disciples as part of the Catholic Church's revitalization during the Counter Reformation.[40] Its economic correlate was corporatism.

This Latin political and economic system was par excellence an enterprise association in Michael Oakeshott's sense. By contrast, the Protestant colonies were relatively indifferent to religious orthodoxy. In the previously cited "Open Letter," Luther maintained that, in the colonies, if a group of Christians had no priest or bishop amongst them they should elect one of themselves as a priest, and this election would not only legitimize their authority but also consecrate it. As Octavio Paz notes "nothing similar exists in all of Catholic tradition."[41]

Thus, in the Protestant North America a pluralist society developed with the view that, Richard Morse writes, "the world is composed not of one highly differentiated society for which certain common forms, acts, and ceremonies are a needed binding force, but of a multitude of unrelated societies, each of them a congregation of similar persons which in finite time and place and ordered by the declarative terms of a compact rather than by common symbolic observances."[42] This allowed the notion of the state as a civil association in Oakeshott's terms to develop, with the state as the umpire between many competing interests. This difference in cosmological beliefs explains the observation by political scientists that, as Gary Wynia writes, "politically, North Americans confine their feuds primarily to selecting officials and debating public policies, but in Latin America feuds are more fundamental . . . democrats, authoritarians, and communists . . . all insist they know what is best for themselves and their neighbors."[43] This "universalism" of the neo-Thomist tradition was further strengthened by the attempt of the Jesuits in Latin America (and in other parts of the world) to promote a religious syncretism which would lead to a "unification of diverse civilizations and cultures . . . under the sign of Rome."[44]

This fundamentalist universalism also provides, in my view, an explanation for the continent-wide swings in political and economic fashions over the last two hundred years.[45] In the postwar era, the pronouncements of the Economic Commission of Latin America (ECLA) have been accorded the status of gospel truth. When it advocated dirigisme, that became the policy for most of Latin America; when it finally endorsed economic liberalism in the early 1990s, that became the new gospel. More than in other parts of the world, a universalist ideology matters in Latin America. Therefore, instead of searching as political economists do in other Western societies for the changing equilibrium of interest groups, in Latin America one needs to explain how these intellectual swings of fashion take place, as they are rather like religious conversions—Carlos Menem in Argentina and Henrique Cardoso in Brazil being outstanding examples.

This penchant for universalist ideological beliefs has also meant that there is a continuing dissonance between the Latin American social reality of the extreme inequalities which are the result of its ecological and political heritage and its Christian cosmological beliefs emphasizing equality (which it, of course, shares with the north). There is no such northern dissonance as for both ecological and political reasons a uniquely egalitarian social and political society developed there.

With the rise of demos, the common people, those societies infected by egalitarianism have a greater propensity for the populism which damages economic performance than hierarchical societies. If, as in Europe, the granting of democratic rights can be phased in with the growing economic and social equality that modern growth helps to promote, then the political effects of the dissonance between an unequal social reality and egalitarian cosmological beliefs can be avoided. In the colonial and nineteenth-century patrimonial states of Latin America, this dissonance was avoided by restricting the polity, in effect, to the property-owning classes. But if, as in this century, while still in the early stages of modern growth, the polity is expanded by incorporating the "dangerous classes" through an extension of democratic rights to the whole populace, then this dissonance can, as it has, lead to political cycles of democratic populism followed by authoritarian repression as the distributional consequences of the populist phase are found unacceptable by the upper classes. By contrast, hierarchical societies can more easily maintain majoritarian democracies, however corrupt and economically inefficient—as the notable example of India shows—despite continuing social and economic inequalities. Thus, as many Latin American commentators[46] have noted, the historic and continuing inequalities of Latin America make democracy insecure, largely—I would argue—because of the dissonance between society and cosmology noted above.

Muslim Societies[47]

There is nothing in its cosmological views which would make Islam incompatible with democracy. But despotism and a disjunction between state and society have been characteristic features of Muslim society since its meteoric rise which smashed the world of antiquity. The reasons for this go back to the origins of Islam. The first problem arose after Mohammed's death in A.D. 632; it concerned political legitimacy, an issue which has subsequently haunted Muslim society and states. The Prophet's decisions while he was alive could be assumed to reflect the will of Allah, so disobedience was tantamount to impiety. But without the prophet's link with God, how could divine guidance of the community be maintained?[48] This led to the split with the Shia's who claimed that the Ummayad caliphate which succeeded Mohammed had usurped power by armed force and perpetuated a hereditary principle supported neither by piety nor tribal custom.[49] The Shia's favored the descendants of Ali, Mohammed's son-in-law. The majority Sunnis came to accept a compromise devised in the Abbasid caliphate which had replaced the Ummayads, again through bloodshed. This too, in the eyes of true believers, was an usurpation. However, through the Abbasid compromise the *ulmma* (a body of religious scholars) became the true heirs of the Prophet, by expounding the sacred law and applying it to particular cases.[50]

It might have been expected that the outcome of these constitutional crises in the early years of the Islamic empire would be a rejection of absolute rule for some form of consultative government.[51] But this was unlikely. Because of the scale of the Arab conquests, the territory could not have been held together without an imperial polity. The polity which emerged was, moreover, one in which the unruly tribal conquerors had to be constantly repressed to maintain order. While being dependent on state handouts for their income,[52] the tribal nobility was unlikely to have much leverage over the caliph. The distribution of public revenues among those entitled to a share became the locus of disputes, not the allocation of the tax burden among those obliged to pay.[53] The leverage exercised by medieval barons against the impoverished sovereigns of Western Europe, which eventually led to these monarchs ceding fiscal and later legislative control to various forms of popular assemblies, was not available to the Arab nobility. Thus, despotism would seem to have been unavoidable in the new Islamic polity, however much it went against the religion Mohammed had founded.

The unique aspect of Islamic polities which allowed long periods of political stability in the millennium since its birth was the induction of slaves as instruments of government. These mamelukes came to form an essential part of the conquest society that Arab arms had created, for it was a conquest society where the conquerors clung to their tribal past. Physically separated from their subjects in the equivalent of modern-day military cantonments, the initial Arab conquerors were faced with the problem of administering and maintaining their new-found empire. The caliphs and sultans who ruled the Islamic state were unable to rely on their tribal clansmen, both because of their limited numbers and their lack of aptitude for civilian pursuits. From the beginning of the Arab empire, Islamic rulers turned to an alternative solution to provide themselves with a loyal and trustworthy military and administrative apparatus. It consisted of slaves.

Islam had household slaves but, except for the "plantation economy" in the marshes of southern Iraq created under the Abbasids, it had no tradition of slave labor in production, with its correspondingly lowly social status. From its earliest conquests Islam had acquired slaves by capture. Many of them were converted, manumitted, and placed in military and administrative positions. This had a number of benefits for the rulers. These manumitted slaves were normally aliens who were completely dependent on their master. The ruler would bring up his foreign slaves as his children, and they existed in the Muslim polity only through him.[54]

Unlike the feudal soldiers of Europe, who were not aliens but members of their own polity, home-born mamelukes who could have acquired a political commitment to Islam were excluded from the army. This mameluke institution spread throughout the Islamic world. The crack troops of settled rulers from the mid-ninth century into modern times consisted of slaves.

But these servile armies needed to be controlled, as an uncontrolled mameluke army could lead to the total disintegration of the state.[55] This happened frequently in Islamic history. The great exception were the Ottomans, who in the Islamic tradition relied on the *dervishme*[56] for their administration and armies. The Ottoman sultans managed to maintain control of the state for a considerable period because of their personal qualities, which were tested in fratricidal wars for succession to be master of the Porte, and which were in the nature of a Darwinian contest for the survival of the fittest. When this system was replaced for humanitarian reasons by the system of the "Cage,"[57] the quality of the sultans deteriorated, and was partly responsible for the Ottoman decline.

Ibn Khaldun[58] praised the mameluke institution as God's gift to save Islam, as he saw them as institutionalized tribal conquerors. As we have seen in chapter 3, the Islamic polity thus never accepted the notion of settled rule,[59] which Ibn Khaldun considered effeminate. This has been the "black hole" of the Islamic polity from its inception. It has retained the lineaments of a conquest society.[60]

The only Muslim society which has been able to escape from this despotic heritage is Turkey. But even there, the democracy which was instituted has till today been supervised by the army, which has in effect vetoed popular Islamist initiatives. In Pakistan, democratic regimes have been toppled by the military which has proved to be less corrupt than the democrats it replaced.

CONCLUSION

Liberal democracy is likely to be a frail flower in much of the world, as it is unlikely to fit the political habits of many cultures. But does this matter? For prosperity, the most important features of a government are civil and economic liberties, or what can be called economic freedom. Unlike political freedom whose value is likely to be determined by the *cosmological* beliefs of different cultures, the value of economic freedom depends on the *material* beliefs of a civilization. With the gradual spread of globalization around the world, and the increasing recognition that economic freedom brings prosperity, many politically illiberal societies are nevertheless gradually changing their material beliefs and introducing economic liberty. The Fraser Institute's Economic Freedom Index shows that since 1980 economic freedom has been rising around the world and has accelerated since the 1990s.[61] Many of the countries or regions where economic freedom is secure are not those which have political freedom. Thus, Hong Kong which tops the list has economic but not political freedom.

Moreover, as the process of globalization spreads, many countries—most notably China—are gradually introducing economic freedom, whose components measured by the index of personal choice, voluntary exchange, freedom to compete, and protection of person and property are precisely the classical liberal liberties which, as argued in chapter 7, define freedom in its most elemental sense. Promoting democracy is not necessary for this extension of liberty. With its accession to the World Trade Organization, China is having to give up many of its illiberal policies—for instance, by changing its legal system to enforce contracts. Thus, in time, even though China is unlikely to become a democracy, it will under the impetus of globalization have to establish many of the institutions of a market economy which ensure the civil and economic liberties comprising economic freedom.

Similarly, in the Islamic world, even though democracy is unlikely to flourish, there is no reason why Muslim countries should not be able to establish economic liberty. Even though it is an autocracy the United Arab Emirates has an economic freedom index which places it number 16 in the rankings, above Belgium, Germany, Japan, and Sweden.[62] Thus, the United States through its imperium should be promoting globalization which will lead to economic freedom. The promotion of the Wilsonian ideals of national self-determination and democracy will not necessarily aid this spread of the liberties that really matter, for it could lead to a backlash as cultural nationalists come to identify globalization with an attack on their cosmological beliefs, and erroneously come to believe that modernizing is going to lead them to lose their souls.

CHAPTER 9

Toward an International Moral Order?

In the early stages of the war in Afghanistan, it was reported that an American military aircraft had the leader of the Taliban, Mullah Omar, in its sight. But before it could fire, clearance had to be obtained from a military lawyer based in Florida, who recommended that it should desist. Mullah Omar has not been captured to date. This must have been the first time in military history that lawyers had the final say on a military operation. It would seem the world is now in an international moral order supervised by lawyers. How has this come to pass?

There are two very different groups who are arguing that an international moral order either already exists or should be created. The first are various international lawyers, activists of NGOs, and officials of UN agencies. They are imbued with the spirit of global salvationism: they seek to bring peace through justice by expanding the role of international law from a body of rules derived from the explicit or implicit obligations of states in an interstate system to one based on the purported human rights of individuals in the world community. The purpose of this "political moralism"[1] is to replace the nationally sovereign state with an emerging international moral order. This order, it is claimed, is emerging spontaneously.

The other group consists of numerous international relations theorists and many politicians of the Third Way who want to pursue an ethical foreign policy. They seek to create a world in which Western "habits of the heart" and particularly democracy are established around the world. They along with the salvationist lawyers claim to be acting in defense of universal values. Their purpose is to use U.S. power in association with various "coalitions of the willing" to promote democracy and human rights around the world. They do not seek the displacement of the state but merely its transformation into that perfect polity, Western liberal democracy.

In this chapter I examine whether an international moral order of either the spontaneous or the imperial kind is likely to emerge, as well as the likely outcome if either of these projects is vigorously pursued.

INTERNATIONAL LAW

As with so much that is wooly in thinking about the modern world, the project of international lawyers to attain peace through justice harks back to Woodrow Wilson. He overthrew the international legal order established by the Treaty of Westphalia of 1648, if not fully in form, at least in spirit. The Treaty of Westphalia that brought the bloody post-Reformation religious wars to an end—in the last of which, the Thirty Years' War, (1618–48) nearly 30 percent of the population of Central Europe was killed—"stopped the merging of domestic and foreign policy," according to Henry Kissinger. "All signatories confirmed the principle *cuius regio, eius religio*—whoever rules determines the religion of his subjects. No other country had a right to intervene in this process. Thus was born the principle of noninterference in the domestic affairs of other states, and it was developed for precisely the opposite reason it is being discarded today. It was the human rights slogan of the period; restoring peace and tranquility was its purpose, not legitimizing domestic oppression."[2] The resulting Westphalian system was concerned with maintaining peace between states, but it had nothing to say about violence within states arising from civil wars, or what are today called violations of human rights. Henry Kissinger writes: "It dealt with the problems of peace and left justice to the domestic institutions. The contemporary human rights activists are arguing the opposite. In their view, peace flows automatically from justice, and the nation-state, or perhaps any state, cannot be relied [on] to deliver justice; it must be put under some kind of supranational authority entitled to use force to make its writ run. On the whole, the human rights activists trust jurists more than they do statesmen. The advocates of the Westphalian principles trust statesmen more than jurists."[3]

As we have seen, Wilson converted the American self-image of a "shining city on the hill" as a moral example for others into a crusade to spread these values worldwide, thereby seeking to abolish both the Westphalian system and the principle of balance of power which over the previous two centuries had provided some order in the anarchical society of European states. Instead of promoting the national interest, Wilson proclaimed a cosmopolitan interest as the only relevant one in foreign policy: "Is it right? Is it just? Is it in the interest of mankind?"[4]

This Wilsonian idealism has remained a vital element in U.S. foreign policy ever since, from Franklin Roosevelt's proclamation of the four freedoms—of speech and of religion, from want and from fear—"everywhere in the world," to John F. Kennedy's inaugural speech. It underlies the views of the international lawyers who have taken up the cause of global salvationism. Without going into the debates surrounding the various schools of international law which have emerged,[5] the important point to note is that historically, international law has not been essential for maintaining international order. As Hedley Bull notes: "Some past international societies—the Greek city-state system, the system of Hellenistic kingdoms that arose after the death of Alexander, the ancient Indian system of states—were without the institution of international law. That modern international society includes international law as one of its institutions is a consequence of the historical accident that it evolved out of a previous unitary system, Western Christendom, and that in this system notions of law—embodied in Roman law, divine law, canon law and natural law—were pre-eminent."[6]

This casts doubt on the validity of the universalist claims of the internationalist lawyers propounding the emergence of a new international legal order.[7] It is claimed that with the growth of the transnational institutions of the UN system, there has been a shift from interstate law to the law of the world community. But I have already cast doubt on the existence of any meaningful world community or the international civil society conjured up by NGOs. All these transnational institutions and NGOs are ultimately beholden to states, which still remain the monopolists of coercive authority within their territories. Until there is a global monopoly of coercion granted to a world government, the rhetorical question to be asked of those who would like to enforce their moral values on the world is that asked of the Pope: how many divisions does he have? The reason why the Pope, nevertheless, was able to enforce his will over temporal sovereigns in the past was because they and their subjects still believed in the Christian God and in the Pope as his viceroy on Earth. The papal nuclear weapon was the power of excommunication, for besides the personal fear that excommunication would lead to the eternal flames of hellfire, there was also the peril to the sovereign's estates. As their excommunication would give their subjects a papal license to rebel. But, once Henry VIII (caught in the entrails of the sixth-century papal revolution Pope Gregory I had wrought in the family domain) decided to accept excommunication as a permanent state—by breaking with Rome and setting up his own Church—the papal weapon of excommunication became a paper tiger. Today's global salvationists cannot count on any universal morality, even in their Western homelands, which will force recalcitrant states to heed their wishes. The attempt by the moralizing international lawyers to promote an international law of welfare rather than the traditional international law of liberty will prove to be a chimera. The perception by international lawyers of the progress of international law in this direction is little more than their "heightened protest against the facts of international politics."[8]

Equally fanciful is the hope of the global salvationists, whose most prominent international relations academic is Richard Falk of Princeton, that the world community they see emerging through the UN and its agencies will spontaneously transform itself into a world government, which will then promote global justice and virtue. The goals of the New World Order System he hopes will be established[9] include not only the preservation of international and internal peace, but also a whole host of idealized social, economic, and environmental conditions. He wants to create a global enterprise association (in Oakeshott's sense) to subserve his moral ends. But such a project for global salvation (like all versions of the enterprise view of the state) involves coercion beyond the limits allowed on classical liberal principles. As Kenneth Minogue has succinctly put it: "Moralizing the human condition is only possible if we can make the world correspond to some conception of social justice. But it turns out what we can only transcend the inequalities of the past if we institute precisely the form of social order—a despotism—which Western civilization has immemorially found incompatible with its free and independent customs. The promise is justice, the price is freedom."[10]

Moreover, the claimed universal moral consensus for the globally centralized legislation of virtue is a mirage. As Hedley Bull remarks of Falk's utopianism: "he . . . bases his prescriptions on a conversion of the whole planet to a comprehensive array of goals that reflect his own detailed preferences, a conversion which is to be brought about simply by his own and his colleagues' powers of persuasion and exhortation."[11] They should be parachuted into Afghanistan to see how far they get in converting the Taliban and Osama bin Laden by persuasion to their preferences! Surely, the world is a dangerous enough place without this lunacy of the global salvationists. The time has come to shut down the transnational institutions of the UN which today provide little help in securing either peace, security, or prosperity, and are instead providing nurture and succor to those who proclaim these as their causes but who are in fact their enemies.

Equally serious are the extraordinary attempts made in the last decade to subject international politics to judicial procedures. The first of these is the creation of an International Criminal Court (ICC), which was adopted in 1998 by 95 states, including most European ones. It has been ratified by about 12 countries and will go into effect when 60 have done so. President Bill Clinton signed the ICC treaty just before leaving office but said neither he nor his successor should send it to the Senate for ratification! The United States has since conducted bilateral negotiations to prevent its citizens being subject to the ICC's jurisdiction if and when it comes into effect.

The second route adopted has been to establish the universal jurisdiction of national courts over other country's citizens who may have violated human rights. This came to a head with the arrest of former Chilean President Augusto Pinochet. Acting on an extradition request from a Spanish magistrate who charged him with crimes against Spanish citizens on Chilean soil, Pinochet was put under house arrest for over 16 months in the UK. On 25 November 1998, Britain's House of Lords concluded that "international law has made it plain that certain types of conduct . . . are not acceptable conduct on the part of anyone."[12] As Henry Kissinger rightly notes: "But that principle did not necessarily oblige the House of Lords to confer on a Spanish magistrate the right to enforce it in a third country. It could have held that Chile or an international tribunal specifically established for crimes committed in Chile on the model of the courts set up for crimes in Yugoslavia and Rwanda were the appropriate forum. The unprecedented and sweeping interpretation of international law in *Ex Parte Pinochet* would arm any magistrate, anywhere in the world, with the unilateral power to invoke a supranational concept of justice; to substitute his own judgement for the reconciliation procedures of even incontestably democratic societies where the alleged violations of human rights occurred."[13] This is precisely what happened in Belgium, which passed a law giving its magistrates the right to start criminal proceedings against any violator of human rights in any part of the world. Its intended targets included Ariel Sharon and Henry Kissinger! The resulting furor in Israel and the United States has led the Belgian government to backtrack and it proposes to rescind this law.

The creation of this legal Frankenstein goes back to the Nuremberg trials and the Wilsonian streak in American foreign policy. In committing the United States to the allied side in the name of his four freedoms, Franklin Roosevelt declared: "Freedom means the supremacy of human rights everywhere."[14] The United States has since used the rhetoric of human rights for political ends. This tactic is not new. But, as Kristin Sellars notes, "the United States was the first nation in history to possess both the power and the interest to pursue an international crusade in the name of all humanity, not just in the war, but also in the peace that followed."[15] The UN and its 1948 Universal Declaration of Universal Human Rights, the genocide conventions of 1948, and the antitorture convention of 1988 were seen as the means for wrapping "the iron fist of global power . . . in the velvet glove of international humanitarianism," Sellars continues. But the real turning point was the final act of the Conference on Security and Cooperation in Europe signed in 1971 by 35 countries and known as the Helsinki Accords. These obliged the signatories to observe various human rights or face sanctions. These accords were used by dissidents in Eastern Europe to undermine Communist rule.

Henry Kissinger, one of the leading lights of the U.S. foreign policy elite, makes it clear that the United States did not see the invocation of human rights as anything more than a diplomatic weapon in its various wars, and as providing a cover in U.S. domestic politics for the exercise of American imperial power. He writes: "It is unlikely that any of the signatories of either the United Nations conventions or the Helsinki Final Act thought it possible that national judges would use them as a basis for extradition requests regarding alleged crimes not committed in their jurisdictions. The drafters almost certainly believed that they were stating general principles, not laws that would be enforced by courts other than those of the countries of the victims or the perpetrators. For example, Eleanor Roosevelt, one of the drafters of the Universal Declaration of Human Rights, referred to it as a 'common standard.' As one of the negotiators of the Final Act of the Helsinki conference, *I can affirm that the administration I represented considered it primarily a diplomatic weapon to use against Soviet pressure on their own captive people*, not as a legal weapon against individual leaders before courts of countries not their own. It was never argued until very recently that the various UN declarations subjected past and future leaders to the possibility of prosecution by national magistrates of third countries without either due process safeguards or institutional restraints."[16] Clearly, the use of universalist moral rhetoric for instrumental purposes has hoist him and the other members of the US foreign policy elite on their own petard!

As I have argued, the notion of universal human rights is a wooly concept. Its use to define the purposes of American imperial policy may give a warm glow to American breasts, but it remains a meaningless concept. The principles advocated under its rubric are neither universally accepted, nor can they be derived from the fact of our common humanity. There are no such human rights as there is no one who has contracted with humanity to take on the obligations which alone can give rise to rights.

ETHICAL IMPERIALISM

Like those promoting human rights through transnational institutions and their incorporation and enforcement in international law, there are two other

groups of Wilsonian moralists who want to use Western arms to bring political freedom, particularly democracy, to the whole world. They differ only on
the role of international institutions in promoting their morality. The first
have been labeled "liberal internationalists," the second, "conservative internationalists."[17]

The liberal internationalists, whose chief recent proponents have been
the Third Way politicians Tony Blair in the United Kingdom and Bill Clinton
in the United States, believe that Western force should be used to right
humanitarian wrongs.[18] Liberal internationalists consider past wars to have
been wrong in principle (being based on selfish national interests, like the
Vietnam War) or tainted by economic interest (like the first Gulf War). They
prefer purely moral wars to uphold universal rights. For them, the war in
Kosovo was thus a just war and they supported it vociferously. By contrast,
they have opposed the recent Iraq war (except for Blair), either because it
smacks of imperialism or because it is seen as tainted with the supposed U.S.
desire to acquire Iraq's oil reserves. No one symbolizes this left-wing liberal
ethos better than the former British Foreign Secretary Robin Cook, who
claimed in 1997 that the incoming New Labour government would follow an
ethical foreign policy. He was a vehement supporter of the Kosovo war to
protect the human rights of the Kosavars but resigned when Tony Blair
decided to take Britain into the Iraq war. As for Blair, who is reported to
claim that Kosovo was the first "progressive war," it would appear that
Saddam Hussein's presumed possession of weapons of mass destruction
rather than strategic reasons loomed large in his decision to wage another
progressive war in Iraq.

The liberal internationalists are also happy to see the erosion of
national sovereignty and to embrace the postmodern notion that the nation-
state is dying and is to be replaced by the pooling of sovereignty into ever
larger transnational groupings, of which many see the European Union as a
paradigm.[19] They take the will of the international community as expressed
by the United Nations seriously—hence Tony Blair's misjudged and ill-fated
embroilment of President George W. Bush in the UN quagmire to provide
legitimacy for the current Iraq war. They are happy to see the legalization of
international affairs as discussed in the previous section.

But it is still a left-wing agenda. Their morality, instead of being universal in its application, seemingly only applies to regimes which are not
progressive. While supposedly right-wing politicians who have violated
their people's human rights, such as Chile's Augusto Pinochet, are to be
prosecuted before the court of world public opinion in the name of universal
rights, a blind eye is turned to the crimes against humanity which continue to
be committed by Cuba's Fidel Castro. Nor is there even a rhetorical attempt

to bring the innumerable officials who were responsible for the Gulags of the Soviet Union and Maoist China to book. Nor are the academic and other scribblers, who were propagandists and apologists for the Communist regimes perpetrating these crimes, asked to explain themselves and their past "inhuman" advocacy. Instead of being excoriated for their support for some of the most tyrannical regimes of the last century, these lifelong apologists for communism have been honored by New Labour with the award of Britain's highest honors.

Nor when it comes to conducting their just wars are the liberal imperialists willing to bear the full costs in terms of loss of men and materiel of their humanitarian interventions. They recognize that if, in upholding a moral principle, too many body bags are retuned, domestic politics will become enraged, thereby giving the lie to the belief that these interventions are based on any deep morality for which people are willing to die. It is easy to be moral when it is costless. As Henry Kissinger tartly remarked about the Kosovo war: "The fear of casualties caused even the bombing campaign to be conducted from altitudes thought to be beyond the range of Serbian anti-aircraft batteries—at fifteen thousand feet or above—suggesting that, in Kosovo at least, the Western democracies confined their risk-taking on behalf of morality to specific altitudes."[20]

By contrast, the conservative internationalists, who are self-identified by their participation in the Project for the New American Century, are strong defenders of the nation-state and its sovereignty. They have no time for the legalization of international law sought by the global salvationists. Nor, rightly, do they care for the multilateral processes and endorsement of the United Nations, which they see as a way to constrain American power. However, they too, like the liberal internationalists, wish to use U.S. power to establish an international moral order. In their influential 2000 book *Present Dangers*, William Kristol and Robert Kagan, two of the leading conservative internationalist thinkers, commend Henry Luce who "spoke for most influential Americans inside and outside the Roosevelt administration when he insisted that it had fallen to the United States not only to win the war against Germany and Japan, but to create 'a vital international economy' and 'an international moral order' that would together spread American political and economic principles—and in the process avoid the catastrophe of a third world war."[21]

Kagan and Kristol wish to see a robust exercise of the U.S.'s overwhelming global power, which they claim "enjoins upon [it] a general obligation to maintain the basic peace and order of the world, and does not lessen its chosen responsibility to promote political regimes based on respect for individual rights and democracies."[22] Their views have been influential. The recent National Security Strategy paper of the Bush administration, embodying what is called the Bush doctrine, besides advocating the maintenance of American military supremacy and claiming the right of preemptive strikes against "rogue states," also states in its foreword signed by the president that "the United States will use this moment of opportunity to extend the benefits of freedom across the globe. We will actively work to bring the hope of democracy, development, free markets, and free trade to every corner of the globe."[23]

Realizing that the moral crusade Kagan and Kristol favor may be looked upon as the global legislation of American habits of the heart, and thus a form of cultural imperialism, they state: "We know from experience that when acting for universal principles as we understand them, we can often count on the support of many allies who have come to share the same fundamental views, not because they are American ideas but because they have a rational claim to universal validity."[24] This claim—as I hope readers of this part of the book will be able to see—has no merit.

This shared desire to create an international moral order, albeit for the liberal internationalists based on transnational organizations and for the conservative internationalists on the nation state, led them to join forces in the Iraq war. But the shenanigans at the UN preceding the war (supported by the U.S. State Dept and the UK's Tony Blair) to obtain the endorsement of the world community to make it legitimate in the eyes of the liberal internationalists embroiled the Bush administration in wholly unnecessary justifications for the war. It did not have to be defended on the grounds of the danger posed by Saddam Hussein's possession of weapons of mass destruction—a claim which now seems to have been based on flawed intelligence. A more cogent justification was that by throwing out the UN weapons inspectors in 1998, Hussein broke an obligation he had entered into as a result of the first Gulf war that he lost. The liberal internationalists Blair and Clinton, instead of robustly upholding the first principle of order—that obligations must be met—and resuming the unfinished 1991 war, lamely hurled a few missiles at him and let him continue in breach of his obligations. Saddam Hussein lost a just war which ended in a cease-fire whose terms he failed to meet for over 12 years. What should have been done?

An analogy helps to clear the mind. A vicious drug dealer has been caught after a firefight with his mafiosi. The judge in his clemency gives him a suspended life sentence with the condition that he goes into a rehabilitation center supervised by a parole officer, whom he has to direct to the stockpile of drugs he has hidden away. After a few years, he gives his parole officer the slip and disappears from the rehabilitation center. When the authorities catch up with him, he is up to his old tricks. What should they do? Just cordon him off and leave him in peace (as those opposing the Iraq war in fact were proposing) or should they capture him (even if it means a firefight with his newly reconstructed mafiosi) and bring him to jail to enforce the judge's sentence? The answer to any law-abiding citizen should be clear, and was all that was needed to justify toppling Saddam Hussein. On the most elementary and universal moral judgment which is also essential for maintaining any social order—the breaking of promises must be punished—this was as just a war as any.

Instead of making this simple and unanswerable case, President Bush gave into the pleas of the liberal internationalists who said they needed to get the blessing of the international community for this otherwise justified war. Their claims about Iraq's continuing possession of weapons of mass destruction, which was a red herring, then became the focus of attention, instead of the much simpler and more obvious one that Hussein had broken the terms of the cease-fire. Giving into the moralism of the liberal internationalists has come to haunt both Blair and Bush with the failure (to date) to find these weapons of mass destruction, which given their rhetoric was lodged in the popular perception as the justification for the war.

There was also (I hope) a strategic reason for the Iraq war. The Islamist threat emanates from numerous regimes in the Middle East, but most of all from the Wahhabism embraced and financed by the Saudi monarchy. But, as its partner in keeping oil flowing to the West, the United States could hardly threaten the Saudis directly. By contrast, Saddam Hussein had provided an obvious *causis belli*. We will have to wait and see if the historians show that the temporary occupation of Iraq and the creation of a pro-Western government and a military presence in the heart of the Arab world is feasible and provides strategic gains. But to a contemporary outside observer the gains seem patent. By eliminating the major threat to the Saudi Arabian oilfields from Iraq, the Americans could withdraw their forces from the Saudi kingdom—as they are doing—thereby assuaging part of the cause for Islamist fury, since one of Osama bin Laden's ostensible reasons for his jihad was the presence of Americans in the kingdom housing Islam's holiest shrines.

With the second largest oil reserves in the world, a friendly Iraq also provides an alternative to reliance on Saudi oil which has been the basis for the Saudi-American alliance. The U.S. military presence in Iraq should give the Americans a freer hand in dealing with the Saudis' inflaming of Islamist passions by their promotion and financing of the export of their virulent anti-Western form of Islam, Wahhabism. Moreover, by placing its military forces right in the middle of the region, and with the demonstration of its military might in a short surgical war with few casualties, the United States has also served notice on the terror-masters (as Michael Ledeen has called them)[25] in Syria and Iran. The other terror-master, Libya's Muammar Qaddafi, has already taken note and come clean about his weapons of mass destruction. Qaddafi clearly does not want to end up in a dirty hole like Hussein. It is these strategic gains which rightly make the successfully conducted war on Iraq truly a part of the war on terrorism—even though Saddam Hussein himself had no truck with Islamists like Osama bin Laden but did fund the intifada in Palestine. These reasons of realpolitik, even if not openly proclaimed, would provide the U.S. imperium obvious strategic gains from the Iraq war.

But the aftermath of the successfully completed military campaign has also shown up the Achilles heel of the American imperium. It has created the military structures to project its power, but it has failed to build the complementary imperial administrative structure required to run an empire. Its failure to establish order in post-Saddam Iraq shows up this lacuna. The simultaneous dismantling of the only two national institutions which had (however brutally) maintained order in the past—the Iraqi army and the Baath party—without having replacements in the wings, shows either a breathtaking naiveté or an erroneous belief based on Wilsonianism—that once freed of the tyrant, Iraqis would flock to the democratic and humanist banner of their liberators, generating a spontaneous order.[26]

Both the conservative internationalists and liberal internationalists want to go further. They are united in their determination to create a liberal democracy in post-Saddam Iraq. Apart from the moral reasons for promoting political liberty, the export of democracy is also advocated by conservative internationalists on instrumental grounds, based on the assertion that the creation of liberal democracies in the Middle East will promote peace, as democracies do not fight each other. I have already questioned this wholly unsubstantiated claim in the last chapter.

Equally questionable is the assumption that constructing liberal democracies is possible in even the most inhospitable cultures. The examples of post–Second World War Germany and Japan are the ones usually cited. But as Marina Ottaway rightly notes: "The transformation of West Germany and Japan into democratic states following World War II is the most successful nation-building exercise ever undertaken from the outside. Unfortunately, this process took place under circumstances unlikely to be repeated elsewhere. Although defeated and destroyed, these countries had strong state traditions and competent government personnel. West Germany and Japan were nation-states in the literal sense of the term—they were ethnic and cultural communities as well as political states."[27]

Iraq shares none of these attributes. Nor do most of the other Middle Eastern states ruled by various forms of despotism. Iraq has large ethnic and religious fault lines, between the majority Arab Shias and minority Sunnis and the ethnically distinct, but by religion Sunni, Kurds. It was not a nation but a country cobbled together by the British after the First World War to provide a consolation prize to the Hashemite descendants of the sherif of Mecca. The British, when they captured Iraq under General Sir Stanley Maude from the Ottomans in March 1917 with an army largely made up of Indian volunteers also looked upon themselves as liberators, not conquerors, and Maude promised his new subjects on 19 March 1917 "'a future of greatness' and invited them 'through your nobles and elders and representatives to participate in the management of your civil affairs.'"[28] These lofty sentiments were of little avail. By the early 1930s Iraq had suffered the first of its many military coups, and rather than a liberal democracy, the British left behind an illiberal autocracy of which the Sunni-dominated Baath party's tyranny under Saddam Hussein was emblematic. Perhaps if the British had been able and willing to maintain their occupation for a lengthy period as in India, democracy might have taken root. But it seems unlikely. The United States and in particular its populace certainly does not have the heart for maintaining direct rule in Iraq for the lengthy period it would take (over a generation) for the necessary democratic political habits to be engendered, and even then it is unlikely that there will be enough of a national feeling to hold the country together.

But there is no reason to hold this artificial state together.[29] It is not a nation. The only conceivable reason to keep it united is its oil wealth, concentrated in the north, controlled by the Kurds, and in the South, by the Shias. In a partition on ethnic and religious lines the Sunni Arabs would be the losers; not surprisingly, along with Islamist terrorists, the Sunnis are the backbone of the guerrilla movement against the occupation. One solution would be to put the revenue from Iraq's oil wealth into the International National Resources Fund (INRF) suggested in chapter 3, and for three autonomous self-governing regions to be created. Over these would be a loose confederal government—similar to that in Switzerland—whose chief responsibility would be to supervise, with the INRF, the deployment of the oil revenues in the three constituent regions.[30]

After the first heady dreams of creating a liberal democratic, unified Iraq, something on the above lines seems to be emerging. As Geoffey Aronson, the director of the Foundation for Middle East Peace, noted, eventually the winners will find a method like that of the British and, now, that of the United States in Afghanistan: accepting the basis of power and providing it with a democratic sheen. The hope of both the conservative and liberal internationalists of creating a liberal democracy in Iraq which will then be emulated by the rest of the Middle East is likely to remain a pipe dream.

The examples of the recent democratization of South Korea, Taiwan, and the Philippines is held out by the ethical imperialists of both the conservative and liberal bent as showing that democracy can be compatible with non-Western cultures. But, as I have argued, this does not prove that they will be able to sustain democracy. Latin America has seen waves of democracy interspersed with autocracy for the last 200 years even though it shares much the same cosmological beliefs as the West. Similarly, the Philippines since it was an American colony has seen the same Latin American cycles. It is too early to tell whether liberal democracy will mature and be sustained in either South Korea or Taiwan. It is even arguable whether Japan is a Western liberal democracy, though it has all the trappings. Despite General MacArthur's ministrations, Japan has returned to a polity very similar to the one created by the Meiji oligarchs after Japan's opening by Commodore Perry.

The desire of both conservative and liberal internationalists to establish true replicas of their own polities across the world is therefore likely to be thwarted. As I have argued, the form of government which is seen as legitimate is governed by the political habits of different peoples which are determined by both their relatively immutable cosmological beliefs and their history.

But while political liberty may thus be unattainable around the globe, the civil and economic liberties which are an even more fundamental aspect of freedom are not. Though also a Western creation arising from Pope Gregory VII's legal papal revolution in the eleventh century, they concern the material beliefs of a culture, which are much more malleable. This papal revolution provided all the legal and institutional infrastructure for a market economy. With the growing worldwide recognition that the market offers the best hope of promoting the truly universal desire for prosperity, countries of disparate cultures, such as the Sinic and Hindu, are embracing the market. This involves establishing the institutional infrastructure pioneered in the West which requires the civil and economic liberties essential for the efficient functioning of the market. Countries can adopt these essential liberties even without political liberty: the Sinic city states of Hong Kong and Singapore attest to this. Though in the West a change in cosmological beliefs—which led to the rise of liberal democracy—was conjoined with a change in material beliefs—which then led to the rise of the market economy and the consequent rise of the West—this conjuncture of what can be labeled Westernization (involving cosmological beliefs) and modernization (involving material beliefs) is not a necessary one. To reiterate, the Rest can modernize without Westernizing.

The attempt by the Western ethical imperialists to launch a jihad on behalf of their cosmological beliefs currently embodied in democracy and

the promotion of human rights could backfire, as other cultures wrongly
come to see—as many of their cultural nationalists are proclaiming—that to
modernize through globalization is also to Westernize and lose their souls.
The jihad to convert the world to American habits of the heart (which
includes democracy) will be resisted as much as Osama bin Laden's jihad to
convert the world to Islam.

Summary

It is time to sum up. Empires have been natural throughout human history. Most people have lived in empires. Empires and the process of globalization associated with them has provided the order necessary for social and economic life to flourish. By linking previously autarkic states into a common economic space, empires have promoted the mutual gains from trade adumbrated by Adam Smith. Therefore, despite their current bad name, empires have promoted peace and prosperity.

Empires need to be distinguished from mere hegemony. Empires seek to control both the domestic and foreign policies of their allies; hegemons, only their foreign policy. Empires can be maintained directly or indirectly. As direct rule which involves some form of colonization is expensive for the imperium and is likely to lead to nationalist revolts, whenever possible imperial powers have sought to create indirect empires.

Empires can be classified normatively as good or bad in terms of a distinction made by the British philosopher Michael Oakeshott between the enterprise association and the civil association views of the state. The former seeks to promote some enterprise of its own (a religion, plunder, or some secular morality); the latter to merely promote civil order. The empires that have survived, even if they began as embodiments of the enterprise view of the state (such as the early Arab and British empires), have in their fullness adopted the civil association view of the state.

The motives for creating empires have been varied: plunder (the early Arab and Mongol empires, the Latin American Iberian empires), glory (Alexander the Great, Ghengis Khan), the creation of geographical defensible borders (the Eurasian agrarian empires).

Empires have arisen because of some asymmetric military and economic advantage which has allowed a part of an anarchical system of states to come to dominate the whole. Most anarchical systems of states have broken down into hegemony or empire whenever these asymmetries in weapons and the economic base for acquiring them have occurred. In Eurasia, two of the ancient imperial states—China and India—survive to our day, the former with an unbroken history as an imperial state for millennia, the latter as an imperial state which has periodically broken down and then been recreated, most often by foreign invaders.

Given their territorial extent, empires have had to create a civil service and establish a legal code and a lingua franca. Empires can be distinguished as being homogenizing (the Chinese) or multiethnic (the Indian and Roman empires). The longevity of multiethnic empires has depended on their opening the instruments of imperial control—the military and bureaucracy—to the talents of all (as in Rome). Failure to do so has often led to nationalist revolts which have destroyed the empire (as with the British empire).

The most common cause for the decline of empires has been an increase in fiscal exactions which by provoking tax resistance, tax avoidance, and evasion led to a fiscal crisis. This in turn resulted in the breakdown of the imperial military and bureaucratic structure and the order it promoted. The end of an empire has led to widespread disorder in the former imperial territories and a fall in the standard of living of its inhabitants as the common economic space (globalization) created by the empire was shattered. Western European standards of living did not return to the levels achieved under the Roman empire for 500 years after the fall of Rome.

Whereas most of the rest of Eurasia continued to live under various imperial systems after the fall of Rome, Western Europe was unique in so far as none of the successor states were able to create another European empire. The resulting anarchic system of European nation-states was thus a major exception in human history. As much of the thinking on international relations was done by Westerners living in this anarchical system of states, much of contemporary academic international relations theory has been developed to deal with this exceptional situation. It is irrelevant in thinking about the new age of empire.

The reason why no European state was able to recreate a European empire was because they were fairly evenly matched in terms of material resources as measured by their gross domestic product (GDP), while any military innovation was quickly disseminated among the various European contestants in the struggle for the mastery of Europe. The overseas empires these European nation-states created, after the voyages of discovery, were an overseas extension of their European wars. The empires they created were based, particularly in Asia, on luck as much as on the improvements in armaments and communications that followed the slowly emerging Industrial Revolution and the rise of the West. This rise was largely due to the papal revolution of Gregory VII in the eleventh century which created all the commercial and legal infrastructure required by a modern economy.

For a brief period from the end of the eighteenth to the late nineteenth century, Great Britain as the pioneer of the Industrial Revolution had an economic lead over its continental rivals, which allowed it after its victory over the French in the Napoleonic wars to create the first truly global empire. This empire sought to promote the interests of the gentlemanly capitalists of the City of London. It created the first liberal international economic order, based on laissez faire, free trade, free mobility of capital and labor, and an international legal order.

Despite nationalist and Marxist cant, this first liberal international economic order (LIEO) was hugely beneficial for the world, particularly its poorest. It saw the integration for the first time of many countries in the Third World into a global economy and the consequent first stirring of modern intensive growth. With the spread of the industrialization promoted by this British-led LIEO to other European countries, particularly Germany and above all the United States, Britain's economic supremacy (in terms of relative GDP) began to slip. By the beginning of the twentieth century, the United States was already the dominant economy in the world. But it was unwilling to take over the imperial task of maintaining a global Pax from the British. Instead, it embraced Wilsonian idealism with its doomed hope to maintain peace through collective security enforced by the sanctions imposed by the newly created transnational League of Nations. The League failed to maintain the peace. When the U.S. Senate failed to ratify the Versailles treaty, the United States retreated into isolationism, hoping its incipient imperial burden would disappear. Arguably, the United States' failure to assume the imperial role, largely because of its domestic politics, contributed to many of the disasters of the last century: two world wars, the Great Depression, and the rise and fall of two illiberal creeds, fascism and communism.

CREATION OF THE U.S. IMPERIUM

Chastened by the experience of the international disorder its isolationism had caused in the interwar years, the U.S. political elite after the Second World War surreptitiously took up the task of building a U.S. imperium, to maintain the Pax which the British since the First World War were unable— and after the Second World War, also unwilling—to undertake.

The United States also sought to create a new LIEO. Unlike the British, the Americans have never accepted the correct economic principle that it is in each country's self-interest to unilaterally adopt free trade. They have erroneously looked upon foreign trade as a zero-sum game and have demanded reciprocal concessions from their trading partners in the name of fair trade. Nor, after the New Deal did they accept the correct British policy of laissez faire (which Britain itself had gradually repudiated with the rise of the common people). What they did try to do, and by and large successfully, was to create a number of transnational institutions to open world markets to trade in goods and markets and the free flow of capital. Many countries in the Third World, partly traumatized by their interwar experience in a globally integrated economy, and partly in thrall to the rapid economic and military rise of the Soviet Union, only joined this new LIEO half-heartedly. But after the debt crisis of the 1980s and the collapse of the countries of "really existing socialism," they have joined the globalization bandwagon—the most notable of the converts being China and India. This latest period of globalization has, as in the nineteenth century, brought unimaginable prosperity to most of the Third World, including to its poorest. The only countries not to experience this economic progress are those in Africa and the Middle East which have failed to become part of this ongoing globalization.

With the defeat of the communist empire, as the country with the largest GDP, whose growth performance (despite various alarms) has continued to lead the industrialized world's, and with an undisputed military superiority gained from its revolution in military affairs, the United States had achieved a global dominance not seen since the fall of Rome. Since 1989 the U.S. imperium has been there for all to see, although it took the events of September 11, 2001, the ensuing wars in Afghanistan and Iraq, and the promulgation of the Bush doctrine for the public to sense that the United States was an imperial power. But the United States and its leaders are still in denial. They refuse to accept the application of the dreaded E word to their republic. And failure to accept the obvious leads to confusion.

Nowhere is this confusion clearer than in the attempt by all the participants in the U.S. foreign policy debate to wrap themselves in the Wilsonian mantle. It seems that Americans find it difficult to give up their moral self-image of the shining city on the hill. There are many who still hanker after creating an international moral order using the post–Second World War transnational institutions and adding to them if necessary. Most of these transnational institutions, I have argued, have served their purpose and should be shut down. This is important as they provide the main platform and succor to those global salvationists seeking to wreck the new LIEO in the name of an imagined international civil society. There is a simple and economically rational response to spike some of the valid economic complaints of the nongovernmental organizations (NGOs) and to end the bad blood caused by U.S. unilateralism and support for preferential trading agreements in the current Doha round of the World Trade Organization's multilateral trade talks. It is for the United States to follow the British nineteenth-century example and unilaterally adopt free trade, except perhaps with the European Union, unless it too fully opens up its economic borders to the world. But will U.S. domestic politics allow it?

The moralism underlying many of the global salvationists' complaints finds an echo in many a Western breast. The NGOs' desire to promote human rights and democracy in the name of universal human values is shared by many who want to see the United States play an imperial role. They want to use U.S. power to legislate Western habits of the heart. In judging these moral claims, a distinction between the *cosmological* and *material* beliefs of different cultures and civilizations is useful. What is currently being touted by Western moralists as universal values are nothing else but the culture-specific values of a monotheistic, egalitarian, proselytizing Christian religion. In particular, they are not in consonance with the cosmological beliefs of other Eurasian civilizations. These Western habits of the heart—particularly in the domestic domain—arose from a change in the West's cosmological beliefs, from the common Eurasian pattern of communalism to individualism. Forcing people with different cosmological beliefs to accept them can only invite fierce resistance and global disorder. Part of the Islamist rage is fueled by what Muslims see as the attempt by the West to use globalization and the modernization it entails as a Trojan horse to change their cosmological beliefs, particularly in the domestic domain concerning sex and marriage.

Similarly, the legitimacy of different political forms is governed by cosmological as much as material beliefs. Democracy, currently touted as the panacea for the world's ills, does not necessarily promote either peace or prosperity. It does promote political freedom, but this is part of a culture's cosmological beliefs, its political habits. Moreover, political freedom is not the most important component of the ambiguous notion of freedom (liberty). We have to distinguish between economic and civil liberties and political liberties. I have argued that the former have greater primacy and, arguably, universal validity than the latter—certainly for those who are classical liberals. Globalization both depends on and promotes these classical economic and civil liberties. Political liberty, particularly in a majoritarian, participatory democracy, might well not.

The attempt to create an international moral order, either by the transnational route advocated by the global salvationists or by the exercise of U.S. imperial power as advocated by the ethical imperialists, is a route to global disorder. Just when some of the great Eurasian civilizations have come to realize that changing their material beliefs and modernizing through globalization does not entail changing their cosmological beliefs by Westernizing and losing their souls, this Western jihad in the name of human rights, democracy, and freedom might lead to a backlash against that very modernization that is promoting the liberties which matter—economic and civil liberties.

GOALS FOR AN AMERICAN IMPERIUM

If it is infeasible and undesirable for the American imperium to create an international moral order, what goals should it subserve? It clearly cannot be the territorial imperative which was the major objective of past empires: to extend the boundaries of sedentary civilizations to the natural borders at which the nomadic barbarians threatening them could be held at bay, or to acquire the booty including continuing revenue from an extension of territory. As my UCLA colleague Richard Rosecrance has argued,[1] since the Industrial Revolution this territorial imperative no longer offers the route to prosperity and power. Given the costs of maintaining a territorial empire, the first of the post–Industrial Revolution empires—the British—always preferred to keep the "barbarians" at bay through indirect rather than direct control of territory. It was, as Jack Gallagher and Robert Robinson labeled it, an "empire of free trade."[2] Its purpose was to spread its gentlemanly capitalism around the world. Today, even more so, the "trading state," as Rosecrance calls it, is increasingly seen as the way to prosperity. Equally important is what economists call human capital, the intelligence and acquired skills embodied in people. As my late friend Julian Simon rightly said, human beings are the ultimate resource.

But for these trading states to operate, someone needs to maintain the channels of commerce free of pirates and predators. The British empire provided this global public good through its Royal Navy—the "gunboats and gurkhas"—in its informal empire and by direct rule in its formal empire. This formal empire was acquired in part as the legacy of its buccaneering mercantile capitalists as in India, and in part by conquest as in Africa, to protect international channels of trade and commerce, where because of the fragility or amorphousness of local institutions indirect imperialism was not feasible. This British Pax was an essential element in the process of globalization which brought modernization to many parts of the world.

As the reluctant successor of this British Pax, the major objective of the American imperium, as the Bush doctrine explicitly recognizes, is to maintain the Pax necessary for globalization. The war on terror can be seen as merely an extension of this task. The terrorists, despite their utopian millennial objectives, are best seen as pirates of yore. As in the past, many terrorists are state-sponsored, and though the currency they deal in is not material booty but universal salvation, their major targets and threats are directed not so much at lives as at the complex market infrastructure of the modernizing world. They are as much warriors against globalization (though more lethal) as the activists marching at the anti-Davos summits of NGOs in Porto Allegre. Both need to be resisted.

A counter to the long-term threat from the Islamist terrorists currently plaguing the world must lie in bringing their homelands into the globalization process. The creation of true market economies in the countries of Islam, which involves the extension of civil and economic liberties in the Muslim world, is more likely to succeed in controlling this virus than the demands to convert them into democracies—witness the outcomes of democratization in Algeria and Iran. The essential purpose of the American imperium must therefore be, as it was for the British, to provide the global order required for the extension of the liberties promoted by globalization.

STRUCTURE OF THE AMERICAN IMPERIUM

Looking at the future of the world in the age of the American imperium, Robert Kagan and William Kristol correctly divide the world into two conceptual zones: "one in which [U.S.] power is clearly superior to that of any local force, and one in which, in a local theater . . . [the US] would be challenged to our limits."[3] The first comprises most of the world for them, the second the superstates of China and India. This conceptualizing is cogent. But their reluctance, along with most of their countrymen, to use the E word for the U.S. role in the first and geographically largest of the zones is not. Some prefer to talk of American hegemony rather than an American empire. But as one scholar has rightly remarked, hegemony is merely "imperialism with good manners."[4]

Kagan and Kristol do not like the words hegemony or imperium to describe the American role in the first of these world zones. This is partly because "they may give offense," but mainly because though "these terms are considered to be purely descriptive and neutral, in fact they carry strong connotations of dominion and empire, . . . [and] they do not describe the kind of enterprise in which the nation is engaged, which is not directly to rule others, but *to maintain a civilized world order and allow the benefits of free government to become known.*"[5] But the italicized passage is confused and confusing. The British empire, as we have seen, was primarily aimed at maintaining a civilized world order for the spread of gentlemanly capitalism around the world. It preferred indirect to direct rule. Direct rule was seen as too costly and only undertaken when circumstances necessitated it to maintain global order. There is no difference I can discern in the goals which the preponderance of British power in the nineteenth century was deemed to serve and those Kagan and Kristol rightly want to see as the goals for the

exercise of American power today—except for the last clause in the italicized passage. If the exercise of British power in the nineteenth century was
rightly described as imperial, so is that of its successor, American power.
Like the British, as the Americans are now increasingly discovering in Iraq,
the goal of maintaining a civilized world order may in fact require direct
rule, if only for a period. The continuing unwillingness of Americans to recognize that their role is now an imperium makes it difficult for them to sensibly discuss the imperial tasks they must undertake. Words do matter, and it is
no aid to clear thinking to avoid calling a spade a spade.

Once the United States recognizes that it is an empire, albeit a benevo-
lent and multicultural one, it might learn, as the British did from the backlash
provoked by their earlier attempts to impose their own habits of the heart on
others, that to prevent disorder in the imperium, it is best to leave people's
cosmological beliefs, including their political habits, alone. A multicultural
imperium maintaining a civilized world order may be incompatible with
"allow[ing] the benefits of free government to become known."

Kagan and Kristol are right, in my view, in looking at the U.S. relations
in the second of their conceptual worlds as being closer to those of the old
European world of sovereign nation-states. Here the traditional concerns of
academic international relations—the possibility of a challenge to U.S.
power and conflict—are of relevance. The two major emerging powers in
this zone are the continental empires of India and China. Their relationship
is similar to that among the imperial states at the time of the ascendancy of
Rome. Given the high costs of traversing distance at the time, the various
empires rarely collided with each other. Both India and China are ancient
imperial states. At the height of Rome's ascendancy they were its only competitors in terms of power and prosperity. They both continued to maintain a
high standard of living for their multitudinous millions for millennia; it was
probably higher than Rome's, and certainly the highest after the barbarians
destroyed the Roman imperium.

As we have seen, it was not any absolute fall in the standards of living
in these ancient civilizational empires which led to their relative decline
from the late Middle Ages forward. It was the economic miracle associated
with the rise of the West which led to the growing gap in income between
what are labeled the North and the South. After their ancient equilibrium was
shattered in the last two centuries by Western arms, both civilizations have
tried to come to terms with the rise of the West. After many twists and turns,
they have recognized that modernization, which involves their full participation in globalization, is the only way to close the still deeply resented dispar-
ity of wealth and power with the West. This has been accompanied by the
realization that this modernization will not require them to Westernize. In

fully participating in the process of globalization, they are having to introduce or strengthen the civil and economic liberties which are required for the
efficient functioning of the market. With their incorporation into the global
economy, these liberties, the most important ones from the viewpoint of
classical liberals, will therefore increase.

The ethical imperialists, however, want to go further by trying to get
them to accept Western habits of the heart. This remains the most likely
future source of conflict between these ancient empires and the West. It is
also a doomed project. In the early phase of nineteenth century Western
imperialism, Christian missionaries bent on saving heathen souls tried to use
imperial gunboats to aid their mission in these ancient Asian civilizations.[6]
But they completely failed and created a cultural nationalist backlash which
made it difficult for domestic modernizers to pursue their project without
being accused of betraying ancient traditions. In both these ancient civilizations, their subsequent attempts to marry tradition with modernity through
various dirigiste means turned out to be a blind alley. Nothing would resurrect this recently resolved conflict in favor of modernization other than an
effort by the U.S. imperium to attempt to change their ancient cultural,
including political, habits. As Henry Kissinger has sagely remarked about
the continuing attempt by the ethical imperialists to link trade access to
China with its human rights record: "the proposition that freedom of speech
and the press, which has never existed in five millennia of Chinese history,
could be brought about through legislation by the American Congress"[7] is
laughable. It can only lead to the far from inevitable clash of civilizations
posited by Samuel Huntington and others. Not merely in its relations
within its imperium, but even more so in its relationship with the other two
continental empires, it is important for the United States to adopt Queen
Elizabeth I's wise dictum that she would not seek to "make windows into
men's souls."[8]

But in this second zone in which U.S. power is not overwhelming, and in
which, with the rising economic weight of the Chinese and Indian economies,
it is likely to be equaled if not surpassed by the end of the century, is there a
future strategic threat posed by these rising imperial states which the United
States needs to forestall? It is indubitable that both China and India will use
their rising national wealth in part to increase their arms, for in the competing
imperial states of the future, guns and plowshares are not substitutes but com-
plements. Will this threaten the American imperium as some fear?

Several points need to be made. Except for two important exceptions,
both India and China have for millennia by and large been territorially status
quo states, once their natural boundaries defined by ancient barbarian threats
from the North had been established. The territorial conflict arising from both

the Chinese occupation of Tibet and the armed incursion into northwestern India followed by the Chinese occupation of territory on a disputed border seem in the process of being settled on the traditional lines of relationships between Great Powers. The Indians have recently recognized Tibet as part of the Chinese sphere of influence, and the Chinese have recognized Sikkim, which India annexed, as part of the Indian sphere of influence. I would expect that the disputed border along the Himalayas will also be settled with some suitable exchange of territory to satisfy both sides' national pride. With the growing Islamist threat in its northwest, China is also likely to cease trying to build Pakistan as a counterweight to India.

The future conflict between these ancient empires is likely to be about spheres of influence in East and South Asia, and possibly Central Asia. The United States will find itself necessarily drawn into this potential conflict as a Pacific and increasingly a Central Asian power. The prize for gaining influence in Central Asia for all the competing powers are the oil riches of the region. There are already signs as indicated in chapter 3 that the United States is now slowly creeping toward a strategic partnership with India, both to check potential Chinese hegemony in Asia and as an ally against Islamist terrorism. The major test of this latter alliance from the Indian viewpoint lies in the U.S.'s success in imposing the only feasible solution to the intractable Kashmir imbroglio: partitioning the disputed province between the two disputing states along the current actual line of control—which has in fact been the de facto border since 1949. The recent thaw in relations between the nuclear armed neighbors, and the accord President Pervez Musharraf and Prime Minister Atal Bihari Vajpayee signed in January 2004, offers some hope that this border dispute might finally be solved. Apart from the pressure from both the United States and China on Pakistan to deal with the Islamists who are conducting their jihad in Kashmir, both Musharraf and Vajpayee faced more significant pressures from the Grim Reaper to settle swiftly, the one from advancing age, the other from a possible assassin's bullet. With the fall of the Vajpayee government in the 2004 Indian elections, it remains to be seen if the new Congress-led alliance government will be able to settle this dispute. This attempt at settlement could fail. The last secret unwritten 1972 Simla Accord between Indira Gandhi and Zulfiqar Bhutto to convert the line of control into the de jure border[9] died with them, one at the hands of an assassin, the other on the gallows. But, the pressures on Pakistan to settle, from the imperial power (the United States) and the other major powers in the region (China and Russia) will be immense. The January 2004 disclosures of the sale of nuclear technology to Iran, Libya, and possibly North Korea by Pakistani atomic scientists have only added to these pressures. If Musharraf is toppled in an Islamist coup, it is unlikely that any of these powers along with India will allow Pakistan's nuclear arsenal to fall into Islamist hands. The future of Pakistan must remain very uncertain.

The other territorial dispute in which the United States will necessarily be involved is Taiwan. Desirous of joining the globalization bandwagon, it is unlikely that the Chinese will attempt to invade Taiwan, which would lead to a direct conflict with the United States. Moreover, once China modernizes, it will have to institute more of the civil and economic liberties required for the market to function. In this respect it will become more similar to Taiwan, except for the question of democracy. But it is possible to think of a future in which a mutually agreed solution is found by Taiwan becoming an autonomous province of China.

The best hope of avoiding future conflict between the geographically colliding U.S., Chinese, and Indian empires is provided by the growing spread of economic liberty in the Asian giants as they become globalized. The United States instead of hindering this process, as some have recommended,[10] should facilitate it. Above all, in its dealings with these rising Great Powers, the United States must keep its moralists at home.

But given the importance of the populace in its polity, is this likely? As General Vo Nguyen Giap who engineered the North Vietnamese victory in the Vietnam war is reported to have remarked, the North Vietnamese did not win the war on the battlefield (where they were defeated in the Tet offensive) but in the streets of San Francisco and Chicago. It is too early to tell whether the exercise of U.S. imperial power in Iraq will have the same outcome.

With its continuing reluctance to recognize its imperial status, and thus to create the necessary imperial civilian infrastructure to match the military infrastructure it has created, can this Imperial Republic survive without collapsing into a military autocracy, as Rome did, as my libertarian friends fear? Will its domestic politics allow the U.S. imperium to follow the correct economic policies followed by its British predecessor, and adopt free trade and laissez faire? Will the growing fiscal burden from burgeoning social entitlements lead to a future fiscal crisis which, as with past empires, will undermine the imperium? Only time will tell. At least in facing these questions intelligently, instead of burying one's head in the sand, it is important that U.S. leaders start a debate about the nature and purpose of their empire.

If the U.S. public does not recognize the imperial burden that history has thrust upon it, or is unwilling to bear it, the world will continue to muddle along as it has for the past century—with hesitant advances, punctuated by various alarms and by periods of backsliding in the wholly beneficial processes of globalization. Perhaps, if the United States is unwilling to shoulder the imperial burden of maintaining the global Pax, we will have to wait for one or other of the emerging imperial states—China and India—to do so in the future. Despite different political systems, both have long experience of running imperial systems. With their recent growing commitment to a liberal international economic order—of which China's massive unilateral reduction of its trade barriers is the most notable—they might be willing to maintain the Pax to provide the order that globalization requires. Till then, we may be fated to live with the ancient Chinese curse, "May you live in interesting times."

Notes

INTRODUCTION

1. Crone (1996), p. 2.
2. Kipling (1899): "The White Man's Burden."
3. Many of the critics of the current period of globalization, who tend to be sociologists, philosophers, and historians rather than economists, characterize it as the product of an ideology called neoliberalism; see Bourdieu (1998), Giddens (1999), Gray (1999). But as the Peruvian novelist and politician Mario Vargas Llosa (2000) has cogently argued, it is a meaningless term: "a 'neo' is someone who pretends to be something, someone who is at the same time inside and outside of something; it is an elusive hybrid, a straw man set up without ever identifying a specific value, idea, regime, or doctrine. To say 'neoliberal' is the same as saying 'semiliberal' or 'pseudoliberal'. It is pure nonsense. Either one is in favor of liberty or against it, but one cannot be semi-in-favor or pseudo-in-favor of liberty, just as one cannot be 'semipregnant', 'semiliving', or 'semidead'. The term has not been invented to express a conceptual reality, but rather as a corrosive weapon of derision, it has been designed to semantically devalue the doctrine of liberalism" (p. 16). The attempt to define a new ideology called the third way between this "neoliberalism" and the failed "really existing socialism" is equally vacuous; see Lal (2000a), and ch. 5 below.
4. See Lal (1998). Intensive growth which leads to a sustained rise in per capita income is to be distinguished from extensive growth where output grows side by side with population leaving per capita income virtually unchanged. The world has seen extensive growth for millennia with the expansion of population leading to rises in agricultural output as more land is brought into cultivation or is used more intensively. In these agrarian organic economies, as Wrigley (1988) has labeled them, the fixed land constraint implied that at some stage diminishing returns would set in, and along with the expansion of population following any rise in per capita on Malthusian lines, there would be no sustained rise in per capita income. The intensive growth due to the extension or creation of empires would lead to a temporary rise in per capita income (Smithian intensive growth), but it was not till the Industrial Revolution and the substitution of mineral energy resources—fossil fuels—for the products of land as the source of the economy's energy that unlimited intensive growth, which I label Promethean, became a possibility first in the West and subsequently in the Rest.
5. Cain and Hopkins (2002), p. 664. Also see Lieven (2001) ch.1, for a succinct account of the different meanings of empire over the ages.
6. See McNeill (1980) p. 23-25.
7. The Russian empire and its subsequent distorted reinvention under the Soviets may seem to be an exception. But as Lieven (2001) argues, the Soviet deviation—and the horrible tyranny it supported—along with Hitler's failed attempt to create a new German empire were in large part the consequence of the First World War. Also, as he notes, though the consequences of the dissolution of the Soviet empire in terms of chaos in the seceding regions are not as yet severe, it is early yet (only about 10 years since the dissolution) as compared with the time it took for the deleterious effects of the dissolution of the other empires, for instance of the British empire in Africa, to be manifest.

8. It should, however, be noted that Jones (1981)—following in the footsteps of Kant (1784), Gibbon (1787), and Weber (1923)—has maintained that the rise of the West was due to the political and institutional competition which existed in the European "states system" after the fall of the Roman empire. But as I have argued (in Lal [1998, 2003]) this explanation is inadequate as India too had a states system for much of its history and that did not lead it to the Industrial Revolution. Instead, the rare periods of political stability under dynastic imperial rule extending over the subcontinent were the most prosperous and glorious periods of Indian history, when innovation and growth occurred. The rise of the West, as I argued in *Unintended Consequences*, cannot be explained in purely materialist terms. It cannot be understood without the distinctive changes in the cosmological beliefs of Western Europe from those of other Eurasian civilizations, changes associated with the twin papal revolutions of Gregory I (concerning the family in the sixth century) and Gregory VII (concerning the law in the eleventh century).

9. Finer (1997), vol. 1, p. 34.

10. Whenever I write "men" it should be taken to mean "men and women" or "persons." Thereby I can avoid the terrible mangling of English prose perpetrated by current politically correct practices of writing spokespersons and women instead of the colloquially correct forms man, mankind, chairman, spokesmen, etc.

CHAPTER 1

1. Michael Flanders and Donald Swann, *At the Drop of A Hat*, EMI Records, 1960.

2. Evolutionary psychologists are now documenting how both the instinct to trade (truck and barter) and to make war (to confiscate) are part of the basic human instinct of a self-interested animal for whom the basic goods—food and sex—further its reproductive success. See Hirshleifer (1998), Chagnon (1983), Harris (1984), Manson and Wrangham (1991), Keeley (1996). Also see Keegan (1994), part 2, for a judicious survey of the evolution of anthropological writings on war, whose authors were largely part of the nurture school of social science who refused to recognize the importance of war. The warring sides were the cultural determinists (e.g., Ruth Benedict and Margaret Mead) and the structural functionalists (e.g., Claude Lévi-Strauss). They were interested in the stability of societies, and though they knew there were disputes about women in primitive societies, they refused to study its consequences—war. The first anthropologist to challenge them in a 1949 book called *Primitive War* was Harry Turney-High. But he did not look at the biological function for primitive warfare. As Jack Hirshleifer (2001) notes: "he minimized the significance of material-resource capture, and the female-capture aspect appears to have escaped his attention entirely. Accordingly, he was inclined to describe primitive war as 'stupid' or 'childish,' aimed at goals he regarded as whimsical or ephemeral, for example prestige." (p. 37, n. 14).

   Steven Pinker has emphasized that the violent components of human nature exist not because violence is a primitive, irrational urge, or a pathology, but because it "is a near-inevitable outcome of the dynamics of self-interested, rational social organisms." Pinker (2002), p. 329. Competition is what drives natural selection, and for the human survival machines holding their immortal genes in trust, other survival machines can be in the way and might need to be eliminated or disabled. Raw self-interest may thus be the major motive for wars, as has been confirmed by a study of 251 conflicts over the last 200 years by Bruce Bueno de Mesquita (1981).

   War will therefore be endemic in human nature, for it is one way of obtaining the goods desired by the self-interested animals who constitute humanity. The other way is through the productive social interactions emphasized by Adam Smith. Thus, the study of war—the economics of expropriation—is as much a part of economics as that of trade, as Jack Hirshleifer (2001) has emphasized. Vilfredo Pareto, the great Italian economist, knew this when he wrote: "The efforts of men are utilized in two different ways: they are directed to the production of or transformation of economic goods, or else the appropriation of goods produced by others." Cited in Hirshleifer (2001), p. 9.

3. Hobbes (1651/1996), pp. 88–89.

4. Ibid.
5. Doyle (1986), p. 40
6. Machiavelli, *The Prince*, p. 18.
7. See Gallagher and Robinson (1953).
8. Lal (1988), ch. 13.2. The model based in part on Findlay and Wilson (1987) was first developed in Lal (1984) and widely circulated as a World Bank discussion paper. It is also reproduced in the appendix to Lal (1998). Later, Mancur Olson (2000) rediscovered this model. See my review of this book in Lal (2001). The tax-cum-public-goods equilibrium which can be derived from the model (but not discussed below) also allows a classification of what I have termed autonomous states (as opposed to factional ones) into predatory, Platonic guardian, and bureaucrat maximizing states. (See Lal and Myint [1996], pp. 264–7.) These differ in the objectives they seek to subserve. The predatory state is only concerned with maximizing its net revenue; the Platonic guardian state, with maximizing social welfare; the bureaucrat, maximizing the number of bureaucrats. It can be shown that the Platonic guardian state provides the optimal level of public goods with the lowest tax rate. The bureaucrat and predatory states' tax rate is determined by the entries to barriers to rivals as shown below, but they differ in the level of public goods provided, with the bureaucrat maximizing state providing more than the predatory state, and perhaps even overproviding them beyond the optimal level. See Lal and Myint (1996). Hirshleifer's model is contained in Hirshleifer (1995/2001).
9. Hobbes, *Leviathan*, p. 223.
10. See Lal (1988) and (1998) for details. A brief outline of the model may be helpful. The best way to look at the state is as a two-good multiproduct natural monopoly providing protection and justice. But this monopoly is contestable, and the height of the barriers to entry to either internal or external rivals will determine the maximum rent it can extract from its prey. The height of these barriers determine the relative differences in costs of the incumbent (TCi) controller of this natural monopoly—the state—and those of new entrants (TCe) who wish to replace it. These costs will consist partly of the variable costs of running the state and the fixed costs in the form of the infrastructure of coercion. The variable costs of running the state can be expected to be the same for the incumbent as well as for any rival seeking to challenge him. But, the incumbent will have an advantage over any potential rival in so far as part of the fixed costs for him will be sunk costs. If the total costs for any new entrant are K, and the sunk costs for the incumbent, inclusive of the geographic and cultural barriers to entry, are a fraction (s) of these, its total cost curve will lie below the new entrants by this fraction sK. Moreover, as the costs of weaponry, fortifications, buildings, etc. are fixed, the average of this fixed cost component will initially decline with respect to the territory controlled. But as the territory to be controlled expands, the average costs of both maintaining or contesting the natural monopoly are likely to rise. This gives us the shape of the total cost curves of the incumbent and new entrant seeking to contest him for the natural monopoly—the state.

Until the state reaches a certain territorial size, the average costs of maintaining/contesting the state are declining, as the fixed cost component is spread over a larger area. But after this critical level, the average costs begin to rise as the rising variable costs of running the larger state and any incremental fixed costs increase total costs.

As long as the territory to be controlled lies in the decreasing average cost part of the total cost curve, the incumbent can find a tax rate which allows him to extract the full monopoly rents from his prey determined by the barriers to entry of sK. So, other things being equal, there will be a disincentive for him to extend his territorial control beyond the decreasing average cost portion of his total cost curve.

Moreover, depending on the shape of the fixed cost curve in controlling a given territory, there may be no tax rate that will prevent entry, and political instability in the territory will be the norm. If the territory is large enough and the fixed costs required to establish a state under one sovereign over the whole region are prohibitive, there may be a number of competing states in an otherwise homogeneous region. Even if all their cost curves are identical, there may also not be a stable equilibrium in the *number* of states in the territory.

11. The designation "predatory" is to show the similarity of the relationships between sovereign and subjects, as in the predator-prey models of the natural world (see Goodwin), where there is a symbiosis in the interests of the predator and the prey, but the predator is not interested in the welfare of the prey except to see it become fatter and tastier before his meal!

12. Hirshleifer sets out a simple model to explain why anarchy need not be chaotic and also the factors which lead it to break down into hegemony. Consider two groups who are rational, self-interested, and only concerned with maximizing their own income. There are two ways of obtaining income: by making or taking. So there are two technologies to produce income: a technology of production and a technology of appropriating through conflict (war). Each group starts off with given resources; each can use these resources in the technology both of production and of war. Each group will choose a preferred balance between productive and conflictual effort in equilibrium. The social outcome will depend on the interactions between these separate optimizing decisions, and thereby the levels of production and war and the distribution of the total product between the two claimants.

The basic structure of the model is as follows. Assume there are two contenders ($i = 1$, 2) who divide their available resources (Ri) between production (Ei) and fighting (Fi). Assuming that the aggregate resource base ($R = R1 + R2$) is constant, and is hence not affected by fighting, and that the unit costs of transforming resources into productive or fighting effort are a and b respectively: $Ri = aiEi + biFi$.

The income which each contender gets is determined by a production function (the same for both): $Yi = (eiRi) \wedge h$ (where $ei = Ei/Ri$).

But as Ri depends in part on how much of the aggregate resources (R) can be obtained by fighting, this will depend on the relative success in fighting (pi), which in turn depends on the technology of fighting. This technology and hence the relative success ratio in fighting ($p1/p2$) will depend on relative fighting effort ($Fi/F2$), and the decisiveness of the fighting outcome (m): $p1/p2 = (F1/F2) \wedge m$.

From these, the equilibrium success ratio in the steady state can be derived as: $P1/p2 = (f1/f2) \wedge (m/1 - m)$, where $fi = Fi/Ri$.

This simple anarchical system will be dynamically stable if (i) $m < 1$, and (ii) $Yi > y$ (subsistence income).

There would be an anarchical social equilibrium, a spontaneous order in the sense of Hayek (1973). There could be total peace or some equilibrium fighting in this anarchic social equilibrium. The most crucial parameter in the model is the one relating to the decisiveness of conflict. This decisiveness (m) factor amplifies the ratio of military inputs (fighting efforts) into the ratio of consequences (division of the loot or power). If this differs between the contestants and is sufficiently high for one of them, even with a small force superiority, the anarchical society will collapse into hegemony. The country with the higher decisiveness parameter will increase its fighting effort, and the other will try and match this by initially increasing its fighting effort (but proportionately less than the country with the improvement in decisiveness), but will eventually give up the unequal struggle and concentrate more of its efforts and resources to producing income instead.

Moreover, if, other things being equal, the aggregate of resources is fixed and the number of contestants rises, then each will have a higher fighting intensity and lower income—as each will have a smaller share of the fixed aggregate resources and more of these will be diverted to fighting. If, with an unchanged decisiveness factor, one agent has a rise in its productivity coefficient in transforming resources into income and/or fighting, it improves its edge against its competitors. But if the improvement is only in the income transforming coefficient, then apart from the increase in the income of the more productive economy, there is no other change in the anarchical equilibrium. But if the improvement is in the technology of fighting, and thus the coefficient of transforming resources into fighting falls, then the country with the fighting improvement sees both its fighting intensity and income rise, while the others will also raise their fighting intensities (but by less than the country with the military advance) and have lower incomes. Furthermore, when the decisiveness of conflict is not sufficiently high, it can pay the smaller and weaker contestant to fight harder—to increase its fighting intensity—by investing more in conflict than productive activity. This leads to what Hirshleifer calls "the paradox of power" whereby poorer or weaker contenders gain at the expense of their richer or stronger rivals. This does not mean that the weaker side defeats the stronger in an absolute sense. Rather, the weaker side does relatively better as it is willing to commit more of its resources to the battle. It does not lose as heavily as might be expected from counting up the resources available.

As Hirshleifer has pointed out to me in a private communication, the model does not explain asymmetrical warfare, such as guerrilla warfare, where the dominant power and the insurgent are fighting in very different ways. This would be similarly true for a sea power fighting a land power. Then, decisiveness one way may differ from decisiveness the other way. One side might be fighting in such a way that it can't gain much, but can't lose much either (low m), while for the other side the opposite holds (high m). In the Napoleonic wars, Britain's island geography meant she could never be successfully invaded, so for her it was a relatively low-m war, which she could fight for a long time. But Napoleon's continental opponents were forced to fight symmetrical wars against him, and they most often rapidly went down to defeat. Napoleon's defeat in Russia was due to asymmetrical warfare. The Russians were fighting in a low-m way—when defeated they could withdraw into the interior—whereas it was a high-m contest for Napoleon, who had to win big if he was to survive.

13. See Finley (1968), Domar (1970). That this was an efficient institution, particularly in the production of crops subject to increasing returns to scale, had been shown by Fogel and Engerman (1974) and Fogel (1989). For the common problems faced by Eurasian civilizations lay in tying scarce labor to abundant land (see Lal [1998]). There is, however, one historical puzzle which Stan Engerman has pointed out to me in personal correspondence. Quincy Wright has estimated that after about A.D. 1300 northern Europeans did not enslave other northern Europeans, yet in the next six centuries they fought numerous wars which killed and wounded more people than were involved in the transatlantic slave trade. I argue in Lal (1988) that as slavery requires either a state which can enforce slave contracts or else an obvious way to differentiate slaves—like the pigmentation of their skins—medieval Europe (with its weak and fragmented states) could not tie labor to scarce land through slavery and instead adopted a much looser form of controlling labor through serfdom. Perhaps it was the common culture of Christendom which prevented one set of Christians from enslaving others, though this clearly did not prevent them from killing them!

14. McNeill (1963, 1991), pp. 33–34.
15. Keegan (1994), p. 128.
16. Ibid., p. 43.
17. Ibid., p. 135.
18. McNeill (1963, 1991), p. 51–52.
19. Keegan (1994), p. 169.
20. Ibid.
21. Ibid., p. 131.
22. Ibid., p. 132.
23. McNeill (1963, 1991), p. 82.
24. Jenner (1992), pp. 22–23.
25. Rothermund (2002), p. 3.
26. Digby (1971), p. 68.
27. See Lal (1988), p. 24–25.
28. The Greek case is based on Fuller (1954), ch. 1–3, Preston and Wise (1979) ch. 1–2, and Thucydides.
29. See note 12 above.
30. Keegan (1994), p. 268.
31. Ibid.
32. Keegan (1994), p. 280.
33. McNeill (1980), p. 47.

34. Keegan (1994), p. 181.
35. See Findlay and Lundahl (2003) for an analytical discussion of the rise and fall of the Mongol empire within an analytical framework similar to that provided here.
36. Keegan (1994), p. 204.
37. Ibid., p. 207.
38. The Turkish exponents of *jihad* (holy war).
39. Keegan (1994), p. 207.
40. Arquilla and Ronfeldt (1997), p. 24.
41. Chambers (1985), p. 43.
42. Ratchnevsky (1991), p. 155.
43. C. Tyler-Smith et al. (2003). See also S. Sailer, "Gene's of History's Greatest Lover Found?" UPI, Feb. 5, 2003, available at www.upi.com.
44. The Y chromosome is found only in men and is passed down patrilineally. In over 90 percent of the Asian men tested, the Y chromosomes were quite diverse showing their diverse family trees. But, a striking 8 percent had Y chromosomes that were virtually identical, indicating a common forefather. The 23 coauthors of the paper were able to establish that this common progenitor lived in Mongolia, and was most likely Genghis Khan (ca. 1162–12227). Genghis had six Mongolian wives and married many daughters of foreign kings who accepted his suzerainty. "The Secret History of the Mongols" which is a near contemporary record notes that Genghis Khan's subordinates explicitly promised him the pick of captured women and horses.
45. Arquilla and Ronfeldt (1997), pp. 36–37.
46. Keegan (1994), p. 211.
47. McNeill (1982), p. 60.
48. Ibid., p. 60.
49. Fernandez-Armesto (1995), p. 94.
50. Pintner (1995), p. 9.
51. see Howard (2000), pp. 8–9.
52. This has led to the second of the traditions of international relations theory which derives from Hugo Grotius's *De Jure Belli ac Pacis*. He and his followers claimed that after the Treaty of Westphalia, natural law would determine the relationships between sovereign states which would entail a system of mutual social rights and duties (see Gierke [1957], p. 85). This Grotian view implied that with natural law being the main source for the law of nations, there was no longer any need for Christian foundations. But, the Grotians nevertheless maintained that "within the wider circle of mankind, bound by the principles of natural law, there was a narrower circle of Christendom, bound by volitional divine law, by the inherited customs and rules of *ius gentium*, by canon and Roman law" (Bull [1995], p. 27). Certainly the Ottomans, with their continuing threat to Christendom, were seen outside this narrower pale.

In the eighteenth and nineteenth centuries with the gradual secularization of Europe, instead of a Christian society, a European society of states emerged. With the worldwide expansion of Europe, this European system was gradually extended to other parts of the world. But the European international system was now not seen as based on some universal natural law binding nations but as a reflection of a specifically European culture. International society was seen as "a European association, to which the non-European states could be admitted only if and when they met a standard of civilization laid down by the Europeans—the test which Turkey was the first to pass when under Article VII of the Treaty of Paris of 1856 she was admitted to 'the public law and concert of Europe' " (Bull [1995] p. 31). It is ironic that while Islamic Ottoman Turkey seems to have met the European test in the nineteenth century, its successor, the secular Turkish state, set up by Kemal Attaturk is yet to meet the European test laid down for its entry into the European Union!

In the twentieth century, with the retreat of the European powers from their former colonies and the colonies' transformation into independent sovereign states, this Eurocentric cultural test for joining international society came to be repudiated. Instead, there was a reversion to versions of Grotian natural law to provide the norms for international relations. Thus, as Bull (1995) says, in the contemporary international society of states, there has been "a return to the tendency that prevailed in the Grotian era to confuse international law with international morality or international improvement" (p. 38).

53. See Gellner (1988).

54. Howard (2000), p. 20.

55. The leading thinker in this tradition who did most to invent the notion of peace was Immanuel Kant in his *Perpetual Peace*. He did not take as rosy a picture of human nature as Rousseau. For he "remarked (in an aside) that out of the crooked timber of humanity no straight thing was ever made" (Berlin [1979] p. 148). But he agreed with the other Enlightenment thinkers that war had become an enjoyable pastime for the aristocratic-monarchical system. Its destruction and replacement by republican states (which could be constitutional monarchies)—where the people who had to die and pay for wars would be consulted—was a necessary condition for maintaining peace. He had no illusions that this was also a sufficient condition. He expected wars would continue. But, over time, the expense and growing horror of war would provide disincentives to wage them. States would eventually be compelled to abandon their anarchical society and establish "a 'league of nations,' which would provide collectively the security that at present each sought individually" (Howard [2000], p. 30). Meanwhile, it remained a moral imperative to strive for peace.

The classical liberals in England and in America believed with Adam Smith and Richard Cobden that with the growth of international trade and investment, the influence of the bourgeoisie—who unlike the old ruling elites had no interest in perpetuating war—would increase, and peace would result. Thus was born the idealist dream for the institution and maintenance of perpetual peace, which still stands in opposition to the realism of Hobbes. Contemporary idealists believe, as the Enlightenment philosophers did, that the world consists of rational and benign individuals, who are only held in situations of conflict because of the system of states. For them, international relations is a cooperative and non-zero-sum game, much as the classical liberals such as Adam Smith argued was true of foreign trade. There are moral imperatives limiting the action of states, and these require not merely state's to coexist and cooperate, but rather "the overthrow of the system of states and its replacement by a cosmopolitan society" (Bull [1995], p. 25).

56. The notes to Maddison (2001) explain in detail the basis of his estimates. Many for the earlier period are based on qualitative judgments.

57. There is an interesting question raised by Stanley Engerman in private correspondence about why military power shifted from the south to the northwest in Europe. I suspect the answer is partly cultural—the south was the area of the Counter Reformation, the north of the Reformation—and partly economic—the slowly rolling industrial revolution emerged in the northwest with its abundance of coal, the major mineral energy resource on which it was based.

58. Keegan (1994), p. 196.

59. Cook (1983), pp. 36, 38.

60. Bull and Watson (1984), p. 3.

61. Watson in Bull and Watson (1984), p. 19.

62. Bull in Bull and Watson(1984), p. 105.

63. Bull and Watson (1984), p. 6.

64. See Diamond (1997). But the technical advantages enjoyed by the conquistadors over the Aztecs and the Incas have been questioned by Howard in Bull and Watson (eds.) (1984). He notes, quoting Parry (1966), that the cannon Cortez took from his ships were "small and not very effective pieces, though no doubt their noise and smoke made a great impression. Apart from the cannon Cortes had 13 muskets." Parry also states: "Cortes had only sixteen horses when he landed and some of those were soon killed in battle. Most of his men fought on foot with sword, pike and crossbow" (Parry, p. 95–96). The Spaniards did have the advantage of fighting with metal weapons against stone, but Howard states that "basically they owed their victories to their single minded ruthlessness, their desperation, and fanaticism. Like their forefathers of the *reconquista* in Spain, they were fighting both for land and for Christ; also of course for gold, if they could find any" (p. 35). So it seems that their victory is another example of Hirshleifer's paradox of power!

65. Keegan (1994), p. 339.
66. McNeill (1982), p. 44.
67. Ibid., p. 45.
68. Lal (1998), pp. 42–44.
69. Keegan, (1994), pp. 42–45.
70. McNeill, (1982), p. 147.
71. Keegan (1994), p. 45.
72. See Rothermund (2002).
73. See McNeill (1982), p. 147, Keegan (1994), p. 45.
74. McNeill (1982), p. 224. The main advance was developing prophylaxis against malaria. See Headrick (1979).
75. Keegan (1994), p. 313.
76. Ibid.
77. Luttwak (2003), Arquilla and Ronfeldt (1997), Owens (2001).
78. Luttwak (2003), p. 13.
79. See Ogarkov (1982).
80. Ibid., p. 15.
81. See note 12 above.
82. These are the assumptions which underlie the UN system and, till the promulgation of the Bush doctrine, were at least rhetorically defended by all governments.
83. R. Cameron (1993), p. 31.
84. The Marxist theories of imperialism which look upon it as a reflection of finance or monopoly capitalism reached their most popular form with Lenin (1916), but even Marxists acknowledge these theories are seriously flawed. See Brewer (1990), Etherington (1984), Warren (1980), Kiernan (1974). Schumpeter (1955) and Hobson (1902) both emphasised the link between capitalism and formal imperialism and shared "the naive idea that it was possible to find a form of capitalism that would bring peace and prosperity to all" (see Cain and Hopkins [2002], pp. 31–33). Neo-Marxists like Wallerstein (1980) and Frank (1998) consider industrialization as having precipitated imperialism. But Cain and Hopkins, (2002) show that this view is unfounded. Also see Tilly (1992).
85. McNeill (1979), p. 36.
86. Ibid., p. 36.
87. Ibid., p. 63.
88. Toynbee (1995), p. 278.
89. Ibid.
90. Ibid., pp. 313–14.
91. See Anderson (1991).
92. Toynbee (1995), p. 288.
93. Thus Toynbee (1995) notes: "The Incas . . . were builders of roads and fortresses; and like the Roman conquerors of Italy, they used these instruments to consolidate each gain of ground in preparation for the next advance in their systematic movement of conquest northward. The completed system consisted of two main roads running parallel north and south, one along the Andean plateau, and the other along the Pacific coast, with transverse connecting roads at intervals. The roads were carried across rivers and ravines by bridges of stone and wood, by suspension bridges of rope, or by cable and basket; they constituted an engineering feat of such magnitude that it was said that the construction of the bridge of Apurimac was alone enough to overawe and subdue the surrounding hostile Indian tribes" (p. 289).
94. See Hallpike (1986), Lal (1998).
95. Toynbee (1995), p. 296.
96. Toynbee (1995), p. 297.
97. Goldsmith (1984), p. 287.
98. See Findlay (1996).
99. Maddison (2001), Table B-21.
100. See Lal (1998), ch. 3.

101. Goldsmith (1984), p. 287.
102. Ibid., p. 263.
103. See Bernardi (1970).
104. Ibid., p. 81.
105. Ibid., p. 73.
106. See Lal (1987a), Lal and Myint (1996).
107. Goldsmith (1984), p. 283.
108. Maddison (1971), pp. 22, 45.
109. See Spear (1963).
110. Tomlinson (1975), p. 338.
111. See Jenner (1992).
112. See L. Colley (1992).
113. See Oakeshott (1993).
114. Tilly (1992) characterizes it as a tribute-taking empire.
115. Lal (2003a, 1998).

CHAPTER 2

1. At the end of the first millennium, it was the Arabs who could have rightly had the same sense of achievement, as sitting in Baghdad they surveyed the world described by the Syrian geographer al- Muqaddasi: "The Islam he beheld was spread like a pavilion under the tent of the sky, erected as if for some great ceremonial occasion, arrayed with great cities in the role of princes; these were attended by chamberlains, lords and foot soldiers, whose parts were played by provincial capitals, towns and villages respectively. The cities were linked not only by the obvious elements of a common culture . . . but also by commerce and in many cases reciprocal obligations. The strict political unity which had once characterized Islam had been shattered in the tenth century . . . yet a sense of comity survived, and travelers could feel at home throughout the Dar al-Islam—or to use an image popular with poets—in a garden of Islam, cultivated, walled against the world, yielding for its privileged occupants, shades and tastes of paradise." Fernandez-Armesto (1995), p. 35.
2. Shakespeare: Richard II, Act 2, scene 1, John of Gaunt's speech.
3. Kings Bell and Acqua to Gladstone, 6 November 1881, F.O.403/18, Public Records Office, Kew, cited in Doyle (1986), p. 162.
4. In 1998 the Fiji government discussed returning to the empire.
5. It also led to the famous Augustan debates about the reality of credit and the legitimacy of the wealth acquired through the speculation that the new financial instruments permitted. See Pocock (1975a and 1975b) and Lal (1985).
6. Colley (1992), p. 56.
7. Ibid., p. 56.
8. Cain and Hopkins (2002), pp. 100–01.
9. Ibid., pp. 4–5.
10. See Hecksher (1955) and Lal and Myint (1996) for the disorder created by mercantilism and neomercantilism.
11. Cain and Hopkins, ibid., p. 84.
12. Ibid., p. 84.
13. See Perkins (1984) for the rise of the professional classes in Britain.
14. Bayly (1989), p. 3.
15. Cited in Cain and Hopkins (2002), pp. 98, 99.
16. Ibid., p. 99.
17. Webster (1951), p. 750–51.
18. Cain and Hopkins (2002), p. 136.
19. He did have a lot to say about the cost and benefit of colonies, particularly in North America. But colonization is only one form of direct imperialism. India, for example, was not a colony (with white settlers) but was a central part of the British empire. Nor

was all of it ruled directly. The princely states which formed a large part of the British Raj were ruled indirectly through British political agents assigned to the native rulers.

20. See Cain (1998). A detailed study of Britain's foreign investment by Davis and Huttenback (1987) shows that the gentlemanly capitalists were the major investors and that till 1880 these foreign investments yielded more than domestic investments.

21. Angell (1911), p. 302.

22. Angell (1911), p. 302.

23. See Ferguson (1998) for an account and references and for the latest revisionist explanation.

24. R. Aron (1974).

25. Mead (2001), pp. 80–84, breaks up the U.S. ascendency into four periods. The first, 1176 to 1823, when the United States gets its independence and tries to work out a modus vivendi with its former colonial master, Britain. The second, 1823–1914, with the United States living in the Pax Britannia. The third, 1914–1947, which saw the decline and collapse of the British Pax, and the United States faced with the choice of replacing it or standing back inside its continental fortress. The fourth, from 1947 to today when the United States concluded that it would have to replace the British Pax with one of its own.

26. Cited in Aron (1974), p. xxvi, from Van Alstyne (1960), p. 1.

27. Aron (1974), p. xxviii.

28. Ibid., p. xxxv.

29. Mead (2001), p. 84.

30. Liska (1967).

31. See Knock (1992), who points out that in an essay written in 1886 (buried in his papers till 1968), Wilson reconciles his Burkean belief in democracy and his affection for socialism by stating "For it is very clear that in fundamental theory socialism and democracy are almost if not quite the one and the same. They both rest at bottom on the absolute right of the community to determine its own destiny and that of its members." Cited in Knock (1995), p. 7.

32. Ibid., p. 10.

33. Ibid., p. 11.

34. Aron (1974), p. xxvi.

35. Skidelsky (1983), p. 325.

36. Keynes (1919, 1971), p. 34.

37. Skidelsky (1983), p. 395.

38. Knock (1992), p. 226.

39. Keynes (1919, 1971), p. 188.

40. Hufbauer et al. (1990), and Lal (2001a).

41. See Davis and Engerman (2003).

42. Dean Acheson, "Ethics in International Relations Today," in Larson, ed. (1966), p. 134–35.

43. Ferguson (1998), p. 440–41.

44. See Collier and Hoeffler (1998).

45. Skidelsky (2000), p. 38.

46. The much derided sociobiology provides some cogent reasons for the survival of these primordial forces. See Gil-White (1999). Evolutionary psychologists and anthropologists maintain that human nature was set during the period of evolution ending with the Stone Age, since there has not been enough time for further evolution. See J. Tooby and L. Cosmides (1989), J. Barkow, L. Cosmides, and J. Tooby (1992) and R. Trivers (1985). One salient feature of this Stone Age environment was that rapid species-relevant judgments had to be made on the basis of quick impressions. Our brains, they claim, have been hardwired to deal with the problems faced in the primordial environment—the savannahs of Africa. Here it was a matter of life and death to judge from whatever signs were available that a dangerous member of a predatory species was at hand. The decision, moreover, had to be instantaneous, without any time being spent on continual sampling to confirm one's conjecture that a yellow shape with stripes in the distance was indeed a tiger. This means that we are naturally primed to make instantaneous species judgments

between "them" and "us." Thus, Sherif and Sherif (1964) find that even when individuals are assigned arbitrarily to groups, and they know this is the case, nevertheless strong group identification commonly emerges.

Given the divergence between different human groups in physiognomy and culture, once our ancestors spread throughout the world and then rarely came in contact with their genetic cousins—as with the ending of the Ice Age when the ice bridges linking the continents melted—it is hardly surprising that when we do come across another ethnic group we are primed to look upon it as a different species. Intermarriage and long familiarity might change these natural instincts, but, as the bloody outcome in the successor states of Yugoslavia demonstrates, this might not be enough because other characteristics like religion might have replaced mere ethnicity as the marker between "them" and "us." This provides an important reason rooted in our biology why the Enlightenment hope of reducing—if not ending— ethnic and cultural differences and conflicts has not been fulfilled.

47. Mead (2001).
48. Mead (2001), p. 87, lists the following as prominent Hamiltonians in American history: Henry Clay, Daniel Webster, John Hay, Theodore Roosevelt, Henry Cabot Lodge Sr., Dean Acheson, George Bush Sr.
49. Ibid., p. 109.
50. These include according to Mead (2001), p. 88, John Quincy Adams, George Kennan, the historian Charles Beard, the novelist Gore Vidal, and, for part of his life, the columnist Walter Lipmann.
51. Ibid., p. 88.
52. Quoted in Mead (2001), p. 185.
53. Mead (2001), p. 88.
54. Rudyard Kipling (1899).
55. Boot (2002), p. xvi.
56. Ibid., p. xvii.
57. Cited in Boot (2002), p. xviii.
58. Mead (2001), p. 224.
59. Ibid., p. 244.
60. Ibid., p. 236.
61. See Lal (1990a).
62. Arizona senator John McCain, the World War Two generals Patton and MacArthur, as well as the ten former generals who became president of the United States appealed to Jacksonian sentiments. The espousal of Jacksonian views by Presidents Nixon and Reagan were responsible for the shift of Jacksonians to the Republican party. See Mead (2001), p. 244. The younger George Bush can also be looked upon as a Jacksonian.
63. See Bacevich (2002).
64. Bacevich (2002), p. 128.
65. Cited in Bacevich (2002), p. 175. Ibid., p. 175.
66. Bacevich (2002) discusses at length the views of historians Charles Beard and William Williams that America from its very beginnings was an empire.
67. A. M. Schlesinger Jr. (1986), p. 141; quoted in Bacevich (2002), p. 30.
68. Kosterlitz (2002), p. 4.
69. Ibid., p. 11.

CHAPTER 3

1. Liska (1967), pp. 9–10.
2. Ibid., pp. 10–12, and 20.
3. Ibid., p. 37.
4. Ibid., pp. 24–25.
5. Kennedy (1989).
6. This is recognized by both idealists and realists. See Nye (2002), Mearsheimer (2001). Aron (1966) distinguished between force and power and identified three fundamental

elements in power: "first of all the *space* occupied by the political units; second the *available materials* and the techniques by which they can be transformed into weapons, the *number of men* and the art of transforming them into soldiers (or, again, *the quantity and quality of implements and combatants*); and last the *collective capacity for action*, which includes the organization of the army, the discipline of the combatants, the quality of the civil and military command, in war and in peace, and the solidarity of the citizens during the conflict in the face of good or bad luck" (p. 54).

7. Feldstein (2003).
8. Ibid., p. 3.
9. Ibid., p. 2.
10. Dibb et al. (1999), quoted in Nye (2002), p. 21.
11. For instance, Nye (2002).
12. J. W. Cole, "Colonial Rule," in Brown and Louis, eds. (1999), p. 232.
13. See Macaulay (1898), pp. 585–86, and Lal (1988).
14. Macaulay (1898), vol. XI, pp. 585–86.
15. Spear (1963).
16. Here strategic realists, who are follower of Hobbes, need to be distinguished from liberal idealists, the followers of Kant and Grotius. Both look upon the present international system as a continuation of the anarchic European states system when it has in fact become imperial. Thus, strategic realist Christopher Layne (2002), from the Cato Institute, recently argued that from the historical record, hegemonic powers are likely to be challenged by a coalition of other states as "when one state becomes more powerful— becomes a hegemon—the imbalance of power in its favor is a menace to the security of all other states" Layne (2002). This is the central prediction of the realist theory of academic international relations. It claims that unipolarity is dynamically unstable. A new coalition of nations will emerge as a balancer against the U.S. hegemon. But some international theorists are now beginning to realize that it is profoundly mistaken to believe unipolarity is unstable; see Donnelly (2003). As Wohlforth (1999) notes, it is mistaken to consider the United States's "unprecedented quantitative and qualitative concentration of power as an evanescent 'moment'. . . . The scholarly conventional wisdom holds that unipolarity is dynamically unstable and that any slight overstep by Washington will spark a dangerous backlash. I find the opposite to be true: unipolarity is durable and peaceful, and the chief threat is U.S. failure to do enough. Possessing an undisputed preponderance of power, the United States is freer than most states to disregard the international system and its incentives. But because the system is built around U.S. power, it creates demands for American engagement. The more efficiently Washington responds to these incentives and provides order, the more long-lived and peaceful the system" (pp. 7–8). Quite!

Nevertheless, theorists do not like anomalies and in their attempt to keep their old wine but put it into new bottles they have invented the notion of "soft power," which is "expressed through international trade regimes, law and organizations such as the United Nations [and is claimed to be] interchangeable with hard power—actual wealth, military strength and the like" (Donnelly, [2003], p. 1). Joseph Nye (2002), of Harvard's Kennedy School of Government and a former Pentagon official in the Clinton administration, is the chief proponent of this theory. He has called for the United States to exercise its "soft power" and not act as an imperial power. But is this soft power real? Power in international relations as Aron (1966) succinctly described it is "the capacity of a political unit to impose its will upon other units" (p. 47). Military force is a major component of such power, and for realists like Mearsheimer there is little else. Nye however argues that there is another aspect of power. "This aspect of power—getting others to want what you want—I call soft power. It co-opts people rather than coerces them. . . . Soft power arises in large part from our values. These values are expressed in our culture, in the policies we follow inside our country, and in the way we handle ourselves internationally" (p. 9). But, as I will be arguing in the third part of this book, though American culture might have appeal to many, any attempt as Nye describes it "of set[ting] the political agenda in a way that shapes the preferences of others" (p. 9) is likely to be a source of international disorder rather than order.

Nor is Nye's analogy of the distribution of power today in terms of a three-dimensional chess game cogent. He agrees with most other observers that on the top chess board military power is unipolar. He then introduces the second board representing economic power. Here he claims "economic power is multipolar." But as the discussion in the previous section has shown, this is just not the case. Moreover, the relevance of this dimension of power is as a correlate of military power. Nye seems to confuse this aspect from the purely economic interactions in the global economy. Here he seems wrongly to believe that economic interactions are a zero-sum game when he writes, "on this economic board, the United States is not a hegemon and often must bargain as an equal with Europe" (ibid., p. 39). It is mercantilist thinking to believe that in international economic relations there are hegemons and satraps. Nye's characterization of his second chess board is thus incoherent. International economic order requires international political order, but whereas for the latter a hegemon may be needed, there is no such need for the former.

His third chess board is also problematic. He claims this third "board is the realm of transnational relations that cross the borders outside of government control. This realm includes non-state actors as diverse as bankers electronically transferring sums larger than most national budgets, at one extreme, and terrorists carrying out attacks and hackers disrupting Internet operations, at the other" (ibid., p. 39). But this is confused and confusing. Bankers independent of state control are precisely what is needed for the efficient functioning of globally integrated capital markets. It is again a form of mercantilism to believe otherwise. To describe their actions as the exercise of power—forcing states to act according to their will—is a canard also made by many of the antiglobalization activists. The actions of these bankers as those of traders involved in international trade are mutually advantageous and thus wholly benign as opposed to the terrorists and hackers who are international criminals and whose power is like that of pirates of yore. The suppression of their power is the very purpose of maintaining international order, and if that is to be maintained by a coalition of states or as today by an imperial power, nothing is added to clarity of thought to lump them with benign bankers and traders and put them on a separate chess board from the traditional military and economic boards. I hope this is enough to show that the notion of soft power is soft-headed, if not meaningless.

17. Donnelly (2003), p. 2.
18. Ibid., p. 30.
19. See Lal (1999b), Feldstein (1997a, 1997b).
20. See, for example, Kissinger (2001).
21. Oliver (1999), p. 170.
22. See Headrick (1979) for a discussion of these tools of imperialism.
23. Oliver, op. cit., p. 211.
24. Oliver, ibid., pp. 202, 218.
25. See Collier and Lal (1986).
26. Oliver, op. cit., p. 293.
27. World Bank (1989), p. 22.
28. UN Population Division (2002).
29. See Lal (1995a).
30. See Rimmer (1992).
31. See Wrong (2000).
32. See Samatar (1999).
33. See Cooper (2001, 2003).
34. He also notes this in B. Lewis (2002), p. 21.
35. Fernandez-Armesto (1995), p. 35; see ch. 2, note 1.
36. See Lal (1998), ch. 4.
37. McNeill (1979), p. 390.
38. Lord Wavell cited in the epigraph to Fromkin (1989).
39. Fromkin (1989), p. 104.
40. Ibid., p. 562.
41. Fromkin (1989), p. 268.

42. Cited in Fromkin (1989), p. 297.
43. Ibid., p. 563.
44. This is also the title of Bernard Lewis's latest book (2002) which makes many of the points made in this section.
45. Fromkin (1989), p. 564.
46. Ibid., p. 565.
47. Crone (1980), p. 81.
48. See Crone and Hinds (1986) and Rahman (1979).
49. Avineri (1972), p. 302.
50. Ibid., p. 304.
51. Ibid., p. 308.
52. Ibid., p. 304.
53. Ibid., p. 301.
54. Hoffman (1995), p. 206.
55. Ibrahim (1985), p. 499.
56. See Hoffman (1995).
57. Ayubi (1991), pp. 176–77.
58. Ruthven (2002), p. 119.
59. Marty and Appelby, eds. (1993), p. 620.
60. Ruthven (2002), p. 124.
61. Easterman (1993), p. 37.
62. Ruthven (2002), p. 126.
63. Ibid., p. 126.
64. Ibid., p. 132.
65. Marty and Appelby (1993), p. 640.
66. B. Lewis (1992), p. 50.
67. Marty and Appelby (1993), p. 640.
68. See Lal (1998) for an account of and references to this papal family revolution.
69. Ruthven (2002), p. 77.
70. Kelly (1980), p. 218.
71. Koran, 9:5.
72. Khadduri (1955), p. 51.
73. Ruthven (2002), p. 60.
74. Maududi (1967), pp. 3–4, cited in Ruthven (2002), pp. 70–71.
75. Gellner (1992), p. 8.
76. Kepel (2002a), p. 49.
77. An excellent account of the tensions and contradictions in the attempt by Arab intellectuals to introduce modernity in their homelands is provided in Ajami (1998).
78. Kepel (2002a), p. 53.
79. Ibid., p. 67.
80. Ibid., pp. 362–63.
81. Ibid., p. 374.
82. A religious reformer, Muhammad ibn Abd al-Wahhab (1703–92) began to preach the need for Muslims to return to the teaching of Islam as understood by the followers of Ibn Hanbal. He enjoined strict obedience to the Koran and Hadith as they were interpreted by responsible scholars in each generation, and rejected all illegitimate innovations. His alliance with Muhammad ibn Saud, the ruler of a small market town, Diriyya, led to the founding of a state which claimed to live under the guidance of the *sharia*. It rejected the claims of the Ottomans to be the protectors of the authentic Islam. By the early years of the nineteenth century, the armies of the new state had sacked the Shia shrines in southwestern Iraq and occupied the holy cities of Hejaj (See Hourani [1991], p. 257–58).
83. Ibid., p. 319.
84. G. Kepel (2002b).
85. See S. Schwartz (2002).
86. See Ledeen (2002), pp. 33–45; 196–209.

87. Stone (1972) points out that "the truncated West Germany, after World War II, absorbed and rehabilitated no less than 9.7 million displaced persons. Small Austria received 178,000 Hungarian refugees in the aftermath of the Hungarian revolution of 1956. Italy provided a home for 585,000 Italians displaced from territory ceded to Yugoslavia, and from various parts of Africa. France gave permanent asylum to 1.4 million refugees (including Algerian Muslims) displaced by the emergence of new sovereign states in North Africa and Indochina. The Netherlands, tiny and crowded, welcomed and settled 230,000 refugees from Indonesia. Turkey resettled 150,000 Turks expelled by the Communist regime in Bulgaria" (pp. 209–10).

88. Stone (1972), p. 210–11.

89. Joseph Nye state in a *Financial Times* article on a possible war with Iraq: "if the U.S. is perceived as an imperialist power in the region, we shall encounter an anti-imperial reaction that could breed a new generation of terrorists," ("Owls Are Wiser about Iraq than Hawks," 21 October 2002). Two points need to be made. First, the region has been ruled by empires for millennia, some long lasting like the Romans and the Ottomans. To think that the mere existence of an empire will in itself breed terrorism, even if it brings peace and prosperity, seems to go against the historical record. Second, the title of his piece seems to suggest that an imperial power has to be a hawk. The effective exercise of imperial power depends upon the circumstances, requiring it to behave sometimes like a hawk, at other times like a dove, and quite often like an owl. It is Nye's failure, along with so many international relations experts in the United States, to recognize and accept that, for good or ill, the United States is already an imperial power which leads to the confusions displayed in this and other similar articles.

90. This is the so-called Dutch disease effects from foreign exchange bonanzas, which lead to a shrinking or retardation of the sector producing traded goods and an expansion of nontraded goods such as services, housing, etc.

91. Lal, "A Force to Lift the Curse of Natural Resources," *Financial Times*, 3 October 2003.

92. Lal (1983, 2002).

CHAPTER 4

1. By liberal I mean classical liberal throughout this book, and not liberal as it is currently used in the political discourse in the United States, where it is sometimes taken to mean socialist. As Joseph Schumpeter (1954) noted: "The term [classical or economic liberal] has acquired a different—in fact almost the opposite meaning—since about 1900 and especially since 1930; as a supreme if unintended compliment, the enemies of the system of private enterprise have thought it wise to appropriate its label" (p. 394). Whenever liberal in the current mistaken U.S. sense of the term is meant, it will be in single quotes.

2. Stiglitz (2002).

3. Lipson (1985), p. 8.

4. Cain and Hopkins (2002), p. 650 (emphasis added).

5. Maddison (2001), p. 100.

6. See Kindleberger (1973). This view has now had a long life as part of the theory of hegemonic stability in academic international relations, but has rightly been abandoned as it is incoherent; see Lake (1993), and Eichengreen (1989). No imperial hegemon is required (except to maintain international property rights) for the correct classical liberal policies of free trade and free capital mobility to be adopted, in their own self-interest, by all participants in the LIEO. This in fact was the correct classical liberal case against empire. The United States in the interwar period not only failed to provide the public good of protecting international property rights and peace, but foolishly failed to maintain the free trade and capital mobility which were clearly in its own self-interest.

7. These are dealt with in greater detail in the companion volume on *International Economic Order.*

8. See Lal (2003b) for why, even in the modern theory of trade and welfare, the two should again be linked. Also see chapter 5.
9. Bairoch (1993), p. 34.
10. See Baldwin (1969) for the flaws.
11. Bairoch (1993), p. 36.
12. See Lardy (2002, 2003, 1998).
13. Corden (1977), p. 2.
14. See Lal (1990d, 1994) for a rebuttal of the flawed arguments made for international monetary cooperation in a floating exchange rate system.
15. W. A. Lewis (1978), p. 49.
16. As shown by the detailed study by Collier et al. (1997).
17. See Lal (1983, 2000, 2002).
18. The distinction between inward-and outward-looking policies was first made by Hla Myint in his inaugural lecture at the London School of Economics; see Myint (1967).
19. Having risen from $4 in 1972 to $30 in 1983, the price of oil collapsed in 1986 but it has risen markedly in the last year because of the boom in Asia and the continuing troubles in the Middle East is now about $33.
20. See Lal and Myint (1996).
21. The costs and benefits of direct foreign investment are outlined and case studies for India and East Africa presented in Lal and associates (1975).
22. See Lal (1996).
23. It is still unclear to what extent the collapse is due to the internal factors resulting from the economic consequences of past dirigisme which impels reform (see Lal [1987a]), or external factors such as the threat of Star Wars which upped the ante in terms of unsustainable defense expenditures for the Soviet Union. Certainly Deng's reforms in China were motivated by a threatened internal economic collapse rather than any external factors.
24. See Lal (1987a), Hecksher (1955).

CHAPTER 5

1. Taylor (1974), p. 51.
2. This is the opinion of Giddens's colleagues as reported in "The Third Man: This Year's Reith Lecturer May Advise Mr. Blair, But He Bewilders Many Others," *Sunday Telegraph* (London), 28 March 1999, p. 41.
3. Bourdieu (1998), Gray (1999).
4. See Judt (1997).
5. Schwab and Smajda (1999).
6. Stiglitz (2002) (emphasis my own), p. 5.
7. World Development Report (2000–2001), p. 3.
8. Cited in Bhalla (2002), p. 27.
9. Activist Ignacio Ramonet cited in Sala-i-Martin (2002a).
10. Bhalla (2002).
11. A more comprehensive discusssion of the issues is contained in my complementary volume on "International Economic Order."
12. Bhalla.
13. Sala-i-Martin (2002b).
14. Bourguignon and Morrisson (2002). Also see Lindert and Williamson (2003), but their conclusions diverge somewhat from Bhalla's though they both use the same data base. This is because they use the same inappropriate methodology criticized by Bhalla in deriving their global inequality measure. Hence, their conclusion that "the world economy has become more unequal over the last two centuries . . . all of the observed rise in world inequality has been driven by widening gaps between nations, while almost none of it has been driven by widening gaps within nations (p. 263)." As Bhalla shows, using the correct method and deriving the correct distribution of income of the world's individuals, neither statement is true.

15. This is derived as follows. Suppose we could line up every human being in ascending order of their income. We then derive a curve called the Lorenz curve which relates (on the X-axis) the percentage of the total population (on the Y-axis) to the percentage of total income in the world. If everyone's income was equal, then the Lorenz curve would just be the diagonal of the box in the accompanying figure. If all the income went to only one person so there was complete inequality, the Lorenz curve would just be the sides of the box. More usually, when there is neither complete equality or inequality, the Lorenz curve will be concave from the origin. The Gini coefficient is then defined as the area between the Lorenz curve and the diagonal (A) divided by the total area under the diagonal (A + B). When there is complete equality and the Lorenz curve coincides with the diagonal, the area A shrinks to zero, hence the Gini is O. If there is complete inequalty so that the area A is the whole of the area below the diagonal A + B, the Gini is 1.

16. Bhalla (2002), p. 187.

17. See the excellent book by Razeen Sally (1998) for a clarification of what classical liberalism stands for and how it has subsequently evolved in discussions of international economic order.

18. Hume (1978, 1740), part III, section III, p. 415.

19. Ibid., p. 26.

20. Smith (1982, 1759), part II, p. 82.

21. Lal (1988), ch. 13, Lal and Myint (1996).

22. Smith (1982, 1759), part II, pp. 184–85.

23. Keynes (1926), pp. 46–47.

24. The Washington Consensus was the term coined by J. Williamson (1990) to describe the policy package which had emerged as best able to promote efficient poverty-alleviating growth as a result of the experience of developing countries in the 1970s and 1980s. It is close to that advocated in Harberger (1984) as constituting the best technocratic advice based on experience. It is also the one emerging from the Lal and Myint (1996) study of 25 developing countries. Recently J. Williamson (2000) has sought to partly disown it as it has become the whipping horse of the antiglobalization brigade, particularly in Latin America. Llosa (2000) has made the Latin America argument presented here. Srinivasan (2000) rightly takes Williamson to task for his partial recantation.

25. Hayek (1960), p. 402. For as Nozick demonstrated brilliantly, "no end-state state principle or distributional patterned principle can be continuously realized without continuous interference with people's lives [as any patterned distribution can be upset by people's voluntary actions in exchange]. The socialist society would have to forbid capitalist acts between consenting adults." Nozick (1974), p. 163.

26. See the discussion in Lal and Myint (1996).

27. Keohane (1984), Ruggie (1993).

28. An excellent account of the Latin American failure, apart from Chile, to implement the Washington consensus and its continuing failure to generate adequate poverty-redressing growth is provided in "Wanted: A New Regional Agenda for Economic Growth." *The Economist*, 26 April, 2003, pp. 27–29.

29. Rockoff (1998), p. 125.

30. Tanzi and Schuknecht (2000), p. 15.

31. In their authoritative survey of global public spending in the twentieth century, Tanzi and Schuknecht (2000) conclude that in the pre-1960 period "the growth in public spending from a very low level generated significant gains in social and economic welfare. For the period after 1960, however, when the rapid increase in public spending became largely of a redistributive kind, the earlier link between growth in government spending and improvements in social and economic objectives seems to have been broken. In our analysis we have found that the industrial countries with small governments and, to some extent, the newly industrialized countries with low public spending, were able to achieve levels of socioeconomic indicators similar to those achieved by countries with much higher levels of public spending. This has led us to the conclusion that there must be considerable scope for redefining the role of the state in industrialized countries so as to decrease public spending without sacrificing much in terms of social and economic objectives" (p. 131).

32. I first realised this when working on the World Banks' World Development Report for 1984. The dangers were spelled out in Lal and Wolf, eds. (1986), and a model developed in Lal and van Wijnbergen (1985) showed how through global interactions, the fiscal deficits in industrialized countries would crowd out investment in the Third World. With China and India now increasingly financing the U.S. trade deficit, this has come to pass.

33. It should be noted that even though there are current worries about the burgeoning U.S. fiscal deficit of $475 billion in 2004, as the chairman of the U.S. Council of Economic Advisers, Gregory Mankiw, has pointed out, this represents only about 4.2 percent of the $11 trillion U.S. economy and is manageable—being smaller than deficits in 6 of the last 20 years in the aftermath of recessions. G. N. Mankiw, "Deficits and Economic Priorities," *The Washington Post,* 16 July, 2003.

34. It has been estimated that, the shortfall between the present value of all the revenue the government can expect to collect in the future and the present value of all its future expenditure commitments, including debt service, is a staggering $44,000 billion, as compared with the current federal debt of $6,500 billion. By Jagadeesh Gokhale of the Federal Reserve Bank of Cleveland, and Kent Smitters, former deputy assistant secretary of economic policy at the U.S. Treasury, as reported in N. Ferguson and L. Kotlikoff, "The Fiscal Overstretch that Will Undermine an Empire," *Financial Times*, 15 July 2003.

35. See Lal and Myint (1996).

36. See Lal (1994), ch. 6.

37. For an explanation based on the agency problems of semi-industrialized countries, see Lal and Myint (1996) pp. 94–99.

38. See Lal (2003c).

39. See Bhagwati (1998), Krugman (1998), Stiglitz (2002).

40. It is true that convincing empirical estimates of these benefits have not been made. But this was also true of the gains from trade liberalization. As liberalized capital markets are a recent phenomenon in developing countries, one hopes that empirical comparative historical studies of the sort which established the incontrovertible case for liberalizing foreign trade will be undertaken for the opening up of the capital account. See my companion volume on "International Economic Order" for a fuller discussion.

41. Realizing this, the advocates of capital controls now seek to influence the composition of controls through a tax system like the one adopted by Chile. But Edwards (1999) detailed examination of the Chilean controls shows that they did not achieve their intended objectives and had deleterious side effects on the efficient functioning of the economy.

42. See M. Goldstein and N. Lardy (2003).

43. This was floated by the Nobel Prize–winning economist James Tobin, for an international tax to be levied on international financial flows. The tax revenue was to be given to the United Nations; not surprisingly, it has been a continued supporter of the proposal.

44. See Lal (1996a).

45. King (1999).

46. Bagehot (1873).

47. Brady bonds were issued in the late 1980s to convert the sovereign debt into a tradeable dollar bond whose market price reflected the discounted value of the foreign debt.

48. Taylor (2002).

49. Eichengreen and Bordo (2002) examine both periods of globalization—pre-1914 and post-1971. Contrary to common perceptions, they find that currency crises were of longer duration pre-1914, but in banking and banking-cum-currency crises, recovery was faster than now. They attribute this to the fact that nineteenth-century banking crises were less likely to undermine the currency, as most countries were expected, in the long run, to adhere to the gold standard rules. Delargy and Goodhart (1999) provide a detailed comparison of pre-1914 crises and the Asian crisis and find great similarities.

50. See Lal (1990d) for a fuller discussion. Minsky (1977) and Kindleberger (1978) view boom-bust cycles as endemic in capitalist economies due to the supposedly irrational behaviour of private speculators, so that speculative bubbles in which there is overlending are followed by collapse and crisis. A lender of last resort is then advocated to mitigate the deflationary impact of financial crises. John Flemming (1982) has commented

on these views and the mechanism they envisage for the boom-bust cycles: "Suppose an economy is subject to random shocks generated in a stationary way. A chance period of stability will be misinterpreted as implying that fewer precautions need to be taken, thus increasing the economy's vulnerability to the next 'normal' shock. As applied to financial structures, enterprises adopt excessively exposed geared, levered positions in a period of stability that does not in fact reflect a favourable shift in the economy's stochastic environment. . . . The argument depends on agents failing to distinguish a run of good luck from a favourable structural shift in their environment. Such errors are not only identifiable but also optimal if agents attach the correct non-zero probability to structural changes. If Minsky believes that people are too willing to believe that such changes have occurred, he should consider suggesting to the authorities that they intervene randomly in financial markets by increasing their variance. Such intervention would hinder the recognition of genuine shifts and should also inhibit false inferences" (p. 40). Rather than rely on irrational speculation to explain the boom-bust cycle, I find the classical and Austrian perspective more persuasive.

51. Cited in Lipson (1985), p. 44.
52. This is called the Stolper-Samuelson theorem in international economics. There is an ongoing and unsettled debate among economists whether the current wage trends in the U.S. and other developed countries are due to the growing economic integration promoted by the current LIEO, in particular of the low wage and abundant labor countries of Asia, or due to technological changes. See Feenstra (1998). In my judgment it is likely to be bit of both, as it is very difficult, empirically, to assign the relative shares to these two increasingly complementary forces. For the empirical evidence on the income distribution effects of the nineteenth-century LIEO, see J. G. Williamson (1998).
53. See Rogowski (1989) for this "factor-price" explanation of changing trade policies in the nineteenth century.
54. See the companion volume "International Economic Order" for details.
55. See Manne (1972, 2002), N. Barry (1998, 2001).
56. Manne (2002).
57. Demsetz (2003).
58. Henderson (2001).
59. Munk (1999), p. 34, cited in Henderson (2001).

CHAPTER 6

1. Henderson (2001).
2. An excellent account of these moral issues and the market is provided in Searle (1998).
3. Among the customs that Tocqueville identified as being most important for maintaining democracy in America were the myriad civil voluntary associations he found in the country:

> The political associations that exist in the United States are only a single feature in the midst of the immense assemblage of associations in that country. Americans of all ages, all conditions, and all dispositions constantly form associations. They have not only commercial and manufacturing companies, in which all take part, but associations of a thousand other kinds, religious, moral, serious, futile, general or restricted, enormous or diminutive. The Americans make associations to give entertainments, to found seminaries, to build inns, to construct churches, to diffuse books, to send missionaries to the antipodes; in this manner they found hospitals, prisons, and schools. If it is proposed to inculcate some truth or to foster some feeling by the encouragement of a great example, they form a society. Wherever at the head of some new undertaking you see the government in France, or a man of rank in England, in the United States you will be sure to find an association. (vol. II, ch. V)

> These myriad of voluntary associations (or NGOs as they would be called today), moreover, provided the bulwark against the tyranny of the central executive in democracies, according to Tocqueville, once the traditional aristocracy with its sense of noblesse

oblige, which usually stood between the rulers and the ruled in the *anciens régimes* in Europe, had been extinguished with the rise of democracy. These voluntary associations were necessary as an intermediating layer between the ruling elites and the masses to prevent the abuse of power by the elites, and to allow the ordinary citizen to participate in the political process. Thus, he wrote: "In aristocratic nations secondary bodies form natural associations which hold abuses of power in check. In countries where such associations do not exist, if private people did not artificially and temporarily create something like them, I see no other dike to hold back tyranny of whatever sort, and a great nation might with impunity be oppressed by some tiny faction or by a single man." (vol. II, ch. 5.)

4. See Bentley (1908), Truman (1953), and Latham (1952). Contemporary political pundits such as Putnam (2000) bemoan the decline of these voluntary organizations and see Americans as increasingly "bowling alone."

5. Schattschneider (1975), pp. 34–35.

6. Barfield (2001), p. 80.

7. These figures are based on an unpublished manuscript by Marguerite A. Peeters, "Hijacking Democracy: Global Consensus on Global Governance," American Enterprise Institute, Washington, D.C. (2001), cited in Barfield (2001), p. 88.

8. Otto (1996), p. 110.

9. Peeters (2001), p. 23, cited in Barfield (2001), p. 78.

10. Barfield (2001), p. 79.

11. Peeters (2001), p. 34, cited in Barfield (2001), p. 80.

12. Kenneth Anderson (2000) notes: "When international NGO's assert that they are the voice of the world's citizens, the assertion makes no sense because the world is not a polity that has ciizens—it has, to be sure, people, many of them with great needs—but to be a 'citizen' is to be part of a constituted polity, not just a supporter of an NGO and its agenda" (p. 108).

13. Martin Wolf, column in *Financial Times*, 1 September 1999, p. 12.

14. Shaffer (2001), pp. 66–67.

15. Burke (1999, 1774).

16. The title of the book by Rauch (1994).

17. Zakaria (2003), p. 171. This book provides the best and most succinct account of the growth of illiberal democracy in the United States.

18. See Raustiala "The Participatory Revolution," cited in Barfield (2001), p. 90.

19. Peeters (2001), p. 2, cited in Barfield (2001), p. 80.

20. Henderson (2001), pp. 40, 47–48.

21. Henderson (2001), pp. 47–48.

22. See Beckerman (1995).

23. Pecuniary externalities occur when one individual's activity level affects the financial circumstances of another. But this does not result in a misallocation of resources. Suppose that some group increases its consumption of whisky, the price rises, and this lowers the welfare of other consumers of whisky. This has no significance for the efficiency of the economy. It is Pareto-irrelevant because it does not affect the Pareto-efficiency of the economy (a definition of an efficient economic state where one person cannot be made better off without making someone else worse off). Pecuniary externalities are ubiquitous in an otherwise Pareto-efficient economy where tastes and technology are changing. They are synonymous with market interdependence and the price system. They do not require any government intervention. By contrast, technological externalities, like the smoke emitted by a factory that raises the costs of a nearby laundry, could damage the Pareto-efficiency of the economy and hence are Pareto-relevant, though as Demsetz (2003b) has noted, this may still not require government intervention.

24. Schneider (1989), while recognizing the "uncertainties and caveats" surrounding the scientific evidence, nevertheless wants scientists to get involved in hyping the evidence because of his and other scientists' desire "as human beings [to] want to leave the world a better place than they found it" (p. x).

25. Lal (1990d).

26. See Lomberg (2001). The witch hunt by environmental scientists against this excellent and very comprehensive survey of the evidence on numerous environmental issues is symptomatic of the religious nature of the Greens movement. See the website which details the Danish Scientific Committee's charges against Lomberg, his response which *Scientific American* refused to publish, and the alternative independent group of scientists who have looked at all the evidence, and absolved Lomberg, and supported his main conclusions.

27. Schneider (1989), p. 37.

28. Schelling (1992).

29. See Beckerman (1995).

30. See Nordhaus, (1994).

31. Simon (1996), p. xxxiii.

32. See Lal (1995a, 2002).

33. World Development Report 1992—World Bank (1992).

34. Lomberg (2001), p. 329.

35. See Wrigley (1988).

36. But there are still a number of treaties and conventions they have already been able to promote which are inimical to the interests of developing countries. These include the Basle Convention on hazardous waste, which threatens one of the most labor-intensive industries in India—ship-breaking; the POPs and DDT treaty which threatens the most cost-effective defense against one of the most deadly diseases in the Third World—malaria; the biodiversity convention which threatens the development of genetically modified foods and which could endanger raising food supplies in the Third World, as well as prevent cheap means of supplying various nutrients such as vitamin A and iron whose lack leads to blindness and death in the Third World. See Lal (2002) for a detailed discussion of this Greens misanthropy.

37. See Lal (2000c); Lal, Kim, Lu, and Prat (2003); Scruton (2000).

38. See Lal (1998a).

CHAPTER 7

1. See Barfield (2001), Bhagwati (2002b), Irwin (2002).

2. Huntington (1993).

3. Bernard Williams (1985) notes that the Socratic question "how one should live," is the start of any thinking about morality. Also see Hallpike (1986).

4. See Lal (1998).

5. From its inception, the Catholic Church grew as a temporal power through gifts and donations, particularly from rich widows. So much so that in July 370 the Emperor Valentinian had addressed a ruling to the pope that male clerics and unmarried ascetics should not hang around the houses of women and widows and try to worm themselves and their churches into their bequests at the expense of the women's families and blood relations (Robin Lane-Fox [1988], p. 310). From its very beginnings, the Church was in the race for inheritances. In this respect, the early Church's extolling of virginity and preventing second marriages helped to create more single women who would leave bequests to the Church.

6. The process of inhibiting a family from retaining its property and promoting its alienation was furthered by the answers that Pope Gregory I gave to some questions that the first Archbishop of Canterbury, Augustine, had sent in 597 concerning his new charges. Four of these nine questions concerned issues related to sex and marriage. Gregory's answers overturned the traditional Mediterranean and Middle Eastern patterns of legal and customary practices in the domestic domain. The traditional system was concerned with the provision of an heir to inherit family property and allowed marriage to close kin, marriages to close affines or widows of close kin, the transfer of children by adoption, and finally concubinage, which is a form of secondary union. Gregory banned all four practices. There was, for instance, no adoption of children allowed in England until the

nineteenth century. There was no basis for these injunctions in Scripture, Roman law, or the existing customs in the areas that were Christianized. See Goody (1983).

7. See Goody (1983), p. 105.

8. See Berman (1983), who shows how the development of both canon and secular law from the eleventh to thirteenth centuries under the aegis of the Church provided the essential legal infrastructure for a modern commercial and industrial economy. This included the *lex mercatora* (the law of the merchant), the invention of chattel mortgage, the development of bankruptcy law, the invention of the bottomry loan, the development of joint venture (*commenda*) as a kind of joint-stock company, the invention of trademarks and patents, the floating of public loans secured by bonds and other securities, the development of deposit banking. Berman (1983), pp. 349–50.

9. The eighteenth-century philosophers of the Enlightenment in their refurbishment of Augustine displaced the Garden of Eden by classical Greece and Rome, and God became an abstract cause—the Divine Watchmaker. The Christian centuries were now taken to be the fall, with the Christian revelations considered a fraud since for the enlightened, God expressed his purpose through his laws recorded in the Great Book of Nature. The enlightened were the elect and the Christian paradise was replaced by Posterity. By this reconfiguration of the Christian narrative, the eighteenth-century philosophers of the Enlightenment thought they had been able to salvage a basis for morality and social order in the world of the Divine Watchmaker. See Becker (1932). But once, as a result of Darwin, the watchmaker was seen to be blind, as Nietzsche proclaimed from the housetops at the end of the nineteenth century, God was dead, and the moral foundations of the West were thereafter in ruins.

Marxism, like the Christian faith, looks to the past and the future. There is a counterpart to the Garden of Eden, i.e., the time before property relations corrupted natural man. The fall is best regarded as "commodification" which leads to a class society and a continuing but impersonal conflict of material forces. This in turn leads to the Day of Judgment with the Revolution and the millennial Paradise of Communism. Marx also claimed that this movement toward earthly salvation was mediated, not as the Enlightenment sages had claimed through enlightenment and the preaching of good will, but by the inexorable forces of historical materialism. Another secular "city of God" had been created.

That Freudianism follows the same Augustinian narrative is shown in Gellner (1993) and in Webster (1995).

Ecofundamentalism is the latest of these secular mutations of Augustine's city of God. It carries the Christian notion of *contemptus mundi* to its logical conclusion. Humankind is evil, and only by living in harmony with a deified Nature can it be saved. See Lal (1995a).

10. The West's current cosmological beliefs, inadequately summarized by the word "liberty," are thus, at present, incoherent. As the philosopher Alasdair Macintyre has powerfully argued, the current Western notion of self has three contradictory elements. The first derives from the Enlightenment; it views individuals as being able to stand apart from the external social influences and constraints, and allows them to mold themselves in accordance with their own true preferences. The second component of the Western self concerns the evaluation of oneself by others. Here the standards are increasingly those of acquisitive and competitive success, as nurtured (so some would believe) by a bureaucratized and individualist market economy. The third element of the Western self derives from its remaining religious and moral norms and, as Macintyre says, is open to various "invocations of values as various as those which inform the public rhetoric of politics on the one hand and the success of *Habits of the Heart* on the other" (p. 492). This aspect of the self harks back to the Christian conception of the soul and its transcendental salvation.

These three elements comprising the Western conception of self are not only mutually incompatible, they are incommensurable. They also lead to incoherence as there are no shared standards by which the inevitable conflicts between them can be resolved. So as Macintyre puts it, "rights-based claims, utility-based claims, contractarian claims, and claims based upon this or that ideal conception of the good will be advanced in different contexts, with relatively little discomfort at the incoherence involved. For unacknowl-edged incoherence is the hallmark of this contemporary developing American self, a self whose public voice oscillates between phases not merely of toleration, but admiration for ruthlessly self-serving behavior and phases of high moral dudgeon and indignation at exactly the same behavior" (p. 492).

Many in the West can be seen as reverting to the worship of the multiplicity of gods and personal moral codes (particularly in the realm of sexuality) which are reminiscent of the pre-Christian Greco-Roman world. The growing popularity of New Age religions which is occurring at a time the traditional churches continue to lose followers is a testa-ment to the growing neopaganism in the West. In the ensuing plethora of moral beliefs—particularly in a cross-cultural context—it is a brave soul who would be able to find any basis for a universal ethic.

11. Various attempts to argue that there is no difference in these civilization's cosmological beliefs and the West's are critically discussed in Lal (2000b) and Lal (2003d).
12. That these two divergent views of the State cannot be reconciled by arguing as Sen (1992) does, that classical liberals are also egalitarians as they are concerned with the equality of liberty, is cogently argued by Sugden (1993).
13. Jasay (1996), p. 21.
14. Plant (1992), p. 124.
15. Jasay (1996), p. 22.
16. See Sugden (1993).
17. Jasay (1996), p. 23.
18. Ibid., p. 23.
19. Ibid., p. 24.
20. Ibid., p. 25.
21. Jasay's position on rights is different from Nozick's (1974). Of one of the senses in which Nozick uses rights—"that is permissions to do something and obligations on others not to interfere" (p. 92)—Jasay rightly notes, "rights are not permissions but claims for per-formance by another. Yet liberties are not permissions either; if they were they would be most confusingly misnamed. Who would be competent to grant permissions and on what authority?" Jasay (1996), pp. 5–31. He also contests Nozick's position on property rights, see his n. 2, pp. 50–51.
22. See Demsetz (1967).
23. Jasay (1996), p. 30.
24. See Minogue (1979).
25. Hart (1967, 1955), p. 53.
26. Isaiah Berlin (1969) refers to human rights as "a frontier of freedom" which no one is allowed to cross (p. 165). But as Little (2002) rightly notes: "an infinite list of rights is not convincing as a frontier. The frontier is properly constituted by the quite limited list of things that one may not do to human beings" (p. 31).
27. Jasay (1996), p. 51.
28. The existence of corporations depends on there being various contracts which cannot be specified at arm's length; see Coase (1988, 1937). Because workers acquire various skills which are specific to the firm through on-the-job training, this form of firm-specific capi-tal is of value to the firm but not to the worker who cannot cash in on it when he moves to another firm. These firm-specific skills are to be distinguished from-the-general skills acquired from on-the-job training which can be marketed outside the firm. Because of the importance of firm-level skills, there will have to be a more permanent relationship between employer and employee than the arm's-length transactions of a spot market for labor. This means that the employer will now have to incur the policing type of transac-tions costs in monitoring the worker to see that they are not shirking. This would require the hierarchical organization of firms. As part of this task, the employer may choose vari-ous forms of contracts with the workers, which could include codetermination with workers on boards of companies. In a free market, as firms face a diversity of conditions, the contracts they offer will also be varied and could include the types advocated by promoters of stakeholder capitalism. What would go against the functioning of the free

market was if a particular type of contract, viz., the stakeholder type, was forced on all employers by legislative fiat.

29. See Lal and Myint (1996) for a fuller discussion.
30. Bentham (1838–43), vol. II, p. 501.

CHAPTER 8

1. Mandelbaum (2002), p. 377.
2. Berlin (1979, 1972), p. 337.
3. The hinge for both the rise of demos (common people) and nationalism is the Reformation. This shattered the ideological unity of Western Christendom, with profound effects both on political thought and action. It provided fertile ground for questioning political legitimacy in a new way not found elsewhere in Eurasia, raising the question of who had the right to make laws. Till then both rulers and ruled were bound by the Common Law of Christendom, and by being God's law there could be no question of disobedience. (McClelland [1996], p. 171.) But after the Reformation who represented God's law—the Catholics or the Protestants—and whose law should you obey if you were a Catholic in a Protestant kingdom or vice versa? The notion of the social contract was born.

The ancient Greeks and Romans had looked upon the State as a unified corporate structure, like a body. Christianity, with its separation and demotion of politics to the maintenance of peace and justice in the temporal world and its emphasis on the care of the individual soul as the basic purpose of life, had shaken this ancient conception of civil harmony. In Aristotle's classical view, man was a political animal. By the thirteenth century, Aquinas had distinguished man as being both a political and a social animal. But it was not till the seventeenth century that the distinction between state and society became a dominant part of Western thought, with social contract theorists distinguishing between the beginning of society—now seen as an autonomous mode of association—and the construction of a state.

Further associations were subsequently abstracted from the state. First, the economy—as the growth of European commerce and industry showed people being also associated with another distinctive set of associations as producers, consumeres, and distributors of commodities. Unlike the set of social and political relationships which seemed to be ruled by unpredictable human decisions, economic relationships seemed closer to the impersonal relationships of nature being uncovered by the new physical sciences. These economic relationships could be seen to be governed—as Adam Smith was the first to show—by abstract laws, resembling the laws of nature.

Second, with the Romantic revolt against the Enlightenment, people also began to see themselves as bearers of a distinctive culture, based on speaking a particular language or dialect, with their own customs, artistic heritage, and cuisines. This separation of culture from society was to lead to nationalism.

Thus, modernity in the West came to distinguish between different forms of human associations. If society was *sui generis*, the three others—the polity, the economy, and the culture—came to be seen in Western thought as equally important but differing forms of association between human beings. But most important, as Minogue (1995) has stressed, these "self-conscious associations set the scene for the dramas of modern political conflict" (p. 49).

But there was a more far-reaching development following from the Protestant claim of the sinfulness of the hierarchy of the Catholic Church. If the traditional interpreters of God's will appointed by the pope were sinful, where were the true interpreters of his word to be found? "If not the Church, then only the congregations" (Minogue [1995], p. 175). These became self-governing, choosing and dismissing their pastors. But if the church is to be governed by its members, why not the state? Thus were the seeds for the rise of demos sown.

4. See Kedourie (1993, 1960), p. 1. Also Berlin (1979, 1972), Plamenatz (1973). This part is based on Lal (1998, 1993, 1985).

5. "Patriotism, affection for one's country, or one's group, loyalty to its institutions, and zeal for its defense, is a sentiment known among all kinds of men; so is xenophobia, which is dislike of the stranger, the outsider, and reluctance to admit him into one's own group. Neither sentiment depends on a particular anthropology and neither asserts a particular doctrine of the state or of the individual's relation to it. Nationalism does both; it is a comprehensive doctrine which leads to a distinct type of politics" (Kedouriee [1993, 1960], p. 68).

6. Ibid., p. 67.

7. "A British or American nationalist would have to define the British or American nation in terms of language, race, or religion, to require that all those who conform to the definition should belong to the British or American state, that all those who do not, should cease to belong, and to demand that all British and American citizens should merge their will in the will of the community" (Kedourie [1993, 1960], p. 68).

8. Kedourie writes that "a tribesman's relation to his tribe is regulated in minute detail by custom which is followed unquestioningly and considered part of the natural or divine order. Tribal custom is neither a decree of the General Will, nor an edict of legislative Reason. The tribesman is such by virtue of his birth, not by virtue of self-determination. He is usually unaware that the destiny of man is progressive, and that he can fulfil this destiny by merging his will into the will of the tribe" (Kedourie, [1993, 1960], p. 69).

   B. Anderson (1991) distinguishes four waves of nationalism. The *first* are the "creole" wars of liberation in the Americas [starting with the American War of Independence in 1776] and the liberation movement headed by Simon Bolivar in South America in the early part of the nineteenth century. Unlike the subsequent nationalisms where the "imagined communities" of the nation were created by the newly acquired status of vernacular languages and their speakers, the creole revolts were led by people who were part of the same cultural and linguistic world as their metropoles. These revolts were partly prompted by the policy of the European powers of barring the entry of the creole elite to higher official and political office in the metropole, even as *"peninsulares"* had access to high positions in both the colonies and the metropole. This led to resentment amongst the creole elites. The accident of birth in the Americas seemed to condemn the "creole" to an inferior status, even though in every other respect- language, descent, customs, religion, manners—he was indistinguishable from the "peninsular". The ideas of the Enlightenment which had spread from the metropole also meant that these new "nations" were opposed to dynastic rule and were pervaded by republicanism. The nation serving demos which has been a defining characteristic of the modern age was born.

   The French revolution brought these principles into fruition in Europe, and was carried across it by Napoleon's armies. This in turn gave rise to a second wave of nationalism. Its origins lay partly in a reaction against the "French cultural domination of the Western world," the Romantic reaction against the "disenchantment of the world" (Anderson 1991) flowing from the scientific revolution and the Enlightenment, but most important as a result of the spread of a vernacular nationalism. The world of Christendom had a common language—Latin—but this was the lingua franca of administration, diplomacy, theology, and scholarship. In the localities there were a multiplicity of tongues. The vernacular languages which most people spoke acquired an importance once a mass market arose for the printed word with the spread of the printing press. This made it commercially profitable to produce books in the vernacular, which in turn gradually raised the literary status of these languages. Two of these vernacular languages, French and early English, had become competitors of Latin as "languages of power" by the sixteenth century. In England early English had become the legal language in 1362, in France in 1539 (Seton-Watson [1977], pp. 28–29; Bloch [1965], vol. 1, pp. 75, 98). But in many other parts of Christendom, Latin survived as the official language for much longer. With the growth of bureaucracies following the post-Renaissance administrative revolution, the expanding bureaus had to extend their recruitment to people of lower social origins, who became clients of the printing press. The emergence, though uneven, of a commercial bourgeoisie also expanded the demand for the products of the vernacular presses.

   Thus began the *second* phase of vernacular nationalism demanding a vernacular language of state. As this demand then required a definition of who comprised the relevant group comprising the nation-state, it was identified with the territorial boundaries containing the speakers of that language. Aided by the examples of the French and American Revolutions, a model of the nation-state had appeared by the second decade of the nineteenth century: "republican institutions, common citizenships, popular sovereignty, national flags and anthems . . . and the liquidation of their conceptual opposites: dynastic empires, monarchical institutions, absolutisms, subjecthoods, inherited nobilities, serfdoms, ghettoes"(Anderson, op. cit., p. 81).

The threat that this vernacular nationalism posed to the dynasts of Europe led to the *third* wave of nationalism—official nationalism (Seton-Watson [1977], p. 148), whereby the dynasts sought to identify themselves with the new-found vernacular nation. The spread of this official nationalism was in turn to lead to the scramble for empire and the First World War.

The final phase of nationalism is that evoked in the areas of the world where directly or indirectly the spread of Western imperialism had damaged the self-respect of indigenous high status groups. The earliest case was of Japan after its opening by Commander Perry, when the Meiji reformers adopted a type of official nationalism modeled on Hohenzollern Prussia-Germany. But the more typical cases were the nation-states that arose when the Treaty of Versailles at the end of the First World War buried the dynastic age and the nation-state became the international norm.

9. Acton (1985, 1862).
10. Mill (1910), p. 362.
11. Mill goes on to say: "Whatever really tends to the admixture of nationalities, and the blending of their attributes and peculiarities in a common union, is a benefit to the human race. The united people, like a crossed breed of animals (but in a still greater degree, because the influences in operation are moral as well as physical), inherits the special aptitudes and excellences of its progenitors, protected by the admixture from being exaggerated into the neighboring vices." Mill (1910), p. 164.
12. As Acton (1985, 1862) wrote: "If we take the establishment of liberty for the realization of moral duties to be the end of civil society, we must conclude that those states are the most perfect which, like the British and American Empires include various distinct nationalities without oppressing them . . . A state, which is incompetent to satisfy different races condemns itself" (p. 432).
13. Kedourie (1993, 1960), p. 129.
14. Gellner (1983) has argued that industrialization requires mobility, literacy, and cultural standardization, which are supplied by nationalism. But Kedourie (1993, 1960) rightly argues against these and other sociological theories of nationalism. He writes: "this attempt to see nationalism as requisite for industrialization, or a reaction to it does not fit the chronology either of nationalism or industrialization" (p. 143). He argues that this sociological temptation needs to be resisted for "whether nationalism—or any other ideology—will spread in a particular society and become a political force, and what outcome this will have, is nothing which can be described in advance of the event. To narrate the spread, influence and operation of nationalism in various polities is to write a history of events, rather than of ideas" (p. 139). Kedourie's seminal book on nationalism has recently been attacked by O'Leary (2002); see Minogue (2003) for a defense and O'Leary (2003). Also see A. D. Smith (1983) and Hutchinson and Smith (1994) on theories of nationalism.
15. Plamenatz (1960).
16. Plamenatz (1960), p. 11.
17. See for instance Hanke and Walters (1997), for those persuaded by the statistical cross-section type of evidence that has proliferated in this field over the last decade. I prefer the more qualitative and historical evidence based on case studies as in Lal and Myint (1996).
18. It should be noted that the formal conditions for democracy—like periodic elections— may be met by many states which do not uphold political or economic liberty. Zakaria (1997) has labeled these "Illiberal Democracies." I am concerned mainly with true, i.e., liberal democracies.

19. Zakaria (1997, 2003).
20. See Lipset (1959).
21. In fact, even in the United States, the supposed paradigm of liberal democracy, many observers see that its gradual move from a representative to participatory democracy—of which California with its popular initiatives and referenda is a shining example—is leading to a form of illiberal democracy, where minority interests are suppressed, all forms of authority and expertise are denigrated as being elitist and hence undemocratic, and an uninformed public veers hither and thither in response to the latest popular fashion. See Zakaria (2003), Berkowitz (2003).
22. Hume, in his essay "Of the Independence of Parliament" noted:

> "Political writers have established it as a maxim that, in contriving any system of government and fixing the several checks and controls of the constitution, every man ought to be supposed a knave and to have no other end, in all his actions, than private interest. By this interest we must govern him and, by means of it, make him, notwithstanding his insatiable avarice and ambition, co-operate to public good. Without this, say they, we shall in vain boast of the advantages of any constitution and shall find in the end that we have no security for our liberties or possessions except the goodwill of our rulers; that is we shall have no security at all.
>
> It is therefore, a just political maxim that every man must be supposed a knave, though at the same time it appears somewhat strange that a maxim should be true in politics which is false in fact. But to satisfy us on this head we may consider that men are generally more honest in their private than their public capacity, and will go greater lengths to serve a party than when their own private interest alone is concerned.
>
> To which we may add that every court or senate is determined by the greater number of voices, so that, if self-interest influences only the majority (as it will always do), the whole senate follows the allurements of this separate interest and acts as if it contained not one member who had any regard to public interest and liberty." Hume (1965, 1777), p. 42

23. Zakaria (2003), p. 115.
24. M. Doyle, "Ways of War and Peace," cited in Zakaria (2003), p. 116.
25. Mansfield and Snyder (1995).
26. This text is based on Lal (2003d).
27. See Gourevitch (1993) for a further elaboration of the tenuous link between forms of government and their promotion of markets.
28. See Przeworski and Limongi (1993) for a survey. The best of these studies is by Helliwell (1992), and the most cogent critique of the econometrics involved by Deaton and Miller (1995).
29. Olson (1965).
30. Olson (1965), p. 167. A more serious challenge to Olson's malign view of interest group activity has been provided by Gary Becker (1983, 1988), who has sought to provide a rigorous formulation of a model of competition amongst pressure groups for political influence. He partially restores the more benign view of such participation held by the political sociologists. But his arguments depend on ignoring the rent-seeking costs associated with pressure group politics. See Lal(1996b, 1999a).

   Olson later (1982) went on to argue that because of the deadweight costs of the taxes and subsidies associated with a pressure group equilibrium, an economy riddled with pressure groups is likely to bear a heavy burden of such costs, and hence likely to have sluggish growth. He blamed the decline of nations on the growth of interest groups, whose aim must necessarily be to use the political process to redistribute income to themselves. This by necessity—given the fixed economic pie at any point of time—is a zero-sum game, a Hobbesian war of all against all. Whether economic history validates this view remains controversial, as can be seen from the conflicting claims in the collection of essays edited by Mueller (1983).

31. Schumpeter (1950), p. 269.
32. Downs (1957).
33. See Lal and Myint (1996) for a survey of the evidence.
34. Jasay (1985), p. 193.
35. See Lal (1998)
36. Whereas much of development economics is concerned with the development of labor surplus economies, particularly relevant for Asia, it is the economics of land abundant, labor scarce economies which is relevant for the New World. A seminal essay by Domar (1970) provides the necessary theoretical framework. He cogently argues that in a land abundant economy, free labor, free land, and a nonworking upper class cannot coexist. Any two can but not all three. This is because with free land there are no diminishing returns to labor, whose marginal and average product are the same. If employers seek to hire labor, they will have to pay a wage equal to this common marginal *and* average product of labor, leaving no surplus rents from land for the employer. Hence, the agrarian form that will emerge is family labor based farms, as any form of hired labor or tenancy will be unprofitable and landlords—who have to depend on one or the other—cannot exist. A government, by taxing this independent peasantry through direct or indirect taxes, could support a nonworking class of retainers; but the latter or an independent nobility of landlords could not support themselves from land rents as none would be available. Economic expansion based on an independent yeomanry was the form that North American development and its agrarian structure took in the colonial period.

    Next, suppose the government wants to create an independent class of landowners and grants the chosen few sole rights of ownership to land. In order to provide the landlords with a surplus, some means will have to be found to restrict or abolish the peasant's freedom to move. Various forms of tying labor down to land—serfdom, slavery and the caste system—emerged in the great agrarian civilizations. They created a landowning class which derived a rent not from land but from the peasants by expropriating a large part of their income above a subsistence level.

    Finally, as the labor force expands from natural increase and/or migration and land becomes scarce relative to labor, diminishing returns to labor appear with labor's marginal product being less than its average. This allows landlords to obtain the rents from land and an assured labor supply to work it through hired labor paid its marginal product, or else through various forms of tenancy.
37. See Engerman and Sokoloff (1994), B. L. Solow (1991). For evidence on the substantial economies in producing certain crops on large slave plantations, see Fogel (1989), Engerman (1983), and Deer (1949).
38. See Kupperman (1993).
39. Paz (1988), p. 27.
40. This provided an ideological justification for the patrimonial state. Society is considered to be a hierarchical system in which every person and group serves the purpose of a transcendental and universal order. This hierarchy is part of a universal and natural order and not the product of any social contract. The sovereign is responsible to God, not to society, even though his authority originates in the people. "Neothomism was a philosophy destined to offer a logical and rational justification of the Christian revelation. In turn the teaching and defense of the Christian revelation formed the basis of the Spanish empire. Religious orthodoxy was the foundation of the political system." Paz (1988), p. 30.
41. Ibid., p. 27.
42. Morse (1964), p. 152.
43. Wynia (1990), p. 3.
44. Paz (1988), p. 39. But there was also a more positive aspect of the common Catholic culture of Latin America. As compared with North America, as Hugh Thomas has rightly pointed out to me, the Latins succeeded socially where the United States failed. This was in part due to the planned cities, the skillful approach to racial matters enabling manumission of slaves, and, of course, a common Catholic culture which left their personal and social mores closer to the communalist ones of the other great ancient civilizations than to those based on the new-fangled individualism of their Protestant brethren. See Lal (1998).

45. Veliz (1994) contrasts this universalism of Latin America with the greater tolerance of diversity in beliefs in North America as between the Baroque hedgehogs of the South and the Gothic foxes of the North in the New World, reflecting Archilochus's maxim: "the fox knows many things, but the hedgehog knows only one thing"—quoted in Berlin (1978).
46. See, for instance, Castaneda (1995).
47. This section is based on Lal (1998), ch.4.
48. Crone and Cook (1977), p. 77.
49. McNeill (1991), p. 431.
50. Ibid., p. 434.
51. As Crone and Hinds (1986) note: "the widespread insistence that the caliphate be elective (*al-amr shura*), the endless demands for observance of kitab and sunna, good practice and past models, the constant objections to Ummayad fiscal policy, and the general readiness to take up arms against what was perceived to be oppressive rule, all these features are indicative of so stubborn a determination to keep government under control that one might have credited it wih a good chance of success" (p. 106).
52. "The caliph Umar created a system of stipends for those who had fought in the cause of Islam, regulated according to priority of conversion and service, and this reinforced the cohesion of the ruling elite, or at least their separation from those they ruled." Hourani (1991), p. 24. In today's Saudi Arabia, the practice continues in modern form, where besides the vast army of princes living off their stipends as members of the Ibn Saud family, much of the military hardware that has been acquired is to provide honorific posts to the favored (with stipends attached), rather than to serve any useful military purpose. See Schwartz (2002).
53. Hourani (1991), p. 107.
54. "It was this extinction of the soldier's autonomy which made the *mamluke* such a superb instrument of his master's will when it was coupled with personal obedience . . . Mamlukes were not supposed to think, but to ride horses, they were designed not to be a military elite, but military automata." Crone (1980), p. 79.
55. Ibid., p. 84.
56. *Dervishme* were Christian children obtained as a tax on Christian subjects in the Balkans, who were then enslaved, converted, and manumitted, and who rose to high office under the Ottomans.
57. With the end of parricide, unelevated princes from among a sultan's children were confined in gilded cages in the harem. "Here pillow talk was of politics, and women and eunuchs conspired to secure the succession for a potential patron from among the sultan's brood . . . For much of the seventieth century the effective chief executives of the state were queen-mothers who knew nothing first hand of the world beyond the harem walls." Fernandez-Armesto (1995), p. 239.
58. Ibn Khaldun (1967, 1379).
59. See Crone and Hinds (1986), Rahman (1979).
60. The "handing over of power to slaves . . . to the more or less complete exclusion of the free males of the community bespeaks a moral gap of such dimensions that within the great civilizations it has been found only in one." Crone (1980), p. 81.
61. Gwartney and Lawson (2003).
62. Ibid., Exhibit 2, p. 11.

CHAPTER 9

1. Minogue (1995), p. 110.
2. Kissinger (2001), p. 236.
3. Ibid., p. 237.
4. Link, ed., "Papers of Woodrow Wilson," vol. 59, pp. 608–9.
5. Philip Bobbit has distinguished two schools of international law: the *formalists* and the *naturalists*. The former hold that the "truth or falsity of a legal proposition [derives] from a act unrelated to its content." Bobbit (2002), p. 641.

The naturalist by contrast "holds that the content of legal rules and the world accounts for their truth or falsity. Legal rules must be in accord with the nature of man."

Both these approaches were challenged in the United States by the Legal Realist school, Llewellyan (1951, 1930). This claimed that it was "virtually impossible to account for past decisions by reference to the body of legal rules alone, let alone to predict what officials would do in actual cases in the future . . . [I]nternational law was manipulated to rationalize rules rather than determine them, that sometimes it was ignored in deference to powerful interests, and that it even appeared indeterminate, leaving its commands to be decided by the changing needs of foreign policy." (Bobbit [2002], p. 642) This Legal Realist critique raised the important question, whether the history of the twentieth century would be different if there had been no international law? Which in turn subsumes two other fundamental questions about international law: "if the body of international legal rules cannot uniquely determine the legality of a particular act by the parties it is supposed to govern, how can it be law? And if international law is law, why doesn't it seem to have any effect?" (Ibid.)

Most of the schools of international law which have arisen subsequently to meet this challenge can be classified as variants of these two major schools. The Legal Process, Nominalist, and Consensualist schools are variants of the formalist schools. They all agree that nothing can be law which has not been created by states, though they differ in determining what states have agreed.

The New Haven school, Neorealists, and Perspectivists, all look "for something in the world, outside the law itself, that validates international law, though they strongly differ as to what that something is, and what relation it must have to law in order for a legal rule to be legitimate." Bobbit (2002), p. 660.

6. Bull (1995), p. 142.
7. The New Haven school—the child of the Natural Law school and of Wilsonianism—is currently the most influential propounding the emergence of a new international legal moral order.
8. Bull (1995), p. 151.
9. Falk (1970, 1971, 1999).
10. Minogue (1995), p. 113.
11. Bull (1995), p. 304.
12. Lord Nicholls of Birkenhead, Appellate Judgment in *Ex Parte Pinochet*, UK House of Lords, 25 November 1998.
13. Kissinger (2001), pp. 276–77.
14. Annual message to Congress, 1 June 1941, cited in Sellars (2002), p. x.
15. Sellars (2002), p. xi.
16. Kissinger (2001), p. 275.
17. Note that the word liberal in this term is now being used in the American sense and not to mean classical liberal.
18. After the Afghanistan campaign, Tony Blair is reported to have "repeated the call that he first made during the Kosovo conflict for a doctrine of 'international community.' 'Some say it is Utopian, others that it is dangerous to think that we can resolve all these problems by ourselves,' he said, 'But the point I was making was simply that self-interest for a nation and the interests of the broader community are no longer in conflict. There are few problems from which we remain immune. In the war against terrorism the moralists and realists are partners, not antagonists.' " "Together we can find Utopia, says Blair," *The Weekly Telegraph,* no. 539.3.
19. The most cogent case for this postmodern imperialism is made by the British diplomat Robert Cooper (2003). But he concedes that his post modern European empire does depend upon the security umbrella provided by the American Pax.
20. Kissinger (2001), p. 258.
21. Kagan and Kristol (2000), p. 10.
22. Ibid., p. 42.
23. The National Security Strategy of the United States of America, White House, September 2002.

24. Kagan and Kristol (2000), p. 39.
25. Leeden (2002).
26. The former Commander-in-Chief of the Central Command, the proconsul overseeing the Middle East, the Horn of Africa, and Central Asia, General Zini, has recently disclosed that the U.S. plan for a post-Saddam Iraq was to "retain the regular army . . . to subdue the chaos [that] would ensue following a successful invasion. . . . So I was surprised when the Iraqi army was disbanded after the invasion. This decision, along with the complete 'deBaathification' of the government, has proved a miscalculation." A. C. Zini, "Iraqi Army Can Ride to the Rescue," *Los Angeles Times*, 1 February 2004, p. M5.
27. Ottaway (2002), p. 17.
28. Aronson (2003).
29. This is the conclusion also reached by the eminent historian Shlomo Avineri (2003).
30. See Basham (2004) for an analysis of the possible political outcomes in Iraq.

SUMMARY

1. Rosecrance (1986), (1999).
2. Gallagher and Robinson (1953).
3. Kagan and Kristol (2000), p. 40.
4. Schwarzenberger (1959), cited in Bull (1995), p. 216.
5. Kagan and Kristol (2000), p. 41, emphasis added.
6. See Lal (2003d).
7. Kissinger (2001), p. 252.
8. Bindoff (1950), p. 224.
9. This was disclosed in the memoirs of P. N. Dhar (2000) who was Mrs. Gandhi's principal secretary at the time and present at the Simla meetings.
10. See Mearsheimer (2001).

References

Lord Acton (1985, 1862): "Nationality," in *Essays in the History of Liberty*, Liberty Classics, Indianapolis.

F. Ajami (1998): *The Dream Palace of the Arabs*, Pantheon Books, New York.

R. D. Alexander (1987): *The Biology of Moral Systems*, Aldine de Gruyter, New York.

B. Anderson (1991): *Imagined Communities*, Verso, London.

K. Anderson (2000): "After Seattle: Public International Organizations, Non-governmental Organizations, and Democratic Sovereignty in an Era of Globalization: An Essay on Contested Legitimacy," mimeo, Washington College of Law, American University, Washington, D.C.

N. Angell (1911): *The Great Illusion*, G. P. Putnam, New York.

R. Aron (1966): *Peace and War*, Weidenfeld & Nicholson, London.

R. Aron (1974): *The Imperial Republic*, Prentice-Hall, New Jersey.

G. Aronson (2003): "A Cautionary Tale from Colonial Baghdad," *Financial Times*, 4 March 2003.

J. Arquilla and D. Ronfeldt, eds. (1997): *In Athena's Camp—Preparing for Conflict in the Information Age*, Rand Corporation, Santa Monica, Cal.

S. Avineri (1972): "Modernization and Arab Society: Some Reflections," in I. Howe and C. Gershman, eds., *Israel, the Arabs and the Middle East*, Bantam Books, New York.

S. Avineri (2003): "Iraq may be wise to forsake unity for democracy," *Financial Times*, Nov. 18, 2003, p. 15.

N. Ayubi (1991): *Political Islam: Religion and Politics in the Arab World*, Routledge, London.

A. J. Bacevich (2002): *American Empire*, Harvard University Press, Cambridge, Mass.

W. Bagehot (1873): *Lombard Street*, William Clowes & Sons, London.

P. Bairoch (1993): *Economics and World History*, University of Chicago Press, Chicago.

R. E. Baldwin (1969): "The Case Against Infant-Industry Tariff Protection," *Journal of Political Economy*, vol. 77, May/June, pp. 295–305.

C. E. Barfield (2001): *Free Trade, Sovereignty, Democracy: The Future of the World Trade Organization*, American Enterprise Institute, Washington, D.C.

J. Barkow, L. Cosmides, and J. Tooby (1992): *The Adapted Mind—Evolutionary Psychology and the Generation of Culture*, Oxford University Press, New York.

N. Barry (1998): *Business Ethics*, Macmillan, London.

N. Barry (2001): "Ethics, Conventions and Capitalism," in B. Griffithsetal: *Capitalism, Morality and Markets*, Institute of Economic Affairs, London.

P. Basham (2004): "Can Iraq be Democratic?" *Policy Analysis*, no. 505, Jan. 5, 2004, Cato Institute, Washington, D.C.

C. A. Bayly (1989): *Imperial Meridian*, Cambridge University Press, Cambridge.

C. L. Becker (1932): *The Heavenly City of the Eighteenth Century Philosophers*, Yale University Press, New Haven, CT.

G. Becker (1983): "A Theory of Competition Among Pressure Groups for Political Influence," *Quarterly Journal of Economics*, August, pp. 371–400.

G. Becker (1988): "Public Policies, Pressure Groups, and Deadweight Costs," in G. Stigler, ed., *Chicago Studies in Political Economy*, Chicago University Press, Chicago.

J. Bentham (1838–43): *The Works of Jeremy Bentham*, vol. II: Anarchical Fallacies, Edinburgh.

W. Beckerman (1995): *Small Is Stupid: Blowing the Whistle on the Greens*, Duckworth, London.

J. Bentham (1838–43): *The Works of Jeremy Bentham*, vol. II: Anarchical Fallacies, Edinburgh.

A. P. Bentley (1908): *The Process of Government*, Chicago University Press, Chicago.

P. Berkowitz (2003): "The Demagoguery of Democratic Theory," *Critical Review*, vol. 15, no. 2, pp. 123–45.

I. Berlin (1969): "Two Concepts of Liberty," in his *Four Essays on Liberty*, Oxford University Press, Oxford.

I. Berlin (1979): *Against the Current*, Hogarth Press, London.

I. Berlin (1979, 1972): "Nationalism," *Foreign Affairs*, 1972; expanded version in his *Against the Current*, Hogarth Press, London, 1979.

I. Berlin (1978): *Russian Thinkers*, Hogarth Press, London.

H. Berman (1983): *Law and Revolution*, Harvard University Press, Cambridge, Mass.

R. Bernardi (1970): "The Economic Problems of the Roman Empire at the Time of Its Decline," in C. M. Cipolla, ed., *The Economic Decline of Empires*, Methuen, London.

J. Bhagwati (1998): "The Capital Myth: The Difference Between Trade in Widgets and Trade in Dollars," *Foreign Affairs*, vol. 77, pp. 7–12.

J. Bhagwati, ed. (2002a): *Going Alone*, MIT Press, Cambridge, Mass.

J. Bhagwati (2002b): *Free Trade Today*, Princeton University Press, Princeton, N.J.

S. Bhalla (2002): *Imagine There's No Country: Poverty, Inequality and Growth in the Age of Globalization*, Institute of International Economics, Washington, D.C.

S. T. Bindoff (1950): *Tudor England*, Penguin Books, Harmondsworth, Middlesex.

M. Bloch (1965): *Feudal Society*, Routledge, London.

P. Bobbitt (2002): *The Shield of Achilles—War, Peace and the Course of History*, Allen Lane, London.

M. Boot (2002): *The Savage Wars of Peace*, Basic Books, New York.

M. D. Bordo, C. Goldin, and E. N. White, eds. (1998): *The Defining Moment*, Chicago University Press, Chicago.

P. Bourdieu (1998): *Acts of Resistance: Against the Tyranny of the Market*, Polity Press, Cambridge.

F. Bourguignon and C. Morrisson (2002): "Inequality among World Citizens: 1820–1992," *American Economic Review*, vol. 92, no. 4, pp. 727–44.

A. Brewer (1990): *Marxist Theories of Imperialism—A Critical Survey*, 2nd ed., Routledge, London.

J. M. Brown and W. M. Louis, eds. (1999): *The Oxford History of the British Empire*, vol. 4, Oxford University Press, Oxford.

J. Buchanan and C. Stubblebine (1962): "Externality," *Economica*, vol. 29, pp. 371–84.

B. Bueno de Mesquita (1981): *The War Trap*, Yale University Press, New Haven, Ct.

H. Bull (1984): "European states and African Political Communities" in Bull and Watson (ed), pp. 99–114.

H. Bull (1995): *The Anarchical Society*, 2nd ed., Columbia University Press, New York.

H. Bull and A. Watson, eds. (1984): *The Expansion of International Society*, Clarendon Press, Oxford.

E. Burke (1999, 1774): "Speech to the Electors of Bristol" in J. Payne, ed., *Select Works of Edmund Burke*, vol. 4, Liberty Fund, Indianapolis.

P. J. Cain (1998): "Was It Worth Having? The British Empire, 1850–1950," *Revista de Historia Economica*, vol. xvi, 351–76.

P. J. Cain and A. G. Hopkins (2002): *British Imperialism 1688–2000*, Longmans, London.

R. Cameron (1993): *A Concise Economic History of the World*, 2nd ed., Oxford University Press, New York.

J. G. Castaneda (1995): *The Mexican Shock*, New Press, New York.

N. A. Chagnon (1983): *Yanomamo: The Fierce People*, 3rd ed., Holt, Reinhart, & Winston, New York.

J. Chambers (1985): *The Devil's Horsemen*, Atheneum, New York.

J.-C. Chesnais (1987): *La Revanche du tiers-monde*, Laffont, Paris.

R. H. Coase (1988, 1937) "The Nature of the Firm," *Economica* 4, November 1937; reprinted in his *The Firm, the Market, and the Law*, University of Chicago Press, Chicago, 1988.

L. Colley (1992): *Britons*, Yale University Press, New Haven, Ct.

P. Collier et al. (1997): "Redesigning Conditionality," *World Development*, vol. 25, no. 9, pp. 1399–1407.

P. Collier and A. Hoeffler (1998): "On Economic Causes of Civil War," *Oxford Economic Papers*, vol. 50, no. 4, pp. 563–73.

P. Collier and D. Lal (1986): *Labour and Poverty in Kenya 1900–1980*, Clarendon Press, Oxford.

M. Cook (1983): *Muhammad*, Oxford University Press, Oxford.

R. Cooper (2001): "The Next Empire," *Prospect*, October, pp. 22–26.

R. Cooper (2003): *The Breaking of Nations*, Atlantic Books, London.

W. M. Corden (1986, 1977): *Inflation, Exchange Rates and the World Economy*, Clarendon Press, Oxford.

P. Crone (1980): *Slaves on Horseback: the Evolution of Islamic Polity*, Cambridge University Press, Cambridge.

P. Crone (1996): "The Rise of Islam in the World," in F. Robinson, ed., *Cambridge Illustrated History of the Islamic World*, Cambridge University Press, Cambridge.

P. Crone and M. Cook (1977): *Hagarism: The Making of the Islamic World*, Cambridge University Press, Cambridge.

P. Crone and M. Hinds (1986): *God's Caliph*, Cambridge University Press, Cambridge.

L. E. Davis and R.A. Huttenback (1987): *Mammon and the Pursuit of Empire*. Cambridge University Press, Cambridge.

L. E. Davis and S. Engerman (2003): "The Economics of Blockades," paper presented at the Eli F. Hecksher a celebratory symposium, Stockholm School of Economics, Sweden.

A. Deaton and R. Miller (1995): "International Commodity Prices, Macroeconomic Performance, and Politics in Sub-Saharan Africa," *Princeton Essays in International Finance*, no. 79, December, Princeton, N.J.

N. Deer (1949): *The History of Sugar*, Chapman and Hall, London.

P. J. R. Delargy and C. Goodhart (1999): *Financial Crises: Plus ça change, plus c'est la même chose*, Special Paper No. 108, LSE Financial Markets Group, London School of Economics, London.

H. Demsetz (1967): "Towards a Theory of Property Rights," *American Economic Review*, vol. 57, pp. 347–59.

H. Demsetz (2003a): "Business Governance and the Institutions of Capitalism," mimeo, University of California Dept. of Economics, June 2003.

H. Demsetz (2003b): "Ownership and the Externality Problem," in T. L. Anderson and F. S. McChesmey, eds., *Property Rights: Cooperation, Conflict and Law*, Princeton University Press, Princeton, N.J.

K. Derringer and L. Squire (1996): "A New Data Set Measuring Income Inequality," *World Bank Economic Review*, vol. 10, no. 3., pp. 565–92.

P. N. Dhar (2000): *Indira Gandhi, The 'Emergency' and Indian Democracy*, Oxford University Press, New Delhi.

J. Diamond (1997): *Guns, Germs and Steel*, W.W. Norton, New York.

P. Dibb, D. D. Hale, and P. Prince (1999): "Asia's Insecurity," *Survivor*, autumn 1999, pp. 5–20.

S. Digby (1971): *War Horse and Elephant in the Delhi Sultanate*, Oxford University Press, Delhi.

E. Domar (1970): "The Causes of Slavery or Serfdom: A Hypothesis," *Journal of Economic History*, March, pp. 18–32.

T. Donnelly (2003): "Brave New World: An Enduring Pax Americana," *National Security Outlook*, American Enterprise Institute, Washington, D.C.

A. Downs (1957): *An Economic Theory of Democracy*, Harper Bros., New York.

M. Doyle (1986): *Empires*, Cornell University Press, Ithaca.

M. Doyle (1997): *Ways of War and Peace*, W.W. Norton, New York.

L. Dumont (1970): *Homo Hierarchicus,* Weidenfeld and Nicholson, London.

D. Easterman (1993): *New Jerusalems: Reflections on Islam, Fundamentalism and the Rushdie Affair*, Verso, London.

S. Edwards (1999): "How Effective are Capital Controls?" *Journal of Economic Perspectives*, vol. 13, no. 4, pp. 65–84.

B. Eichengreen (1989): "Hegemonic Stability Theories of the International Monetary System," in R. N. Cooper et al., *Can Nations Agree?* Brookings Institution, Washington, D.C.

B. Eichengreen and M. Bordo (2002): "Crises Now and Then: What Lessons from the Last Era of Financial Globalization?" *NBER Working Paper*, No. 8716, National Bureau of Economic Research, Cambridge, Mass.

S. L. Engerman (1983): "Contract Labour, Sugar and Technology in the Nineteenth Century," *Journal of Economic History*, vol. 43, pp. 635–59.

S. L. Engerman and K. L. Sokoloff (1994): "Factor Endowments, Institutions and Differential Paths of Growth among the New World Economies: A View from Economic Historians of the United States," *NBER Working Paper*, Historical Paper No. 66, National Bureau of Economic Research, Cambridge, Mass.

N. Etherington (1984): *Theories of Imperialism: War, Conquest and Capital*, Croom Helm, London.

R. A. Falk (1970): *The Status of Law in International Society*, Princeton University Press, Princeton, N.J.

R. A. Falk (1971): *This Endangered Planet*, Random House, New York.

R. A. Falk (1999): *Predatory Globalization—A Critique*, Polity Press, Cambridge.

R. C. Feenstra (1998): "Integration of Trade and Disintegration of Production in the Global Economy," *Journal of Economic Perspectives*, vol. 12, no. 4, pp. 31–50.

M. Feldstein (1997a): "The Political Economy of the European Economic and Monetary Union: Political Sources of an Economic Liability," *Journal of Economic Perspectives*, vol. 11, pp. 23–42.

M. Feldstein (1997b): "EMU and International Conflict," *Foreign Affairs*, vol. 76, pp. 60–73.

M. Feldstein (2003): "Why Is Productivity Growing Faster?" *NBER Working Paper*, No. 9530, Feb. 2003, National Bureau of Economic Research, Cambridge, Mass.

N. Ferguson (1998): *The Pity of War*, Allen Lane, London.

F. Fernandez-Armesto (1995): *Millennium*, Scribner, New York.

R. Findlay (1996): "The Emergence of the World Economy," Discussion Paper No. 9596–08, Dept. of Economics, Columbia University, New York.

R. Findlay and M. Lundahl (2003): "The First Globalization Episode: The Creation of the Mongol Empire, or the Economics of Chingiz Khan," mimeo, Dept. of Economics, Columbia University, and Stockholm School of Economics.

R. Findlay and J. Wilson (1987): "The Political Economy of Leviathan," in A. Razin and E. Sadka, eds., *Economic Policy in Theory and Practice*, St. Martin's Press, New York.

S. E. Finer (1997): *The History of Government*, 3 vols., Oxford University Press, Oxford.

M. I. Finley (1968): "Slavery," in D. L. Sills, ed., *International Encylopedia of the Social Sciences*, vol. 14, Macmillan, New York, pp. 307–13.

J. S. Flemming (1982): "Comment on Minsky," in C. P. Kindleberger and J. P. Laffague (eds), *Financial Crises—Theory, History and Policy*, Cambridge University Press, Cambridge.

F. W. Fogel (1989): *Without Consent or Contract*, Norton, New York.

F. W. Fogel and S. L. Engerman (1974): *Time on the Cross*, Little, Brown, New York.

A. G. Frank (1998): *Reorient: Global Economy in the Asian Age*, University of California Press, Berkeley.

D. Fromkin (1989): *A Peace to End All Peace*, Henry Holt, New York.

J. F. C. Fuller (1954): *From the Earliest Times to the Battle of Lepanto*, Da Capo, New York.

J. Gallagher and R. Robinson (1953): "The Imperialism of Free Trade," *Economic History Review*, vol. 6. no.1, pp. 1–15.

E. Gellner (1983): *Nations and Nationalism*, Blackwell, Oxford.

E. Gellner (1988): *Plough, Book and Sword—The Structure of Human History*, Collins Harvill, London.

E. Gellner (1992): *Postmodernism, Reason and Religion*, Routledge, London.

E. Gellner (1993): *The Psychoanalytic Movement: The Cunning of Unreason*, Northwestern University Press, Evanston, Ill.

E. Gibbon (1985, 1787): *The Decline and Fall of the Roman Empire*, Penguin Classics, London.

A. Giddens (1999): *The Third Way: The Renewal of Social Democracy*, Polity Press, Cambridge.

O. Gierke (1957): *Natural Law and the Theory of Society 1500 to 1800*, Beacon Press, Boston.

F. J. Gil-White (1999): "How Thick Is Blood? The Plot Thickens. If Ethnic Actors Are Primordialists, What Remains of the Circumstantialist/Primordialist Controversy?" *Ethnic and Racial Studies*, vol. 22, no. 5, pp. 789–820.

R. W. Goldsmith (1984): "An Estimate of the Size and Structure of the National Product of the Early Roman Empire," *Review of Income and Wealth*, September, pp. 263–88.

M. Goldstein and N. Lardy (2003): "A Modest Proposal for China's reminbi," *Financial Times*, 26 August 2003.

R. M. Goodwin (1967): "A Growth Cycle," in C. Feinstein, ed., *Socialism, Capitalism and Economic Growth*, Cambridge University Press, Cambridge.

J. Goody (1983): *The Development of the Family and Marriage in Europe*, Cambridge University Press, Cambridge.

P. A. Gourevitch (1993): "Democracy and Economic Policy: Elective Affinities and Circumstantial Conjunctures," *World Development*, August, pp. 1271–80.

J. Gray (1999): *False Dawn: The Delusions of Global Capitalism*, New Press, New York.

H. Grotius (1925): *De Juri Belli ac Pacis*, Clarendon Press, Oxford.

J. Gwartney and R. Lawson (2003): *Economic Freedom of the World—2003 Annual Report*, Fraser Institute, Vancouver.

C. R. Hallpike (1986): *The Principles of Social Evolution*, Clarendon Press, Oxford.

S. H. Hanke and S. J. K. Walters (1997): "Economic Freedom, Prosperity and Equality: A Survey," *The Cato Journal*, vol. 17, no. 2, pp. 117–46.

A. C. Harberger, ed., (1984): *World Economic Growth*, ICS Press, San Francisco.

M. Harris (1984): "A Cultural Materialist Theory of Band and Village Warfare," in R. B. Ferguson, ed., *Warfare, Culture and Environment*, Academic Press, New York, pp. 111–40.

H. L. A. Hart (1955): "Are There Any Natural Rights," *Philosophical Review* 64, reprinted in A. Quinton, ed. (1967): *Political Philosophy*, Oxford University Press, Oxford.

F. Hayek (1931): *Prices and Production*, Routledge, London.

F. Hayek (1941): *The Pure Theory of Capital*, Routledge, London.

F. Hayek (1954): *Capitalism and the Historians*, University of Chicago Press, Chicago.

F. Hayek (1960): *The Constitution of Liberty*, Routledge, London.

F. Hayek (1973): *Law, Legislation and Liberty, vol.1: Rules and Order*, Chicago University Press, Chicago.

D. R. Headrick (1979): "The Tools of Imperialism: Technology and the Expansion of European Colonial Empires in the Nineteenth Century," *Journal of Modern History*, vol. 51, June, pp. 231–63.

E. Heckscher (1955): *Mercantilism*, 2 vols., Allen and Unwin, London.

J. F. Helliwell, (1992): "Empirical Linkages between Democracy and Economic Growth", *NBER Working Paper*, No. 4066, National Bureau of Economic Research, May, Cambridge, Mass.

P. D. Henderson (2001): *Misguided Virtue*, Institute of Economic Affairs, London.

J. R. Hicks (1969): *A Theory of Economic History*, Clarendon press, Oxford.

J. Hirshleifer (1994): "The Dark Side of the Force," *Economic Inquiry*, vol. 32, pp. 1–10. Reprinted in Hirshleifer (2001).

J. Hirshleifer (1995): "Anarchy and Its Breakdown," *Journal of Political Economy*, vol. 103, pp. 26–52. Reprinted in Hirshleifer (2001).

J. Hirshleifer (1998): "The bioeconomic causes of war," *Managerial and Decisions Economics*, vol. 19, pp. 457–66. Reprinted in Hirshleifer (2001).

J. Hirshleifer (2001): *The Dark Side of the Force—Economic Foundations of Conflict Theory*, Cambridge University Press, Cambridge.

T. Hobbes (1996, 1651): *Leviathan*, Cambridge University Press, Cambridge.

J. A. Hobson (1902/1948): *Imperialism: A Study*, revised edn., Allen and Unwin, London, 1948.

V. J. Hoffman (1995): "Muslim Fundamentalists: Psycho-Social Profiles," in M. E. Marty and R. Scott Appelby, eds., *Fundamentalisms Comprehended*, University of Chicago Press, Chicago.

A. Hourani (1991): *A History of the Arab Peoples*, Harvard University Press, Cambridge, Mass.

M. Howard (2000): *The Invention of Peace*, Yale University Press, New Haven, Ct.

G. Hufbauer, J. Schott, and K. Elliot (1990): *Economic Sanctions Reconsidered*, Institute of International Economics, Wahington, D.C.

S. P. Huntington (1993): "The Clash of Civilizations," *Foreign Affairs*, vol. 72, no. 3. pp. 22–49.

D. Hume (1965/1777): *Essays: Moral, Political and Literary,* Liberty Fund, Indianapolis.

D. Hume (1975, 1750) : *An Enquiry Concerning the Principles of Morals*, Oxford University Press, London.

D. Hume (1978, 1740): *A Treatise on Human Nature*, Clarendon Press, Oxford.

J. Hutchinson and A. D. Smith, eds. (1994): *Nationalism*, Oxford University Press, Oxford.

S. P. Huntington (1993): "The Clash of Civilizations," *Foreign Affairs*, vol. 72, no. 3.

S. P. Huntington (1991): *The Third Wave*, University of Oklahoma Press, Norman.

Sa'd al-din Ibrahim (1985): "Egypt's Islamic Militants," in S. Ibrahim and N. S. Hopkins, eds., *Arab Society: Social Science Perspectives*, Cairo.

H. Inalcik and D. Quataert, eds. (1994): *An Economic and Social History of the Ottoman Empire,* Cambridge University Press, Cambridge.

Ibn Khaldun (1967, 1379): *The Muqaddimah: An Introduction to History*, Princeton University Press, Princeton, N.J.

D. A. Irwin (2002): *Free Trade Under Fire*, Princeton University Press, Princeton, N.J.

A. de Jasay (1985): *The State*, Blackwell, Oxford.

A. de Jasay (1996): *Before Resorting to Politics*, Shaftesbury Papers 5, Edward Elgar, Cheltenham.

W. J. F. Jenner (1992): *The Tyranny of History*, Penguin, London.

E. L. Jones (1981): *The European Miracle*, Cambridge University Press, Cambridge.

R. Jones and S. Engerman (1996): "Trade, Technology and Wages: A Tale of Two Countries," *American Economic Review*, vol. 86, no. 2, pp. 35–40.

T. Judt (1997): "The Social Question Redivivus," *Foreign Affairs*, vol. 76, no. 5, pp. 95–117.

R. Kagan and W. Kristol, eds. (2000): *Present Dangers: Crisis and Opportunity in American Foreign and Defense Policy,* Encounter Books, San Francisco.

I. Kant (1983, 1784–95): *Perpetual Peace and Other Essays*, Hackett Publishing, Indianapolis.

E. Kedourie (1993, 1960): *Nationalism*, 4th exp. ed., Blackwells, Oxford.

E. Kedourtie, ed. (1970): *Nationalism in Asia and Africa*, Weidenfeld and Nicolson, London.

J. Keegan (1994): *A History of Warfare*, Vintage Books, New York.

L. H. Keeley (1996): *War before Civilization*, Oxford University Press, New York.

J. B. Kelly (1980): *Arabia, the Gulf and the West*, Weidenfeld & Nicholson, London.

P. Kennedy (1989): *The Rise and Fall of the Great Powers*, Fontana Press, London.

R. O. Keohane (1984): *After Hegemony*, Princeton University Press, Princeton, N.J.

G. Kepel (2002a): *Jihad*, Harvard University Press, Cambridge, Mass.

G. Kepel (2002b) "The Jihad in Search of a Cause," *Financial Times*, 2 September, 2002.

J. M. Keynes (1971, 1919): *The Economic Consequences of the Peace*, Macmillan, London.

J. M. Keynes (1926): *The End of Laissez-Faire*, Hogarth Press, London.

J. M. Keynes (1936): *The General Theory of Employment, Interest and Money*, Macmillan, London.

M. Khadduri (1955): *War and Peace in the Law of Islam*, Johns Hopkins University Press, Baltimore.

V. G. Kiernan (1974): *Marxism and Imperialism*, St. Martin's Press, New York.

C. P. Kindleberger (1973): *The World in Depression, 1929–39*, University of California Press, Berkeley.

C .P. Kindleberger (1978): *Manias, Panics and Crashes,* Basic Books, New York.

M. King (1999): "The Evolving Role of Banks in International Capital Flows," in M. Feldstein, ed., *International Capital Flows*, University of Chicago Press, Chicago.

R. Kipling (1899): "The White Man's Burden."

H. Kissinger (2001): *Does America Need a Foreign Policy?* Simon & Schuster, New York.

T. J. Knock (1992): *To End All Wars*, Princeton University Press, Princeton, N.J.

J. Kosterlitz (2002): "Empire Strikes Back," *National Journal*, 13 December 2002, pp. 1–13.

A. O. Krueger (2001): "International Financial Architecture for 2002: A New Approach to Sovereign Debt Restructuring", mimeo, IMF, Washington DC.

P. Krugman (1998): "Saving Asia: It's Time to Get Radical," *Fortune*, 7 September 1998, pp. 74–80.

K. O. Kupperman (1993): *Providence Island, 1630–1641: The Other Puritan Colony*, Cambridge University Press, Cambridge.

D. A. Lake (1993): "Leadership, Hegemony, and the International Economy: Naked Emperor or Tattered Monarch with Potential?" *International Studies Quarterly*, vol.37, pp. 459–89.

D. Lal (1978): "Poverty, Power and Prejudice: The North-South Confrontation," Fabian Society, London; reprinted in Lal (1994).

D. Lal (1980): "A Liberal International Economic Order: The International Monetary System and Economic Development", *Princeton Essays in International Finance*, No.139, October; reprinted in Lal (1993).

D. Lal (1980a): *Prices for Planning*, Heinemann Educational Books, London.

D. Lal (1981): *Resurrection of the Pauper Labour Argument*, Thames Essay No. 28, Trade Policy Research Center, London; reprinted in Lal (1994).

D. Lal (1983, 2000, 1997, 2002): *The Poverty of Development Economics*, Institute of Economic Affairs, London, 1st, 2nd, 3rd editions; U.S. editions, Harvard University Press, 1985, 2nd ed., MIT Press, Cambridge, Mass., 2000; Indian edition, Oxford University Press, New Delhi, 2000.

D. Lal (1984): "The Political Economy of the Predatory State," DRD Discussion Paper No. 105, World Bank, Washington, D.C.

D. Lal (1985): "Nationalism, Socialism and Planning: Influential Ideas in the South," *World Development*, vol. 13, no. 6, pp. 749–59; reprinted in Lal (1993).

D. Lal (1987a): "The Political Economy of Economic Liberalization," *World Bank Economic Review*, vol. 1, no. 2, pp. 273–99; reprinted in Lal (1993).

D. Lal (1987b): "Markets, Mandarins and Mathematicians", *Cato Jornal*, vol. 7, no. 1, pp. 43–70; reprinted in Lal (1994).

D. Lal (1988): *The Hindu Equilibrium*, vol. 1, Clarendon Press, Oxford.

D. Lal (1990a): "Manners, Morals and Materialism: Some Indian Perceptions of America and Great Britain," in L. and N. Glazer, eds., *Conflicting Images: India and the United States*, Riverdale Publishing, Glenn Dale, Maryland; reprinted in Lal (1994).

D. Lal (1990b): *Fighting Fiscal Privilege*, Social Market Foundation, Paper No. 7, London; reprinted in Lal (1994).

D. Lal (1990c): *Political Economy and Public Policy*, Occasional paper no. 19, International Center for Economic Growth, San Francisco; reprinted in Lal (1993).

D. Lal (1990d): *The Limits of International Cooperation*, Twentieth Wincott Memorial Lecture, Occasional Paper No. 83, Institute of Economic Affairs, London.

D. Lal (1993a): *The Repressed Economy*, Economists of the 20th century, Edward Elgar, Aldershot.

D. Lal (1993b): "Does Openness Matter? How to Appraise the Evidence" in H. Siebert, ed. *Growth in the World Economy*, J. C. B. Mohr, Tubingen reprinted in Lal (1994).

D. Lal (1994): *Against Dirigisme: The Care for Unshackling Economic Markets*, ICS Press, San Francisco.

D. Lal (1995a): "Eco-Fundamentalism," *International Affairs*, vol. 71, pp. 515–28.

D. Lal (1995b): "Policies for Economic Development: Why the Wheel has Come Full Circle," *South African Journal of Economics*, vol. 63 (4) pp. 489–517.

D. Lal (1995c): *Poverty, Markets and Democracy*, The 1995 Nestle Inaugural lecture on the Developing World, Nestle, U.K.

D. Lal (1996a): "Foreign Aid: An Idea Whose Time Has Gone," *Economic Affairs*, Autumn 1996, pp. 9–13.

D. Lal (1996b, 1999a) : "Participation, Markets and Democracy," in M. Lundahl and B. J. Nudulu, eds., *New Directions in Development Economics*, Routledge, London; reprinted in Lal (1999a).

D. Lal (1998): *Unintended Consequences: The Impact of Factor Endowments, Culture, and Politics on Long Run Economic Performance*, MIT Press, Cambridge, Mass.

D. Lal (1998a): "Social Standards and Social Dumping," in H. Giersch, ed., *Merits and Limits of Markets,* Springer, Berlin.

D. Lal (1999a): *Unfinished Business: India in the World Economy*, Oxford University Press, New Delhi.

D. Lal (1999b): *EMU and Globalization*, Policy Series No. 17, Politeia, London.

D. Lal (2000a): "The Challenge of Globalization: There Is No Third Way," in I. Vasquez, ed., *Global Fortune*, Cato Institute, Washington, D.C.

D. Lal (2000b): "Does Modernization Require Westernization?" *Independent Review*, vol. 5, no. 1, Summer, pp. 5–24.

D. Lal (2000c): *Smoke Gets in Your Eyes: The Economic Welfare Effects of the World Bank-World Health Organization Global Crusade against Tobacco*, FMF Monograph No. 26, Free Market Foundation, Sandton, South Africa.

D. Lal (2001): "How To Get Rich," *Prospect*, March 2001, pp. 32–35.

D. Lal (2001a): "The Development and Spread of Economic Norms and Incentives," in R. Rosecrance, ed., *The New Great Power Coalition,* Rowman and Littlefield, Lanham, Maryland.

D. Lal (2002): "The New Cultural Imperialism: The Greens and Economic Development," *Humane Studies Review*, vol. 14, no. 3.

D. Lal (2003a): "India" in P. Bernholz and R. Vaubel, eds., *Political Competition and Decentralization as Preconditions for Economic Freedom, Innovation and Development in Asian Civilizations*, Springer, Berlin (in press).

D. Lal (2003b): "Free Trade and Laissez-faire—has the Wheel Come Full Circle?" *The World Economy*, vol. 26, no. 4, pp. 471–82.

D. Lal (2003c): "The Japanese Slump" in R. Pethig and M. Rauscher, eds., *Challenges to the World Economy—A festschrift for Horst Siebert*, Springer, Berlin.

D. Lal (2003d): "Is Democracy Necessary for Development?" in S. Ramaswamy and J. W. Cason, eds., *Development and Democracy*, University Press of New England, Lebanon, N.H.

D. Lal (2003e): "A Force to Lift the Curse of Natural Resources," *Financial Times*, October 23.

D. Lal, S. Bery and D. K. Pant (2003): "The Real Exchange Rate, Fiscal Deficits and Capital Inflows: India 1981–2000," *Economic and Political Weekly*, vol. XXXVIII, no. 22, pp. 4965–4976.

D. Lal, with M. Cave, P. Hare and J. Thompson (1975): *Appraising Foreign Investment in Developing Countries,* Heinemann Educational Books, London.

D. Lal, H. Kim, G. Lu and J. Prat (2003): "The Welfare Effects of Tobacco Taxation: Estimates for 5 Countries/regions," *Journal des Economistes et des Etudes Humaines*, vol. 30, no. 1, pp. 3–20.

D. Lal, R. Mohan, and I. Natarajan (2001): "Economic Reforms and Poverty Alleviation: A Tale of Two Surveys," *Economic and Political Weekly*, vol. XXXVI, no. 12, pp. 1017–1028.

D. Lal and H. Myint (1996): *The Political Economy of Poverty, Equity, and Growth*, Clarendon Press, Oxford.

D. Lal and I. Natarajan (2001): "The Virtuous Circle: Savings, Distribution and Growth Interactions in India," in D. Lal and R. Snape, eds, *Trade, Development, and Political Economy: Essays in Honour of Anne O. Kruege*, Palgrave, Basingstoke.

D. Lal and S. Rajapatirana (1987): "Foreign Trade Regimes and Economic Growth in Developing Countries," *World Bank Research Observer*, vol. 2, no. 2, pp. 189–217; reprinted in Lal (1993).

D. Lal and M. F. Scott, eds. (1990): *Public Policy and Economic Development: Essays in Honour of Ian Little*, Clarendon Press, Oxford.

D. Lal and R. Snape, eds. (2001): *Trade, Development, and Political Economy: Essays in Honour of Anne O. Krueger*, Palgrave, Basingstoke.

D. Lal and S. Wijnbergen (1985): "Government Deficits, the Real Interest Rate and LDC Debt: On Global Crowding Out," *European Economic Review*, vol. 29, pp. 157–91; reprinted in Lal (1993).

D. Lal and M. Wolf, eds. (1986): *Stagflation, Savings, and the State*, Oxford University Press, New York.

R. Lane- Fox (1988): *Pagans and Christians,* Penguin, London.

W. Langewiesche (2000): "The Shipbreakers," *The Atlantic Monthly*, August 2000.

N. Lardy (1998): *China's Unfinished Economic Revolution,* Brookings Institution, Washington, D.C.

N. Lardy (2002): *Integrating China into the Global Economy,* Brookings Institution, Washington, D.C.

N. Lardy (2003): "Trade Liberalization and its Role in Chinese Economic Growth," Paper for IMF-NCAER conference "A Tale of Two Giants—India and China's Experience with Reform and Growth," New Delhi, November 14–16, 2003.

D. L. Larson, ed. (1966): *The Puritan Ethic in United States Foreign Policy*, Van Nostrand, Princeton, N.J.

E. Latham (1952): *The Group Basis of Politics*, Cornell University Press, Ithaca.

C. Layne (1993): "The Unipolar Illusion: Why New Great Powers will Arise," *International Security*, vol. 17, no. 4.

C. Layne (1997): "From Preponderance to Offshore Balancing: America's Future Grand Strategy," *International Security*, vol. 22, no.1.

M. Ledeen (2002): *The War against the Terror Masters*, St. Martin's Press, New York.

V. I. Lenin (1916/1939): *Imperialism: The Highest Stage of Capitalism* (Russian edition 1916), English edition, Lawrence & Wishart, London, 1939.

B. Lewis (1992): "Muslims, Christians, and Jews: The Dream of Co-existence," *New York Review of Books*, vol. 39, no. 6.

B. Lewis (2002): *What Went Wrong?* Weidenfeld & Nicolson, London.

W. A. Lewis (1978): *The Evolution of the International Economic Order*, Princeton University Press, Princeton, N.J.

D. Lieven (2001): *Empire*, Yale University Press, New Haven, Ct.

P. H. Lindert and J. G. Williamson (2003): "Does Globalization Make the World More Unequal?," in M. D. Bordo, A. M. Taylor and J. G. Williamson, eds, *Globalization in Historical Perspective,* University of Chicago Press, Chicago.

A. S. Link, D. W. Hirst, J. E. Little, M. F. Boemeke, D. Thompson and F. Aandahl, eds., (1966): *The Papers of Woodrow Wilson,* 67 vols., Princeton University Press, Princeton, N.J.

S. M. Lipset (1959): *Political Man*, Heinemann, London.

C. Lipson (1985): *Standing Guard*, University of California Press, Berkeley.

G. Liska (1967): *Imperial America: The International Politics of Primacy*, Johns Hopkins Press, Baltimore.

I. M. D. Little (2002): *Ethics, Economics and Politics*, Oxford University Press, Oxford.

K. N. Llewellyn (1930/1951): *The Bramble Bush—On Our Law and Its Study,* Oceana Publications, New York.

Mario Vargas Llosa (2000): "Liberalism in the New Millennium," in I. Vasquez, ed., *Global Fortune*, Cato Institute, Washington, D.C.

B. Lomberg (2001): *The Sceptical Environmentalist*, Cambridge University Press, Cambridge.

E. N. Luttwak (2003): "What the Sergeant Never Told Us," *Times Literary supplement*, 31 January 2003, pp. 13–15.

J. Lynch (1973): *The Spanish-American Revolutions*, Norton, New York.

T. B. Macaulay (1898): *The Complete works of Lord Macaulay*, 12 vols., London.

N. Machiavelli (1513 /1950): *The Prince and the Discourses,* Modern Library, New York.

A. MacIntyre (1990): "Individual and Social Morality in Japan and the United States: Rival Conceptions of the Self," *Philosophy East and West*, vol. 40, no. 4, pp. 489–97.

A. Maddison (1971): *Class Structure and Economic Growth: India and Pakistan since the Moghuls,* Allen and Unwin, London.

A. Maddison (2001): *The World Economy—A Millennial Perspective*, Organization for Economic and Co-operation Development, Paris.

J. H. Makin (1984): *The Global Debt Crisis*, Basic Books, New York.

N. Malcolm (1995): "The case against 'Europe,' " *Foreign Affairs*, vol. 74, no. 2, pp. 52–68.

M. Mandelbaum (2002): *The Ideas that Conquered the World*, Public Affairs, New York.

H. Manne (1972): *The Modern Corporation and Social Responsibility*, American Enterprise Institute, Washington, D.C.

H. Manne (2002): "Bring Back the Hostile Takeover," *Wall Street Journal*, 26 June 2002.

E. D. Mansfield (1994): *Power, Trade and War*, Princeton University Press, Princeton N.J.

E. D. Mansfield and J. Snyder (1995): "Democratization and War," *Foreign Affairs*, vol. 74, no. 3, pp. 79–97.

J. H. Manson and R. W. Wrangham (1991): "Intergroup Aggression in Chimpanzees and Humans," *Current Anthropology*, vol. 32, pp. 369–90.

M. E. Marty and R. Scott Appelby (1993): *Fundamentalisms and the State*, University of Chicago Press, Chicago.

J. S. McClelland (1996): *A History of Western Political Thought*, Routledge, London.

W. H. McNeill (1991, 1963): *The Rise of the West*, University of Chicago Press, Chicago.

W. H. McNeill (1979): *A World History*, 3rd ed., Oxford University Press, New York.

W. H. McNeill (1982): *The Pursuit of Power*, University of Chicago Press, Chicago.

W. H. McNeill (1992): *The Global Condition*, Princeton University Press, Princeton, N.J.

M. Mead (1964): "Warfare is Only an Invention" in L. Bramson and G. Goethals,: *War: Studies from Psychology, Sociology, Anthropology*, New York, pp. 269–74.

Walter Russell Mead (2001): *Special Providence*, Knopf, New York.

J. E. Meade, (1955): *Trade and Welfare*, London: Oxford University Press.

J. J. Mearsheimer (2001): *The Tragedy of the Great Powers*, W.W. Norton, New York.

J. S. Mill (1910, 1861): *Representative Government*, Everyman Library, London.

K. Minogue (1979): "The History of the Idea of Human Rights," in W. Laquer and R. Rubin, eds., *The Human Rights Reader*, New American Library, New York.

K. Minogue, (1993): *The Constitutional Mania*, Policy Study No. 134, Centre for Policy Studies, London.

K. Minogue (1995): *Politics*, Oxford University Press, Oxford.

K. Minogue (2003): " 'Managing' Nationalism," *New Left Review*, 23, Sept./Oct., pp. 95–99.

H. P. Minsky (1977): "A Theory of Systematic Fragility," in E. I. Altman and A. W. Sametz, eds., *Financial Crisis: Institutions and Markets in a Fragile Environment*, Wiley, New York.

R. M. Morse (1964): "The Heritage of Latin America" in L. Hartz, ed., *The Founding of New Societies*, Harcourt, Brace & World, New York.

J. Morris, ed. (2002): *Sustainable Development*, Profile Books, London.

D. C. Mueller, ed. (1983): *The Political Economy of Growth*, Yale University Press, New Haven.

N. Munk (1999): "How Levi's Trashed a Great American Brand," *Fortune*, 12 April 1999.

H. Myint (1967): "The Inward and Outward-looking Countries of Southeast Asia," *Malayan Economic Review*, vol. 12, pp. 1–13.

W. D. Nordhaus (1994): *Managing the Global Commons*, MIT Press, Cambridge, Mass.

R. Nozick (1974): *Anarchy, State, and Utopia*, Basil Blackwell, Oxford.

J. S. Nye Jr. (2002): *The Paradox of American Power*, Oxford University Press, New York.

M. Oakeshott (1993): *Morality and Politics in Modern Europe*, Yale University Press, New Haven, Ct.

N. V. Ogarkov (1982): "Always in Readiness for the Defense of the Fatherland," *Voyenizdat*.

B. O'Leary (2002): "In Praise of Empires Past," *New Left Review*, 18, Nov./Dec., pp. 106–30.

B. O'Leary (2003): "Staus Quo Patriotism," *New Left Review*, 23, Sept./Oct., pp. 100–4.

R. Oliver (1999): *The African Experience*, revised edn, Weidenfeld and Nicolson, London.

R. Oliver, ed. (1976–84): *Cambridge History of Africa*, 8 vols., Cambridge University Press, Cambridge.

M. Olson (1965): *The Logic of Collective Action*, Harvard University Press, Cambridge, Mass.

M. Olson (1982): *The Rise and Decline of Nations,* Yale University Press, New Haven, Conn.

M. Olson (2000): *Power and Prosperity*, Basic Books, New York.

D. Otto (1996): "Non-governmental Organizations in the United Nations: The Emerging Role of International Civil Society," *Human Rights Quarterly*, vol. 18, Ottaway, no. 1, pp. 107–41.

B. Owens (2001): *Lifting the Fog of War*, Johns Hopkins University Press, Baltimore.

J. H. Parry (1966): *The Spanish Sea-borne Empire*, Hutchinson, London.

O. Paz (1988): *Sor Juana*, Harvard University Press, Cambridge, Mass.

M. A. Peeters (2001): *Hijacking Democracy: Global Consensus on Global Governance*, mimeo, American Enterprise Institute, Washingon, D.C.

H. Perkins (1984): *The Rise of the Professional Classes*, Routledge, London.

H. Phelps-Brown (1983): *The Origins of Trade Union Power*, Clarendon Press, Oxford.

S. Pinker (2002): *The Blank Slate*, Viking, New York.

W. Pintner (1995): "The Future of Russia in Historical Perspective," Working Paper No. 9, Center for International Relations, University of California, Los Angeles.

J. Plamenatz (1960): *On Alien Rule and Self-Government*, Longmans, London.

J. Plamenatz (1973): "Two Types of Nationalisms," in E. Kamenka, ed., *Nationalism*, Arnold, London.

J. G. A. Pocock (1975a): "Early Modern Capitalism—the Augustan Perception," in E. Kamenka and R. S. Neale, eds., *Feudalism, Capitalism and Beyond*, Arnold, London.

J. G. A. Pocock (1975b): *The Machiavellian Moment*, Princeton University Press, Princeton, N.J.

S. W. Polachek (1992): "Conflict and Trade: An Economic Approach to Political International Interactions," in W. Isard and C. H. Anderton eds. *Economics of Arms Reduction and the Peace Process*, North holland, Amsterdam, pp. 89–120.

M. A. Pollock and G. C. Shaffer eds (2001): *Transatlantic Governance in the Global Economy*, Rowman and Littlefield, Lanham, Md.

K. Pomeranz (2000): *The Great Divergence*, Princeton University Press, Princeton, N.J.

R.A. Preston and S.F. Wise (1979): *Men in Arms*, 4th ed., Holt, Reinhart and Winston, New York.

A. Przeworski and F. Limongi (1993): "Political Regimes and Economic Growth," *Journal of Economic Perspectives*, vol. 7, no. 3, pp. 51–69.

R. D. Putnam (1993): *Making Democracy Work*, Princeton University Press, Princeton, N.J.

R. D. Putnam (2000): *Bowling Alone*, Simon and Schuster, New York.

F. Rahman (1979): *Islam*, 2nd ed., University of Chicago Press, Chicago.

J. Rauch (1994): *Demosclerosis*, Random House, New York.

P. Ratchnevsky (1991): *Genghis Khan*, Oxford University Press, Oxford.

K. Raustiala (1996): "Democracy, Sovereignty, and the Slow Pace of International Negotiations," *International Environmental Affairs*, vol. 8.

K. Raustiala (1997): "States, NGO's, and Environmental Institutions," *International Studies Quarterly*, vol. 20, pp. 719–740.

L. G. Reynolds (1985): *Economic Growth in the Third World*, Yale University Press, New Haven, Conn.

D. Rimmer (1992): *Ghana's Politcal Economy 1950–1990*, Pergamon Press, Oxford.

L. Robbins (1952): *The Theory of Economic Policy in English Classical Political Economy*, Macmillan, London.

J. M. Roberts (1990): *The Penguin History of the World*, Penguin books, London.

H. Rockoff (1998): "By Way of Analogy: The Expansion of the Federal Government in the 1930's," in Bordo, Goldin and White, eds., *The Defining Moment*, Chicago University Press, Chicago.

R. Rogowski (1989): *Commerce and Coalitions*, Princeton University Press, Princeton, N.J.

R. Rosecrance (1986): *The Trading State*, Basic Books, New York.

R. Rosecrance (1999): *The Rise of the Virtual State*, Basic Books, New York.

D. Rothermund (2002): "From Chariot to Atom Bomb: Armament and Military Organization in South Asian History," University of Heidelberg, mimeo.

J. G. Ruggie, ed. (1993): *Multilateralism Matters*, Columbia University Press, New York.

M. Ruthven (2002): *A Fury for God*, Granta Books, London.

X. Sala-i-Martin (2002a): "The Disturbing 'Rise' of Global Income Inequality," *NBER Working Papers*, No. 8904, National Bureau of Economic Research, Cambridge, Mass.

X. Sala-i-Martin (2002b): "The World Distribution of Income (estimated from individual country distributions)," *NBER Working Papers*, No. 8933, National Bureau of Economic Research, Cambridge, Mass.

R. Sally (1998): *Classical Liberalism and International Economic Order*, Routledge, London.

A. I. Samatar (1999): *An African Miracle*, Heinemann, Portsmouth, N.H.

S. B. Saul (1976): *The Myth of the Great Depression 1873–1896*, Macmillan, London.

Sayyid Abu Ala Maududi (1967): *The Religion of Truth*,? Lahore.

E. E. Schattschneider (1975): *The Semi Sovereign People*, Dryden, Hinsdale, Ill.

T. C. Schelling (1992): "Some Economics of Global Warming," *American Economic Review*, vol. 82, no. 1, pp. 1–14.

A. M. Schlesinger Jr (1986): *The Cycles of American History*, Houghton Mifflin, Boston.

S. H. Schneider (1989): *Global Warming*, Sierra Club, San Francisco.

J. A. Schumpeter (1950): *Capitalism, Socialism and Democracy*, Harper & Row, New York.

J. A. Schumpeter (1954): *A History of Economic Analysis*, Oxford University Press, New York.

J. A. Schumpeter (1955): *Imperialism and Social Classes*, Meridian, New York.

K. Schwab and C. Smadja (1999): "Globalization Needs a Human Face," *International Herald Tribune*, January 28, p. 8.

S. Schwartz (2002): *The Two Faces of Islam*, Doubleday, New York.

G. Schwarzenberger (1959): "Hegemonial Intervention," *Yearbook of World Affairs*, Stevens and Son, London.

R. Scruton (2000): *WHO, What and Why?* Institute of Economic Affairs, London.

G. R. Searle (1998): *Morality and the Market in Victoriam Britain*, Clarendon Press, Oxford.

K. Sellars (2002): *The Rise and Rise of Human Rights*, Sutton Publishing, Stroud, Gloucestershire.

A. K. Sen (1992): *Inequality Reexamined*, Clarendon Press, Oxford.

A. K. Sen (1999): *Development and Freedom*, Oxford University Press, Oxford.

H. Seton-Watson (1977): *Nations and States*, Westview Press, Boulder, Col.

G. Shaffer (2001): "The World Trade Organization under Challenge: Democracy and the Law and Politics of the WTO's Treatment of Trade and Environment Matters," *Harvard Environmental Law Review*, vol. 25.

M. Sherif and C.W. Sherif (1964): *Reference Groups: Exploration into Conformity and Deviation of Adolescents*, Harper & Row, New York.

J. Simon (1996): *The UIltimate Resource*, Princeton University Press, Priceton, N.J.

R. Skidelsky (1983): *John Maynard Keynes*, vol. 1, Macmillan, London.

R. Skidelsky (2000): *John Maynard Keynes*, vol. 3, Macmillan, London.

A. Smith (1982, 1759): *The Theory of Moral Sentiments*, Liberty Fund, Indianapolis.

A. D. Smith (1983): *Theories of Nationalism*, 2nd ed., Holmes and Meier, New York.

A. D. Smith (2000): *The Nation in History*, Oxford Unviesity Press, Oxford.

B. L. Solow (1991): "Slavery and Colonization" in Solow ed., *Slavery and the Rise of the Atlantic Economies*, Cambridge University Press, Cambridge.

T. G. P. Spear (1963): *The Nabobs*, Oxford University Press, Oxford.

T. N. Srinivasan (2000): "The Washington Consensus a Decade Later: Ideology and the Art and Science of Policy Advice," *The World Bank Research Observer*, vol. 15, no. 2, pp. 265–70.

J. Stiglitz (2002): *Globalization and Its Discontents*, Allen Lane, London.

E. Stokes (1959): *The English Utilitarians and India*, Oxford University Press, Oxford.

J. Stone (1972): "Self-determination and the Palestinian Arabs," in I. Howe and C. Gershman, eds., *Israel, the Arabs and the Middle East*, Bantam Books, New York.

R. Sugden (1993): "A Review of *Inequality Reexamined* by Amartya Sen," *Journal of Economic Literature*, vol. 31, no. 4, pp. 1947–86.

V. Tanzi and L. Schuknecht (2000): *Public Spending in the 20th Century*, Cambridge University Press, Cambridge.

C. Taylor (1974): "Socialism and Weltanschauung," in L. Kolakowski and S. Hampshire, eds, *The Socialist Idea—A Reappraisal,* Weidenfeld and Nicholson, London.

J. Taylor (2002): "Sovereign Debt Restructuring: A U.S. Perspective," mimeo, U.S. Dept. Treasury, Washington, D.C.

J. Taylor (2003): "Increasing Economic Growth and Stability in Emerging Markets," *Cato Journal,* vol. 23, no. 1, pp. 127–34.

P. Temin (2003): "Mediterranean Trade in Biblical Times," paper for Hecksher Symposium, Stockholm School of Economics, 2003 (to be published in the conference volume).

C. Tilly (1992): *Coercion, Capital, and European States A.D. 990–1992,* Blackwell, Oxford.

B. R. Tomlinson (1975): "India and the British Empire, 1880–1935," *Indian Economic and Social History Review,* vol. 12, no. 4.

J. Tooby and L. Cosmides (1989): "Evolutionary Psychology and the Generation of Culture, Part 1," *Ethnology and Sociobiology,* vol. 10, pp. 29–49.

A. Toynbee (1995): *A Study of History,* abridged edition, Barnes & Noble Books, New York.

R. Trivers (1985): *Social Evolution,* Benjamin Cummings, Menlo Park, Cal.

D. B. Truman (1953): *The Government Process,* Knopf, New York.

H. H. Turney-High (1971): *Primitive War,* 2nd ed., University of South Carolina Press, Columbia, S.C.

C. Tyler-Smith et al. (2003): "The Genetic Legacy of the Mongols," *American Journal of Human Genetics,* vol. 72, electronically published Jan. 17, 2003.

UN Population Division (2002): *World Population Prospects: The 2002 Revision,* United Nations, New York.

R. W. Van Alstyne (1960): *The Rising American Empire,* Blackwell, Oxford.

J. Vasquez (1992): "The Steps to War: Toward a Scientific Explanation of Correlates of War Findings," in J. A. Vasquez and M. T. Henehan, eds., *The Scientific Study of Peace and War,* Lexington Books, New York.

A. Vayda (1976): *War in Ecological Perspective,* New York.

C. Veliz (1980): *The Centralist Tradition of Latin America,* Princeton University Press, Princeton, N.J.

C. Veliz (1994): *The New World of the Gothic Fox,* University of California Press, Berkeley, Cal.

I. Wallerstein (1974, 1980, 1988): *The Modern World System,* 3 vols., Academic Press, New York.

K. Waltz (2001, 1954): *Man, the State, and War,* Columbia University Press, New York.

B. Warren (1980): *Imperialism: Pioneer of Capitalism,* New Left Books, London.

A. Watson (1984): "European International Society and Its Expansion," in Bull and Watson, eds. (1984), pp. 13–32.

M. Weber (1961, 1923): *General Economic History,* Collier, New York.

C. K. Webster (1951): *The Foreign Policy of Palmerston,* London.

R. Webster (1995): *Why Freud Was Wrong,* Harper-Collins, London.

B. Williams (1985): *Ethics and the Limits of Philosophy,* Fontana Press, London.

J. Williamson (1990): "What Washington Means by Policy Reform," in J. Williamson, ed., *Latin American Adjustment: How Much Has Happened?* Institute for International Economics, Washington, D.C.

J. Williamson (2000): "What Should the World Bank Think About the Washington Consensus?" *The World Bank Research Observer,* vol. 15, no. 2, pp. 251–64.

J. G. Williamson (1998): "Globalization, Labour Markets and Policy Backlash in the Past," *Journal of Economic Perspectives,* 12 (Fall), pp. 51–72.

W. Wohlforth (1999): "The Stability of a Unipolar World," *International Security,* vol. 14, no. 1.

World Bank (1989): *Sub-Saharan Africa: From Crisis to Sustainable Growth,* World Bank, Washington, D.C.

World Bank (1992): *World Development Report 1992: Development and the Environment,* Oxford University Press, New York.

World Bank (2001): *World Development Report 2000–2001: Attacking Poverty,* Oxford University Press, New York.

E. A. Wrigley (1988): *Continuity, Chance and Change,* Cambridge University Press, Cambridge.

M. Wrong (2000): *In the Footsteps of Mr. Kurtz: Living on the Brink of Disaster in Mobutu's Congo*, Fourth Estate, London.

A. Wyatt-Walter (1996): "Adam Smith and the Liberal Tradition in International Relations," *Review of International Studies*, vol. 22, no. 1.

G. Wynia (1990, 1984): *The Politics of Latin American Development*, Cambridge University Press, Cambridge.

F. Zakaria (1997): "The Rise of Illiberal Democracies," *Foreign Affairs*, vol. 76, no. 6, pp. 22–43.

F. Zakaria (2003): *The Future of Freedom*, Norton, New York.

Index